Elementary Education in India

This book examines the policy shifts over the past three decades in the Indian education system. It explores how these shifts have unequivocally established the domination of neoliberal capital in the context of elementary education in India.

The chapters in the volume:

- Discuss a range of elementary education policies and programmes in India with a focus on the policy development in recent decades of neoliberalism.
- Analyse policy from diverse perspectives and varied vantage points by scholars, activists and practitioners, illustrated with contemporary statistics.
- Introduce the key curriculum, assessment and learning debates from contemporary educational discourse.
- Integrate the tools and methods of education policy analysis with basic concepts in education, like equality, quantity, equity, quality and inclusion.

A definitive inter-disciplinary work on a key sector in India, this volume will be essential for scholars and researchers of education, public policy, sociology, politics and South Asian studies.

Jyoti Raina is Associate Professor, Department of Elementary Education, Gargi College, University of Delhi, New Delhi, India. Her main teaching focus is educational studies, learning theory and science education. She also looks after the work of equal opportunity, Gandhi studies and anti-discrimination at the college.

'*Elementary Education in India: Policy Shifts, Issues and Challenges* constitutes an urgent challenge not only to India's educational system but to the underpinnings of the crisis in which it is perilously enmeshed – the roots and branches of capitalist overproduction and consequent immiseration. Jyoti Raina has assembled a distinguished group of Indian and international educational scholars whose critiques of neoliberalism and education sound the death-knell of efforts to repurpose education to accommodate a capitalist system reeling on its transnationalist heels. Equally important, the book provides readers with new vantage points from which a new system can be built. This stunning work will be of interest to critical educators worldwide.'

– Peter McLaren, Distinguished Professor in Critical Studies,
The Attallah College of Educational Studies, Chapman University;
and Chair Professor, Northeast Normal University, China

'The period 1990 to the present has seen a major neoliberal turn in public policy in India in all sectors of education. The policy shifts in elementary education have been of the greatest impact because these touch the very base of India's highly stratified society. There has been a dearth of competent documentations and analyses that set out the causes, trajectories and consequences of these major shifts. The present collection of essays attempts to fill this vacuum by bringing together the perspectives of several Indian and international scholars and practitioners on the contemporary realities of policy and practice in elementary education. This book promises to serve as an important resource world-wide for students and educators as well as for those who work in policy spaces.'

– Shyam B. Menon, Professor of Education, Central Institute
of Education, University of Delhi, Delhi; Founder
Vice-Chancellor, Ambedkar University, Delhi, India

'This is an important book that brings together a rich collection of essays on a range of issues that are critical to the present and future of education in India. The larger context is the neoliberal restructuring of education and its fallout as reflected in the changes we are witnessing in schooling especially in the last two decades. The themes dealt with relate to policy shifts in education, privatisation, transformations in curriculum and pedagogical practices, exclusion and discrimination in schooling and so on. There is also an engagement with education as a public good and the challenge of public education, social justice and democratic citizenship, concerns that are increasingly marginalized today. This makes the book a timely contribution as well.'

– Geetha B. Nambissan, Professor of Education, Zakir Husain
Centre for Educational Studies, School of Social Sciences,
Jawaharlal Nehru University, New Delhi, India

'At a time when discourse on the public education system is dominated by activist foundations and the practical urge [for] "fixing things" the collection of essays in this book bring back the focus on the underlying national and transnational force field within which the Indian constitutional promise of the Right to Education is playing out. The collection of essays presents fresh historical and political analysis and commentary on education in society.'
– *Padma M. Sarangpani, Professor of Education, Tata Institute of Social Science, Mumbai, India*

'This volume edited by Jyoti Raina is a direct and critical engagement with the ideas and practices of neoliberalism as they restructure education with devastating consequences for the institutions of public education. Even more, Raina advances the theory that neoliberalism and the global ideas of the Washington Consensus find their partner in the Indian state. This state has abandoned its role of redistribution in favour of the poor, and advancing the conditions for growth of private capital in education. The contributions in the volume highlight myriad themes of these arguments. A must read for scholars and researchers of Indian education.'
– *Manisha Priyam, Associate Professor, National Institute for Educational Planning and Administration, New Delhi*

Elementary Education in India

Policy Shifts, Issues and Challenges

Edited by Jyoti Raina

LONDON AND NEW YORK

First published 2020
by Routledge
2 Park Square, Milton Park, Abingdon, Oxon OX14 4RN

and by Routledge
52 Vanderbilt Avenue, New York, NY 10017

Routledge is an imprint of the Taylor & Francis Group, an informa business

© 2020 selection and editorial matter, Jyoti Raina; individual chapters, the contributors

The right of Jyoti Raina to be identified as the author of the editorial material, and of the authors for their individual chapters, has been asserted in accordance with sections 77 and 78 of the Copyright, Designs and Patents Act 1988.

All rights reserved. No part of this book may be reprinted or reproduced or utilised in any form or by any electronic, mechanical, or other means, now known or hereafter invented, including photocopying and recording, or in any information storage or retrieval system, without permission in writing from the publishers.

Trademark notice: Product or corporate names may be trademarks or registered trademarks, and are used only for identification and explanation without intent to infringe.

British Library Cataloguing-in-Publication Data
A catalogue record for this book is available from the British Library

Library of Congress Cataloging-in-Publication Data
A catalog record for this book has been requested

ISBN: 978-1-138-32231-8 (hbk)
ISBN: 978-0-429-32879-4 (ebk)

Typeset in Sabon
by Apex CoVantage, LLC

Contents

List of figures	x
List of tables	xi
List of contributors	xii
Acknowledgements	xvi
List of abbreviations	xvii

Introduction: mapping the exacerbated crisis in elementary education: issues and challenges	1
JYOTI RAINA	

PART I
Neoliberal restructuring of education   23

1 Neoliberal policy shifts in elementary education in India	25
JYOTI RAINA AND PARUL	

2 Extending the neoliberal agenda to forbidden territory: public–private partnership in school education in India	43
SUMAN LATA	

3 Public education: can it be fixed?	55
ATISHI	

4 Equitable elementary education as a public good: what is left of it?	66
JYOTI RAINA	

viii Contents

PART II
Understanding knowledge and curriculum 89

5 Draft NEP 2016: education for 'citizenship' or 'resource
development for a pliable workforce'? 91
ROHIT DHANKAR

6 Bin bhay hoye na preet: resilience of the fear-based
examination-detention policy in the Indian education system 108
DISHA NAWANI

7 Indian modernity as the problem of Indian education 122
NITA KUMAR

PART III
Schooling, social justice and critical pedagogy 135

8 *Sanskara*: the notion of hereditary educability and
changing behaviour of the teachers 137
SANJAY KUMAR

9 Consensualised reproduction and the fascised rule of
capital: the responsibility of critical pedagogy 154
RAVI KUMAR

10 A strategy for exclusion: how equality and social justice
have been derailed in Indian elementary education 177
MADHU PRASAD

PART IV
**Transnational perspective on neoliberalism and
education** 201

11 The reactionary right and its carnival of reaction: global
neoliberalism, reactionary neoconservatism: Marxist
critique, education analysis and policy 203
DAVE HILL

12 The agonies of neoliberal education: what hope progress? 220
TOM G. GRIFFITHS

Contents ix

13 Analysing educational change: towards an understanding
of patterns of historical and cultural refraction 235
IVOR GOODSON

14 Combating educational inequality: competing frameworks 249
VIKAS GUPTA

Index 285

Figures

4.1	Social backgrounds of children attending different types of schools in primary grades, academic year 2014–15	69
4.2	Social backgrounds of children attending different types of schools in primary grades, academic year 2011–12	70
8.1	Vicious circle of exclusion of children from marginalised communities	139
8.2	Parameters of action research	141
13.1	Juxtaposing system narratives and work–life narratives	240

Tables

4.1	Increase in number of private schools providing elementary education from 1979 to 2009	78
4.2	Increase in number of new private schools versus state schools from 2010 to 2016	79
4.3	Children attending private unaided schools in India by age and region for the academic year 2014–15	79
8.1	Percentage of children by social category and education of father	143
8.2	Percentage of children by social category and education of mother	144
8.3	Percentage of children by social category and household landownership	145
8.4	Percentage of children by social category and occupation of father	146
13.1	Periodisation in national contexts	237
13.2	Main features of public service restructuring in the case studies	238

Contributors

Atishi is a political leader belonging to the Aam Aadmi Party. She has been an advisor to the deputy chief minister of Delhi, primarily on education. She has a master's degree in education curriculum from Oxford University and has worked in the field of alternative education and curriculum. She spent some time teaching at Rishi Valley School in Andhra Pradesh before moving to a small village near Bhopal in Madhya Pradesh, India. There she was involved with developing organic farming and progressive education systems. She has worked with several non-profit organisations on public policy issues.

Rohit Dhankar is Professor of Philosophy of Education at Azim Premji University, Bengaluru, India. He has been a member of several NCERT initiatives to develop material and curriculum for school education. He trained as a teacher under David Horsburgh in the Neelbagh School, and taught in elementary schools for 15 years. He is the founder secretary of Digantar, a voluntary organisation in Jaipur, India, that is engaged in providing alternative education to rural/urban slum children.

Ivor Goodson has worked in universities in England, Canada and the United States, and is currently Professor of Learning Theory at the Education Research Centre, the University of Brighton, UK. He has authored more than 50 books and 600 articles, including *Negotiating Neoliberalism: Developing Alternative Educational Visions* (2018); *Routledge International Handbook on Narrative and Life History* (2017); *The Limits of Neoliberal Education. Refraction, Reinterpretation and Reimagination* (2017); *Critical Narrative as Pedagogy* (2014); *Developing Narrative Theory: Life Histories and Personal Representations* (2012); *The Life History of a School* (2011); *Through the Schoolhouse Door* (2010); and *Professional Knowledge, Professional Lives: Studies in Education and Change* (2003). Among the key ideas that he has contributed to the study of education include notions of Historical Periodisation, Refraction, Narrative Capital, Narrative Learning, Narrative Pedagogy and Curriculum Form. He has received the Michael Huberman Award at the American

Educational Research Association for his work on teachers' lives and was made a laureate of the Phi Delta Kappan Society in the United States.

Tom G. Griffiths is Associate Professor of comparative and international education at the University of Newcastle, Australia. His recent books include a co-authored volume, *Mass Education, Global Capital, and the World: The Theoretical Lenses of István Mészáros and Immanuel Wallerstein*, and the co-edited *Logics of Socialist Education: Engaging with Crisis, Insecurity and Uncertainty*. His research is focused on the relationship between education and projects to construct a more democratic, equal, peaceful and just world-system.

Vikas Gupta teaches in the Department of History at the University of Delhi, India. His broad area of academic engagement includes historical and contemporary aspects of education in modern India, with a special focus on curriculum knowledge, social inequalities, state policies and school practices. He is a member of the All-India Forum for Right to Education and Associate Editor of its quarterly newsletter, *Reconstructing Education for Emancipation*. He is currently also engaged in building up a nation-wide public campaign in support of the Common School System and spearheads this work through the All-India Forum for Right to Education.

Dave Hill is a socialist political activist, trade union leader and twice a Labour parliamentary candidate in England. His academic work focuses on issues of neoliberalism, capitalism, class, socialist education, critical pedagogy and resistance. He is Research Professor (Emeritus) of Education at Anglia Ruskin University, Chelmsford, England; Visiting Professor at the Kapodistrian and National University of Athens, Greece; and in the Social Policy Research Centre at Middlesex University, London, UK. He is series editor for the *Routledge Studies in Education, Neoliberalism and Marxism* series, which has published 18 books. He founded and is editor-in-chief for the *Journal for Critical Education Policy Studies*, which has had more than a million downloads in the last 10 years. He is co-organiser of the annual International Conference on Critical Education (founded in 2010). His recent works include *Marxism and Education: International Perspectives on Theory and Action* (2018); *Class, Race and Education Under Neoliberal Capitalism* (2017); *Eleştirel Eğitim ve Marksizm (Critical Education and Marxism)* (2016); *Marxist Essays on Education: Class and 'Race', Neoliberalism and Capitalism* (2013); and *Immiseration Capitalism and Education: Austerity, Resistance and Revolt* (2013), among many others.

Nita Kumar is Professor of South Asian History at the Department of History, Claremont Mckenna College, United States. She also runs a school and an organisation, NIRMAN, in Banaras, India, which is a postcolonial education research centre devoted to sponsoring intellectual and change-oriented activity on the subjects of children, education, women and civic and environmental values. She has written several books on history, education and gender studies, including *Educating the Child in India: The Family and the School*; *Lessons from Schools: A History of Education in Banaras*; *Exploring Indian Precolonial and Colonial Intellectual History*; and *The Politics of Gender, Community and Modernity: Essays on Education*. She has produced and scripted a forthcoming film, *Shankar's Fairies*.

Ravi Kumar teaches at the Department of Sociology, South Asian University, New Delhi, India. His recent works include *Neoliberalism, Critical Pedagogy and Education* (2016); *Education, State and Market: Anatomy of Neoliberal Impact* (2014); and *Education and the Reproduction of Capital: Neoliberal Knowledge and Counterstrategies* (2012). He co-edits the book series on *Social Movements, Dissent and Transformative Action* (2014), *Conversations on/for South Asia* and *Sociology/Anthropology Across Borders*. His area of research includes political economy of identity politics, social movements, neoliberal impact on education and processes of knowledge production. He is also an associate editor of *Society and Culture in South Asia* and a member of the editorial board of *Journal of Critical Education Policy Studies*.

Sanjay Kumar is a scholar, practitioner and founder of the Deshkal Society, Delhi, India. He has been working in the area of social diversity, inequality and education for more than one and half decades, both in practice and scholarship. His articles, monographs and occasional papers have been published in journals and magazines. He is a co-editor of various books: *Interrogating Development: Insights from the Margins*, *School Education Marginality and Pluralism Comparative Perspectives* and *Dynamics of Inclusive Classroom: Social Diversity, Inequality and School Education in India*.

Suman Lata teaches at the Department of Elementary Education, Gargi College, New Delhi, while also a doctoral candidate at the Jamia Milia Islamia, New Delhi, India. Her areas of interest include curriculum studies and school educational policies and practices. She is a member of the Parents Forum for Meaningful Education, India, an organisation that works for child rights and progressive practices in the elementary school system all over the country.

Disha Nawani is Dean, School of Education, Tata Institute of Social Sciences, Mumbai, India. Her research interests include curriculum, teacher education, educational policy and resources for school education. She has been a member of various teacher education review committees set up by Ministry of Human Resource Development and the National Council of

Teacher Education. She has been writing on the contemporary discourse of educational policy and assessment. She has also edited the volume *Teaching-Learning Resources for School Education* (2016).

Parul is a doctoral candidate at the Tata Institute of Social Sciences, Mumbai, India, in the area of Teachers Professionalism in the context of policy changes. Her research interests include Teachers Professional Development, Gender and Education, Policy Studies and Curriculum Studies.

Madhu Prasad has been actively involved with issues of education policy for more than two decades. She has analysed the impact of early 19th-century colonial education policy from archival material on Delhi's Madrasa Ghaziuddin/Delhi College, contributed chapters to volumes on the Education Commission (1964–66) and on India's neoliberal policy in education, and writes on education for academic journals and the print media. She is a member of the editorial board of the journal *Social Scientist* and is Executive Editor of *Reconstructing Education for Emancipation*, a quarterly newsletter of the All-India Forum for the Right to Education.

Jyoti Raina is Associate Professor, Department of Elementary Education, Gargi College, University of Delhi, New Delhi, India. Her main teaching focus is educational studies while her research interests include learning theory, cognitive education and initial teacher education. She also looks after the work of equal opportunity, Gandhi studies and anti-discrimination at the college.

Acknowledgements

I am grateful to all the chapter authors for their contributions, which made this volume possible at the current juncture of unprecedented crisis in elementary education in India. The friendships formed in bringing the chapters together has provided me several insights on the role elementary education can potentially play in building an inclusive society.

I thank all the contributing authors for letting me experience this thread of interconnectedness that has enriched me personally. I thank anonymous reviewers of the manuscript for pointing out some missing aspects of policy analysis, as well as for ideas on addressing them. I want to express my gratitude to Dave Hill, Ravi Kumar, Suman Lata and Parul for their encouragement, support and optimism that provides me with strength to carry on my teaching, writing and action. I thank Manju Rajput for inviting me to various meetings, activities and programmes at Raghubir Singh Junior Modern School, New Delhi – each visit illuminated me with valuable insights on school education policies and practices.

My colleagues at Gargi College have been a constant source of fellowship. I particularly thank Anjana Neira Dev for her constant advice that enabled me to sharpen the manuscript and members at the Department of Elementary Education for always being available to discuss my ideas. My students at the department continue to challenge me with their questions, teach me new things and expect me to generate readings for them, which compelled me to bring out this volume. They are too many to be named, but I need to make special mention of the B.El.Ed. fourth-year students of the 2018–19 session.

I am grateful to Aakash Chakrabarty and Brinda Sen of Routledge for helping at each step of turning the draft manuscript into this edited volume. They have not only been patient and cooperative but have also made useful suggestions. Their de-bureaucratic approach combined seriousness with a lightness that made the work of this volume a pleasurable experience.

Finally, I owe a debt of gratitude to my teacher, Professor Bharati Baveja, for initiating me into educational studies and teaching me the willingness to learn.

Abbreviations

AAP	Aam Aadmi Party
ABVP	Akhil Bharatiya Vidyarthi Parishad
AHC	Allahabad High Court
AIE	Alternative and Innovative Education
AIFRTE	All-India Forum for Right to Education
AISF	All India Students Federation
AKP	Adalet ve Kalkinma Partisi, Justice and Development Party
ASER	Annual Status of Education Reports
BDO	block development officer
B.Ed.	Bachelor of Education
B.El.Ed	Bachelor of Elementary Education
BJP	Bhartiya Janata Party
BO	beat officer
BPS	budget primary/private schools
BRC	block resource centre
BRP	block resource person
CBSE	Central Board of Secondary Education
CCS Rules	Central Civil Services (Conduct) Rules
CCE	continuous and comprehensive evaluation
CCS	Centre for Civil Society
CPI	Communist Party of India
CRC	cluster resource centre
CRP	cluster resource person
CSR	corporate social responsibility
CSSNS	common school system based on the concept of neighbourhood schools
CUG	Central University of Gujarat
DBT	Direct Benefit Transfers
DIET	District Institute of Education and Training
DISE	District Information System for Education
DoE	Directorate of Education

xviii Abbreviations

DPEP	District Primary Education Programme
EFA	Education for All
EGS	Education Guarantee Scheme
EIC	East India Company
EWS	economically weaker section
GATS	General Agreement for Trade in Services
GDP	gross domestic product
GER	gross enrolment ratio
GoI	Government of India
HM	headmaster/headmistress
HRD	human resource development
ICT	information and communication technology
IEC	Indian Education Commission
IIT	Indian Institute of Technology
ILO	International Labour Organisation
IMF	International Monetary Fund
INC	Indian National Congress
ISA	ideological state apparatus
JNU	Jawaharlal Nehru University
KBES	knowledge-based economy and society
LFPS	low-fee private schooling
LGBT	lesbian, gay, bisexual and transgender
LLO	learning level outcome
LO	learning outcome
MBC	most backward class
MDG	Millennium Development Goal
MDM	mid-day meal
MHRD	Ministry of Human Resource Development
MLL	Minimum Levels of Learning
NAR	net attendance ratio
NAS	National Achievement Survey
NCERT	National Council of Educational Research and Training
NCF	National Curriculum Framework
NCFR	National Curriculum Framework Review
NDP	no-detention policy
NEET	national eligibility cum entrance test
NEP	National Education Policy
NER	net enrolment ratio
NFE	non-formal education
NGO	non-governmental organisation
NISA	National Independent School Alliance
NITI Aayog	National Institution for Transforming India
NPE	National Policy on Education
NPM	new public management

NSP	non-state providers
NSSO	National Sample Survey Organisation
NUEPA	National University of Educational Planning and Administration
OBC	other backward class
OBE	outcome-based education
OoSC	out-of-school children
PISA	Programme for International Student Assessment
POA	Programme of Action
PPP	public-private partnership
PROBE	Public Report on Basic Education in India
PSU	public sector undertaking
PTM	parent-teacher meeting
RMSA	Rashtriya Madhyamik Shiksha Abhiyan
RPA	repressive state apparatuses
RSS	Rashtriya Swayamsevak Sangh
RTE Act	Right of Children to Free and Compulsory Education Act
SAP	structural adjustment programme
SC	scheduled caste
SCNC	School Choice National Conference
SDG	Sustainable Development Goal
SEQI	School Education Quality Index
SMC	school management committee
SSA	Sarva Shiksha Abhiyan
TaRL	Teaching at the Right Level
TDC	Teacher Development Coordinator
UEE	Universalisation of Elementary Education
UIS	UNESCO Institute for Statistics
UKIP	United Kingdom Independence Party
UNDP	United Nations Development Programme
UNESCO	United Nations Educational, Scientific and Cultural Organisation
UNICEF	United Nation's Children's Fund
UNO	United Nations Organization
UP	Uttar Pradesh
WB	World Bank
WHO	World Health Organisation
WTO	World Trade Organisation

Introduction

Mapping the exacerbated crisis in elementary education: issues and challenges

Jyoti Raina

The Indian constitution envisioned elementary education as a public good that contributes to the building of an egalitarian, just and democratic social order by providing free schooling of equitable quality to all the children of our country up to 14 years of age. This was viewed as the means to secure equality of opportunity for all citizens while upholding constitutional principles of social justice, diversity and inclusion. The educational policies of the post-independence years did not reflect the social justice intent towards securing this, by detailing an operational framework, to actualise elementary education into a public good. Moreover, subsequent educational policy shift(s) have cumulatively moved further from this constitutional commitment, following the twin trends of increased abdication of constitutional obligation and steady dilution of policy thrust on ensuring the public good of a free elementary education (Sadgopal, 2006: 93). The priorities of India's constitutional commitment to public elementary education have been wholly restructured in the past three decades as a result of the economic policy decisions for the liberalisation of the Indian economy under the influence of World Bank (WB)–World Trade Organization (WTO) mandates following the Washington Consensus in 1989. The consensus consists of a list of ten policies and reforms that include reordering public expenditure priorities, trade liberalisation, liberalisation of inward foreign direct investment, privatisation and deregulation (Williamson, 2009: 10). These international policy prescriptions and reforms were primarily economic but had wide-ranging implications for political economy as well for the social infrastructure domains, including education. They emanated from the ideology of neoliberalism that continues its dominance in shaping political and economic practices mediating a common sense that believes:

> [W]e are best served by maximum market freedom and minimum intervention by the state. The role of government should be confined to creating and defending markets, protecting private property and defending the realm. All other functions are better discharged by private enterprise,

which will be prompted by the profit motive to supply essential services. By this means, enterprise is liberated, rational decisions are made and citizens are freed from the dehumanising hand of the state.

(Monbiot, 2007)

Following the announcement of the New Economic Policy, since 1991 the International Monetary Fund (IMF) and the WB dictated a structural adjustment programme (SAP) and downsized welfare sectors, with a consequent reduction in the public financing of elementary education. This was reflected in the planning, organisation and pedagogy of WB-sponsored state programmes like the District Primary Education Programme (DPEP), beginning in 1994, but later covering 18 states and more than half of the districts in the country; it was characterised by replacing regular teachers with inadequately prepared contractual para-teachers, single-teacher schools with multi-grade teaching and the beginning of an outcome orientation (Ayyar, 2017: 26) with a curriculum consisting mainly of mere foundational skills, such as numeracy and literacy, as well as wreaking major havoc upon the elementary education system. The serious shifts in educational policy had already begun with the National Policy on Education (NPE) in 1986, which in itself heralded the policy wisdom in favour of privatisation (or non-state stake holding), reducing the role of the state and its commitment to public education. It continued to speak, as did previous policies, about equalising educational opportunities through the strengthening of the common school system, but without delineating how the state proposed to actualise this vision. More importantly, it continued to ignore an analysis of why the egalitarian idea of a common school system had continued to remain mere policy rhetoric on paper. The process of policy implementation into practice was simply passed over. The NPE in 1986 also introduced the category of 'pace-setting schools' on the premise that,

> It is universally accepted that children with special talent or aptitude should be provided opportunities to proceed at a faster pace, by making good quality education available to them, irrespective of their capacity to pay for it.

(MHRD, 1986: 13)

This brought further structural distortion to the already multi-layered school system, as if the state was responsible for provisioning 'good quality education' only for some children with the necessary aptitude in a separate layer of government schooling that was above the common school in an ascending hierarchy of school education. The children who belong to this category would typically be from the relatively advantaged sections of rural/ semi-urban society. This represents a selective kind of thinking, a tapered inclusion (Gupta, 2016) of a symbolic few, which awards policy legitimacy to the point of exacerbating already deep hierarchies in terms of access in the Indian multi-layered, graded, non-egalitarian schooling system. The policy also proposed, and in fact popularised, a multi-track, parallel, discriminatory, non-formal education system of elementary education while adversely affecting public institutional teaching and learning, leading to a deterioration of the state education system. The underlying assumption was that formal schooling is not necessary for every child. The subsequent ambitious state flagship educational reforms, like Sarva Shiksha Abhiyan (SSA), in 2000 continued to offer inferior norms and standards, further increasing the stratification among government schooling systems, while popularising the non-formal system in the trajectory of educational policy and practice, particularly for children who were not yet in the fold of school education. Ravi Kumar highlights how incremental policy changes and reforms (I wonder why they are called reforms!) moving further from the constitutional vision of equitable elementary education continue to reflect the segregation of an already differentiated typology of school systems, because the

> transition from a promise of universal free and compulsory education (read equality in access and access to quality education) by leaders of the freedom movement to the current division into formal and nonformal schools, with trained and well-paid teachers on one hand, and partially trained and ill-equipped, underpaid teachers on the other, has come about.
>
> (Ravi Kumar, 2006b: 14)

The outcome orientation embedded in the policy shifts aligned with a techno-managerial model for educational planning and management in which the notion of quality education was quantified to the achievement of measurable learning outcomes (LOs). The prevailing status of education in any district of the country was assumed to be indicated by the assessment of the LOs in the school academic domains of reading and arithmetic (ASER, various years). These kinds of large-scale assessments resulted in the development of a binary between public and private school performances, which instead of taking a school as the unit of analysis, has tended to show public schools as failures. This further aggravates the multi-faceted attack on the public education system, which is now not only turned into but is even known as the colony of the 'underprivileged' section of our society. This has continued to draw attention away from systemic constraints and other structural bottlenecks associated with the functioning of government schools, circuitously further supporting the political economy of privatisation. Empirical research has demonstrated that the systemic deterioration of the public education system in the name of educational reforms, following SAP, led to the proliferation of a burgeoning economy of private schools euphemistically termed low-fee private schooling (LFPS) by the end of the 1990s (Valaskar,

2017), adding further layers in the existing graded hierarchy of access to schooling. Another precarious outcome of this alleged deterioration of government schools was the diversion of public finances to private players in a hidden agenda of privatisation in the name of public–private partnership (PPP). The WTO–General Agreement for Trade in Services (GATS) regime had already come to India in 1995, following the Washington Consensus, turning education into a legally 'tradeable commodity' and distorting the role an equitable system of schooling could play in building a democratic society. The Right of Children to Free and Compulsory Education, or RTE Act (2009), in pursuit of a rights-based approach to elementary education as an entitlement that every child deserves, continued with the existing hierarchies of schooling which were established as legitimised by earlier policies, cumulative shifts and reforms. Although the act was created with the intention of expanding the state's responsibility for providing education to the children of India, it preferred to outsource expansion in the non-public sector instead of achieving it via a public and universal system of elementary education. This intent belied the impact, as the act did not focus on qualitative improvement in a 'universal' government school system, but on quantitative expansion, enrolling each child in the system, establishing norms and creating a token space for children belonging to economically weaker sections (EWS) of society and choosing to co-opt private schools in the policy framework of a private schools–based market society. The exploratory studies examining the status of implementation of this provision of including EWS children in private unaided schools in cities have identified gaps in administrative processes in terms of their complexity, whereby inclusion is ensured only at the level of granting admission to the school and does not provide inclusive education beyond the mere physical presence of the child in the school (Mehendale et al., 2015). Anil Sadgopal, has pointed out how the act succumbed to the neoliberal trap by providing an escape route for the state and indirectly supported the withdrawal of the state governments in ensuring public education for all, as well as diffused the struggle for a common school system (Sadgopal, 2016a: 34). The entrenchment of a multi-layered school system from the mid-1980s for each separate section of our stratified society has contributed to the sharp divisions in school education, as well as the decline of the state system, which is being attended, in recent years, mostly by children from the marginalised social segments (Sadgopal, 2016b: 18).

Thus, the trajectory of the constitutional vision of equitable elementary education has continued to remain mere rhetoric or sloganeering for more than seven decades. This parallels the worrying trend in post-colonial schooling systems in several other parts of the world, where schooling is increasingly class based, with children of the elites and well-to-do attending schools with better physical infrastructure and other resources, and those of the peasantry and working class lacking access to such schools (Bloch, 2009).

The social differences based on economic class and school education are not cross-cutting but overlap in Indian society, leading to profound social divisions while perpetuating graded social hierarchies, regional disparity and educational inequality. This merits importance, as social scientists in India have emphasised caste–class, rural–urban and gender-based distinctions but have not paid sufficient attention to the sharp divisions produced in society by the multi-layered, graded structures that distort our school education system (Kumar, 2009). The outcome of the neoliberal policy changes since the liberalisation of the economy has been the operationalisation of the process of developing and entrenching further hierarchies of schooling systems which not only reproduce the existing social inequalities but also exacerbate another set of graded inequalities in our stratified social structure with its overlapping social differences. School education has become a class-based process. This has debilitating consequences for our society, as there are disturbing resemblances between the densely, multi-layered graded hierarchies of schooling and the exacerbating structural social hierarchies of the neoliberal economy, which is irreparably shaping the lives, aspirations and aims of our young learners. The lack of thrust on public education with each policy 'reform' has accentuated social divisions by unequivocally establishing the domination of private capital (with increasing privatisation) in the context of elementary education policy and practice in India. The state, irrespective of political dispensation, has continued to be a facilitator of this shift (in the name of reform), leading to a convergence of economic and educational discursive regimes aimed at adjusting education to fit the prevailing neoliberal socio-economic order since the two and a half decades following liberalisation. The wilful lack of policy thrust on public education, accentuation of existing hierarchies of access, contractualisation of teaching, increasing non-state stake holding, involvement of private players, proliferation of private capital and a shift of value by the state from public to private have precipitated an educational crisis since education came under neoliberalisation.

However, at the current historical juncture, the state of crisis in elementary education has exacerbated to an unprecedented urgency since a new political-ideological context is becoming more sharply defined. The post-colonial capitalism complemented welfare policies (in education as in other social domains) for the seven decades following independence, but the state gradually eschewed this welfarism in favour of the market as the socio-political determinant shaping public policy – so much so that at the current juncture there are hardly any incremental aspects left that provide continuity to the 'policy history' (Rizvi and Lingard, 2009: 9) of previous policy concerns of egalitarianism, social justice and commitment to a public good. The nature of the state has shifted with the diminishing operative distinction between state and market. The direction of policy shifts culminates into a new paradigm of unprecedented privatisation/quasi-privatisation of schooling, driven by both the market and the neoliberal state. The agenda of marketisation/privatisation and abdication of direct state responsibility for elementary education is not even hidden anymore, but rather working towards increased accommodation of the demands of private capital in/from school education. With the increasing commodification, marketisation, privatisation and commercialisation of society and education, whatever remains of public schooling in this country is endangered and is on the cusp of being turned into a privatised service in a free-market model of elementary education, accompanied by the broader social, cultural, economic and political changes supporting it.

This new policy context is sorely appropriate to the workings of neoliberal capital underwritten within contemporary reform practices. The country has not had a national policy on education for more than three decades. The trends reflected in executive pronouncements and policymaking projections are based on the underlying assumptions of a 'market-based economy' in 'a regulatory framework that maximises the efficiency of markets' (NITI Aayog, 2017: 123). This calls for an education that '[orients] the system towards outcomes' (NITI Aayog, 2017: 131), 'will amalgamate globalization with localization' (MHRD, 2016a: 1), giving 'new impetus to skill development through vocational education in the context of the emergence of new technologies in a rapidly expanding economy in a globalised environment' and 'encouraging ways of enhancing private investment and funding' (MHRD, 2016a: 2), involving strategies of privatisation, marketisation and centralisation coupled with minimum state power and oversight (Ramamurthy and Pandiyan, 2017). The worrying effects include an outcome-based curriculum which provides opportunities to aspire for 'excellence in learning outcomes' which can be 'comparable to student learning outcomes in high-performing international education systems', designing a common national curriculum for the subjects: Science, Mathematics and English; and introduction of information and communication technology (ICT) as another subject in grade 6 (MHRD 2016b: 21). There is an affirmation of the neoliberal common sense, as the structural inequality prevailing in school education and what it means in terms of a redistributive elementary education policy – a fundamental concern – has been side-stepped. The earlier genre of policies at least paid symbolic lip service to the social aims of education and reconstruction of Indian society on egalitarian premises. There was no shying away from at least expressing disquiet at the class basis of school education and its role in reproducing the societal class divide (NCERT, 1970: 449). The topic of education for equality and, more importantly, a common school system (which is an instrument in the quest for equality) to which full chapters were dedicated in earlier policies cease to receive space in the current policy text, or rather the policy regime, as no formal education policy has been pronounced for three decades now. The urgent crisis in elementary education has been cumulatively building up but has peaked at the current juncture, as policymaking is looking like an official participant of the global neoliberal project, a new version of the class phenomenon, re-posing faith in a stratified society with concomitant sharp divisions in the school education system. It is insightful to contextualise what we want to make of our society as these policy changes threaten to further divide Indian society in which social differences are not cross-cutting but typically overlap in graded hierarchies.

Educators in the Indian tradition have held the aim of education to be nothing short of the highest aim of life itself, to discover the higher and wider significance to life, to seek an intelligent understanding of the world (Krishnamurti, 1992: 11) and to experience the unity of life. To critical educators, the goal of education is to invite students to think about varied disciplinary domains, their society and learning how to learn so that education becomes the place where the individual and society are co-constructed. This co-construction is based on a social pedagogy, a mutually created dialogue developed by teachers posing problems to students that may be derived from their own personal and social lives and the disciplinary academic domains. Such a critical education 'challenges teachers and students to empower themselves for social change, to advance democracy and equality as they advance their literacy and knowledge' (Shor, 1993: 25). In contrast the neoliberal policy framework of a market society with techno-managerial competency–based knowledge systems undermine knowledge in its true meaning by merely functioning to prepare students to take their place in the existing consensuses of the corporate hierarchy and serve as submissive human capital, tolling the bells for a globalising polity that envisages to build 'obedient productive units in so called knowledge based economy, and society consisting of an uncritical citizenry (Dhankar, 2016). The neoliberal educational policies and reforms have attempted to understand learning, knowledge and curriculum in mere utilitarian terms of measurable standards and targets – so much so that learning outcome performances are centre stage in most of the mainstream education debates, blurring the distinction between classroom learning experiences and LOs and in alignment with the changing aims of education that restrict it merely to uncritical skill building in the national and international context.

The policy shifts, issues and challenges that the study of elementary education during the last three decades in India brings to the fore contour the four section divisions of this book. These consist of theory, policy analysis, empirical research, ethnographic data, field experiences and critical explorations, which are presented in the 14 chapters that have been brought together in this anthology plumbing diverse disciplinary viewpoints while engaging with structures of elementary education across policy contexts, dividing the range of section-division deliberations as follows:

- Policies, programmes and practices have played a devastating role by a **neoliberal restructuring of education**, beginning with the SAP unleashed by the Washington Consensus, which imposed a reform regime in the developing context of India. This has resulted in policy-led dilutions, detractions and distortions in the nationalist vision of educational progress underlying constitutional ideals. An overview of the history of the neoliberal shifts, an explanation of what neoliberalism means in policy parlance, its assault on democratic polity and commitment to public good (including elementary education) are basic to undertaking an analysis of the restructuring of elementary education, while raising questions related to policy emphasis, strengths and shifts. A direct engagement with various policy texts on specific matters is useful in fleshing out the exact terms of policy discourse, putting it in a societal context and outlining worrying trends and policy outcomes.

- Transactions of **knowledge and curriculum** in the classroom and its assessment are trivialised to literacy, numeracy and mechanical skill development and shorn of criticality. The aim of education is to prepare a docile workforce for a graded labour market, so knowledge, too, depends on whether the market wants or does not want the specific skills to exist. There is *fragmentation* of knowledge into marketable competencies, its *alienation* from its social and material base, exacerbated by the fetish for information and communication technology (ICT) in school education and *increasingly* shaping the character of knowledge by global market trends (Kumar, 2017: 10). The economic rationale underlying 'input' considerations within curricular practice and accompanying assumptions of knowledge 'output' frequently remain unexamined in policy and practice. The examination system, based on a conception of education as the acquisition of a given body of knowledge, continues the spectacle of reproducing social asymmetries legitimised by school systems that make differential resources available to children from different sections of our hierarchical society who attend different types of schools.

- Critical education engenders possibilities to mitigate the structures of oppression, dominance and inequality inherent in the existing society, with special reference to **schooling, social justice and critical pedagogy.** The emphasis on critical pedagogy makes for a counter-hegemonic examination of the exclusion inherent in neoliberal policies for the masses, with an eye for a wider transformative egalitarian vision that educators can catalyse. The National Curriculum Framework Review (NCRF) 2005 proposes a new vision of pre-service teacher education 'to create reflective practitioners who would have the promise of bringing about radical changes in the process of schooling for hundreds of millions of our children' (NCFR, 2005: 101). Such reflective practitioners cannot remain apolitical by framing pre-defined questions from existing textbooks dissuading schools to teach young children from raising their own questions (Sleeter et al., 2004). Critical pedagogy thus positions elementary school teachers as transformative educators in an explicit emancipatory role (Hill and Boxley, 2007: 54), offering possibilities that can potentially lead to fissures in the neoliberal common sense.

- There is agreement that private capital, with its overriding aim of maximising profit under neoliberal capitalism, accumulates globally. Its consequences for elementary education, though global, vary for various countries, depending upon uneven levels of resistance based on each country's own balances of class forces (Hill and Kumar, 2009) and class interests. Marxist educational analysis and world-systems analysis (Wallerstein, 1994) provide as one of its many theoretical arguments a lens to look at **transnational trends on neoliberalism and education**, recognising both the power of resistance and the need for more fundamental economic, political and social change. The ubiquitous prevalence of human capital theory as the basis for educational planning and policy-making further supports the neoliberal logic, with its recognition of education as an instrument of future economic return. Research has revealed the robust evidence of fissures in the neoliberal common sense with the finding that neoliberal restructuring has not necessarily improved even 'educational standards', its avowed goal (Goodson and Lindblad, 2011).

Neoliberal restructuring of education

In Chapter 1 Jyoti Raina and Parul present an overview of the educational policy changes that have taken place in the last three decades since neoliberalisation of school education. The chapter examines the dominant wave of policy reform, quality, an idea which has been reduced to completing targets in the name of achieving LOs, and proxy indicators that 'show off' learning have become centre stage. It concludes by highlighting the emergence of a new political-ideological policy context framed around the concepts of quality and accountability in contemporary times that seeks to legitimise the neoliberal common sense in spite of the devastating role it has played in restructuring educational policy and practice in India.

The Bombay Plan (1945) advocated a capitalist model of development, using the resources of the public sector for its own advancement, a phenomenon that Suman Lata examines in Chapter 2 while looking at the extension of the neoliberal agenda by governments across the world in involving private players in big public projects in the name of utilising the managerial expertise and capital from the private market for efficient delivery of public services, supposedly, in the larger interest of people. The term public–private partnership (PPP) is a euphemism for this scourge and is one of the depredations associated with liberalisation of the economy in the arena of social infrastructure. Her multi-pronged analysis of the origin, rise and models of the concept in the Indian context concludes with the argument for not only its undesirability but also possible fallout in school education.

Atishi, who is a leader from a political party that is currently in office in the capital's state government, speaks in a voice that is unusual for a politician. In Chapter 3 she does not hesitate to make several against-the-grain admissions which merit special attention for two reasons. The first is their unambiguous candour and the second is the fact that they are made by a politician at the helm of affairs in a state. She states that the 'deep politician-private school nexus means that [the] executive has little or no incentive to fix public education', the 'political establishment that profits from [the] increasing enrolment of children in private schools has a vested interest to keep government schools dysfunctional' and 'public education is closely linked to the class divide prevailing in the country'. She looks at the steady decline in the quality of public education as a 'national crisis' of the government's own making (without hesitating to term it nothing short of a *national crisis*), which further coincides with the widening inequality India has witnessed over the last three decades. She makes a call that research on land allocations to private schools during different political regimes would provide an interesting insight into why there is a breakdown of the public education system. Who would undertake such a research? The doctoral students fishing for scarce employment opportunities in the private sectors of education (the state is hardly recruiting anymore) or civil society/research organisations that depend on state largesse in the name of funding.

She speaks of possibilities to a better public schooling system, simply through honest governance and political will. The Aam Aadmi Party (AAP) made school education an election issue, and since coming to power in February 2015 accorded highest priority to it. The immediate huge hike in allocation to education (in 2015–16, the government allocated Rs 9,836 crore to education) was a whopping 106% over the previous government's allocation. Over the next two years, the allocation to education has been maintained at around a quarter of the total budget of the Delhi government. Atishi presents a poignant account of some of these efforts to 'fix' public education through a four-pronged approach involving modernising infrastructure, building capacity for schoolteachers and principals, making the school administration accountable and improving LOs. The hurried policies and programmes of the AAP government, particularly ability grouping, opposition to continuous and comprehensive evaluation (CCE), equating quality with better LOs and looking up at private schools in the name of standards, have attracted censure from progressive educators, but her chapter reflects an uncompromising political commitment to saving public education, particularly at the school level. Ironically, the policies have provided a fillip to non-state actors in the name of outsourcing several school services, deflecting the increased budgetary allocation to private players, while recruitment of teachers to vacant posts has not been undertaken for eight years now. Yet the intent in school improvement processes by taking up the underlying challenges and opportunities is undeniable.

The central argument of Chapter 4 by Jyoti Raina is that both the stance of the state and the neoliberal assault on education are in conflict with the constitution's vision of elementary education. The cumulative policy shifts in the direction of non-state stake holding are explicated through a direct engagement with policy text(s) revealing how a lack of thrust on elementary education as a public good, increasing privatisation of school education and indifference to increasing hierarchies of schooling in policy parlance is serving to exacerbate the class divisions underlying Indian education. The chapter undertakes a policy analysis examining the worrying outcomes of contemporary trends in India's national trajectory and what we intend to make of our society with them as school education emerges as an overlapping social difference providing another category of social division.

Understanding knowledge and curriculum

In some of the recent policy deliberations, there was talk of the need to educate the youth as per the industry demand while lamenting the gap between industry requirements and the goals of education. It was argued that institutions should be prepared according to a list of industry requirements (ASSOCHAM, 2017) evidently reflecting the policy impact of the market on the content of education. These changing aims of education ignore the entrenched inegalitarianism, oppressive power structure and neoliberal depredation of our society. The function of education should be to develop critical citizens who sustain a society through their economic and cultural contribution and have a responsibility to offer constructive criticism to counter its ills. Rohit Dhankar, Chapter 5, argues that historically education policy documents in India emphasise both these functions. However, the current policy shifts seem to be heavily tilting towards the 'citizen as a resource', reducing the idea of a 'democratic citizen' to a 'subject of the state'. One strategy to achieve this tilt that is being used in the recent state initiatives is a surreptitious 're-definition of knowledge'. The chapter focuses on this tilt in the conception of knowledge in a supposedly knowledge-based economy and society (KBES) and its implications for social justice in a democracy.

If the purpose of knowledge in forming a formal curriculum and its assessment is understood as grading and ranking of learners in a culture of competition, enterprise, employability and managerialism, a Marxist analysis would see this process as natural to a class society (Rustin, 2016: 148). The understanding of assessment, which is a key aspect of the examination-centred Indian school education system, follows from the behavioural paradigm, which is in alignment with the neoliberal approach. Assessment is aimed at evaluation of LOs on scholastic parameters and criteria by using paper-and-pencil methods rather than building a learning culture where assessment is a continuous process of and for learning (Shepard, 2000).

Such an approach to learning and assessment have been declining in educational theory for several decades, and its underlying assumptions about the nature of the learner and the learning process are unacceptable to most progressive educators. The examination system with a sole focus on LO performances assumes a narrow, behavioural view of learning as an external observable product, ignoring the holistic processes of learning and knowledge construction during classroom and out-of-classroom experiences. In Chapter 6, Disha Nawani contests the narrow product-oriented viewpoint which implies that learning can be ensured by holding learners back and testing them in standardised, time-tested, reliable ways via a centralised examination system where students had to per force learn (read and memorise), pass the exam and get promoted to a higher grade. Part of the chapter carries an interview with eminent educationist Krishna Kumar explaining how the examination system tries to provide a legitimate veneer of fairness to the participation of children from different social backgrounds in a supposedly objective certification process under common conditions, irrespective of the social or educational background they come from. The interview speaks of this supposed fairness as something that can be read as silence to the deep inequalities that prevail in the broader structure of our school education system. The performance in the examination ignores the supply-side asymmetries within schooling systems, including academic resources, physical plant and infrastructural resources, among others. The chapter highlights that socially, the examination system, just like the other social systems, is working for a society which is divided hierarchically, legitimising the prevailing social hierarchies of our society, a process that is exacerbated by education under neoliberalisation. The struggle for improvement in the examination system needs to be situated in the wider background of other unjust aspects of our educational systems in our society, where social differences of economic class, caste and gender do not cross-cut, but overlap, leading to sharp social divisions that are reflected in school education.

In Chapter 7 Nita Kumar argues that we must understand longer political trends since independence and the relationship of the school to the family to be able to deal with neoliberal shift towards privatisation in schooling. She presents ethnographic data from a large research study conducted in one of the schools in a representative small town, Varanasi, in Uttar Pradesh, to describe that the present failure of egalitarianism and democracy in education at several levels in living up to the constitutional policy of equality is due to our very understanding and practices of modernity. If we understand the longer trends, if we break up schools and technical practices, if we focus on the relationship between the school and community and, most of all, if we look, apart from numerical data, at thick ethnographic data, we will come closer to understanding the shift towards privatisation as a problem and find a solution.

Schooling, social justice and critical pedagogy

In Chapter 8 Sanjay Kumar interrogates and interrupts caste-based exclusionary processes in select rural Bihar schools, situating the questions of social justice and structural discrimination with an eye for anthropological detail, in a critical framework emphasising first-hand inclusive teaching and learning methodology. He presents some revelatory truths about the deep-rooted caste-based prejudices in schools by a rigorous engagement with some of the structures of belief that condition classroom practice, especially teaching activity, and end up making elementary education double up for a renewed performance of caste-, class- and community-based discrimination. The chapter is based on an action research study focused on the key question of how teachers can be made aware of the problems around the notion of heredity-based educability, reflected through *Sanskara,* and the ways in which teachers can be enabled to reflect on their own beliefs and assumptions about the key concepts of education, learning and the notion of caste. The methodology consisted of small-group workshops, classroom demonstrations and training modules engaging some 1,000 primary and upper primary school teachers from the Wazirganj block of the Gaya district of Bihar. The findings of the action research study inform policies and practices in making classrooms inclusive for all children in particular, and the professional development of the teachers in general, in order to attain the larger goal of social justice and equality in a teacher education programme. Prior to deployment of the intervention programme of inclusive teaching and learning methodology, the teachers lacked an understanding of the doctrine of inherent educability of children, which is central to the history of ideas in educational theory. It is further disturbing to note that the key findings of the study based on the micro-context correspond to the macro-level understanding and perception prevalent in the public knowledge domain. A similar study in a village in Bihar more than a decade ago also concluded that 'unequal structural realities of village life play a very important role in producing and reproducing educational inequality in the village' (Kumar, 2006a: 319). This seriously implicates teacher education for absence of a critical pedagogy that interrogates the deficit assumptions of educability among socially disadvantaged children. The social realism underlying the chapter is a grim reminder of the dehumanisation that is implicit in caste hierarchy, social exclusion and the consequent discriminatory practices. The flush of educational reforms in the uncritical framework of the techno-managerial model does not provoke teachers to interrogate such structures and practices of the deep social inequalities, but rather to potentially reinforce, promote and validate the deficit assumptions about educability that often stem from discriminatory attitudes which underlie the class, caste and gender hierarchies in wider society.

In a Marxist educational analysis, the possibilities for social justice exist only by doing away with an unjust, exploitative and oppressive capitalist social order. This has greater relevance at the current historical juncture in which the sharper avatar of capitalism-neoliberalism dominates the social, economic and political life, coupled with the dismantling of the social justice agenda in official policy trends. Dave Hill (in this volume) argues that because neoliberalism is simply the current stage of capitalism, its critique is essentially a critique of capitalism itself. Slavoj Zizek (2018) reiterates the same when he writes that

> not only is Marx's critique of political economy and capitalist dynamics still fully relevant, but rather it is only today, with global capitalism, that it is fully relevant.

Ravi Kumar's critical essay in Chapter 9 resonates these words with a hammer while presenting an incisive critique of the shifting aims of education. The aims have moved beyond the idea of knowledge that even capitalist welfare regimes conceived to mere skilling; which in turn is about training an individual to be unconcerned about the oppression prevailing around her or him. This is a tacit consensualisation for the existing order of things in times of what he calls a 'fascisation of society' – so much so that he even considers the question, are we living in a fascist state, worthy of asking. Critical pedagogy can be an instrument to counter these processes of consensualisation, which is something that mobilisation aimed to counter. Ravi argues that critical pedagogy, while locating itself within the labour-capital dialectic, must also move towards exploring the possibilities of how its teachings can lead to a situation of counter-mobilisation. In the education battlefield, therefore, possibilities of being neutral, quiet and non-partisan do not exist (Ravi Kumar, 2016: 2). The chapter states that unequivocally *we need to decide which side we are on*, which can be very simply read as either standing for the status quo or challenging it. In a penetrative analysis, the chapter shows that educational discourses are inherently political, in which the mainstream schooling systems are dedicated towards a consensus-building exercise based upon the status quo, consisting of existing social formations. The possibilities to challenge the status quo are compromised if, for example, one is dependent on the state for survival (economic wages for work) or in precarious contractual work buffered by a wide pool of unemployment, as is increasingly the case in both the arenas of school education and higher education. The adjustment with neoliberal policies starts with this fear, which in turn helps the capitalist status quo to thrive (Marcuse, 1969). Also in India supposedly under cover by Central Civil Services (Conduct) CCS Rules, academics, although not owing direct allegiance to any political party, understandably seek personal and academic protection against discrimination that being a critic of government policy might bring. Where then is the direct possibility for entering a pedagogical war to counter, subvert and resist the processes of consensualisation by a practice of freedom from the logic of the present system? Nine teachers of the Central University of Gujarat (CUG) were issued show cause notice under Rule 5 of CCS Rule number 5, which prohibits government employees from associating with any political party or campaigning for elections. The clarification offered by the teachers in this matter was finally accepted by the university administration, and the matter has been since closed (IE, 2018). The CCS Rules have been in force since 1964 with unwritten ambiguity about whether teachers are covered under these rules or not. Rule 5 states

> No Government servant shall be a member of, or be otherwise associated with, any political party or any organisation which takes part in politics nor shall he take part in, subscribe in aid of, or assist in any other manner, any political movement or activity.

Rule 9, in fact, prohibits criticism of the government. Critical educational policy analysis is political in nature, as the making of public policy is a political activity and can be looked at as a violation of CCS rules. Coupled with this, even if teachers as transformative intellectuals and critical citizens were to realize that education is the battlefield on which possibilities of being neutral are non-existent, educational issues have been rendered invisible in the party manifestos by competitive electioneering over other popular political issues in the public imagination. Even if academics review party manifestos, policies and programmes, in various fora like academic books and journals, raising concerns about the core issues related to schooling, social justice and equality, their voice, inputs and scholarship more often than not fall on deaf ears in political policymaking arena. This is evident as the plethora of writings and research on how neoliberal restructuring has devastated educational systems and practices, with the loss of equity, democracy and critical thought, and has not received any political recognition in state policymaking, which continues to shift in the opposite direction. This is notwithstanding the social imaginary underlying the aim of public policy for inclusive development through equitable elementary education.

Exclusions based on caste and status have existed in Indian society, and Madhu Prasad, in Chapter 10, provides a synoptic account of pre-colonial exclusions, colonial subjugation, radical goals of our freedom movement and their subversion in the politics of an independent citizenry. In a democratic society, all sections of the population, including children, have legitimate rights to equality and claims on the state not merely to 'protect' those rights but also to ensure that they are realised in ways that comply with the principles of equality and social justice. She argues that India's attempt to leap-frog over this democratising phase of capitalist development, with its concomitant increased employment and mass provisioning of essential social services such as education, health, public utilities, etc., and adopt the contemporary phase of neoliberal 'jobless growth' and privatisation/corporatisation of all essential services with user-pays principles of efficiency, has resulted in a massive 'exclusion' of those who simply cannot afford to pay. This contemporary sense of 'exclusion' in the Indian context de-legitimises existing sites of debate against oppression, threatens the autonomy and self-governing capacity of the people and ultimately endangers the democratic unity of society itself.

Transnational trends on neoliberalism and education

The final section opens up the debate for a comparative understanding through an analysis of some of the recent policy trends in some parts of the world as an index for measuring neoliberal 'common sense' and its relative degree of failure. This section is also aimed at deepening the response to emerging challenges in India through a wider international and comparative lens.

Locating contemporary developments more theoretically within the Marxist fold continues to highlight the enduring relevance of Marxist educational analysis to the current neoliberal era. Class analysis as an intellectual tool with abiding significance central to a social understanding of education can also contrastingly explain reflective departures that emphasise two-way relations between ideas and material realities or conditions. The recognition of the latter relationship is increasingly contrasted with a view of Marx's theory as one which defines ideas being determined by economic conditions (Sen, 2018). Marxian analysis remains pervasive in education discipline because it continues to inspire extraordinary contributions from other radical left, non-Marxist educators ranging from Anton Gramsci, to Henry Giroux, to Michael Apple and enable anyone with egalitarian beliefs, including the non-Marxist reader, to draw insights from Marxist theory. It also inspires the reader to move beyond 'deconstruction' to 'reconstruction' by offering a doctrine for action, while recognising both the power of resistance and the need for more fundamental economic, political and social change in the hope of building a new world. It is against this background that Dave Hill, in Chapter 11, critically examines neoliberal and neoconservative policy globally and how it differs in different national contexts. The chapter concludes by suggesting a socialist policy for education, delineating facets of its ownership and control, funding, organisation of students, the curriculum, the hidden curriculum, secular education and relationship with communities. This suggestion of a socialist policy for education is important because a central theme in educational studies, particularly programmes of teacher education, is student-teachers building their own personal theory of education. This theoretical chapter provides valuable conceptual tools, techniques and perspectives on educational policy analysis for education workers across political affiliations.

Engagement with ideologies across political dispensations in the public sphere is part of a democratic citizenship. The conservatives in India have been running schools through non-profit religious and cultural trusts, but have recently become increasingly articulate about their economic world-view as well, which includes a general opposition to privatisation. The chief of Rashtriya Swayamsevak Sangh (RSS) was invited to speak on the Indian economy at the Bombay Stock Exchange, Mumbai, on 16 April 2018, where he highlighted that enslavement to a theory or an ideology like socialism or capitalism was unwise, as each country must pick policies suited to its own unique circumstances. He spoke of 'leading' the world economy through India's own model of development; reflecting how neoconservativism is some-times in conflict with neoliberalism, which Dave Hill points out in his chapter.

Tom Griffiths's theoretical analysis in Chapter 12 further argues that neo-liberal policy for education gains legitimacy from, and in turn reinforces, aspects of human capital theory, through its construction of education not as a public and social service, nor as a universal human right, but as a private, individual responsibility to be purchased by individuals for their personal social and economic benefit. The chapter concludes by noting how advocacy for increased public expenditures on education often cites eco-nomic returns, which risks supporting the neoliberal logic and policy that we seek to replace. Instead, it calls for critical educators and activists to emphasise and build support for alternative primary purposes of mass edu-cation that more firmly support high-quality, public, universal systems with the potential to contribute to wider anti-systemic movements.

Even though neoliberal restructuring, resembling a world movement ema-nating from the global financial institutions (Meyer, 2000), started in most of the countries of the world in the 1990s, it has varied historical founda-tions. The historic trajectory of each nation-state has therefore 'refracted', translated and diffused the neoliberal reform agenda in different ways. The post-liberalisation neoliberal regimes have thus increasingly sought the tech-nocratic weight of evidence in favour of restructuring. Ivor Goodson, in Chapter 13, based on seminal research, presents evidence that is otherwise. The chapter aims to understand patterns of historical and cultural 'refrac-tion' by reporting some of the findings from four-year qualitative national case studies of educational reforms in seven European countries. The empir-ical findings from this seminal qualitative research can be read as an index for the measurement of this neoliberal common sense, as well its assault and paradoxically also a relative failure at 'implementation' policies. The global neoliberal frameworks get re-worked, re-enacted and re-formulated by international and national actors alike, and particularly professionals like teachers, often ending up getting fissured in unintended directions, like the refracted rays of light through an optical medium.

The comparative understanding of transnational trends of neoliberalism and its consequences for education is useful in re-visiting the current elementary education policy context in India through the lens of competing frameworks for combating educational inequality in the concluding chapter. The judgment dated 18 August 2015 by Justice Sudhir Agarwal of the Allahabad High Court (AHC) directing the Uttar Pradesh (UP) government to ensure that government servants and all such persons who receive any perk, benefit, salary, etc., from state exchequer or public fund to send their children to primary schools run by the UP Board of Basic Education can be read as an attempt by the Indian judiciary to mitigate sharp educational inequality. In Chapter 14 Vikas Gupta examines this audaciously radical legal development. He develops his line of argument using the context provided by the AHC judgment and further validated through a very brief survey of the chequered transnational historical trajectories of the Western world to combat educational inequalities through state intervention. The chapter draws attention to the radicalness of the judgment, which was ahead of its time in comparison to the RTE 2009, which is often facetiously hailed in Indian educational debates as a progressive piece of legislation. This is against the backdrop that 'neoliberalism poses a more serious threat not only to the diversity of knowledges and languages, but to the entire society by augmenting existing inequalities' (Gupta, in this volume) by ignoring the wider structural concerns.

The pending issues and contemporary challenge that the judgment poses resonate in many of the chapters in this volume that highlight the indifference and now increasing complicity of the state in the policy-led deterioration of state schooling systems. The vision of an egalitarian, democratic and inclusive society, of development of the country through an equitable system of elementary education, cannot be realised without an uncompromising thrust on public education, an ideal that neoliberalisation in education works against. If hope is the thing that features our burdens, then the fact that the judgment has to date continued to remain only a non-mandatory declaration on paper, without implementation, begs the question: Is there hope for a greater thrust on public education in India at the current juncture of neoliberal depredation? But what is left of life without hope? 'So the sailor sails on, though he knows he will never touch the stars that guide him' (Galeano, 2011). It is hoped that the chapters gathered in this volume will contribute to the timely debates on elementary education policy and practice at the present juncture of an unprecedented crisis. The volume aspires not just to analyse the policy shifts in recent years but also to offer possibilities and egalitarian alternatives to the educational crisis generated by the neoliberalisation of education. More importantly, it hopes to re-kindle a constitutional renaissance by re-vitalising the diffused struggle for a common school system among teachers, academicians, researchers, activists, policymakers, students and other education workers, which alone holds the promise to create an equitable elementary education policy and practice that can serve as the foundation of an inclusive society.

References

ASER. (various years). *Annual status of education report*. New Delhi: ASER Centre, Pratham.

Associated Chambers of Commerce and Industry of India (ASSOCHAM). (2017). *Keynote address at education summit by Shri Manish Sisodia, Minister of Education*, Government of National Capital Region of Delhi (Accessed on 25 October 2017).

Ayyar, R. and Vaidyanatha, V. (2017). Inclusive elementary education in India: The journey. In: M. Tiwary, K. Sanjay Kumar and A. K. Misra, eds., *Dynamics of inclusive classroom: Social diversity, inequality and school education in India*. New Delhi: Orient Blackswan.

Bloch, G. (2009). *The toxic mix: What's wrong with South Africa's schools and how to fix it*. Cape Town: Tafelberg.

Dhankar, R. (2016). Dumbing Down a Pliable Workforce. *The Hindu*. Available at: www.thehindu.com/opinion/lead/Dumbing-down-a-pliableworkforce/article1456 2308.ece (Accessed on 10 August 2016).

Galeano, E. (2011). *Mirrors: Stories of almost everyone*. London: Portobello Books.

Goodson, I. F. and Lindblad, S. (2011). Conclusions: Developing a conceptual framework for understanding professional knowledge. In: I. F. Goodson and S. Lindblad, eds., *Professional knowledge and educational restructuring in Europe*. Rotterdam: Sense Publishers.

Government of India. (2009). *The right of children to free and compulsory education act*. New Delhi: Ministry of Law and Justice, Legislative Department.

Gupta, V. (2016). Politics of the guarded agenda of national education policy 2015–16. *Economic and Political Weekly*, 51(42), 15 October 2016, pp. 59–69.

Hill, D. and Boxley, S. (2007). Critical teacher education for economic, environmental and social justice: An ecosocialist manifesto. *Journal for Critical Education Policy Studies*, 5(2).

Hill, D. and Ravi, K. (2009). *Global neoliberalism and education and its consequences*. New York and London: Routledge.

Kumar, K. (2009). Bring Everyone On Board: India's School System Must Be More Egalitarian. *The Times of India*. New Delhi (Accessed on 19 June 2009).

Kumar, R. (2006a). Educational deprivation of the marginalised: A village study of the Mushar community in Bihar. In: R. Kumar, ed., *The crisis of elementary education in India*. New Delhi: Sage.

———. (2006b). Introduction: Equality, quality and quantity-mapping the challenges before elementary education in India. In: R. Kumar, eds., *The crisis of elementary education in India*. New Delhi: Sage.

———. (2016). Introduction. In: R. Kumar, ed., *Neoliberal, critical pedagogy and education*. New Delhi: Routledge.

———. (2017). Introduction. In: D. Hill, ed., *Class, race and education under neoliberal capitalism*. New Delhi: Aakar.

Krishnamurti, J. (1992). *Education and the significance of life.* Chennai: Krishnamurti Foundation India.

Marcuse, H. (1969). *An essay on liberation.* Boston: Beacon Press.

Mehendale, A. R., Mukhopadhaya, R. and Namala, A. (2015). Right to education and inclusion in private unaided schools: An exploratory study in Bengaluru and Delhi. *Economic and Political Weekly,* 50(7), pp. 43–51.

Meyer, J. (2000). The world institutionalisation of education. In: J. Schriewer, ed., *Discourse formation in comparative education.* Frankfurt: Peter Lang, pp. 112–132.

MHRD. (1986). *National policy of education 1986.* New Delhi: Ministry of Human Resource Development, Government of India.

———. (2016a). *National policy on education, 2016: Report of the committee for evolution of the new education policy,* Ministry of Human Resource Development, Government of India, New Delhi.

———. (2016b). *Some Inputs for Draft National Policy on Education (Draft NPE), ministry of human resource development,* Government of India, New Delhi, http:// mhrd.gov.in/sites/upload_files/mhrd/files/Inputs_Draft_NEP_2016.pdf (Accessed on 12 June 2017).

Monbiot, G. (2007). How the Neoliberal Stitched up the Wealth of Nations for Themselves. *The Guardian,* 28 August 2007. Available at: www.theguardian.com/commentisfree/2007/aug/. . ./comment.buisnesscomment (Accessed on 20 March 2017).

NCERT. (1970). *Education and national development: Report of the education commission 1964–1966* (Kothari Commission). New Delhi: NCERT.

NCFR. (2005). National Curriculum Framework Review (NCFR). National Focus Group Position Papers Systemic Reform Vol. II *Draft, teacher education for curriculum renewal.* New Delhi: NCERT (National Council for Educational Research and Training), 89–116.

NITI Aayog. (2017). *Three Year Action Agenda 2017–18 to 2019–20.* New Delhi: Government of India.

Ramamurthy, S. and Pandiyan, K. (2017). National policy on education 2016: A comparative critique with NPE 1986. *Economic and Political Weekly,* 52(16), 22 April 2017.

Rizvi, F. and Lingard, B. (2009). *Globalizing education policy.* New York and London: Routledge.

Rustin, M. (2016). The neoliberal university and its alternatives. *Soundings: A Journal of Politics and Culture,* 63(3), pp. 147–176.

Sadgopal, A. (2006). Dilution, distortion and diversion: A post – Jomtien reflection on the education policy. In: R. Kumar, ed., *The crisis of elementary education in India.* New Delhi: Sage.

———. (2016a). Skill India' or deskilling India: An agenda of exclusion. *Economic and Political Weekly,* LI(35), pp. 33–37.

———. (2016b). Common classrooms, common playgrounds. In: M. Prasad, ed., *Newsletter.* New Delhi: All India Forum for Right to Education.

Shepard, L. A. (2000). The role of assessment in a learning culture. *Educational Researcher,* 29(7), pp. 4–14.

Shor, I. (1993). Education is politics: Paulo Freire's critical pedagogy. In: P. McLaren and P. Leonard, eds., *Paulo Freire: A critical encounter*. New York and London: Routledge.

Sen, A. (2018). Karl Marx 2.00. *The Indian Express*. New Delhi, 5 May 2018.

Sleeter, C., Torres, M. and Laughlin, P. (2004). Scaffolding conscientization through inquiry. *Teacher Education*, 31(1), pp. 81–96.

The Indian Express (IE). (2018). Showcause to 9 teachers closed: Gujarat varsity. *The Indian Express*, 10 May 2018.

Velaskar, P. (2017). Neo-liberal policy and the crisis of state schooling. In: Avinash Kumar Singh ed., *Education and empowerment in India: Policies and practices*. New Delhi: Routledge, pp. 251–267.

Wallerstein, I. (1994). The agonies of liberalism: What hope Progress?. *New Left Review*, (204), pp. 3–17.

Williamson, J. (2009). A short history of the Washington consensus. *Law and Business Review of Americas*, 15. Available at: http://scholar.smu.edu/lbra/vol15/iss1/3 (Accessed on 18 July 2017).

Zizek, S. (2018). *Voices*. www.independent.co.uk/voices/karl-marx-200-years-uk-politics-elections-working-class-slavoj-zizek-a8335931.html (Accessed on 4 May 2018).

Part I

Neoliberal restructuring of education

Chapter 1

Neoliberal policy shifts in elementary education in India

Jyoti Raina and Parul

Education under neoliberalisation

Neoliberalism is a global policy framework characterised by marketisation that has led to privatisation/quasi-privatisation, commoditisation and managerialisation; in social and economic life it has led to an unapologetic degradation of public services. It has established itself as the dominant political and ideological trend of the contemporary era while unabashedly seeking to cast all human actions in the mould of the market. The frequently cited definition of neoliberalism by David Harvey views it as a distinct universalist theory of political and economic practices that proposes that human well-being can be augmented by a release of individual entrepreneurial freedom in an supportive institutional framework characterised by strong property rights, free markets and free trade (Harvey, 2005: 2). Neoliberalism views the market with its corporate domination of society and polity as an entity that offers the advantages that can never be achieved by planning and in the process views citizens as human resources. Its early classical liberal roots advocate freedom for the pursuit of self-interest, wealth and capital accumulation in a 'possessive individualism' (Hall, 2011: 13) supported by a limited form of the state. Classic liberalism advocated a state roll-back so as to allow private enterprise cost-cutting legislations while minimising its tax burdens for a welfare state (Hayek and Caldwell, 2007), while the contemporary version of neoliberalism contrastingly demands a strong interventionist state to promote the interests of private capital (Ahmed, 2017: 276). According to Ravi Kumar neoliberalism involves:

> the effort by capital to survive by initiating a process of simultaneity wherein the individual, the collective and the processes that bind them together are targeted in such a way that the processes of accumulation can be facilitated in the most effective manner. It gives us the illusion of being democratic by touting how well it represents diversity and difference in society but without allowing us to extend our penetrative analysis that could tie together the liberal-bourgeois ideas of democracy

to processes of accumulation, surplus generation and wealth appropriation by few.

(Kumar, 2016: 2)

The role that it seeks for the state is that of creating, preserving and fos-
tering an institutional framework appropriate to such accumulative economic practices. Its widespread embrace by fields ranging from banking,
mass media, healthcare and education across countries and continents can
be looked at as the 'common-sense way many of us interpret, live in and
understand the world' (Harvey, 2005: 3) and can be termed as the neoliberal
common sense.

The educational agenda followed by neoliberalism is based on a concept
of education as that of a tradeable service, a commodity for profit, to be
sold at a price that is as high as possible and an institutional cost that is as
low as possible. This commodification is aimed at subsequent profit generation by educational institutions/schools that are commercial ventures. For
the neoliberal educators, education is just another transactional commodity
in the market (Tooley, 2001). In a blasé attack on public-funded education, the World Trade Organization (WTO) background paper on education
(1998) and the General Agreement for Trade in Services (GATS) lamented
the dominance of government's provisioning for education and spoke of
'reclaiming' education. A neoliberal political economy of privatisation of
school education has sprung from these arguments and is seeking justification on a variety of grounds, including parental freedom of choice, 'quality'
education, performativity, user accountability and an effective demand for
such institutions from certain sections of society. Or, in other words, the
neoliberal argument is that provisioning of education is best left to the market (Tooley, 2000).

Neoliberalism does not desist from drawing an analogy between commerce
and education, projecting a strong association between education and the
private sector (Winch 1996: 13). The neoliberalisation of education has been
operationalised by the approach of new public management (NPM) geared
to increasing market responsiveness. The NPM approach is based upon a
techno-managerial model of education reform seeking to recast the 'structure
and culture of public services' so as to 'entrench the mechanisms of the market
form and forms of privatisation' (Ball and Youdell, 2007: 14) in a competitive manner akin to corporate business. The assumption here is that education is no different from any other business entity in the private sector. Critics
have pointed out that NPM in education recasts management of education
around performance, control and accountability (Olssen et al., 2004), replacing trust and self-regulation with contract and surveillance (Chattopadhyay,
2016: 251). This undermines teachers' autonomy and de-professionalises
teaching sorely aligning with behaviouristic assumptions that regard teaching and learning as an externally observable, measurable activity.

Critical educators, on the other hand, do not regard education as a commodity to be bought and sold (Hill, 2003: 16). They argue that the goals of the market and education are orthogonal as the structures of appropriation that they employ are opposing. The market operates on the principle of private profit, whereas education is acquired by a structure of appropriation that is not designed to exclude others, but rather flourishes with sharing (McMurtry, 1991: 212). In an analysis of the relationship between neoliberalism and education, it has been argued that the market in fact suppresses education itself, unless one considers mere literacy and uncritical learning of skills for a graded labour market as knowledge. Marketisation reduces the aim of education merely to an uncritical, utilitarian instrument of the development of a knowledge-based economic society consisting of human resources (Hill, 2009: xiii). Such an uncritical education cannot aim towards an intelligent understanding of the world or offer possibilities for recovery of critical thought.

This chapter undertakes an analysis of elementary education policy shifts in India during the last three decades. The chapter is divided into three parts. The first part locates the policy changes to their national, international, regional/state and school locations where the neoliberal agendas originate. The second part identifies the dominant emphasis underlying these neoliberal changes, which are not limited to a particular period but transcend beyond a specific period to an extended phase. This key emphasis at the current juncture in India is identified as quality, of which accountability is an important aspect. The third section examines the impact of these policy changes upon notions of teacher accountability that are increasingly shaded by NPM. The discernible policy shifts have unequivocally established the domination of the neoliberal approach, which underwrites the broader policy framework at the current juncture, in the socio-political context of elementary education. The chapter concludes with a brief discussion of the emergence of a new policy context in contemporary times that legitimises the neoliberal common sense, in spite of the devastating role it has played in restructuring educational policy and practice in India.

The location

The changes in elementary education policy during the last three decades at the national level can be traced to the international economic policy decisions to which India committed in 1990. The opening of the economy was because of the economic problems that the government faced and not the aspirations of the people, or even the long-term development objectives of the country (Nayyar, 2017). This particular period was a turning point when a sagging economy and an alarmingly negative balance of payments forced the government of India (GoI) to come up with a New Economic Policy while approaching international monetary organisations for assistance in return for 'opening' the economy to foreign players in a hitherto regulated system aimed at reducing the budgetary deficit to a sustainable level. There was consequently a restructured state financing of social sectors, including elementary education, supported in the name of 'policies that have valorised parental choice in a commercialised education sector' (Jeffery, 2005: 38). This resulted in a structural adjustment programme (SAP) and educational 'reforms' that downsized public spending on elementary education, arguably marking the beginning of the era of liberalisation, globalisation and economic reforms which India had to opt for and which have continued unabated since 1991. The SAP aligned educational reforms, beginning with the flagship District Primary Education Programme (DPEP) in 1994 and the Sarva Shiksha Abhiyan (SSA) in 2000, funded by international agencies like the World Bank (WB), created a big dent in the public education system by developing parallel systems of lower quality, such as alternative schools for specific sections of society. The policy framework for alternatives to regular schooling was already laid by the NPE in 1986, as DPEP and SSA supported such alternatives. These included alternative schools, non-formal schooling and initiatives like the Education Guarantee Scheme of Madhya Pradesh in the 1990s. A significant part of educational development (increased enrolment of children in schools) accrued from this arena. However, the SSA framework was subsequently revised for non-provisioning for alternative schooling, such that all centres have since 2011–12 have been closed or turned into regular schools. Yet the direction of the state policy shift in school education is reflected in the continued emphasis on state programmes, like SSA, as its ten-year completion led to the formulation of a similar programme for secondary education: Rashtriya Madhyamik Shiksha Abhiyan (GoI, 2009). These parallel systems have quantified the notion of quality education by defining learning as achieving measurable standards and targets, while adversely affecting public institutional teaching and learning.

The signpost RTE Act on 2009 ostensibly emerged from the constitutional rights framework, but in fact restricted the constitutional entitlement (free compulsory elementary education of equitable quality to all children) that our constitution already provides (Sadgopal, 2010). The specification of input norms and standards in terms of physical infrastructure and academic resources, including teachers, etc., was not supported by adequate financial allocation by central or state governments, and the economically weaker sections (EWS) provisions provide for mere symbolic inclusion of economically disadvantaged children in private schools. The consequences of the former have been widespread closure of government schools which were serving the most disadvantaged children in 'underdeveloped' and remote regions (where private players would not like to operate), and the latter has further widened inequality in an already stratified school system. The act has had a devastating effect on the state schooling system,

Neoliberal policy shifts 29

taking elementary education in our country in the direction opposite from that envisioned through a common school system by the erstwhile Indian Education Commission (IEC) (GoI, 1968). Recent empirical research has highlighted the structural distortion brought about in school education as a regional consequence ensured by the international and national policy changes accompanying neoliberalisation, particularly abetted by the RTE Act. One such research study highlighted that in the municipal elementary education system of the regional Mumbai metropolis in the state of Maharashtra, there has been a 'complete disappearance' of municipal/other government schools (at regional/state levels), turning the public system 'into a profitable private ventures by state functionaries' themselves because of gradual as well as selective withdrawal of the state's educational functioning while there was abdication from the 'primary responsibility of direct delivery' (Velaskar, 2017). This systemic deterioration of the public education system has supported the political economy of private schools, particularly low-fee private schooling (LFPS). The emergence of LFPS and stratification among government schooling has exacerbated the hierarchies of schooling which have become even more densely multi-layered. LFPS, with its minimum facilities, infrastructure, academic resources and utilitarian aims of education, has been marked as a substitute for government schools in terms of providing education in the name of an 'English medium' school. This has legitimised the intra-internal parallel systems of education existing since colonial times. Not only the colonial state but the independent Indian state has not refrained from establishing, legitimising and perpetuating multi-layered, class-based hierarchies of schooling, accentuating structural distortions to the elementary school system from the 1990s to the present as

> neoliberal policies led to the dismantling of state-funded educational institutions, accompanied by the opening up of an ever-expanding market for profit-hungry, corporate-controlled, commercialised education from 'K.G. to P.G' (Kindergarten to post graduation).
>
> (Sadgopal, 2016)

The wider international agendas shading the policy shifts at all the other locations began with the General Agreement on Trade and Tariff (GATT) that was established in 1947, the same year as the WB and International Monetary Fund (IMF), aimed at regulating trade and tariff on industrial goods. After eight rounds of negotiations among the member countries, the regulations and restrictions upon legally enforceable international trade were progressively lowered. A multi-lateral trade regime in agriculture, textiles, intellectual property rights and services was established to take effect on 1 January 1995. The GATT's radically expanded version, the WTO, was created with trade operations organised into the major groups of goods, services and intellectual property rights emerged, has 164 members now. India is a member of the WTO-GATT's regime that covers education, converting it into one of twelve tradable service sectors, alongside other service sectors, including business, tourism, travel and finance. Economists using the goods and services metaphor have traditionally viewed education as non-traded along axes of distinction between traded services, non-traded services and tradeable services. Under neoliberalism, however, 'trade in education' has become a legitimate term to use as per the central product classification that recognised five sub-sectors in education: primary education, secondary education, higher education, adult education and other education. The exercise of governmental authority is an exception to it, and it is pertinent to point out that a service falls out of the GATS rules only when it is provided entirely by the state, which would be a non-possibility in the Indian education system, as private education has already established its increasing presence over the last two centuries in colonial and post-colonial India. The GATS defines four modes of supply by which educational services can be traded. In the first mode there is consumption of a service abroad in which, for example, the student consumer travels to another member supplier country to receive the service of education by payment of requisite service charges. The second mode is cross-border supply in which there is consumption abroad of a service (education) by a consumer (student), with neither of the two moving anywhere. This is the e-education, open and distant mode where the student-customer pays the charges for the traded commodity. The third mode consists of the commercial presence of the supplier of educational services in the consumer country by establishing its institutions/branches there. This can be plainly seen in the outskirts of the metropolitan cities with their adjoining countryside dotted with a plethora of offshore foreign universities. The fourth mode involves the presence of natural persons (teachers) outside their own country in a consuming country. All of these four modes of supply are market driven and reduce education to the legal status of a tradable commodity. This international economic policy global framework aligned with the dictates of the market ensured the concomitant elementary education policy shifts at the national, regional, state and school levels. The shifts are interlinked at various locations, operationalising as a burgeoning neoliberal political economy at the level of schools, particularly LFPS, in a free market, destroying the idea of public elementary education for all.

The enigma of 'quality'

Educational policy analysts have distinguished between two phases of elementary education policy changes in India's national trajectory: the first one began with the introduction of the National Policy on Education (NPE) in 1986 and the second with the economic liberalisation of 1991, which involved systemic interventions and changes shaped by global international forces, including the SAP (Velaskar, 2010: 70). The fetish for quality accentuated in the second phase operationalised with the WB-sponsored DPEP,

Neoliberal policy shifts 31

beginning in 1994 (Ayyar, 2017: 26) as dominant wave of reform restructuring policy change, with a key focus on measurement, monitoring and assessment of performance through learning outcomes (LOs). This was associated with regulatory mechanisms of surveillance, contract employment and precariousness aimed at monitoring delivery mechanisms. This mix of outcome orientation with education delivery mechanisms, on the deviated road of market principles, has brought about a new policy paradigm located around the twin themes of quality and accountability, with the latter viewed as an aspect of quality itself since the second phase of policy change.

'Quality' in education

The notion of quality appeared in the first phase of policy change as the NPE in 1986 spoke of incorporating changes 'in the quality and range of education,' arguing that '[a]ll teachers should teach and all students study.' Among the quality measures to make the system work were a 'provision for improved students' services and insistence on observed norms of behaviour' and 'creation of a system of performance appraisals of institutions according to standards and norms set at the National or State level' (GoI, 1986: 20). Notwithstanding the publication of the seminal volume *Equality, Quality and Quantity: The Elusive Triangle of Indian Education* (Naik, 1975), the term 'quality' as something extrinsic to education did not appear in any educational policy literature until the 1990s. The Programme of Action (POA) in 1992, which primarily aimed to assess the implementation of the NPE, introduced performance and outcomes at an administration level in a quest for 'quality.' The introduction of a section titled 'Management of Education' in the POA at the outset of the second phase of policy change indicated a shift from inputs to performance and outcomes, proposing that consideration of cost-effectiveness should inform all levels of educational administration and planning (GoI, 1992: 112). The subsequent policies and programmes like DPEP and SSA funded by international agencies like the WB and IMF brought elementary education in India as per a neoliberal approach in alignment with the emerging international notions of quality underlying global policy frameworks (GoI, 1995, 2004). In this international scenario, the Dakar framework (World Education Forum, 2000) accorded centrality to the notion of 'quality' and posited it to be not just at the heart of education but also the fundamental factor shaping student enrolment, retention and achievement. Quality of education is emphasised as one of the six Education for All (EFA) goals. The Global Monitoring Report 2013–14 mentioned the term in its title itself *Teaching and Learning: Achieving Quality for All*. Interestingly, the report does not separate quality from equity, arguing that until an education system is equitable with respect to access, enrolment, gender parity, retention and completion, it can hardly be described as being of good quality.

Quality of education thus became a key concern, a dominant wave of reform, beginning with the first phase of policy change in India, becoming more pronounced (or, even central) in the second phase. This was coupled with the emphasis on the development of tools, techniques, indexes, processes and instruments to monitor quality, which have been used by state agencies and other actors for educational review and assessment. Educational policy in India has sought to view parity in quality as an aspect of equality itself, particularly in the context of universalising elementary education through state financing, even regarding it as a pre-condition for the expansion of access (Kumar and Padma, 2004). This can be seen in the definition of equity as a reduction in gender and caste disparity for access and achievement, which is looked at as a component of quality itself in the qualitative and quantitative provisioning under the schemes of the DPEP and SSA (Velaskar, 2010: 74–75). The status reports on the progress of education in our country have identified quality as one of the two key concerns, the other being equity (Govinda and Sedwal, 2017).

Yet the term 'quality' remains an enigma because it lacks a definition. In the absence of a clear definition, deploying the term quality causes ambiguity (Alexander, 2015). The lack of clarity is so because its quest is accompanied by the search for specific observable indicators and measures. This quest for indicators and measures of quality has led to a focus on input and output in terms of attendant attributes like student–teacher ratio, retention, male and female teacher ratio, relative percentage of trained and untrained teachers, expenditure per pupil as percent of gross domestic product (GDP), net enrolment ratio, infrastructure provisioning, cost per child and the number of years spent in school, adult literacy rate and, most of all, learning achievement/LO, which has been considered the vital indicator. These learning achievement measures have been based on language, numeracy and science paper-and-pencil test scores. This is a deliverology framework, with quality of education looked at as if it were a material good produced through the factorisation process and therefore needs to be measured in terms of, quality in market terms which is shaping the educational agenda of our country through accountability measures that are sought to be standardised through regular testing, as well as technology-oriented solutions to teaching-learning issues, while ignoring the very process of education (Batra, 2015). The classroom processes may not always be directly measurable and in fact have not even been considered so in the cognitivist psychological tradition located 'firmly in the territory of non-measurable indicators' (Alexander, 2015: 2). Such flawed notions of quality in education have resulted in the development of proxy indicators, an example of which is the Programme for International Student Assessment (PISA) that regards the test results of a sample of 15-year-old students a reliable and valid measure characterising an entire country's education system.

Quality is not a value-neutral notion. In its literal meaning it is inherent to the process of education itself, as education is a normative and purposeful process. Quality in education cannot be viewed without reference to the socio-political context of education (Kumar and Padma, 2004). The flawed international quality agenda which has proliferated nationally with a body of work aimed at assessing quality at state, district and school levels is based solely on the dictum 'measure to understand' (ASER, 2017) with a focus on LO performances, raising national alarm that poor LOs that are supposedly continuously declining in language and mathematics for elementary grades among children all across the country. The quality of education has been reduced to externally observable LO performances and completing targets in the name of achieving LOs and proxy indicators that 'show off' that learning has become the focus within this redefined discourse. Clearly, it reflects the 'objectification' of the child and undermining the capabilities of the learner to be able to construct knowledge using his or her intellectual faculties. The focus is on standardisation for all instead of recognising diversity is required to cater to the various needs of learners. It is being done by measuring outcomes with the parameter of expected and fixed behaviour in the child.

The current projected policy trend (GoI, 2016a; GoI, 2016b) uses the phrase 'quality upgradation' in order to 'revamp the education sector' (Subramaniam, 2016), expressing concern at 'a decline in learning levels among school students' (GoI, 2016a: 3). While the NPE of 1968 and 1986/92 had sections on 'education for equality,' 'common school system,' 'regional imbalances' and 'equalisation of educational opportunity,' the draft NPE dedicates several sections to quality education and governance in education, including the use of information and communication technology (ICT) in school management. There is a marked shift from the policy goals of equality, access and equity in education to a thrust on quality and governance. In this approach, quality is limited to 'improved governance,' as well as something to be achieved through improved governance, steering the notion of quality away from concerns related to equality in education. This ignores the socio-political context of school education and the attendant learning, curricular and pedagogical issues in a narrow posing of 'quality.' The quest for quality is associated with the demand for accountability that has emerged as its important facet, as is reflected in United Nations Educational, Scientific and Cultural Organization's (UNESCO's) 2017–18 Global Monitoring Report titled *Accountability in Education: Meeting Our Commitments.*

Accountability ambit: academic or administrative?

Accountability is a moral and political issue (Winch, 1996). This further confirms the idea of situating accountability as the mutual obligation of internal/personal ethics with structures of institutionalised processes. However, the neoliberal approach, in aiming to minimise the role of the state as much as possible, advocates placing public and private goods under the purview of the market, negating the moral and political facets. This supposedly ensures both 'freedom of choice' and quality of service, as the mechanism of accountability is immediate and transparent in its operation. Accountability is thus viewed as a market mechanism, and its manifestation is located externally to the actors and depends exceedingly upon the visible proofs of performances. There is inherent mistrust on the ethics/practical rationality of actors and heavy reliance on the tangible indicators, proofs and measures through which it operates.

This was evident towards the end of the first phase of policy change in India when the POA in 1992, in the newly introduced section titled 'Accountability and Efficiency,' emphasised that norms of performances, and achievement of these norms of performance, be linked with the incentives. The policy spoke of '[m]onitoring of all educational programmes for implementation at the district will take place at the state level and relevant indicators for inter-district comparison will need to be worked out' (GoI, 1992: 114). This reflects how the POA diluted its own policy of decentralisation (which was situated in the wider policy thrust of decentralisation of educational planning and administration ascendant at that time), as it reduced the monitoring structures as centralised to the upper levels of educational planning and administration. Nowhere does it mention that parameters/indicators will be made at a district level or block as per the needs of the locale. Therefore, it can be said that the educational management it opted for was the standardised approach, which again decontextualised the life in school and reduced it to programme implementation at school level.

The involvement of non-governmental organisations (NGOs) was seen as an appropriate solution for the successful implementation of programmes. The POA seemed to be presenting conflicting standpoints when it came to the functioning of schools: on one side, it focussed on programme implementation indicators; on the other side, it showed the concern for maintaining networks like school and educational complexes to promote professionalism among teachers. It was envisaged that these institutions would work as the smallest viable unit, like a cluster, further taking on the responsibility of inspection, exchanging resource materials, and each state could adopt their own model of working of school complexes as per their needs. It also recognised the need for greater teacher autonomy in managing the school as a proposed action in the elementary education section (GoI, 1992: 42). This situation at the level of educational administration introduced the parallel structures working together: programme implementation vs. strengthening a school system, highlighting the inherent tussle between 'decentralisation' and 'centralisation' visible in the POA.

In contrast, in the second phase of policy change, policy shifts and programmes reduced the notions of accountability to financial audits of expenditure of funds coming through sponsoring agency/WB projects. This brought about a new commercialised bureaucratic culture (Velaskar, 2017: 267) in the state system in the name of quality and raising the learning achievements of its underprivileged children. As a consequence of the SAP-aligned, WB-funded national educational reforms, the ambitious SSA aimed at Universalisation of Elementary Education (UEE) in a mission with financial allocation linked to decentralisation and district-specific plans in a process-based, time-bound implementation strategy (GoI, 2004), but this idea of decentralisation lost its meaning by providing mere signatory authority to the community for the purpose of auditing paperwork.

Due to the DPEP and SSA reforms, parallel structures have already been infused into the system and reporting lines have become blurred. The new structures and initiatives such as the block resource centre (BRC) and cluster resource centre (CRC), which were established to bring decentralisation and were aimed to be school support institutions, have become data delivery service centres. The role of BRC and CRC has been reduced to uncritical 'messengers' for collecting proofs of financial expenditure, proxy indicators or parameters of LOs, where the structured pedagogies have been introduced, like in the states of Tamil Nadu and Karnataka (Sarangapani, 2010). In-service teacher trainings were visualised through these block and cluster institutions as more localised and contextualised, but it turned out to be more tokenised and centralised in approach. These reforms failed to improve LOs or even 'quality' as they focused more on administrative and financial audits and increased corruption further, as the data can be fudged internally to show the proper documentation of expenditures. Block resource persons (BRPs) and cluster resource persons (CRPs) also did not have any decision-making power or autonomy to take any action if required, as their 'position' in the education system does not allow them to do so. The capacities and capabilities of BRPs and CRPs was another weak area because whether they are equipped with or capable of providing support to elementary teachers remains unscrutinised. The work of data collection (of expenditure and documentation) and communication of the same becomes the core of the system, and hence full monitoring and mechanisms move around it by making it a means and ends in itself in the name of accountability.

The development of these parallel systems in the NPM work culture also influenced the earlier system of inspections, which has its roots in the colonial era. This system was eroded due to a dearth of the required number of personnel; hence, fewer inspectors were working for more schools. The earlier system of inspection withered because newer ways brought a focus on documentation, data handling and creating reports. Inspectors' work was reduced from inspection/supervision of schools to ensuring proper documentation of each and every task and communication of circulars and notices coming from the higher authorities. There was a sanction on materials necessary for the schemes to be implemented from the district to school level and approval of administrative requirements by again making it a centralised process. This shifted the accountability focus away from the classroom discourse/engagements and away from efforts at making learning

Teacher accountability in the NPM era

The accountability ambit, instead of examining the systemic problems and nature of working conditions, particularly those aligned with international financial institutional agendas, blames employees/teachers for being irresponsible (Kremer et al., 2005). Teachers have particularly been the target of this attack, which has brought the 'deprofessionalisation' of teaching (Sarangapani, 2010). This process of 'deprofessionalisation' is not only restricted to contractual appointments or reduced salary; it has also extended to degrading their role to 'implementers' where critical thinking, professional growth and so-called curriculum development–related work is not viewed as the responsibility of the teacher. There is a lot of micro-management of teaching through the introduction of defined and restrictive pedagogies. Hence, teachers are not understood as responsible intellectuals, but there is shift of focus on developing newer ways of extrapolating to find solutions through monitoring. This is how the discourse of governance is brought to the fore, where monitoring becomes the essential part of industry to bring efficiency as per the techno-managerial approach. The focus has shifted to creating 'proofs' of performances. The idiosyncratic turbulence here is that the parameters of monitoring have been reduced to measurement of the teaching-learning process by defining certain fixed proxy indicators which are aimed at converting teaching learning performance into numbers or even simply multiple choice/yes-or-no measures. This also excludes any professional development support to the teacher, which could nurture a culture of teaching and learning. This creates a kind of culture where teachers are expected to be uncritical implementers of educational administration and communicate the same to students without aiming at critical thinking.

An ethnographic study of reforms conducted in Karnataka schools articulates how teachers finds themselves pulled between the frameworks of 'activity-based learning' and expectations of bureaucratic and inspectorial systems of hierarchy, which expect them to show an increase in the performance level instead of activity processes. It is further argued that 'managerial cultures' that are 'governing teachers' work legitimise the imposition of strong regulatory controls over their activities and practices as 'the presence of officers seemed to militate against the ethos of the child-centred reforms in these schools' (Sriprakash, 2011: 28).

Another research study conducted in Mumbai's municipal corporation schools has revealed that for teachers there has been major transformation in the work expectations from their supervisors-headmasters (HM) and beat officers (BOs). They are now expected to produce statistics of records of the provisions, activities and schemes which are ongoing in the school, and BOs closely monitor the same. Teachers are expected to be responsible for the maintenance of adequate student levels, and this has seen in the light of the concern to attain full enrolment and attendance goals (Velaskar, 2017: 264). Teachers find themselves feeling guilty and frustrated because they are not able to prioritise their teaching due to an unfair amount of administrative and logistic work. This study also revealed that recent neoliberal accountability measures have made teachers the object of greater surveillance and control than before. The aforesaid research studies highlight how teachers' accountability is getting re-conceptualised since the historical hierarchical inspectorial structures (established during colonial times) to the current context of NPM. This becomes a point of tension and constant negotiation because the teachers' own conception of teaching locates the accountability in academic and pedagogic processes which further draws from the ethics of personal formation. The accountability of a professional is at the core of personal formation, which is embedded in its professional identity (Green, 2011). The ethics of this personal formation draw from several experiences, which neoliberalism, with its NPM approach, does not consider. It recognises accountability only in terms of visible indicators and in financial audits and documentation specifically in Indian national, regional, state, district and school contexts.

New policy context

At the current juncture in our national educational trajectory, both of the erstwhile phases of policy change in elementary education, the first beginning in 1986 hinting at privatisation/quasi-privatisation and the second with the liberalisation of India's economy bringing education under neoliberalisation, are arguably over. The wider framework of the post-colonial era of developmental planning, aimed at democratic socialism that began in 1951, has significantly ended at the expiry of the twelfth Five-Year Plan in March 2017, accompanied by the disbanding of the Planning Commission. The establishment of NITI Aayog, aimed at designing long-term policy, strategies, programme frameworks and initiatives, heralds a new era of policy wisdom. In keeping with this wisdom, the Aayog plans to prepare a fifteen-year vision document, a seven-year strategy and action agendas for three years. The latter document (NITI Aayog, 2017) outlining the agenda for policy reform situated in neoliberal economics speaks of the role of the government as follows:

> India's choice to build a socialist pattern of production during several post-independence decades has resulted in the government entering many activities that do not serve any public purpose and are best performed by the private sector.

(113)

The increasing faith posed by the neoliberal state of contemporary India in the market is unambiguously stated in the following words:

> As a market-based economy, it is essential that the government puts in place a regulatory framework that maximises the efficiency of markets. Often laws, rules and regulations enacted by the government inadvertently build into them provisions that restrict competition and harm efficiency of markets. This has happened in India as well.
>
> (123)

In this policy text or action agenda, education has not merited even a full separate chapter out of the 182 pages constituting its twenty-four chapters, but appears under the broad theme in the part title 'Social Sector,' where school education has been included, strategised with the title 'Education and Skill Development.' If policymaking is a political process and neoliberalism a political ideology, then the neoliberal common sense of the assumption that a free market leads to quality is defining the new policy context in an unapologetic grouping of education with skilling.

The policy text speaks of not merely improving LOs but to 'orient the system towards outcomes' which has turned the outcome orientation into the central objective of school education (Kundu, 2018: 24). The action agenda further speaks of a process for measuring LOs for each child (22). The underlying assumption is that the abysmally poor levels of learning and the continuing deterioration of LOs among schoolchildren in primary and upper primary grades (ASER, 2017, various years; Pratham, 2016) is the gravest concern in school education. A new construct, the School Education Quality Index (SEQI), reminiscent of an earlier second policy change that emphasised the development of such instruments as a measure of quality in education, has been explicitly introduced. The construct is designed as a competitive lever that drives school quality by tracking outcomes. The action agenda is envisaged to operationalise an essentially outcome approach to school education.

The earlier phases of policy change initiated the shift in emphasis from inputs to a focus on performance, outcomes and delivery mechanisms, on the deviated road of market principles, but the contemporary policy context essentialises it. Policymaking has not even considered the counter-factual aspect that in spite of the policy-led flawed overemphasis on LOs across school systems for several decades, the outcomes have not shown any improvement. Rather, survey research continues to highlight the deterioration in the quality of elementary education. Quality as a dominant theme of reform has continued to remain an elusive enigma in school education as per the criteria of the neoliberal instruments that aim to monitor it. This reflects a fundamental fissure in the neoliberal approach itself and points to its many failures.

Some reasons to understand this failure are evident. Learning occurs in a specific context. Theory and research in the discipline of learning and cognition have established conclusively that contextual factors mediate children's learning and consequently their LOs. LOs result from classroom learning processes and experiences, which are not independent of the wider social context of schooling, something which an isolated focus on the LOs in the neoliberal approach to policy reform does not take into account. Also, teacher education as a catalyst in the improvement of LOs has been relatively ignored in the policy emphasis upon quality and accountability.

What the new policy context also ignores is structural concerns located around the social and regional disparity in elementary education that have distorted the school system into unequal layers. The quest for equitable schooling, equalisation of educational opportunity and education for social justice seem to have been dropped from the policy agenda, as these issues do not receive explicit space in the policy text. The faith in a free market with unprecedented privatisation that aligns with the outcome approach of a behaviouristic paradigm that is even moribund in progressive educational theory is reiterated in full measure. It is ironic that the concluding chapter in the part on 'Social Sector' is titled 'Towards Building a More Inclusive Society', but how can this take place without addressing the graded structural inequality in the elementary education system? The creation of an inclusive society, as the post-independence years' education policy has recommended, can occur through an equitable system of school education in which the state needs to play a significant role. This mandates a policy thrust on qualitative improvement in state schooling, an important issue that has not merited the attention of the action agenda. Even while speaking of 'Empowering through Education' the agenda ignores this fundamental policy prescription, which has now been officially abandoned in the upcoming new policy paradigm even symbolically. How can the socially disadvantaged and the other marginalised be empowered through education unless free schooling of equitable quality is available to them?

Conclusion

The economic liberalisation of 1991 in India began the process of bringing education under neoliberalisation, even though some policy shift towards non-state stake holding, privatisation and pruned public financing had in fact begun prior to this opening of the economy. The dominant wave of reform in the last three decades following a key shift from 'inputs' to 'outcomes' has been on 'quality' in education with a focus on measurement, monitoring of delivery mechanisms and assessment of performance in a quest for visible proofs of performance. The quality of education underlying the neoliberal policy shifts has been reduced to completing targets in the name of achieving LOs and a quest for proxy indicators that 'show off' learning. Aligned with this neoliberal approach, accountability in its professional setting manifests externally to the actors and depends exceedingly upon the visible proofs of performances. This has decontextualised learning in terms of the basic aim of education, namely connecting home and school life by making it more meaningful for the learner. The overemphasis on LOs has neglected the very processes of education, including systemic issues of supply-side bottlenecks, classroom teaching-learning processes and teacher education. Accountability matters have been ignoring the very change in working conditions which has further expected professionals to re-form the idea of work in terms of technical documentation, and this has further led to undermined teaching-learning processes. Research studies conducted to study the local context of these policy implementations shows how policy gets translated in different contexts and settings. It gets re-enacted and re-interpreted by the actors, including teachers and bureaucrats involved in the system. It does not remain as homogenous as it is sought to appear and ignores the actors' interpretation of policy dynamics involved in the process. It has been shown in the various studies how actors develop their coping mechanism and contestation in this kind of disempowering context (Mukhopadhaya and Sriprakash, 2010). Be that as it may, cumulative neoliberal policy shifts have played a devastating role in restructuring educational policy and practice. At the current juncture, a new policy context is emerging on our national trajectory. The erstwhile phases of policy change were merely shaded by the neoliberal common sense, but the current policy context is essentialising the neoliberal approach characterised by unprecedented marketisation and indifference to social aims of education, as well as to the structural concerns related to equalisation of educational opportunity, social disparity and equitable schooling. This heralds a distinct break from the state-led policy wisdom of post-independence years in favour of an uncertain policy-led neoliberalisation of elementary education.

References

Ahmed, P. R. (2017). Neoliberal education and critical social movements: Implications for democracy. In: R. Kumar, ed., *Neoliberalism, critical pedagogy and education*. London: Routledge India.

Alexander, R. J. (2015). Teaching and learning for all? The quality imperative revisited. *International Journal of Educational Development*. Elsevier, 40(C), pp. 250–258.

ASER. (various years). *Annual status of education report*. New Delhi: ASER Centre, Pratham.

———. (2017). *Annual status of education report (Rural) 2016*. New Delhi ASER Centre (Accessed on 18 January 2017).

Ayyar, R. and Vaidyanatha, V. (2017). Inclusive elementary education in India: The journey. In: M. Tiwary, K. Sanjay Kumar and A. K. Misra, eds., *Dynamics of inclusive classroom: Social diversity, inequality and school education in India.* New Delhi: Orient Blackswan.

Ball, S. J. and Deborah, Y. (2007). *Hidden Privatisation in Public Education*, Preliminary Report, prepared by Institute of Education, University of London presented at Education International, 5th World Congress, July 2007.

Batra, P. (2015). *Quality of Education and the Poor: Constraints on Learning*. TRG Poverty and Education Working Paper Series 4: Max Weber Stifung Foundation.

Chattopadhyay, S. (2016). Neoliberal approach to governance reform. In: R. Kumar, ed., *Neoliberalism, critical pedagogy and education*. London: Routledge India.

GoI. (1968). *National Policy of Education* (NPE), Department of Education, Ministry of Human Resource Development, Government of India.

———. (1986). *National Policy of Education*, Department of Education, Ministry of Human Resource Development, Government of India.

———. (1992). *National Policy on Education 1986 Programme of Action 1992*, Department of Education, Ministry of Human Resource Development, Government of India

———. (1995)._*DPEP guidelines*. New Delhi: MHRD, Government of India.

———. (2004). Sarva Shiksha Abhiyan, a programme for universal elementary education, a manual for planning and appraisal. New Delhi: MHRD, Department of Elementary Education and Literacy.

———. (2009). *Rashtriya Madhyamik Shiksha Abhiyan, framework for implementation*. New Delhi: Ministry of Human Resource Development (MHRD).

———. (2016a). *National policy on education, 2016: Report of the committee for evolution of the new education policy*. New Delhi: Ministry of Human Resource Development, Government of India.

———. (2016b). *Some Inputs for Draft National Policy on Education, 2016*. New Delhi: Ministry of Human Resource Development, Government of India, http://mhrd.gov.in/sites/upload_files/mhrd/files/Inputs_Draft_NEP_2016.pdf (Accessed on 28 June 2017).

Govinda, R. and Sedwal, M. (2017). *India education report: Progress of basic education*. New Delhi: Oxford University Press.

Green, J. (2011). *Education, professionalism and quest for accountability: Hitting the target but missing the point*. London: Routledge.

Hall, S. (2011). The neo-liberal revolution. *Cultural Studies*, 75(6), pp. 705–728.

Harvey, D. (2005). *A brief history of neoliberalism*. Oxford: Oxford University Press.

Hayek, F. A. and Caldwell, B. (2007). *The road to serfdom: Text and documents-The definitive edition* (The collected works of F.A. Hayek). Chicago: University of Chicago Press.

Hill, D. (2003). Global Neo-liberalism, the deformation of education and resistance. *Journal of Critical Education Policy Studies*, 1(1).

———. (2009). Foreword. In: D. Hill and E. Rosskam eds., *The developing world and state education: Neoliberal depredation and egalitarian alternatives*. London: Routledge.

Jeffery, P. (2005). Introduction: Hearts, minds and pockets. In: R. Chopra and P. Jeffery eds., *Educational regimes in contemporary India*. New Delhi: Sage.

Kremer, M., Nazmul, C., Halsey, R., Karthik, M. and Jeffery, H. (2005). Teacher absence in India: A snapshot. *Journal of the European Economic Association*, 3(2–3).

Kumar, K. and Padma, M. S. (2004). History of the quality debate. *Contemporary Education Dialogue*, 2(1), Monsoon.

Kumar, R. (2016). Introduction. In: R. Kumar, ed., *Neoliberalism, critical pedagogy and education*. London: Routledge India.

Kundu, P. (2018). NITI Aayog Three Year Action Agenda: What is there for education?. *Economic and Political Weekly*, 53(18), 5 May 2018.

McMurtry, J. (1991). Education and the market model. *Journal of Philosophy of Education*, 25(2), pp. 209–217.

Mukhopadhaya, R. and Sriprakash, A. (2010). Global frameworks, local contingencies: Policy translations and education development in India. *Compare: A Journal of Comparative and International Education*, 41(3), pp. 311–326.

Naik, J. P. (1975). *Equality, quality and quantity: The elusive triangle of Indian education*. Bombay: Allied Publishers.

Nayyar, D. (2017). 25 years of economic liberalisation. *Economic and Political Weekly*, 52(2), 14 January 2017.

NITI Aayog. (2017). 'Three Year Action Agenda 2017–18 to 2019–20, April, Government of India, New Delhi.

Olssen, M., Codd, J. and O'Neill, Anne-Marie. (2004). *Education policy, globalization, citizenship and democracy*. London: Sage Publications.

Pratham. (2016). *ASER: Annual status of education report*. Delhi: Pratham.

Sadgopal, A. (2016). Skill India' or deskilling India an agenda of exclusion. *Economic and Political Weekly*, LI(35).

———. (2010). Right to education Vs Right to education act. *Social Scientist*, 38(9–12), pp. 17–50.

Sarangapani, P. (2010). Quality concerns: National and extra national dimensions. *Contemporary Education Dialogue*, 7(1).

Sriprakash, A. (2011). Being a teacher in contexts of change: Classroom reforms and the repositioning of teachers' work in India. *Contemporary Educational Dialogue*, 8(1), pp. 5–31.

Subramaniam, T. S. R. (2016). Education in disarray: Need for quality upgradation and inclusivity. *Economic and Political Weekly*, 51(35), 27 August 2016.

Tooley, J. (2000). *Reclaiming education*. London: Cassell.

———. (2001). *The global education industry*, 2nd ed. London: Institute for Economic Affairs.

Velaskar, P. (2010). Quality and inequality in Indian education: Some critical policy concerns. *Contemporary Education Dialogue*, 7(1).

———. (2017). Neo-liberal policy and the crisis of state schooling. In: A. K. Singh, ed., *Education and empowerment in India: Policies and practices*. New Delhi: Routledge, pp. 251–267.

Winch, C. (1996). Manufacturing educational quality. *Journal of Philosophy of Education*, 30(1), pp. 1–24.

World Education Forum. (2000). *The Dakar Framework for action: Education for all: meeting our collective commitments*. Dakar, Senegal: World Education Forum.

World Trade Organisation (WTO). (1998). *Education services: Background note by the Secretariat*. 23 September 1998. Available at: www.wto.org/english/tratop_e/serve_e/w49.doc (Accessed on 15 June 2017).

Chapter 2

Extending the neoliberal agenda to forbidden territory

Public–private partnership in school education in India

Suman Lata

Governments across the world are involving private players in big public projects in order to utilise the expertise and capital from the private market for expediting and efficiently managing the projects or services, supposedly in the larger interest of people. Popularly known as a public–private partnership (PPP), the concept of governments and private sectors getting in to mutually agreed upon arrangements has gained equally in developed and developing countries. As a result, boundaries between public and private economic activities have blurred. Instead of working independently in their separate spheres, government and the private sector work together in various combinations to complete and run projects and services. It is

> a long term contract between a private party and a government agency, for providing a public asset or service, in which the private party bears significant risk and management responsibility.
> (World Bank Institute, 2012: 11)

PPP is reflective of the overall rise of capitalism and decline of socialism or communism all over the world.

After independence in 1947, India experimented with a unique Nehruvian model of development known as a 'mixed economy' consisting of both public and private sector. The assumption underlying the adoption of this model was that the private sector, driven solely by profit, would not contribute to nation building in sectors that required huge investments and much less profit. Public-sector undertakings (PSUs) were run by the government to boost production. The privatisation of many sectors and PPP gained momentum in the 1990s, generally coinciding with the liberalisation of the economy. It is a buzzword now, and both the union government and the state governments separately have initiated major projects under PPP and involved the private sector in development, financing and infrastructure development and providing services to citizens. The government of India now maintains a dedicated website for PPP, and so do most of the state governments. The website proudly declares,

> India has systematically rolled out a program for the delivery of high-value priority public utilities and infrastructure and over the last decade or so, developed what is perhaps one of the largest programs in the world . . . according to the World Bank, India is one of the leading countries in terms of readiness for PPPs.

As per the 2015 Infrascope Report of the Economist Intelligence Unit, 'India ranks first in the world in "Operational Maturity" for PPP projects, third for sub-national PPP activity and fifth overall in terms of having an ideal environment for PPP projects'.[1] A majority of mega-projects undertaken bear the stamp of PPP and so do future projects. Prime Minister Narendra Modi endorsed the concept of PPP even as chief minister of Gujarat and has added another P standing for 'people', to make it PPPP in his inimitable style.[2]

The following features of PPP can be derived as follows:

It is a long-term contract between the government and private players.
The areas of intervention and policy perspective are initiated by the government.
It is governed by mutually agreed upon terms and conditions.
It is supposed to be mutually beneficial for both the parties, generally, though not always, in the form of financial benefits for the private sector and efficiency and cost-effectiveness, quality and expediency for the government sector.
The ultimate stated objective is the welfare of citizens.

PPP in education

PPP as a neoliberalistic model of development has caught the fancy of governments across globe. The concept has its supporters as well as detractors. However, as of now, the trend is here to stay. In 2015, for example, the State of Victoria in Australia entered into a contract with Learning Communities, Victoria, 'to finance, design, construct and maintain 15 schools in some of Victoria's key growth areas' (State of Victoria, 2016). But the extension of the concept to the areas of education and health, hitherto considered the major responsibility of the state, is certainly problematic. PPP in education has many dimensions. Although it is a growing phenomenon all over the world, yet apart from the main thrust towards privatisation, there is no uniformity, as the socio-economic context is different. National ideology and social policy, apart from the economic considerations, are major factors in 'fashioning the terrain of public-private partnerships' (Fennell, 2007).

Again in education, there is a difference in the application of the concept, and its consequences are different in the area of higher education and school education. Though privatisation of higher education also is considered anti-poor, the dynamics of PPP in higher education are different compared to school education, as higher education is looked at as a privilege, whereas school education is considered a basic necessity. The Supreme Court of India has declared elementary education as a fundamental right flowing from the basic right to life itself.[3]

In the Indian context, participation of the private sector in school education is not a new phenomenon. Schools have always been run by trusts and charitable entities, as facilitating education for children has always been considered a noble philanthropic venture. The state has always welcomed such initiatives by providing subsidies in such not-for-profit ventures. The public and the private exist simultaneously, though mainly separately. Hence, we have a multi-layered system of school education with a lot of diversity. But unfortunately, this diversity has a dimension of disparity. The majority of the schools are run by the government at different levels. Education in these schools is almost free. Within government schools also, there are many layers in terms of quality. Some types of schools such as Kendriya Vidayalays, Navodaya Vidayalays, etc., can be called elite government schools with access limited to a few. Then there are private schools run by societies, trusts, non-government organisations (NGOs) and schools run by minorities, which enjoy special privileges and exemptions granted to them by the constitution of the country. All the schools differ widely in terms of infrastructure, performance indicators of learners, co-curricular activities and fee structure and socioeconomic background of children studying in these schools. Private schools, referred to as 'public schools' because of the colonial legacy, are considered in the public imagination to be superior to government schools, though within the private schools also there is lot of disparity. Still as things stand today, given a chance, no parent would like to send their children to government schools if they could afford private schools. 'It is a commonplace, at least among the Indian urban middle class that the state education system is beyond repair' (Narayan, 2010). The standard of government schools is deteriorating, and the government has failed to universalise elementary education despite declaring education as a fundamental right. The number of children shifting to private schools is increasing every year. According to the Tenth Annual Status of Education Report (ASER) 2014, 30.8% of rural enrolments in the ages six to fourteen groups were in private schools, marking an increase of 22% over eight years. The poor quality of education in government schools has been reported in all educational surveys. According to the ASER 2016 report, of all children enrolled in standard V in rural areas, only 24.5% could read simple sentences in English. This figure has remained almost unchanged since 2009. In the upper primary grades, there has been a continuous decline in the reading of English. Whereas in 2009, 60.2% of children could read simple sentences, only 46.7% in 2014 and 45.2% in 2016 could do so! According to the ASER 2017 report focusing on the group of children ages fourteen to eighteen, 25% of learners could still not read a basic text fluently in their own language. More than half struggle with simple division problems. These factors have led the government to look to the private sector for both the expansion and improvement in the quality of schools. In fact, ASER reports that are widely circulated and discussed have played a crucial role in raising the pitch for increased involvement of the private sector in schooling.

As mentioned earlier, PPP in education is a growing phenomenon, both in developed and developing countries. Though the developed countries have a robust system of public education, increasingly a need is being felt to involve private players to improve the falling standards of public education. In developing countries like India, there are a variety of reasons for inviting private players to manage schools. When the constitution of independent India was being drafted, the idea of making elementary education (up to fourteen years of age) a fundamental right was debated.[4] Eventually the right to education could find its way only in the non-justiciable directive principles of state policy. The main reason for this development was the lack of resources available to the government to open such a large number of schools for this purpose. Ironically, this reason remains valid even today. Despite the judiciary-driven constitutional amendment to include the right to elementary education as a fundamental right and the subsequent enactment of the Right of Children to Free and Compulsory Education (RTE) Act of 2009, the government has not been able to make education accessible to all. The minimum specified infrastructural requirements in the RTE Act are far from being met even after more than eight years of implementation. The contribution of the private sector is sorely sought in order to achieve this mammoth task.

Apart from access, the issue of equity is equally important in the field of education. The public school system has miserably failed in our country However, the concept of PPP in school education is quite different from PPP in other areas, as education in India is a not-for-profit venture. Schools cannot be run as a business enterprise, and no financial benefits can accrue to the private sector in this partnership. Here, it would be more appropriate to look at it as a partnership between state and non-state actors such as non-government organisations and philanthropic activities undertaken by trusts and business houses.

PPP models in school education

There are many models of PPP in school education. The most common are transferring existing schools to private management and establishing new schools. In the former, poorly performing government schools are handed over to private school managements or non-government organisations with a track record of school education to improve the quality of education. The handing over is based on certain terms and conditions. Generally improved learning outcomes (LOs) are expected, and private players are granted lot of flexibility in meeting these. The latter model has many variants. It could be a BOT (Build–Operate–Transfer) model or the more popular one in India: BOO (Build–Own–Operate). Globally, the voucher version of PPP is prevalent wherein instead of funding schools, the government funds students with vouchers to enable them to study in a school of their choice. As part of PPP, government could outsource the services and expertise of non-state actors to enhance infrastructure or introduce better pedagogical practices.

Variants of PPP in school education in India

Various types of PPP models have been conceptualised in school education. An inadvertent PPP model covering a large number of children comes out of the RTE Act. As per a significant provision of the act, all private unaided schools will have to admit at least 25% of children from the economically weaker section (EWS) of the society at the admission stage in class one. Government would reimburse 'expenditure so incurred by it (private school) to the extent of per child expenditure incurred by the state, or the actual amount charged from the child, whichever is less in such manner as may be prescribed'.[5] This inclusion of EWS children in private unaided schools has turned out to be biggest model of PPP in education 'the world's largest voucher programme' (Shaw, 2010).

Another long-standing example of PPP in the Indian context is the type of schools known as private aided schools. This variant existed long before the phenomenon of PPP came into existence. These schools are run by private trusts but are almost fully funded by the government. The fee and salary structure of these schools is similar to the government schools, but they have autonomy in the day-to-day functioning of the schools. It is interesting to point out that these schools are supposedly doing much better than the schools solely run by the government.

Another contribution of the private sector in the area of school education is through corporate social responsibility (CSR). Big private companies all over the world are involved in CSR activities on a voluntary basis. Such activities are an indispensable part of any big enterprise. But India is the only country so far to make a fixed percentage of the net profit mandatory as CSR spending for companies above a certain defined limit of profit.[6] It has been documented that contribution towards school education is the most preferred area for most of the companies. For example, the Azim Premji Foundation of the company WIPRO is a big project in the field of school education. The foundation works in collaboration with state governments in eight states, which together have more than 350,000 government schools.

It has established schools for the specific 'purpose of demonstration'. These schools provide quality free education to the local community at costs and constraints similar to that of rural government schools.[7] Non-state actors are also involved in providing services of different kinds to existing schools, for example, providing the mid-day meal (MDM) to the students in the government schools. The MDM is the flagship programme of the government of India (GoI) for children studying in the government schools. All children studying up to the elementary level are provided a free cooked meal in the school. The scheme has now been extended up to the secondary level. Many non-government organisations are providing this service to the schools on behalf of the government (Kaushal, 2009). Akshay Patra is one such organisation running 'the world's largest NGO-run mid-day meal programme serving [a] wholesome school lunch to over 1.6 million children in 13,579 schools across 12 states in India'.[8] 'Teach for India' is another variant of PPP on the lines of the Teach for America model. It was established in 2008. This organisation places volunteers to teach full time in 'under-resourced' schools with an objective to eliminate educational inequality in the country.[9]

Establishing model schools

In November 2008, the central government announced the opening of 6,000 model schools with the help of private players for providing good-quality education to children from educationally backward areas, on par with good private schools, which were to be modelled on the central government's Kendriya Vidyalayas. Later the Ministry of Human Resource Development (MHRD) delinked itself from the project and passed it on to the states. The model school concept is akin to the government's other initiatives in the form of Navodaya Vidyalayas in the rural areas and Sarvodaya Vidyalayas in the urban areas, which provide a good infrastructure and other facilities to bright economically weaker children who otherwise cannot afford to join expensive private schools. But these schools do not fall in the category of PPP. The difference is that in case of model schools the government has, with certain conditions, handed over the control of the schools to private players, whereas other category of schools is run by the government itself. Another difference is that the model schools would cater to a heterogeneous group of students, as there would be government-sponsored students, as well as students admitted by the private operators independently. The initial proposal was to open 2,500 schools in the country.

The government proposed to set up 6,000 model schools, mainly in the backward regions, with good infrastructure and other facilities. Initially, it was proposed that 2,500 such schools would be set up by partnering with private players. This PPP model is called DBFO (Design–Build–Finance–Operate). In such schools, the government would sponsor children from scheduled castes, scheduled tribes, other backward castes and other children belonging to low-income families. These students would be charged only a nominal fee. Private players would be free to admit and determine the fee structure from other students. Non-state actors were given lot of autonomy in administrative matters.

Now the central government has delinked itself from the scheme and handed it over to the states. States have responded to the scheme and have come up with their own versions within the broad framework proposed by the central government. Existing NGOs working in the area of school education have entered into this partnership with the government. Bharti Foundation, through its Satya Bharti School Program, is running five schools in Punjab as per the state government's PPP policy. The foundation has also adopted existing government schools in Rajasthan on the manage and operate model of PPP. The Rajasthan government came up with a version of PPP schools along the Adarsh schools scheme, with a proposal to have 10,000 good-quality schools in a phased manner. Many other states in the country have adopted the PPP model for schools.

The concept of PPP in school education has its supporters as well as staunch critics. Those who support involvement of non-state actors in education put forth many arguments in its favour. Thus, a UNICEF report (2011) on PPP in school education states:

> [N]on-state providers (NSPs) play an important role in the delivery of education services, both generally and to the poor. Indeed, at times, private and non-state schools are the *only* educational option for disadvantaged and marginalized households and communities.
>
> (Emphasis added)

Another World Bank document that studied the impact of PPP in education across countries points out its benefits on the basis of some research studies.

> The few studies that have been carried out so far suggest that contracting out to the private sector can have several benefits, including greater efficiency, increased choice, and wider access to education, particularly for those households who have been poorly served by traditional methods of providing education.
>
> (World Bank Report, 2009)

The general refrain is that public schools and children unable to afford private schooling would be better off with the involvement of non-state players (Chaudhary and Uboweja, 2014).

When the Indian government came up with the proposal of model schools in collaboration with the private sector, the MHRD circulated a note in September 2009 on PPP in school education and invited comments from the stakeholders and concerned citizens. The rationale provided in the note sums up the points in favour of PPP in schools generally propounded by those supporting the need for PPP in school education. Accordingly, involvement of non-state actors is required to meet the huge cost involved in universalising education. As mentioned earlier, one of the major arguments for not declaring education as a fundamental right was a lack of sufficient resources. Now that the constitutional amendment has granted the right to free and compulsory elementary education to all children up to fourteen years of age, the government needs to pump in immense resources to meet this requirement. The government may not be able to do so on its own. It is justifiable to seek assistance from non-state actors to execute this immense task.

Another argument is based on the popular assumption that private schools are in a better position to provide quality education. Therefore, children must benefit from their expertise and efficiency. The HRD Ministry's report on the setting up of model schools states the benefits of PPP in terms of financial investment and the 'functional efficiency of private entities' to deliver quality education. (MHRD, 2010: 4). Such is the popularity of private schools in comparison to public schools that neoliberal educators (Tooley and Dixon, 2005) look at private schools as the only hope for realising the millennium goal of universalising elementary education in the developing world.

Further, a PPP in school education would remove much of the red-tapism associated with the public sector. The expertise of the private sector would help in cost reduction and economical management of the schools, as they would enjoy autonomy in terms of hiring of staff and deciding on the fee structure. PPP in general also is an instrument of risk sharing. The PPP model of a voucher system wherein the government funds children and not the schools gives a wider choice to the children. It would give impetus to competition, and the public schools would be shaken out of their complacency.

However, the concept of PPP in education, and specifically in school education, has been strongly criticised by educationists. The PPP model in education is in sync with the larger neoliberal agenda of the governments the world over. Gradual withdrawal of the state from its welfarist stance to giving in to the market forces in the name of wider choice and more efficient services is a cover-up for the government's failure to provide basic education to all its citizens. As Krishna Kumar (2008) critiques, PPP is 'not an idea, but rather an ideology which promotes privatization as a means of reducing the government's responsibility to increase the number of schools'. In response to the note by the MHRD, a consultation meeting was held at the National Council for Education Research and Training (NCERT). The concept of model schools as a PPP model was criticised on many grounds. Similarly, when Adarsh Vidayalayas were proposed by the state of Rajasthan, thirty-three educationists and activists wrote an open letter to the chief minister against the proposal, citing the faulty premise that private schools are sure-shot providers of quality education (Rai, 2015). Although the provision in the RTE Act reserving 25% of seats in the private unaided schools for EWS was welcomed by and large, except, of course, the schools in question, some educationists termed the move a whitewash and an abdication of responsibility by the state (Sadgopal, 2011, 2013). Similar moves in the United States and UK have been criticised (Apple, 2006, 2013; Whitty et al., 1998; Winch, 1996) as unleashing conservative market forces in the area of school education.

The main argument against PPP in education and school education in particular is that education is the responsibility of the state. For an egalitarian system of education, a robust public school system run by the government is essential. In India, after the enactment of RTE, constitutionally, the state is obligated to provide free and compulsory education to all children up to fourteen years of age. The state cannot pass the buck to private players. Instead of improving its own system, the government is letting it further deteriorate by handing over the schools to private players. The concept of PPP in other areas cannot be simply extended to education, as education is not a commercial venture like other enterprises. PPP in school education is a clear violation of constitutional tenets.

The assumption implicit in handing over government schools to the private sector is that private schools are better, which is a misguided notion. Not all private schools are good. There is lot of variation in their quality. Similarly, it is not true that all government schools are not good. Schools like Kendriya Vidayalays have proven that government, too, can run quality schools. Neoliberal educators like Tooley (2004), who extol the virtues of private schools and cite the mushrooming of private schools in every nook and corner of the country as evidence of growing parental preference for low cost, low-fee private schools over poorly performing government schools, fail to see the reasons behind the phenomenon. Utter neglect of the government schools, coupled with the aspiration to acquire proficiency in the language that could ensure upward socio-economic mobility, are the real reasons behind this. So, the future does not necessarily lie in unleashing low-cost schools if the state were to own its responsibility to some fundamental needs of its citizenry.

Seeking assistance from community or non-state actors for achieving the desired goals is one thing, and giving a free run for profiteering another thing. The regulatory mechanism in the given models leaves out many details and gives free hand to private players, thus risking corruption and exploitation of staff and students. Because private operators can hire the staff on their own terms and conditions, teachers are the 'sacrificial lamb' and get very low salaries compared to their counterparts in the government schools (Sarangapani, 2009). Such efficiency at the cost of teachers is not healthy for an education system. No wonder there is lot of resistance on behalf of the stakeholders whenever an attempt is made to hand over the government schools to private operators. Recently, in Rajasthan, the government had to shelve a move to privatise fifteen schools after widespread protests by the teachers and parents.[10]

Such policies are likely to cater to only few, leaving a large number of children without access to quality education and widening disparities in the process. The MHRD's own note on the concept of model schools states that this:

> [The] scheme should not be viewed as a means to reform the entire system of school education. It should be viewed as an initiative that create some centres of excellence in support of the wider agenda for reform in school education.
>
> (MHRD, 2010: 2)

Such initiatives just serve the purpose of diverting people's attention from the pathetic conditions of state-run schools (Sadgopal, 2013). Even well-intended initiatives like Teach for India end up producing inequality rather than 'eliminating' it, as the volunteers happen to take charge of only a select few classes in a school. Unless the state takes upon itself the responsibility of improving providing quality education to all, such piecemeal efforts will deliver only a few success stories.

Although PPP in other areas is evaluated on issues like share of profit of the private players, regulatory mechanism and consumer interest, etc., the model 'falters . . . in offering a wholesale package, which is supposedly as good for education as it is for transport' (Kumar, 2008). PPP in school education and basic health services are condemned as areas which should not be handed over to private players at all (Derez and Sen, 2013, Harma, 2009). In India, educationists had long been demanding a common school system for all, regulated by the state. Tilak (2010) writes:

> [The] earlier models of PPP, including the aided school system, aimed to encourage philanthropy and generate voluntary contributions to the education sector. But the objectives of the present mode seem to be altogether different. It invites commercial companies, whose ulterior motives often conflict with educational goals and for whom there is no difference between education and, say, the production of cars, refrigerators and soaps, as long as it ensures attractive profits.

To conclude, we can say that given the present scenario, PPP in school education is likely to advance a neoliberal common sense in some form or another across nations, irrespective of their developmental status. Not much evaluation of the impact of PPP in education has been done so far, mainly because of the diffused as well as contested notion of quality education. Private initiatives may arguably yield better measurable LOs, but that is little consolation when looking at the larger picture of school education.

The role of private players in education has to be regulated differently in comparison to other areas. Education, particularly elementary education, which is now a fundamental right, cannot be equated with other economic activities. Wholesale transfer of a concept applicable to commercial activities is a dangerous trend. Education, being the most important life-changing tool, has to be made available to all on an equal footing, which the latest version of PPP can never accomplish.

Notes

1 www.pppindia.gov.in
2 www.narendramodi.inpeople-public-private-partnership-3163
3 Article 21 of the constitution is a fundamental right pertaining to right to life and liberty. In various judgments the Supreme Court expanded the right to life to mean the right to live beyond mere physical existence and to be able to live with dignity. Eventually, the right to education was declared a fundamental right by associating it with the right to life. Now the right to free and compulsory education from six to fourteen years of age has been added as Article 21-A. See *Mohini Jain v. State of Karnatka* (1992)3 SSC 666 and *Unnikrishnan J.P. v. State of Andhra Pradesh* (1993) 1 SCC 594, 603, 605, 645.
4 During drafting of the constitution, a sub-committee on justiciable fundamental rights recommended inclusion of the right to free and compulsory education in the list, but the advisory committee later put the right in the directive principles of state policy, which are guiding principles for the state to follow. (righttoeducation.in/how-was-original-article-45-constitution-arrived).
5 The Right of Children to Free and Compulsory Education Act, 2009, Chapter iv, section 12(2).
6 As per the Companies Act of 2013, every private or public limited company with a net worth of Rs. 500 crore or a turnover of Rs. 1000 crore or a net profit of Rs. 5 crore has to mandatorily spend at least 2% of its net profit on CSR activities. The activities have been specified in the act. An analysis of 300 big companies for the financial year 2016–17 shows that the maximum spending (32%) has been on education. See www.mca.gov.in/SearcheableActs/Section135.htm and India CSR Outlook Report 2017 at ngobox.org.
7 www.azimpremjifoundation.org
8 www.Akshaypatra.org
9 https://teach4india.wordpress.com
10 The state of Rajasthan is a front-runner when it comes to PPP in schools. But of late, the government's move to hand over even those government schools that are doing well to private operators has led to lot of resentment among teachers and parents. See the news reports 'In Rajasthan, villagers protest as government plans private management for schools it did not build' at https://scroll.in/article 863718 and 'Protests forced govt to shelve PPP model in state' at www.dnaindia. com/jaipur/report

References

Apple, W. M. (2006). *Educating the 'right' way: Markets, standards, god, and inequality*, 2nd ed. New York: Routledge.
——. (2013). *Can education change society?* New York: Routledge.

Chaudhary, S. and Uboweja, A. (2014). *Public-private partnerships in school education: Learnings and insights for India.* Central Square Foundation, Working Paper. Available at: www.centralsquarefoundation.org (Accessed on 12 March 2017).

Dreze, J. and Sen, A. (2013). *An uncertain glory: India and its contradictions.* New Delhi: Penguin Books.

Fennell, S. (2007). *Tilting at windmills: Public-private partnership in Indian education today.* Research Consortium on Educational Outcomes and Poverty, RECOUP WP07/05

Harma, J. (2009). Can choice promote education for all? Evidence from growth in primary schooling in India. *Compare: A Journal of Comparative and International Education*, 39(2), pp. 151–165. https://dx.doi.org/10.1080/03057920902750400

Kaushal, S. (2009). *A study of the best practices in the implementation of mid-day-meal programme in Rajasthan.* New Delhi: National University of Educational Planning and Administration.

Kumar, K. (2008). Partners in education? *Economic and Political Weekly*, 43(3), pp. 8–11.

Rai, A. (2015, 18 July). Misguided education policy in Rajasthan: A critique of the public private partnership in school education. *Economic and Political Weekly*, 50(29).

Sadgopal, A. (2013). Inclusion vs. Equality in right to education. *Restructuring Education*, 2(2), April-June.

———. (2011). Neoliberal Act. *Frontline*, 28(14), July, pp. 2–15.

Sarangapani, P. (2009). Quality, feasibilty and desirability of low cost private schooling. *Economic and Political Weekly*, 44(43), pp. 67–69.

Shah, P. J. (2010). Where private and public co-exist: The opportunity in the right to education act, *Pragati*. March 2010. Available at: www.schoolchoice.in/media room/ articles by supporters/201003-pragati-parth.php (Accessed on 22 December 2016).

Ministry of Human Resource Development (MHRD). (2010). *Scheme for augmenting school education through public private partnership: Report of the sub-group of the round table on school education.* MHRD, May 25, 2010. Accessible at Planningcommission.gov.in/sectors/ppp_report_guidelines.

State of Victoria (Department of Education and Training). (2016). *Project Summary: New Schools Public Private Partnership (PPP) Project.*

Tilak, J. B. G. (2010). Public Private Partnership in Education. *The Hindu*, 24 May 2010.

———. Tooley, J. (2004). Private education and education for all. *Economic Affairs*, 24, pp. 4–7. doi: 10.1111/j.1468-0270.2004,00506.x

Tooley, J. and Dixon, P. (2005). *Private education is good for the poor: A study of private schools serving the poor in low-income countries.* Cato Institute. https:// object.cato.org/pubs/wtpapers/tooley.pdf (Accessed on 20 August 2017).

UNICEF Report. (2011). *Non-state partners and public-private partnerships in education for the poor.* ADB UNICEF, Available at: www.unicef.org/eapro (Accessed on 24 March 2017).

Venu, N. (2010). The private and the public in school education. *Economic and Political Weekly*, 45(6).

Whitty, G., Power, S. and Halpin, D. (1998). *Devolution and choice in education: The school, the state and the market.* Buckingham: Open University Press.

Winch, C. (1996). Quality and education. *Journal of Philosophy of Education*, 30(1)

World Bank Institute. (2012). *Public-private partnerships reference guide version 2.* Washington, DC: World Bank Publications.

Chapter 3

Public education

Can it be fixed?

Atishi

Public education in India has received stepmotherly treatment from state governments across the country. Barring a few states that have had Left rule and some others in South India, most states have only made marginal progress, if any, when it comes to the quality of education provided in government schools. The eleventh ASER Report 2016, released in January 2017, provides an insight into learning levels in government schools across the country. The study uses reading ability up to Class 2 textbooks as a metric (the highest level assessed in the survey) for learning levels and shows that one out of every four children enrolled in Class 8 is not able to read the Class 2 textbooks (Aiyar et al., 2018). In August 2016, the Delhi government's Directorate of Education (DoE) released the findings of its own study of learning assessment that was commissioned by the state government. The study assessed basic language and mathematics levels for 201,997 children studying in Standard 6 from 1,011 schools of the DoE. The survey was carried out by Bachelor of Elementary Education (B.El.Ed.) and Bachelor of Education (B.Ed.) students who were associated with all nine District Institutes of Education Training (DIETs) for their practicum and other courses located in the various districts of Delhi. It was found that:

- Seventy-four percent of children could not read a paragraph from their own Hindi textbook.
- Forty-six percent of children could not read a simple story of Standard 2–level competency.
- Eight percent of children could not identify the letters of the alphabet.

Similarly, in mathematics:

- Sixty-seven percent of children could not do simple three digits by one digit division.
- Forty-four percent of children could not do two-digit subtraction with borrowing.
- Five percent of children could not recognize single-digit numbers.

Further, in basic English:

- Seventy-five percent of children could not read a story of Standard 2–level competency.
- Thirteen percent of children could not identify the alphabet.

The condition of schools in the national capital is consistent with that of schools in states across the country. This is nothing short of a national crisis: entire generations of children, with few or no opportunities to begin with, are being condemned to fail.

The health of India's public education is closely linked to the class divide prevailing in the country. Elementary education policy in post-independence India has highlighted this social reality and recommended that a common school system be established so as to provide equitable education to all children (GoI, 1966, 1986). But this has continued to be mere policy rhetoric so far, as the structure of school education – particularly the differential arrangements of layers within schooling: high-fee-charging private schools, budget schools, layers within the government system like Navodaya Vidyalayas, Kendriya Vidyalayas, Pratibha Vidyalayas, etc. – reflects.

The stigma attached to government schools is so deep that the moment parents are able to afford the fees charged by private schools, they transfer their children from government to private schools. Private schools have come to be seen as doorways to prosperity. Private schools are associated with an opportunity for upward social mobility, and public schools with a resignation to one's economic reality. The steady decline of public education has undoubtedly coincided with the widening inequality India has witnessed over the last three decades. It is implicit therefore that unless an effort is made to rescue government schools from further decline, there will continue to be a sharp divergence between the haves and the have-nots.

How have we come to this? At the risk of oversimplifying a complicated problem, the root of this crisis is a concerted neglect of public education by the state. The deep politician–private school nexus means that the executive has little or no incentive to fix public education. In Delhi, the list of major politicians owning and/or managing private schools is long. There is an obvious conflict of interest at play. A political establishment that profits from increasing enrolment of children in private schools has a vested interest in keeping government schools dysfunctional. The key to a better public schooling system is, quite plainly, honest governance.

The National Sample Survey Organisation's (NSSO) 71st round of the survey on education reveals that 42% of all children in Delhi at the primary level are studying in government or government-aided institutions. This figure goes up to 49% for upper primary and 28% for secondary and higher secondary levels of education. What this indicates is that the quality of education being provided to almost half of all children of the country's capital is consistently poor because they are enrolled in government schools. Private entrepreneurial budget private schools (BPS) with low fees that mushroomed in the late 1980s in India just as in other developing countries (allegedly as substitutes to dysfunctional state-run schools) had become popular in the educational landscape of Delhi's poor. The condition of a large number of BPS in Delhi is as bad or worse than Delhi's government schools. The survey also reveals that the wealthiest quintile of households spends as much as eight times the amount spent by the poorest quintile on primary education. What these statistics mean is that only the wealthiest Indians today have access to high-quality education. This has made social inequality increasingly acute over the years and has widened the class divide in society. The only way to reverse this is to improve the quality of education offered in government schools.

The right intent is the foundation on which a sound school education policy can be formulated. In Delhi, the Aam Aadmi Party (AAP) government, which took charge in February 2015, made education its top budgetary priority. In 2015–16, the government allocated Rs 9,836 crore to education, an increase of 106% over the previous government's allocation. Over the next two years, the allocation to education has been maintained at around a quarter of the total budget of the Delhi government. The allocation for education for the year 2017–18 was Rs 11,997 crore, 26% of the total budget of the state.

How has the government used the increased allocation? The plan of action for school improvement processes was shared in the public sphere with all the stakeholders: parents, teachers, students and the community (Directorate of Information and Publicity, 2016). In the first year, there was a thrust on improving infrastructure, both in terms of upgrading existing school buildings and constructing new ones. However, as the learning assessment conducted in 2016 revealed, the core of the crisis in government schools was not in its infrastructure, but in the learning deficits. The government developed a four-pronged strategy: (1) modernising infrastructure, (2) capacity-building of schoolteachers and principals, (3) making school administration accountable, and (4) improving learning outcomes.

Infrastructure

When one entered a government school in Delhi a few years back, the unbearable stench of the toilets would be the most striking feature. The toilets were in disrepair, taps were broken, and running water was a luxury in many schools. The coat of paint on walls, both within classrooms and outside, was peeling off. The windows were either missing or broken, and desks were from another century.

The visual that this description invokes is commonplace in a large majority of public schools across the country. Although restoring crumbling infrastructure is a lower-order problem when compared with the larger learning-level deficit crisis, learning cannot take place in an unpleasant environment. Such an environment is emblematic of a non-serious institution. Children who stepped into such schools were made to think that they were second-class citizens who did not deserve any better.

In 2015, the government identified 54 pilot schools, which received special attention on infrastructure development in the first two years. After detailed deficiency analyses, surveys, and visits to top private schools, plans were drawn up for the construction of new buildings for the existing schools. The new buildings now resemble any of India's world-class private schools: aesthetically designed, airy, well-lit classrooms; smart boards; beautiful desks; clean bathrooms; swanky libraries; laboratories; and large auditoriums. Some schools have been equipped with swimming pools, athletic tracks, football fields, and field hockey turfs. The problem of overcrowding in classrooms has also been brought under control, with unprecedented expansion of capacity. Eight thousand new classrooms have been added to existing schools in a span of two years, and 10,000 more are in various stages of completion. Each new classroom resembles those being built in the pilot schools.

Several regions of Delhi are so underserved that children have been forced to travel several kilometres to reach the closest government school. This has been addressed by building and operationalising 25 new schools, including five 'Schools of Excellence' which will have English as the primary medium of instruction.

In order to ensure that the buildings are maintained and cleaned regularly, the government hired a new sanitation contractor, increased the number of sanitation staff allotted to each school, and provided them with advanced cleaning equipment. Several months went into calculating seemingly unimportant details like the quantity of cleaning supplies needed by each school, but this is what has made schools significantly cleaner than they used to be. It might seem counter-intuitive, but often, policymaking is about getting these little things right.

Most importantly, the role of supervising the upkeep of schools was divested from the principal's office. Principals were asked to hire estate managers of their choice, who were entrusted with the job of supervising the school's building infrastructure maintenance. Every day, estate managers report the condition of their school through an app closely monitored by officials in the directorate and by the education minister.

The government has also made more efficient use of existing infrastructure. Delhi's government schools occupy large swathes of prime land across the city. Utilising this land only in the first part of the day is a waste of this resource. Early in 2018, indoor and outdoor spaces in all schools were thrown open to private institutes providing training in arts and sports.

These institutes are mandated to train at least 50% of all children from the government schools, who will be enrolled for free.

Capacity-building of staff

Elementary education policy in post-independence India has underscored the need for continuous teacher education. The Kothari Commission spoke of teacher education as a continuous process, of which the pre-service and in-service components are inseparable.

In-service teacher training has been given a major push by the Sarva Shiksha Abhiyan (SSA) and the Rashtriya Madhyamik Shiksha Abhiyan (RMSA). As a consequence of these two programmes and other allocations by the state government, Delhi too was training a large number of teachers every year. However, despite more than 30,000 teachers getting trained annually, there was virtually no impact on classroom practices. Studies in education discipline have highlighted that the field of teacher education has been characterised by inertia and an isolation from the classroom realities prevailing in schools. The fact that hardly any impact was discernible upon classroom practices in the DoE schools points towards the fossilisation of the in-service programmes that were designed for the teachers. On speaking to teachers, we identified two reasons for this: first, training was conducted by faculty from universities who had little or no idea about the ground conditions faced by teachers; second, even if the teachers found some innovative methods, they would not have any help in resolving challenges they faced in its implementation.

In the summer of 2016, the government introduced a radical change to teacher training with the launch of the mentor teacher program. A cadre of 200 dynamic, committed teachers from among existing government school-teachers called 'mentor teachers' was selected. Mentors are provided with specialised training in their subjects of instruction and are brought up to speed with the advancements in pedagogy. This is done through workshops and exposure trips. All 200 mentors attended a programme at the National Institute of Education in Singapore. They were also sent to some of the finest educational institutions of the country on similar trips. They were sent to Anupam Moti Dau Primary School, Mahesana Block, Gujarat state; Gyan Shaala Programs; Dream a Dream, Centre of Educational Innovations, Bangalore; Digantar, an alternative school in Rajasthan; Uday Community Schools; and The Gateway School, Teach For India program in cities in different parts of India, all of which are institutions at the forefront of progressive school reform. The cadre of mentors is now responsible for facilitating teacher training sessions, both annually and throughout the year. During the summer vacation, mentors conduct four-day-long workshops with teachers of their subjects in small groups. In these workshops, teachers prepare

60 Atishi

supplementary material for the syllabus they are expected to teach over the course of the year. When such an exercise was first carried out in the summer of 2016, both mentors and regular teachers had a liberating experience. A science teacher said during a feedback session,

> After teaching for 22 years in government schools, these workshops made me realise that what I was doing for so many years was not teaching at all. This workshop has started to make me think and innovate. I am sure my class is going to be much more engaging next year.

After several years of serving in government schools, for the first time teachers got an opportunity to engage in a dialogue on pedagogy and teaching-learning methodologies with their peers. Small groups of four to six teachers, facilitated by mentors, worked to come up with innovative techniques to teach topics. The summer training workshops have been taking place every year since the summer of 2016. After the second summer workshop ended in 2017, teachers expressed a need for more regular interactions on pedagogy on a smaller scale. The annual workshops left teachers with interesting ideas for the year, but to implement them inside schools, they needed more active support from the community of teachers of their subjects. In keeping with this demand, from the academic year of 2017–18 onwards, the summer training sessions have been followed up by bimonthly subject-level workshops on immediate syllabus goals linked to learning outcomes.

Mentor teachers, along with being resource persons for capacity-building sessions, are also required to visit the five to six schools allotted to them at least once a week. The idea was to begin a conversation with teachers on a weekly basis about their challenges in the classroom. Although this programme helped many teachers improve their classroom teaching, the mentor programme was limited by the fact that the mentor teacher was an outsider to the school's ecosystem. It was felt that a similar person was needed within the school. This prompted the development of the Teacher Development Coordinator (TDC) program, which was launched in 2017. As an extension of the mentor program, a TDC is in charge of developing an academic discourse among the teachers. A regular teacher from each school was appointed the TDC of that school. To achieve their mandate, TDCs hold regular half-hour sessions after school hours with teachers to discuss their challenges and potential solutions.

Developing effective school leadership has been a crucial piece of the puzzle. School leaders need to be able to anchor reforms in their own schools for them to reach the grassroots level. For schools to truly accept and implement reforms, heads of schools have to be motivated to achieve shared objectives and drive them at their own levels. Principals attend a monthly session with in-house facilitators in small groups of ten principals each to share concerns and strategies for running schools with one another. This has significantly transformed the ability of principals to adapt to change and find effective solutions to problems faced in the administration of schools through the knowledge-sharing approach of small group sessions. Because principals are the most powerful stakeholders in government schools, they are best placed to create lasting change in schools. The principal of a school in Hari Nagar, west Delhi, has established a student representative body, which has been empowered to play a role in school administration. Another principal of a school in Lajpat Nagar, south Delhi, has been solely responsible for preventing children from dropping out by encouraging them to use their crafts to make decorative items in the school itself, which the school helps them to sell. The government also joined with the Indian Institute of Management, Ahmedabad, where principals are enrolled in a course on school leadership development. Some batches of principals have also completed a course in school leadership at Cambridge University.

Accountability structures

The systemic inertia in the government needs to be countered on all levels through effective accountability structures. Government schools have also been a victim of the weight of government bureaucracy. Towards this end, the government introduced three levels of oversight and supervision. The message to all schools to perform well comes right from the top – the education minister visits at least three to four schools every week without notice. The surprise inspections have resulted in some senior officials, including principals, being suspended for corruption and purposeful negligence in administration. The knowledge that the minister could turn up at any school without notice has forced some to shed their customary lethargy. District officials of the directorate have also been pushed to make school visits a regular feature of their workdays. Monitoring and tracking the management of schools under their jurisdiction have been made more rigorous. Although these two levels of accountability are the only means that are under direct control of the government, it is unrealistic to expect a district education official with a hundred schools under her or him to visit each school more than once in three or four months. The education minister will take years to make even one round to each school. Moreover, it is a fact that all government employees may not be working at their full potential. The only way to keep public schools accountable, therefore, is by involving those who have the most crucial stake in the running of these schools: the parents. The third and most important level of monitoring has been a strong network of school management committees (SMCs).

The SMCs, which comprise parents, are mandated by the RTE Act 2009, with a view to make school administration more accountable to parents and the communities which they serve. Before September 2015, SMCs in Delhi government schools either didn't exist or were defunct. The government, with the help of civil society, mobilised parents to participate in elections to the SMCs. On 5 September 2015, elections were conducted for the first time in all 1,023 schools run by the Delhi government. SMCs consist of members who live in the vicinity of the school. They are therefore able to visit and monitor the functioning of the school on a regular basis. They feel a sense of ownership in this process because their work as SMC members directly affects the quality of education their own children have access to. Due to the fact that male parents are more likely to be engaged in full-time work, SMCs are filled with more women than men. Many of these are women who, until their election to the SMCs, may never have occupied a position of significance in public fora. Because a large number of children in government schools are first-generation school-goers, their parents are also more likely to be illiterate. Over the last three years, it has been this class of parents which has been empowered to play a role in the running of their children's schools, and the results have been extremely positive. In one school in Shahdara, east Delhi, members of the SMC physically placed themselves at the school exit gate to prevent certain teachers who had a habit of leaving early to catch their trains back to their homes in Sahibabad. After a few weeks, the teachers stopped the practice of leaving before the working hours ended. In another school in Okhla, southwest Delhi, an SMC member who happened to be acquainted with a professor of economics at the Delhi University connected the school to the professor, who filled in voluntarily for a short period when an economics teacher's position was vacant. Such promising stories of community involvement in running the schools can be found from schools all across the city. SMCs have also altered the parent–school dynamic. By empowering these committees, the government gave parents a seat at the table. The class divide between parents and teachers and principals and teachers is acute and used to result in casual mistreatment of parents at the hands of staff. In an encouraging development, this has indeed changed. Educating a class of citizens about the rights they did not know existed can be a challenge. It can be an even bigger challenge to encourage them to exercise these rights. With significant progress on these fronts being made over the last three years, SMCs have become a part of the culture of schools.

Grievances of parents in SMCs are now resolved at SMC Mahasabhas – public meetings organised on the Vidhan Sabha level, attended by officials from several relevant government departments and the local MLA. SMC members confront officials with their issues, who find ways to resolve them at the meeting itself. In one such SMC Mahasabha in Burari, north Delhi, a school principal notified a Delhi Jal Board (DJB) official present at the meeting that she had raised a complaint to his office several times in the previous months. The DJB official denied having received such a complaint. The principal approached the stage with copies of her 14 letters to the DJB and requested the local MLA and education department official to escalate the matter. Faced with public pressure, the DJB official was forced to address the matter and resolved it within a week of the meeting.

Parent involvement has also been increased through Parent–Teacher Meetings (PTMs). The first mega-PTM was organised in July 2016. It was preceded by a large campaign to create awareness among parents through radio jingles and newspaper ads. Children made personalised invitation cards for their parents. A small welcome party was set up to serve tea and biscuits to parents near the school entrance as well. For many parents, the July 2016 mega-PTM was the first time they set foot in their children's schools. Over several more mega-PTMs, the idea of such parent–teacher engagement has become institutionalised in Delhi's government schools.

Learning outcomes

In 2016, over 50% of all Class 9 students failed to pass their examinations. The no detention policy (NDP) ensured that the Class 9 exam was their first detrimental test on which their promotion was dependent. Unfortunately, the NDP was not supported by mechanisms to ensure that both teachers and parents continue to take academic prowess seriously in middle school. However, because there was no institutional incentive for teachers to focus on children's learning levels, the learning deficit kept widening year after year, resulting in the debacle we see in the Class 9 results.

To remedy this, the government launched the 'Chunauti 2018' reforms in 2016. The Chunauti reforms were based on the model developed by the Abdul Latif Jameel Poverty Action Lab (J-PAL), termed Teaching at the Right Level (TaRL), which follows a pedagogy that groups children according to their learning level instead of the conventional age or grade-specific grouping alone (Banerjee et al., 2016). The teaching of the groups begins with the current competency level and consequent tailor-made teaching-learning activities. This pedagogical approach had already been pioneered in India by *Pratham* and had encouraging results.

The classrooms in schools were fundamentally altered to ensure children are taught based on their ability to grasp the syllabus. The large variance in learning levels in a single class, as revealed by the baseline assessment, impeded the standard age-appropriate model of teaching. Theory and research from the fields of learner studies, educational psychology, and child development provide the rationale for Teaching at the Right Level as a general maxim in education. The path-breaking cognitive development theory of Swiss educator Jean Piaget recommends that teaching methods be matched to children's abilities and teachers' understanding of how they think (Piaget, 1974). On the basis of Piaget's theory the term 'problem of the match' emerged in the context of how the psychology of learning could be applied to teaching (Hunt, 1961). It refers to the principle that the cognitive tasks presented to students should be appropriate to encourage growth – neither too simple to bore/disinterest them nor so hard that students lack the mental structures to make sense of them.

Children enrolled in Classes 6 to 8 are now grouped based on their learning levels into Neo-Nishtha, Nishtha, and Pratibha classes; they are taught the syllabus at differing levels of complexity. Nishtha teachers focus on building reading, writing, and basic math competency, and those in Pratibha carry on with the regular syllabus. The grouping helps teachers address the needs of children, no matter how basic. In addition to this, since 2017, the pattern of assessments was changed to encourage teachers to focus on achievement of learning outcomes for all subjects while teaching classes. An assessment unit consisting of motivated and dynamic teachers has led the assessment reform over the past year.

In order to improve children's overall reading ability, in September 2016, the Every Child Can Read campaign was started by the education minister. A systematic effort towards teaching children to read was carried out in every government school. Over a period of eight weeks, more than one lakh child across Delhi moved from being a non-reader to a reader. Over 1,000 Reading Melas were held across the capital, where community members (young and old) volunteered to help children with reading on weekends. A visible change in the classroom environment was perceived, with innovative teaching replacing 'chalk and talk'. Several teachers voluntarily adopted a small bunch of non-reader children to provide them personalised support in learning to read.

The enormity of the crisis that our country faces when it comes to educating our children is so massive that despite all our efforts, the Delhi government has only just begun to address the problems. And yet the past three years have shown that change is possible and that public education can be fixed. The policy solutions involved are not rocket science, but often common-sense fixes that need to be implemented well. And driving this implementation requires political will. Herein lies the crux of the education crisis of our country: Will citizens demand high-quality education of their elected representatives? Will politicians dread facing their electorate if the government schools of their constituency are not functional? It is when this transformation takes place that all governments will marshal the political will to transform the public education system.

References

Aiyar, Y., Banerji, R., Chavan, M., Bhattacharjea, S. and Wadhwa, W. (2018). *annual status of education report 2016 – National findings*. New Delhi: ASER Centre, January 2018.

Banerjee, A., Banerji, R., Berry, J., Duflo, E., Kannan, H. and Mukerji, S. et al. (2016). *Mainstreaming an effective intervention: Evidence from randomized evaluations of 'teaching at the right level' in India.* Cambridge: Abdul Latif Jameel Poverty Action Lab, August.

Directorate of Information and Publicity, Govt of NCT of Delhi. (2016). *Press release.* Available at: http://delhi.gov.in on (Accessed on 9 August 2016).

Government of India. (1966). *Report of the education commission: Education and national development.* New Delhi: Ministry of Education.

———. (1986). *National policy of education.* New Delhi: Ministry of HRD.

———. (10 March 2016). *Education in India.* New Delhi: National Sample Survey Organisation.

Hunt, E. (1961). *Intelligence and experience.* New York: Ronald Press.

Piaget, J. (1974). *Understanding causality.* New York: Norton.

Chapter 4

Equitable elementary education as a public good

What is left of it?

Jyoti Raina

The constitution of India held out the promise of egalitarianism, equality of opportunity and social justice, envisioning quality equitable elementary education as a public good for the people in aiming to build a democratic republic. As it came in force on 26 January 1950, it also attempted to address the post-independence prevailing challenges of poverty, population and illiteracy (85% of the people could not read and write) in our stratified, hierarchical and inegalitarian society, as well as the complexities of reaching out to educate children from diverse social, regional, religious, linguistic, ethnic and economic backgrounds. The constitutional vision of elementary education is that of a public good which serves a social agenda, with the hope that the public good of elementary education would become a reality through distributive and redistributive policies that would intervene against structures of inequality by positive discrimination. This vision necessitated a dominant role by the state in provisioning for elementary education, as reflected in Article 45, a directive principle of state policy that highlighted the role of the state in providing within a period of ten years from the commencement of the constitution free and compulsory education for all children until they complete the age of fourteen years. The preamble provides the underlying framework which envisages that education must serve as a moral force to build a democratic citizenship for a socialist, egalitarian and just society (Sadgopal, 2010). The years following independence witnessed considerable progress, particularly quantitative expansion of education. However, the constitutional vision of free education for all did not turn into a reality, as issues of equality, quality and equity remained. This is the only constitutional provision with a time frame which ended in 1960 even though its aim remained unaccomplished. On the passing away of the deadline, India's then education minister M. C. Chagla (1964) spoke of the national failure of Universalisation of Elementary Education (UEE):

> Our Constitution fathers did not intend that we just set up hovels, put students there, give untrained teachers, give them bad textbooks, no playgrounds, and say, we have complied with Article 45 and primary

education is expanding. They meant that real education should be given to our children between the ages of 6 and 14.

Article 45 remained mere symbolic policy, as the state had an escape route justifying its poor performance in elementary education (Seetharamu, 2002) through Article 41 that reads

> The State shall, within the limits of its economic capacity and development, make effective provision for securing the right to work, to education and to public assistance.

On 23 April 1947 the advisory committee of the constituent assembly rejected the idea of free and compulsory education as a fundamental right on the grounds that there would remain an uncertainty if the state did not have sufficient funds to make arrangements for free and compulsory education of all children. It consequently added elementary education to the list of 'nonjusticiable fundamental rights' classified later as directive principles of state policy in the constitution.

In the seven decades since, there has been unprecedented expansion of elementary education in India, particularly the impressive educational development in the last one and a half decades, leading to increased enrolment and access to improved schooling facilities. This is reflected in a promising Net Enrolment Ratio (NER) in the primary stage of elementary education. The enrolment exclusion is almost over, with NER as per the government's District Information System for Education (DISE) data for 2010–11 in the primary stage of elementary education at 99.6%. More than 27 million children were enrolled in Class I in the year 2015–16 (State Report Cards, 2015–16, 2017: 29). Yet the euphoria generated by the statistics on enrolment, availability of schooling facilities and inclusion of children from marginalised groups, as advertised by a steadily increasing Gross Enrolment Ratio (GER) for marginalised caste groups, celebrating the inclusion of historically excluded socially disadvantaged children into the fold of formal schooling deflates the constitutional promise of equitable elementary education as a public good for two principal reasons.

The first is the structural distortion of elementary education, which continues to conform to the hierarchy prevalent in our stratified society by socialising learners through an unequal schooling system embedded in existing inequalities in society and differences in educational opportunities. Sharp divisions are inherent in the school education system because of the many kinds of schools that it consists of, making school education inegalitarian and failing to bring different sections of society in the common space of a school classroom. The 'hierarchical educational streams for different social segments' (Ravi Kumar, 2017: 11) of the multi-layered, hierarchical school education streams consist of flagship government school systems like

Pratibha Vikas Vidyalayas, Sainik Schools, Kendriya Vidyalayas, Navodaya Vidyalayas and many others to ordinary village/small town/slum-located schools under rural/urban local self-government bodies like Gram Panchayats/municipalities, to elite, sought-after day/residential private schools in urban and non-urban areas which charge exclusionary high fees; the LFPS system run by individual businessmen, religious trusts, corporate houses, NGOs and politicians; and open schooling, non-formal and alternative education for students from particular segments. The sharp divisions have been accentuating into a disturbing fault line separating children belonging to socially disadvantaged backgrounds from other children in society. The former are attending government schools in inordinately greater numbers in comparison to the latter. Also, the proportion of children belonging to non-disadvantaged backgrounds is much higher in private schools in comparison to government schools. The more severely disadvantaged sections of SCs and STs are underrepresented in the private schools in spite of a 25% quota reserved for children belonging to the EWS under the RTE Act since 2010. Further, even though there is a substantial increase in the enrolment of children from the disadvantaged sections of society in all types of schools, a comparison between the enrolment figures for government and private schools shows that the highest increase in the enrolment of socially disadvantaged children has taken place in the government school system recently. This is coupled with the decrease in the proportion of students from the general non-disadvantaged category in government schools, being attended mostly by children from the marginalised social segments, including Dalits, SCs, STs and other minorities (Sadgopal, 2016a: 18), turning state schools into a colony of the underprivileged. This is corroborated by an analysis of educational statistics shown in Figure 4.1 and Figure 4.2, showing percentage enrolment by social category in government, private aided and private schools from Grades I through V.

As Figure 4.1 shows, almost 82% of children who attend government schools belonged to socially disadvantaged sections of society in the academic year 2014–15. This is a whopping increase of the same statistic for the year 2011–12, which stood at 55%, as shown in Figure 4.2. Further, the number of children from the general category attending private unaided schools is double that of those who attended government schools for this academic year. The state schools turning into mainly a colony of the underprivileged is a debilitating consequence of a lack of thrust on public education. The overlapping social differences of class, caste and gender in our stratified society contain possibilities of deep social divisions. Added to this is the social reality that the differences in school education are not cross-cutting, but overlap with the other social differences, the outcome of which is further social division on another basis: school education.

Second, the Indian elementary education system has failed to align itself with the contemporaneous notion of 'inclusive classrooms' that can mitigate

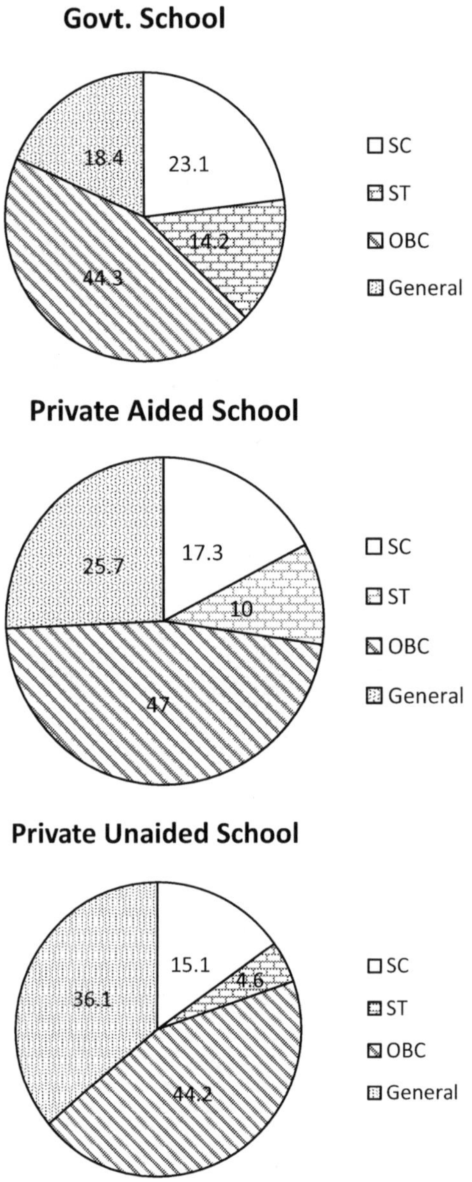

Govt. School

- □ SC
- ▣ ST
- ◹ OBC
- ▦ General

Values: 23.1, 14.2, 44.3, 18.4

Private Aided School

- □ SC
- ▣ ST
- ◹ OBC
- ▦ General

Values: 17.3, 10, 47, 25.7

Private Unaided School

- □ SC
- ▣ ST
- ◹ OBC
- ▦ General

Values: 15.1, 4.6, 44.2, 36.1

Figure 4.1 Social backgrounds of children attending different types of schools in primary grades, academic year 2014–15

Source: District Information System for Education (DISE), National Institute of Educational Planning and Administration (NUEPA), raw data for years 2013 and 2015. http://udise.in/drc2013-14.htm and http://udise.in/drc2015-16.htm (2013–14; 2015–16) under enrolment statistics category % enrolment by caste.

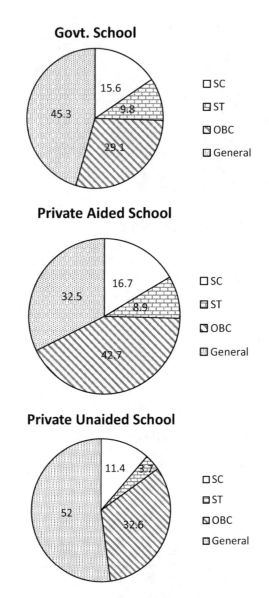

Figure 4.2 Social backgrounds of children attending different types of schools in primary grades, academic year 2011–12

Source: District Information System for Education (DISE), National Institute of Educational Planning and Administration (NUEPA), raw data for years 2013 and 2015. http://udise.in/drc2013-14.htm and http://udise.in/drc2015-16.htm (2013–14; 2015–16) under enrolment statistics category % enrolment by caste.

I am grateful to B.El.Ed 3rd year students of class of 2017–18, Gargi College, New Delhi, for assistance in compiling raw DISE data in preparing this figure.

the deeply ingrained social inequality that children experience outside the school (Tiwary et al., 2017). The celebratory end of enrolment exclusion appears flawed when pitted against deep inequities in educational participation, particularly the data on dropout rates. As per the most recently reported DISE data, GER stands at 99.2% for 2015–16, with the dropout rate for primary school level for the same year, at 4.10% (State Report Cards 2015–16, 2017: 39). The dropout rates are disturbingly higher for children belonging to socially disadvantaged sections, which are at 4.81% for SCs, 7.46% for STs and 7.45% for Muslims (Ibid, 2017: 37). The quest for social justice through school education implies retention, meaningful school participation and learning of all children within the framework of social diversity (Singh and Kumar, 2010). This quest is belied in spite of the increasing social diversity in school education because of the structural barriers erected by deep-rooted, entrenched hierarchies that are embedded in intricate structures of caste, class, community, gender and patriarchy. Discrimination based on class, caste, gender, ethnicity and linguistic background is prevalent, accompanied by denial of equal opportunity, beginning with not the primary but rather the pre-primary stages of school education (Bandyopadhyay, 2017: 46). There is a plethora of evidence highlighting that even the children who are admitted to aided and unaided private schools under the 25% EWS quota reserved for children from economically poor backgrounds undergo neglect, humiliation and insensitive treatment, leaving them with no choice but to drop out of the school (Choudhary, 2014; Nag, 2018). The social divisions are the basis of the hierarchical social inequality that leads to social exclusion, which is deepened due to school education hierarchies, which is further accompanied by the process of educational exclusion wrought by non-participation of socially disadvantaged children in the classrooms, learning performance disparity and high dropout rates. These divisions/hierarchies have kept the marginalised at the margins rather than moving them centre stage, let alone acknowledge their presence by providing democratic space to incorporate, respect and legitimise their worldviews within the epistemic folds of schooling inside inclusive classrooms. The charge of intellectual damage wrought by histories of systemic discrimination has often turned elementary education into a spectacle of reproducing the existing relations of social production. The logic of meritocracy serves as an adequate ruse for it. The last child in the classroom continues to remain the last concern, while social justice begs him to come first. The hitherto excluded children are entering the formal school system with dreams and hopes of simply improving their lives. They do not find rescue from the social stigma, discrimination and prejudice of caste that is attached to them, but rather often find themselves silenced in the classroom by the prevailing structures of oppression. Besides, there still are 6.064 million out-of-school children (OoSC) in our country, of which a staggering 76% are SCs, STs and religious minorities (Ansari, 2016). There is no gainsaying that elementary education of equitable quality is not available to the children belonging to disadvantaged sections of society (Bandyopadhyay, 2012). Both of these disconcerting facets of the educational development in last two decades accentuate the systemic concern of inequality and inequity in terms of social structure, as Ravi Kumar (2006: 40) explains:

> Inequity in education, as in other cases of social concern, reflects sharply the structural inequalities of our social system and its structures. These structures are driven by economic differentiation and corresponding cultural and social features, and which create hurdles for many down the structure in accessing education. It is manifested on one hand in the accessibility to formal schooling system due to lack of purchasing power, while on the other hand social and cultural norms are reinforcing this further.

This chapter undertakes an analysis of policy text(s), revealing how a lack of thrust on elementary education as a public good, increasing privatisation and indifference to increasing hierarchies of schooling in policy parlance, underlying both the stance of the state and the neoliberal assault on education, is in conflict with the constitution's vision of equitable elementary education. The chapter is divided into two parts. The first traces the elementary education policy shifts in the last three decades that have incrementally compromised the state schooling system, denting public institutional teaching-learning, with the consequence of increasing privatisation of schooling. The second part examines the worrying outcomes of contemporary policy trends in India's national trajectory and what we intend to make of our society with them as they continue to exacerbate the social divisions in Indian elementary education, belying the ideal of equitable elementary education for all.

Tracing educational policy shifts

The early years of educational development in independent India neglected elementary education in policy deliberations, with the thrust on higher education as a vehicle for the industrial development–led growth needs of the nation, without emphasising a policy 'on those who were already in the net of basic education and could be included in the growth-led economic agenda of the day' (Bhatty, 2014). The IEC (1964–66) report that presented India's first NPE envisioned education as a tool for the realisation of national objectives, keeping in mind the problems of national development, including the equity agenda. The commission's report recommended a structural reorganisation of school education into a national system of education of 10 +2 + 3 years (which meant 10 years of general education in school in all the disciplinary domains followed by 2 years of specialised school education in a given disciplinary stream and 3 years of undergraduate tertiary education) through a common school system for all children, dedicating a full chapter 'towards equalization of educational opportunity' (GoI, 1966: 181–239). However, the comprehensive, voluminous and painstakingly detailed IEC report, while speaking about equalising educational opportunities through the strengthening of the common school system, provided a broad framework only, without delineating the specific necessary organisational and financial support structures required from the state. There already existed a historic trajectory of an egalitarian imagination of Indian society, which was inherited at the time of Indian independence, since India's first common school system was established by Rajarshi Shahuji Mahararaja in his Kolhapur state (the late 1890s) and Gokhale's Free and Compulsory Education Bill (1911) challenged the British reluctance to universalize elementary education.

The NPE 1986 marked the first phase of serious policy change in the Indian national context about the role of the state and the commitment to public education (Velaskar, 2010: 70). It spoke of community involvement, decentralisation of educational planning and administration (which by itself is not undemocratic) and greater involvement of non-state actors in public education, reiterating the preceding NPE 1968 concerns, including a 'common school system', 'national system of education', 'vocationalisation' and 'education for equality', but ignored an analysis of why these egalitarian ideas about schooling continued to remain only on paper. It also spoke of delinking jobs and degrees and taking India to the 21st century with the help of technology. This was the beginning of replacing education with skill-based training. The development of Minimum Levels of Learning (MLL), aimed at transforming a knowledge and education process to the skill-based approach to learning, not only shifted the focus from conceptual learning but also decontextualised learning by generalising standards for each child (GoI, 1986). These 'minimum' levels in its implementation became a 'maximum' marker to represent learning, which reflects the deficit orientation towards what constitutes students' learning. This notion of skill-based learning is a complete departure from the revolutionary vision of craft-based basic education that was proposed by Mahatma Gandhi in the late 1930s. Productive work involving the locale-specific craft, including agriculture, was the basis of schooling in the basic education scheme with which all the school subjects were correlated. This would mean not only learning by doing, the psychological efficacy of which is undoubted, but would also lead to a re-vitalisation of the local village economy. Education through productive work would thus become an instrument to establish a resurgent socio-economic order in an egalitarian society. Craft was accorded the status of certified knowledge in the school curriculum, a notion that was trivialised to 'vocationalisation' and 'socially useful productive work' in the report of the IEC. The cumulative policy shifts have further reduced this path-breaking concept of learning through productive work to the linking of the contemporary NPE 2016 to the 'Skill India' mission.

The NPE 1986 introduced another major policy shift by advocating for parallel discriminatory non-formal education (NFE) in the name of 'organisational flexibility, relevance of curriculum, diversity in learning activities to relate them to learners' needs and decentralisation of management' (GoI, 1986: 25). The assumption that formal schooling is not even necessary for every child received wide currency, giving 'a big boost to various alternatives to regular schooling' (Ayyar, 2017: 24). The member secretary of the IEC from 1964–66, J. P. Naik, who was influential in shaping policy in subsequent decades, was a votary of NFE for OoSC and drew upon the Mao metaphor to continue the argument that UEE could be achieved by walking on the twin legs of formal schools and NFE (Naik, 1975). The divisive school education system that had existed since colonial times, consisting of different types of schools, was distorted with further segregation because of policy support for non-formal and alternative education, taking attention away from ensuring universal elementary schooling (Acharya 1994: 27), augmenting inequalities within the existing divisive school system further into formal and non-formal segments. This heralded a policy wisdom in which the state abdicated its constitutional responsibility of providing equitable and quality education to all children until fourteen years of age by awarding policy legitimacy to further layers to existing hierarchies of access in the multi-layered, graded, non-egalitarian schooling system. The policy text was candid in its admission of the failure at UEE:

> While these achievements are impressive by themselves, the general formulations incorporated in the 1968 policy did not, get translated into a detailed strategy of implementation, accompanied by the assignment of specific responsibilities and financial and organisational support. As a result, problems of access, quality, quantity, utility and financial outlay, accumulated over the years, have now assumed such massive proportions that they must be tackled with utmost urgency.
>
> (GoI, 1986: 2)

The changed policy wisdom in favour of privatisation or, non-state stakeholding, deflected the policy commitment to public elementary education with the following words:

> Resources, to the extent possible, will be raised by mobilising donations, asking the beneficiary communities to maintain school building and supplies of some consumables, raising fees at the level of higher education and effecting some saving by efficient use of resources. . . . All these measures will be taken not only to reduce the burden on State

resources but also for creating a greater sense of responsibility within the educational system.

(GoI, 1986: 28)

The constitutional vision of equitable elementary education as a public good leading to creation of an egalitarian society was diluted as NPE 1986 concluded by according education a multi-faceted role in the nation-wide effort in 'Human Resource Development'. Two noteworthy nuggets about the formulation of NPE 1986 are that, first, unlike the NPE 1968, it was not preceded by any expert commission of educationists, and the policy was perhaps developed by officials from the concerned HRD ministry, reflecting a bureaucratic rather than an educational vision. It is not clear how such an approach could reflect the elementary education needs and aspirations of a burgeoning multi-lingual, multi-cultural population in the diverse regions of the country. Second, the ruling party of that time came to power in December 1984, forming the Congress government, and was ready with the policy proposals with unusual alacrity by August 1985, which were submitted to the public domain for discussion, and by May 1986 the final policy, NPE 1986, had emerged. The POA 1992, while aiming to assess the implementation of NPE 1986, highlighted continuing regional imbalances, inequities and caste and gender inequalities in schooling. The resolution appointing the Acharya Ramamurti committee that submitted POA 1992 states,

Despite efforts of social and economic development since attainment of independence, a majority of our people continue to remain deprived of education. It is also a matter of grave concern that our people comprise 50 percent of the world's illiterate, and large sections of children have to go without acceptable level of primary education. Government accords highest priority to education both as a human right and as the means for bringing about a transformation towards a more humane and enlightened society.

(GoI, 1992)

Right to Education Act, 2009: a neoliberal trap

It has been said that the Indian state's inability to mitigate illiteracy, low school enrolments, high dropout rates and child labour stemmed from belief systems of the state bureaucracy, which did not call for compulsory education even in NPE 1986. This belief system was shared by educators, social activists, researchers and, more broadly, people belonging to the Indian middle class, cutting across political orientations who occupy policymaking positions. The belief was in a uniquely Indian view of the social order, according to which the role of education was that of a means of maintaining differentiation among social classes (Weiner, 1991). The constitutional policy commitment to UEE sounded like rhetoric, because as late as 1981, the literacy rate of children in the age group of five to nine was an abysmal 30.6%. India's policy pronouncements and 'what obtained in reality' (Priyam, 2017: 161) have been different from the educational development of many other countries that have attained UEE.

The committee of state education ministers examined the implications of the proposal to make elementary education a fundamental right (GoI, 1997). It held the view that entitlements that are sanctioned by the constitution cannot be deferred by the state, regardless of the reasons (GoI, 2002). The state is obliged to make the required reallocation of resources by superseding other claims, if necessary, so that justiciable entitlement 'can become a reality' (Government of Bihar, 2007: 24). This may warrant restructuring all government expenditures, even curtailing what would otherwise be considered essential but not covered by any of the fundamental rights guaranteed by the constitution. The committee further set up an expert group to assess the financial resource requirements for operationalising the fundamental right to education, with respect to the financial requirements of the states/union territories. The report of the expert group (GoI, 1999) delineated the financial requirements for making elementary education a fundamental right. The committee estimated that an additional investment of Rs.1, 37,000 crores would have to be made over a ten-year period to bring all OoSC into the school system (not parallel streams) and enable them to complete the elementary stage. This amount comes to an average investment of Rs. 14,000 crores a year, which in 1999 amounted to a mere 0.78% of the gross domestic product (GDP), namely 78 paise out of every Rs. 100 India then earned (GoI, 1999; Sadgopal, 2003).

Policy analysts have read the passing of the act as a failure to fulfil the constitutional promise to provide free elementary education, giving rise to the need for the RTE Act (Tilak, 2010). The policy intended to expand the state's responsibility for providing quality education to all the children of India, but not necessarily through a public and universal system of elementary education, choosing instead to divert public resources directly to the private schools in the name of the 25% EWS quota. In a press release by the then minister of Human Resource Development on 12 August 2010, a projected amount of about Rs. 1,50,000 crore was estimated for implementing the RTE Act for all children between the ages of six and fourteen. In the same press release he admitted that this presents a huge challenge to the nation, as there will be a shortfall of Rs. 60,000 crore, while speaking of the policy priority to harmonise the SSA with the RTE Act, which in an incisive critique of the act is pointed out with the words

> Few realise that the Constitution (86th Amendment) Act 2002 and the consequent Right to Education (RTE) Act, 2009 were designed to legitimise the aforesaid neoliberal agenda. The much-hyped '25% quota' for

the weaker sections and the disadvantaged in the enrolment of private unaided schools amounts to the provision of a farcical space for no more than 3%-4% of the deprived classes and castes. For this façade, the government shifts public funds to private schools under public-private partnership (PPF). For the rest, the acts promise an inferior quality, ill-managed and discrimination-based government school system, where only the children of the impoverished and oppressed castes are destined to study. Through this '25% quota' provision, the state has also attempted to diffuse the emergent movement for a state-funded, entirely free . . . common school system.

(Sadgopal, 2016b: 34)

The underlying assumption is that the provision of free and compulsory education of satisfactory quality to children from economically lower sections is the obligation not merely of schools run or supported by the state but also of schools which are not dependent on state funds, as well as the ones that are privately managed. Schools of the latter kind also need to provide education to such children at least to the extent of 25% of their intake, irrespective of whether they received concessions including subsidised land from the state or not. This indirectly belies the constitutional vision according a dominant role to the state in particular to provide access to social justice to the disadvantaged sections of society. The act thus supported the withdrawal of the state governments in ensuring public education for all. This neoliberal trap is evident, as even the demand has been raised that reimbursements for the 25% seats reserved for the 'poor' children in private schools, instead of being paid to the schools, be given to the child in a direct benefit transfer on the grounds that

It would be a scholarship which gives the student a choice to attend any private school. Since the student would bring revenue to the school it would give her dignity as she walks into the school with her head held high.

(Das, 2018)

The tacit assumption is that the student needs to provide revenue to a school in order to receive an education, which the state facilitates through a voucher system for the poor that private schools can claim. This is an unapologetic vision of a voucher society (a euphemism for the marketisation of elementary education) without public goods, where education is bought and sold in a private market. This is a distortion of the constitutional vision of elementary education, as

The voucher system is no alternative to the state taking responsibility for providing free and quality education to all. A voucher system

78 Jyoti Raina

legitimizes and reinforces the idea that, instead of being a 'public good', school education is a commodity for sale.

(Nag, 2018)

Privatising school education

The cumulative policy wisdom of non-state stakeholding has been blowing its own trumpet of 'quality' measured solely through metrics of observable LOs in schools, disregarding systemic constraints and leading to the schooling space being vacated for private players since the 1980s. This vacant space was consolidated by the RTE 2009, opening a flurry of dormant possibilities with regard to investments in elementary education. The thrust on non-state stakeholding in school education has led to the current policy context, so much so that the debate on the direction of policy change is situated in a state or private schooling framework, reflecting a 'definitive shift to neoliberalism in state educational policy' (Velaskar, 2017: 251). This is notwithstanding the fact that the state school system consisting of 1.1 million schools, 143 million students and 4.9 million teachers (Nallur and Thomas, 2018: 4) still constitutes the major part of the elementary education system in India and is one of the largest in the world. The increasing privatisation of school education is sorely evident by an increase in the numbers of new private schools that are opening up, as well as the relative increase in the number of children that attend these schools, as is shown by the secondary data drawn from DISE in Tables 4.1 and 4.2.

The whopping increase in the number of private schools from 1979 to 1986 can be read as a by-product of the non-state stakeholding ushered in during the first phase of policy change.

The DISE data show that in the four-year period from 2010–11 to 2014–15 the number of private schools that opened in comparison to state/

Table 4.1 Increase in number of private schools providing elementary education from 1979 to 2009

Year	Government	Private	Total	Private schools as percentage of total
1979	5,34,260	45,780	5,80,040	7.9
1986	7,05,560	1,13,404	8,18,964	13.8
2002	7,55,792	1,40,594	8,96,386	15.7
2003	7,94,265	1,25,842	9,20,106	13.7
2005	8,80,545	1,57,268	10,37,813	15.2
2007	10,02,915	2,43,895	12,50,775	19.5
2008	10,35,178	2,49,920	12,85,576	19.4
2009	10,48,046	2,54,178	13,03,812	19.5

Source: DISE data, Elementary education in India: Progress towards UEE, National University of Educational Planning and Administration, New Delhi (2007 and 2009).

Table 4.2 Increase in number of new private schools versus state schools from 2010 to 2016

Years	Number of new private schools	Number of new state schools
2010–11	71,360	16,376
2015–16	77,063	12,297

Source: DISE data, Elementary education in India: Progress towards UEE, National University of Educational Planning and Administration, New Delhi.

I thank B.El.Ed 3rd-year students of the 2017–18 class, Gargi College, New Delhi, for assistance in compiling raw DISE data in preparing this table.

Table 4.3 Children attending private unaided schools in India by age and region for the academic year 2014–15

Age	Rural	Urban	Total
6–10	20.8	48.9	31.8
11–14	17.5	40.7	27.0
15–18	24.5	36.1	29.6
Total	20.8	42.1	29.6

Source: National Sample Survey raw data, 71st Round, 2014–15.

other schools was 71,360 vs. 16,376 – four times more. Subsequently in the next year 2015–16 the number of the former increased to 77,063 while the number of the latter decreased to 12,297, reflecting the same trend. This corresponds with an increase in enrolment in private schools by 16 million children and a drop in that for government schools by 11 million from the period 2010–11 to 2014–15. This fast-developing and proliferating economy by itself is the outcome of policy shifts, as a result of which India has the largest number of children attending private schools in the world. The National Sample Survey data for 2014–15 indicate (as shown in Table 4.3) that 30% of India's children attend private schools (NSSO, 2016). In most of the OECD countries, the proportion of children attending private schools is not more than 10%.

This general all-around trend towards private schools defines the emerging political-ideological context, with the worrying outcome of distorting, diluting and even abandoning the vision of equitable elementary education as a public good in a democratic society, something in which neoliberal educators revel:

> The middle class abandoned state schools a generation ago but now even the poor are doing so. They are able to do so because affordable private schools have come up whose median fee is only Rs 417 per month.
>
> (Das, 2018)

80 Jyoti Raina

> Even if private schools were no more effective than public schools in imparting learning, they would still be several times more *cost*-effective than public schools, simply because their salary costs are much lower. Private schools pay market-clearing wages, taking advantage of educated unemployment that exists in the country.
>
> (Kingdon, 2011)

The current crisis

Almost immediately after the present BJP government came to power, in an analogous bureaucratic approach characterising the development of NPE 1986, the HRD Ministry appointed a five-member committee, consisting mainly of retired civil servants which submitted the 217-page report (referred to as GoI 2016a) with alacrity within a few months in May 2016, based on which a brief 43-page document, 'Some Inputs for Draft National Education Policy, 2016' (Draft NEP, 2016b), was placed in the public domain, the future status of which is ambiguous. The thirteen themes which were put up in the public domain for a wide-ranging consultative process pertaining to the constitutional goals of social justice, equity and protection of fundamental rights received little attention (Mehendale and Dewan 2015). The NPE 2016 reported the state of education in our country to be in disarray and recommends a two-fold emphasis on 'quality upgradation' and 'inclusivity' to 'revamp the education sector' (Subramaniam, 2016), expressing alarm at the declining learning taking place at all levels of school education (2016: 3). The Draft NPE 2016 envisions an outcome-based curriculum which provides opportunities to aspire for 'excellence in learning outcomes', which can be 'comparable to student learning outcomes in high-performing international education systems', designing a common national curriculum for science, mathematics and English, aligned with the NPM of the neoliberal approach (GoI, 2016b: 21). At the very outset the NPE 2016 speaks of education that 'will amalgamate globalization with localization' (GoI, 2016a: 1), giving 'new impetus to skill development through vocational education in the context of the emergence of new technologies in a rapidly expanding economy in a globalised environment' and 'encouraging ways of enhancing private investment and funding' (2016: 2). It has taken the road of standardising the curriculum instead of making it locale-specific and ignoring the local, contextual nature of educational processes, leaving behind even its own promise of amalgamation of local and global. The report laments the 'absence of requisite disaggregated data, particularly at sub-national and institutional levels for evidence-based management of education' (GoI, 2016a: 170). It presents data about the status of elementary education in its discussion of the context and objectives of the emerging education policy (2016: 23–31). These relate to enrolment, literacy rates, MDGs, number of elementary schools and teachers, children's learning levels, percentage of children across public–private schools, children's attendance and reading, as well as arithmetic levels. Yet these data are disaggregated only superficially in cursory references to merely two statistics. The first is the differential average achievement levels of students between states, as revealed in the National Achievement Survey (NAS), the methodology and assumptions of which are not detailed, and second the differential achievement between students in the highest- and lowest-performing categories. A commitment to inclusivity in the elementary schools would require an analysis of the disaggregated empirical field data on educational disparities and imbalances across diverse social groups, as well as on differential, graded levels, with access, dropouts and learning outcomes across them. Schools are potentially the sites of inclusion, but a symbolic inclusion with the mere physical presence of select children from varied socio-economic backgrounds, rather than meaningful participation, which cannot lead to the creation of inclusive classrooms. Empirical evidence continues to point at the lack of equitable inclusion in elementary education, stating that 'out of the children admitted in class 1, only about 6 of STs, 8% of STs, 9% of Muslims and 10% of OBCs are able to cross the crucial barrier of Class 12' and are forced to remain in 'caste-based and patriarchal parental occupations' (Sadgopal 2016b).

Be that as it may, there is no gainsaying that our classrooms reflect more than ever before the socially diverse demographic reality, with children from socially marginalised communities enrolling in elementary schools close to the level of their demographic share. The disaggregated composite data analysed during research studies reveal that although low LOs cut across children from all social categories, children from marginalised communities score much lower in the learning achievement count. A study conducted in the districts of Gaya and Katihar, Bihar, concluded that in each of the districts 46.02% and 47.12% of Scheduled Caste children in Std. II can read nothing. The literacy levels of their upper-caste classmates in Std. II is higher, with only 22.37% and 23.64% failing to read anything (Deshkal, 2012). Although the NPE 2016 points that 'greater local decision making authority and accountability have better learning outcomes' in school governance and management (2016a: 181), a viable school-based governance system with an appropriate framework of autonomy as well as accountability will need to take into account a complex range of systemic, institutional, learning, pedagogical and social factors in seeking a more nuanced understanding of what 'quality upgradation' and 'inclusivity' mean. With its lack of thrust on public education, coupled with the 'minimalist expansionism' (Gupta, 2016) oriented techno-managerialism of NPM, the report recommends a merger, conversion and consolidation of schools with low enrolment and poor infrastructure. The critical issue of how this change in school boundary and closure can be discriminatory to the already disadvantaged, marginalised or excluded and is likely to further reduce access, particularly in remote, backward and underdeveloped regions of the country, is left unexamined (or is an outdated concern?). The report unapologetically argues this facetious pretext of 'rationalization' for closing of government schools:

> There were 15 lakh schools in the country with an enrolment of 26 crore (DISE 2014–15). Nearly 33% of schools have less than 50 students and 54% less than hundred. The preponderance of small schools not only affects the quality of teaching and learning but also makes school education inequitable and expensive in terms of per-pupil expenditure. Such schools are neither academically not financially viable.
>
> (GoI, 2016a: 177)

An empirical research study examining the impact of school closures and merger policy on the public education system in some of the states clarifies who such policies disadvantage:

> Even a cursory look at the social composition of students who are enrolled in the government schools that were closed or merged is enough to tell us which groups are affected the most by the closures. Needless to say, there is an overwhelming presence of Scheduled Castes, Scheduled Tribes, Other Backward Classes and the religious minorities such as Muslims in the government schools. Among them the percentage of girls is higher. A combination of factors such as poverty, under-development, poverty induced migration, are already responsible for educational backwardness of these communities. Therefore, when a school is closed in a Dalit or tribal concentrated region it further excludes them from the opportunity of schooling. Moreover, in the present context where a hierarchy of so-called 'good' quality private schools and poor quality government schools exist, closing the only accessible and affordable government school will further entrench the educational inequalities.
>
> Save the Children (2017: 52)

These trends continue to be reflected in contemporary policy proclamations, which propose a school reform agenda that essentialises an outcome orientation into the central objective by developing instruments to measure the quality of education in schools (NITI Aayog, 2017) and deploying them for its quantification. This reform agenda further ignores structural distortions, systemic inequalities, classroom processes and development of critical educators, which are the key aspects of an equitable system of schooling.

At the current juncture, the prescribed direction of policy change is an unparalleled crisis for public education. With the diminishing operative distinction between the state and the market, even the struggle between state and society is becoming attenuated, with restructuring of the very idea of welfare while people 'adjust' to a market society. The new policy context of unprecedented privatisation/quasi-privatisation of schooling, driven by both the market and the neoliberal state, are regularly reflected in news reports in national dailies and in other fora, based on the vision of a dynamic, globalising and knowledge-based economy and society. There has been not just acceptance and even 'wide currency' (Krishna Kumar, 2011) of profitability as a legitimate aim of educational enterprise, but rather the current neoliberal state is seeking to re-structure or even do away with 'the idea of public itself' (Ravi Kumar, 2017: 9). The recent debates on the elementary education policy shifts have highlighted the waning egalitarianism and decreasing design to mitigate the prevailing structures of injustice, inequality and exclusion (Gupta, 2016). The new genre of policies, framed in alignment with neoliberal ideology, is not aiming to be redistributive, even symbolically, let alone in material terms, but lacks social purpose. The state is no more a facilitator of education as public good, but withdraws from direct delivery while actively evolving a new paradigm of control and deregulation (NITI Aayog, 2017). In this new policy context there is a diversion of public finance towards increased accommodation of the demands of private capital in/from school education in the name of PPP, state support for educational entrepreneurship and similar neoliberal policies (Velaskar, 2017: 254). The projected population of children ages six to ten according to statistics put forth by the HRD Ministry for 2016 is more than 130 million and of the age group eleven to thirteen is more than 72.8 million. The Draft NPE 2016 even speaks of the government's inability to educate such a large young citizenry. Are these millions of young children to be left to the vagaries of the EWS quota education window of private schooling? Or to their substitute LFPS, on the assumption that private schooling does not need any 'quality reforms' and is working effectively? Or education vouchers which are nothing but a euphemism for marketisation?

The country has not had a national policy on education for more than thirty years, since NPE 1986. The long-overdue New Education Policy (NEP) is currently being formulated by the HRD Ministry and the government of India (GoI). The HRD Ministry has since appointed a nine-member committee to further prepare the final draft of the NEP, which is due for submission any time now. The Press Information Bureau released a statement on 26 June 2017 that this new committee will derive detailed inputs from the report of the 2016 committee, as well as the numerous suggestions expressed by the various stakeholders in the last two years. The executive pronouncements – as evident by statements issued by the state think tank NITI Aayog, the officials of the MHRD and other industrial/economic/commerce groups including neoliberal economists, who are the new players getting involved in formulating public policy – seem to reiterate the definitive neoliberal shifts. The criticality of the current juncture is evident by this news item from the national daily *The Times of India* of 26 July 2017, also available at https://timesofindia.indiatimes.com/india/

hand-over-schools-colleges-jails-to-private-sector-amitabh-kant/article-show/59782227.cms:

> There is no need why jails, schools and colleges should be run in government sector. At least experience of many countries like Canada and Australia shows that the private sector is capable of doing very good work in creation of quality infrastructure over a long period of time in social sector.

These were the words of the CEO of NITI Aayog, Amitabh Kant, at a conclave organised by a corporate trade association at New Delhi. This viewpoint is a decimation of the constitutional vision that the state should play a significant role in providing education to its citizens so as to facilitate access and quality of education for the disadvantaged sections of society. This continued hesitancy towards public schooling, accompanied by continued inadequate public finance (Jha and Parvati, 2017: 190) and the state ambivalence to the class-based polarisation of education into an anti-egalitarian market of selection and exclusion, has worrying and wide-ranging outcomes affecting not only elementary education but also society and polity (World commission on social dimensions of globalisation, 2004) with the creation of a market society accompanied by a culture of materialism, consumerism, consumption and pursuit of material well-being as a desirable ideal.

The exponentially widening social and economic inequality in our country, coupled with the direction in which the new genre of educational policy shift is occurring, accentuate the inequality, stratification and graded hierarchy in the elementary education system. The market society will provide educational resources to the children and young citizenry, according to the demands of the market and their economic capacity to pay. This ability to pay will correlate with the increasing socio-economic inequality, while many research studies conclude that currently inequality in India is at its highest since 1922 (Chancel and Piketty, 2017). The downsizing of public education will further convert education into a class-based social privilege. How children and youth access this privilege will depend directly upon which section of society they belong to (read: ability to pay). This graded structural inequality will determine accessibility/inaccessibility to hierarchies of schooling depending upon purchasing power (or lack of it). The LFPS, for example, has turned elementary education in an affordable commodity, but again according to the financial status of the child's family. The entrenchment of a class-based system of education in a market society will add greater asymmetry in social relations that will shape the everyday lives of millions of our children in a strategy for exclusion. The near collapse of the previous genre of welfare policies, with professed social justice orientation being replaced by market-driven capital policies, presents an impeding dystopia. This is in contrast with the democratic constitutional thrust on equality, social justice and inclusion and is a cause of worry for education workers or anyone with egalitarian beliefs. Even in comparison to the SAP of the early 1980s, the present shifts present a re-structuring of the very idea of welfare in educational policy.

The increasing privatisation of school education distorts whatever is left of elementary education as a public good, as there is increasing inequity within the elementary education system, which is getting more and more institutionalised by policy shifts, accompanied by social consequences such as differentiated wages, employment probabilities and poverty, whereby the

> unintended impact of such increasingly unequal schooling facilities may prove to be too damaging to the society in several ways. For instance, schools are getting gradually ghettoized and a veritable hierarchy is emerging virtually dividing the society based on social and economic considerations. The downstream effects and intergenerational costs of such increasingly unequal schools and learning opportunities would prove to be serious in a society which is already stratified on social lines and is experiencing increasing economic inequality arising out of globalization.
>
> (Govinda and Sedwal, 2017: 25)

This has been a systemic concern in the past, but at the current juncture the state apparatuses are not merely indifferent to but in fact are becoming tacit participants of the neoliberal project. Also, the entire economy is gradually getting privatised and the exclusionary hierarchies of access in schooling will arguably parallel the hierarchies in employment. In our country, at least 270 million people are estimated to live in extreme poverty, while fifty-seven billionaires possess as much wealth as the poorest 70% of the country (Oxfam, 2017). Is this doomsday scenario what we intend to make of our society and the world, with elementary education under neoliberalisation, particularly in view of the forthcoming unique demographic dividend (or time bomb?) of a young citizenry? Growth and equality are two inseparable aspects of development. The simplistic policy goal in the current national project of aiming at increasing GDP growth (as if techno-economic progress were unlimited) continues to ignore the need to design policy to improve the living conditions of the poor people living on the margins. To the majority who live on the margins, public elementary education alone is the alternative, the absolute moral force that can offer hope of a better life chances and thereby contribute to the creation of an egalitarian, just and democratic social order, as the constitution makers envisioned. However, the idea of equitable elementary education as a public good at the current juncture of India's educational trajectory stands has withered because of the stance of the state coupled with the neoliberal policy shifts; instead of striving to reinstate the constitutional vision of equitable elementary education, it stands in conflict with it.

References

Acharya, P. (1994). Universal elementary education: Receding goal. *Economic and Political Weekly*, 29(1), pp. 27.

Ansari, H. (2016). *Inaugural speech in the conference on Factors of poor learning: Challenges, opportunities, and practices for learning improvement in socially diverse schools of India* in. New Delhi, organized by Deshkal Society, New Delhi on 2 September, 2016.

Ayyar, R. and Vaidyanatha, V. (2017). Inclusive elementary education in India: The journey. In: M. Tiwary, K. Sanjay Kumar, and A. K. Misra eds., *Dynamics of inclusive classroom: Social diversity, inequality and school education in India*. New Delhi: Orient Blackswan.

Bandyopadhyay, M. (2012). Social Disparity in Elementary Education. *Seminar*, October, pp. 21–25.

Bandyopadhyay, M. (2017). Social and regional inequality in elementary education in India: Retrospect and prospect. In: M. Tiwary, K. Sanjay Kumar, and A. K. Misra eds., *Dynamics of inclusive classroom: Social diversity, inequality and school education in India*. New Delhi: Orient Blackswan.

Bhatty, K. (2014). Review of elementary education policy in India: Has it upheld the constitutional objective of equality? *Economic and Political Weekly*, 49(43–44), 01 Nov, 2014.

Chagla, M. C. (1964). *Presidential address*. Bangalore: Thirty-first, meeting of the Central Advisory Board of Education, 11 and 12 October 1964.

Chancel, L. and Piketty, T. (2017). *Indian Income Inequality, 1922–2014: From British Raj to Billionaire Raj?* CEPR Discussion Paper No. DP12409. Available at: SSRN: https://ssrn.com/abstract=3066021 (Accessed on 11 March 2018).

Choudhary, S. (2014). Right to education act 2009: Letting disadvantaged children down? *International Research Journal of Social Sciences*, 3(8), pp. 1–7.

Das, G. (2018). *License Permit Raj, renewed: Industry was liberated in 1991, but education's Shackles are growing heavier*. New Delhi: The Times of India, 17 April 2018.

Deshkal Society. (2012). *Findings of household survey and baseline learning assessment of children in government primary and primary with upper primary schools in Bihar* (Mimeo.). Delhi: Deshkal Society.

Government of Bihar. (2007). *Report of the Bihar common school system commission*. Patna: Common School System Commission, Govt. of Bihar.

GoI. (1966). *Report of the education commission: Education and national development*. New Delhi: Ministry of Education.

———. (1986). *National policy of education*. New Delhi: Department of Education, Ministry of Human Resource Development, Government of India.

———. (1992). *National policy on education1986 PROGRAMME OF ACTION 1992*. New Delhi: Department of Education, Ministry of Human Resource Development, Government of India.

———. (1997). *Report of the committee of state education ministers on implications of the proposal to make elementary education a fundamental right*. New Delhi, Chairman: Muhi Ram Saikia, Ministry of Human Resource Development, Department of Education.

———. (1999). *Expert group report on financial requirements for making elementary education a fundamental right* (also known as Tapas Majumdar Committee Report of 1999). New Delhi: Department of Education Ministry of Human Resource Development, GoI.

———. (2002). *Report of the national commission to review the working of the constitution*. New Delhi: Ministry of Law, Justice and Company Affairs, Department of Legal Affairs, GoI.

———. (2016a). *National policy on education, 2016: Report of the committee for evolution of the new education policy*. New Delhi: Ministry of Human Resource Development, Government of India.

———. (2016b). *Some inputs for draft national policy on education, 2016*. New Delhi: Ministry of Human Resource Development, Government of India. http://mhrd.gov.in/sites/upload_files/mhrd/files/Inputs_Draft_NEP_2016.pdf (Accessed on 10 April 2017).

Govinda, R. and Sedwal, M. (2017). Introduction. In: R. Govinda and M. Sedwal eds., *India education report*. New Delhi: Oxford University Press.

Gupta, V. (2016). Politics of the guarded agenda of national education policy 2015–16. *Economic and Political Weekly*, 51(42), 15 October 2016.

Hill, D. (2016). Transformative education, critical education, Marxist education: Possibilities and alternatives to the restructuring of education in global neoliberal/neoconservative times In: K. Ravi, ed., *Neoliberal, critical pedagogy and education*. India: Routledge.

Jha, P. and Parvati, P. (2017). The challenges of public finance. In: R. Govinda and M. Sedwal eds., *India education report*. New Delhi: Oxford University Press.

Kingdon, G. (2011). Private Versus Public Schooling in India. *Seminar # 626*.

Kumar, K. (2011). Teaching and the neoliberal state. *Economic and Political Weekly*, XLVI(21), 21 May 2011.

Kumar, R. (2006). Introduction: Equality, quality and quantity-mapping the challenges before elementary education in India. In: R. Kumar, eds., *The crisis of elementary education in India*. New Delhi: Sage.

———. (2017). Introduction. In: H. Dave ed., *Class, Race, and education under neoliberal capitalism*. New Delhi: Aakar.

State Report Cards 2013–14 (2015). *Elementary education in India where do we stand?* Vols. I and II. New Delhi: NUEPA.

State Report Cards 2015–16 (2017). *Elementary education in India where do we stand?* Vols. I and II. New Delhi: NUEPA.

Mehendale, A. and Hridaykant, D. (2015). Towards a new education policy: Directions and considerations. *Economic & Political Weekly*, 50(48).

Nag, S. (2018). The skew in education. *The Indian Express*. New Delhi. 28 June 2018.

Naik, J. P. (1975). *Equality, quality and quantity: The elusive triangle of Indian education*. Bombay: Allied Publishers.

Nallur, V. and Alex, M. T. (2018). Urgency of inclusive education. *The Book Review*, LII, 5 May 2018.

NSSO (2016) *National sample survey, 71st round, 2014–15*. New Delhi: National Sample Survey Organisation, Ministry of Statistics and Programme Implementation.

NITI Aayog. (2017). *Three Year Action Agenda 2017–18 to 2019–20, April*. New Delhi: Government of India.

Oxfam. (2017). *One percent of Indians own 58% of country's wealth: Oxfam inequality report*. Available at: www.oxfamindia.org/newsclipping/1781 (Accessed on 24 March 2018).

Priyam, M. (2017). Policy Reform and Educational Development: Reflections on the uneven process of change in Bihar. In: A. Kumar Singh ed., *Education and empowerment in India: Policies and practices*. London: Routledge New Delhi South Asia, pp. 160–178.

Sadgopal, A. (2003). Education for too few. *Frontline*, 20(24), 22 November–5 December.

———. (2010). The world bank in India: Undermining sovereignty, distorting development. In: K. Michele and D. D'Souza, eds., *Dependent people's tribunal on the world bank in India*. Hyderabad: Orient Blackswan, pp. 296–324.

———. (2016a). *Common classrooms, common playgrounds*. In: M. Prasad, ed., April 2016: New Delhi: All India Forum for Right to Education.

———. (2016b). Skill India' or deskilling India: An agenda of exclusion. *Economic and Political Weekly*, LI(35), pp. 33–37.

Save the Children. (2017). *Report on school closures and mergers: A multi-state study of policy and its impact on public education system*. Telangana, Odisha, Rajasthan, New Delhi: Save the Children.

Seetharamu, A. S. (2002). Fundamental right status for education: Opportunity or eyewash? *Deccan Herald*. 9 February 2009. Available at: www.deccanherald.com/ (Accessed on 2 March 2018).

Singh, P. D. and Kumar, S. (2010). *Social hierarchy and notion of educability: Experiences of teachers and children from marginalised and non marginalised communities. Dalit Studies-3*. New Delhi: Deshkal Society.

Subramaniam, T. S. R. (2016). Education in disarray: Need for quality upgradation and inclusivity. *Economic and Political Weekly*, 51(35), 27 Aug 2016.

Tilak, J. B. G. (2010). *RTE Act 2009 – Illusory promises*. Available at: http://educa tionworldonline.net/index.php/page-article-choicemore-id-2288. (Accessed on 6 July 2010).

Tiwary, M. K., Sanjay, K. and Misra, A. K. (2017). Introduction. In: M. K. Tiwary, K. Sanjay and A. K. Misra, eds., *Dynamics of inclusive classroom: Social diversity, inequality and school education in India*. New Delhi: Orient Blackswan.

Velaskar, P. (2010). Quality and inequality in Indian education: Some critical policy concerns. *Contemporary Education Dialogue*, 7(1).

———. (2017). Neo-Liberal Policy and the crisis of state schooling. In: A. K. Singh, ed., *Education and empowerment in India: Policies and practices*. London: Routledge New Delhi South Asia, pp. 251–267.

Weiner, M. (1991). *The child and the state in India; Child labour and education policy in comparative perspective*. Princeton: Princeton University Press.

World Commission on Social Dimensions of Globalisation. (2004). *A fair globalisation: Creating opportunities for all. Geneva*: International Labour Organisation.

Part II

Understanding knowledge and curriculum

Chapter 5

Draft NEP 2016

Education for 'citizenship' or 'resource development for a pliable workforce'?

Rohit Dhankar

On the heels of the Subramanian committee report, which was made public against the wishes of the government (MHRD, 2016a), the MHRD has revealed its own curiously titled draft version of the National Policy on Education (MHRD, 2016b). There is some ambiguity generated by the title of the document as to whether it is 'the draft version of the policy' or only 'Some Inputs for Draft National Education Policy'. However, the country is treating it as 'A Draft National Education Policy' and so am I in this chapter. The MHRD has become even more unsure about National Education Policy, and even the document under consideration in this chapter is no longer presented as 'the government document'. However, it still remains relevant to discuss the thinking expressed in it, as it expresses the favoured line of thought taken up by the present government.

At the very first glance, the lack of care in the language used in a national document is somewhat disconcerting, but perhaps not a serious cause of concern. What is really worrying is the conceptual confusion in articulating vision and mission and in scattered hints at the aims of education. It is not that the draft policy does not have any merits – actually, many of the recommendations are very appropriate, for example, an emphasis on quality and equity in education and raising educational expenditures to 6% of GDP. Similarly, there are many issues that need serious discussion and critique, for example, the stance taken on a no-detention policy, school leadership and teacher accountability. But this chapter does not aim at a comprehensive response to the draft policy. It has only a limited purpose of looking closer at the vision and aims of education in the document.

The importance of articulating aims

There are very few official documents in India in which the aims of education are given a serious and rigorous treatment, except the very first two commission reports after independence. The University Education Commission (1948–49) and the Secondary Education Commission (1952–53) are the two documents which pay adequate attention to the aims of education

(GoI, 1962). Other documents often gloss over and confuse aims with national goals, on one side, and curricular objects, on the other. It is believed in India, at least by some educators, that aims are built into the overall educational plan and process and do not need a specific and clear articulation.

Therefore, it would be interesting for an Indian to note what the philosopher of education John Dewey had to say about the role of aims in educational reform. Dewey was invited by the Turkish government to advise it on educational reforms right after the collapse of the Ottoman Empire. He submitted his report with the opening sentence: '[T]he first and most important point is to settle upon the aim and purpose of the schools of Turkey'. He further says that only after settling the aims will it become possible to 'be clear upon the means to be used and to lay down a definite program' for educational development (Dewey, 1983: 273).

This is not a philosopher's penchant for systematic articulation. Dewey thinks that it is necessary to protect the schools from frequent superfluous changes; in his own words

> [A] clear idea of the ends which the schools should attain will protect the schools from needless changes which are no sooner effected than they are undone by other so-called reforms, which lead nowhere.

Unfortunately, that sounds rather familiar in our country. Elsewhere Dewey says that acting with an aim is synonymous with acting with a mind – an aimless activity is also a mindless activity (Dewey, 2004: 111). He also thinks that

> a clear idea of the end will reveal the steps which need to be taken, afford a check and test for measures proposed, and reveal the order in which the successive steps in education should be taken.

Without clarity on aims, then, any further plan is arbitrary and has no logic, and the progress cannot be assessed. The system then becomes a blind and fumbling system, of which no one knows where it is going and why.

An education system with arbitrary recommendations and unable to work out clear justifiable steps is bad enough. Not articulating aims clearly, however, produces more sinister results: it further marginalises the weaker sections. C. Winch argues that if the major aims of education are not clear, there is a danger that covert aims defined by those in power will guide the system. And that

> [I]f a society does not have clear and agreed aims for its education system, there will be a danger that not only will it fail to have a healthy system that is respected and functions well, but there will also be

widespread and damaging discontent among those groups whose interests are not well served.

(Winch, 1996: 33)

Not articulating the aims of education clearly can be used by the powers that be to have an education system of their own choice even without an explicit social agreement on this. Dearden's critique of the lack of clarity on the aims in progressive education is equally valid in terms of evasion of the discussion for other reasons, including political. He states:

The implicit structure of the evasion is this: (i) leave alone any attempt thoroughly to discuss the aims you have in mind; (ii) at a more concrete level, enter into discourse which can in fact be engaged in only if your aims are already tacitly presupposed; (iii) then everyone will be so absorbed in the detail as not to notice the overall direction in which you are going [,]

(Dearden, 2012: 52)

a neat strategy to go into a description of concrete recommendations on the basis of unclear and unanalysed vision. The Draft National Education Policy is guilty on all three counts: Dewey's caution that without getting clear on aims, one cannot work out details of action; Winch's charge that lack of clarity on aims may further marginalise the disadvantaged; and Dearden's charge of taking education in a chosen direction without explicit social agreement. We will see why next.

The aims in NPE 1968 and NPE 1986

In the light of the previous discussion, then, let us first see how the two earlier education policies deal with the issue of aims.

NPE 1968 is a very brief document, all of seven and a half pages. The first one and a quarter pages of that is devoted to what the document sees as the role of education in the national development and how it can play that role

According to NPE 1968, the leaders of the national freedom movement 'stressed its [education's] unique significance for national development' (1998, MHRD, 1986: 38). In the '[P]ost-independence period', according to it, 'the Government of India and of the States' gave 'increasing attention to education as a factor vital to national progress and security' (38). It further states that the major reconstruction of education 'is essential for economic and cultural development of the country, for national integration and for realising the ideal of a socialistic pattern of society' (38). The document recognises the key role 'education, science and research play in developing the material and human resources of the country'.

94   Rohit Dhankar

These quotes reflect how policy sees education as playing a very important role in national development, security, progress, development of resources, national integration and realisation of the pattern of society.

One notes that they all are social or national goals to be achieved through education. Here education is seen as an instrument of realising national goals. But how does education play this role? How does education help in developing national resources, in national progress and so on?

The NPE 1968 believes that education helps in all this by cultivating 'moral and social values' (38) in individuals and by producing 'young-men and women of character and ability committed to national service and development'. It says that

> [O]nly then will education be able to play its vital role in promoting national progress, creating a sense of common citizenship and culture, and strengthening the national integration.

NPE 1968, then, is based on the belief that national goals (of progress, socialist society, integration, etc.) can be achieved by producing individuals of character, moral values, ability, commitment to the nation and common citizenship. The earlier ideals in this sentence (progress, socialist society, integration, etc.), as said, are national goals – we can also call them social goals. The later (individuals' character, moral values, ability, commitment to the nation and value of common citizenship) are aims as philosophers of education use the term. The aims of education are capabilities and qualities of individuals which can be developed through learning. The national or social goals are states of affair in the society – they are not abilities of individuals. But such states of affairs can be achieved only through the abilities and qualities of individuals. Thus, the aims of education are closely connected with national/social goals, but they are not the same thing. The University Education Commission (1948–49) is quite clear on this issue:

> Our educational system must find its guiding principle in the aims of the social order for which it prepares, in the nature of the civilisation it hopes to build. Unless we know whether we are tending, we cannot decide what we should do and how we should do it. Societies like men need a clear purpose to keep them stable in a world of bewildering change.

> (1949: 31)

NPE 1986 starts with the same idea of achieving the national goals of economic, social and political development through education, but emphasises the individual a little more compared to NPE 1968. It is aware of the distinction between national gaols and capabilities of individuals, though it does not use the term 'aims of education'.

According to NPE 1986, '[E]very country develops its system of education to express and promote its unique socio-cultural identity and also to meet the challenges of the times' (MHRD, 1986: 2). It expresses concern over several social/political problems, like '[T]he goals of secularism, socialism, democracy and professional ethics are coming under increasing strain.' Note that here they all are listed as 'national goals'. And then it sees the remedy in the development of capabilities and dispositions of individuals through education:

> The coming generations should have the ability to internalise new ideas constantly and creatively. They have to be imbued with a strong commitment to humane values and to social justice. All this implies better education.
>
> (4)

The following statement frames the relationship between individual abilities (aims of education) and national goals very neatly:

> Education has an acculturating role. It refines sensitivities and perceptions that contribute to national cohesion, a scientific temper and independence of mind and spirit – thus furthering the goals of socialism, secularism and democracy enshrined in our Constitution.
>
> (4)

If we want to list some of the components of the social vision as expressed in NPE 1986, it would be: *a society that is secular, democratic, multicultural, peaceful, cohesive and harmonious, and socialistic.* The qualities that are needed in the citizens to create and sustain such a society are: *having a national identity, commitment to human values, to social justice, with refined sensitivities and perception, independence* of mind, scientific temper, etc. Of course, the social vision includes economic prosperity, and capabilities include those required for appropriate economic action as well. The vision of the society and the aims of education are closely connected, and both of the earlier policies see that connection. They do not use the term 'aims of education', but constantly list individual capabilities that good education should be able to develop, and those capabilities in turn will help achieve the national/social goals.

The aims and vision in Draft NEP 2016

The vision

The vision and aims in the Draft NEP 2016 have to be analysed in light of the earlier considerations: one, the importance of clearly articulating aims, and, two, how the issue was dealt in the earlier policies.

The NEP 2016 starts with a preamble and then lists key challenges in Chapter 2. Both of these chapters need to be discussed in detail, but we will start with Chapter 3, which is titled 'Vision, Mission, Goals and Objectives'. One naturally expects aims as well as a vision of education and society in this chapter. The vision is stated in a paragraph, which is actually a single compound sentence. Much is packed into this long sentence; therefore, it is worthwhile to break it into separate but interconnected components.

1   It is the vision of a policy, that is, of NEP 2016.
2   The NEP 2016 'envisions a credible and high-performing education system'.
3   This education system should '[ensure] inclusive quality education and lifelong learning opportunities for all'.
4   This learning is to produce 'students/graduates equipped with the knowledge, skills, attitudes and values'.
5   The knowledge, etc., 'that are required'

   a   'To lead a productive life',
   b   To 'participate in the country's development process' and
   c   To 'respond to the requirements' of society.

6   A society that is 'fast-changing [and] ever-globalising', has a 'knowledge-based economy' and itself is 'knowledge-based'.

It is clear that points 2 and 3 are the *objectives of the policy*. Point 3 describes qualities of the kind of system the policy wants to create. Points 4 and 5 define the proper *aims of education* at two different levels. Point 5 defines the kind of behaviour or actions that are expected from an individual, and point 4 hints at what people have to acquire/learn to be able to behave in the desired manner. Point 6 hints at the kind of society the framers of this document see as emerging and are preparing for. By implication, this is their definition of either a desirable society or of an inevitable society, over which they have no control.

To understand the full import of this statement, we should see it in the reverse order: the vision of the society is that of a 'fast-changing, ever-globalising, knowledge-based economy and society'. We should note that the forces that are changing the society, making it 'fast', 'ever-globalising', 'knowledge-based', etc., are accepted as given. They just are – some kind of a mystery beyond our ken. Not to be questioned, not to be challenged. That is what the society is going to be, and it is made this way by someone else. All we have to do is 'cope' with it.

So, what does our education system do in this? It produces graduates that are prepared to 'respond to its requirements'. The requirements are, of course, defined by the fast pace of the change. Our job is to be prepared to respond to them. And that is what 'development' means: to be 'prepared', to 'respond', to find a place in this emerging order. One can find one's place in this emerging order by 'leading a productive life'.

To lead a productive life in this order one needs 'knowledge, skills, attitudes and values'. That is where education comes in: to produce people who have the 'knowledge, skills, attitudes and values' that are required by the knowledge-based economy (whatever that might mean) and society. This system should ensure participation of all and opportunities for lifelong learning for all. That is necessary for the national development; otherwise, the human resource is wasted.

One may ask: Where is the personal autonomy to live a life of one's own choosing in it? Where is the political space to participate in decisions regarding what kind of society we want to create? What kind of economy do we want? Where is democracy? The votaries of NEP 2016 may answer: 'ensuring inclusive quality education and lifelong learning opportunities for all' spells equality and, therefore, democracy, as it is 'for all'. But it actually does not. Because the society for which these 'opportunities' are to be provided is being defined by some other forces and knowledge, etc. this policy's recommendations are only to cope with that emerging society.

No wonder the NEP 2016 has its focus on the skills – knowledge is only a necessary base needed for skills and values to decide for what purpose those skills are to be used. This policy envisions an education to develop all this to cope with the society formed by the economic forces. It is not for an education to examine, challenge and change the direction of those developments. Therefore, the emphasis on employable skills is understandable.

The mission

The mission of (policy? – most probably) is stated in four bullet points. The first one is simply a repetition of the first part of the vision. The third bullet emphasises reform in curricula, pedagogy, management, teacher education, etc., to achieve the same objectives as mentioned in the vision.

Bullets two and four make some statements that can be construed as aims of education. Therefore, we will discuss them together with some other statements of aims scattered in the policy at various places. We need to collect them first.

But before that it would be useful to see what the policy itself calls 'objectives of education'.

Goals and objectives

The section on goals and objectives starts with a statement of the objectives of the policy or of the system of education. They are laudable, at least in part, for example, improving quality, ensuring equitable access, raising the credibility of the system, etc. The focus here is also on employability of the 'products' of the schools and higher education. The term 'product' is repeatedly used for human beings – one could pass it off as a simple way of talking, but the absence of democratic values and autonomy of these 'products' in the *key statements* reveals that humans are seen as 'human resources' much more than autonomous critical citizens who also shape the processes and purposes for using that resource. But we will return to this point in due course.

The main point in this section I want to discuss is the so glaringly revealed confusion between various kinds of 'objectives'. The sections give a list of 13 'objectives of education for the fulfillment (sic) of the vision and mission'. The problem is that only two and a half of these thirteen points can be seen as aims or objectives of education; all the rest are either social purposes (in the sense we defined earlier) or objectives of the system of education. Before we go to educational aims, it will be useful to see some of these statements.

Bullet point two in the draft states:

> Achieving universal elementary and secondary education and ensuring that all secondary education graduates have access to higher secondary education and all higher secondary education graduates have equitable access to higher education and that all enrolled students are supported to successfully complete their education with all of them achieving expected learning outcomes.

It is very clear that it might be defining the targets of the government or education system or of MHRD, but this statement does not define any aims of education in the sense of capabilities of individuals. One can universalise an elementary education that *aims* at developing vocational skills alone, or that *aims* at developing religious zealots, or that *aims* at developing knowledge base for becoming an independent critical citizen. All these aims *can* be different. The reach alone can be considered 'targets' to achieve, but not 'aims of education'.

Out of the 13 points under the heading 'main objectives of education' 10 define targets to achieve. The targets may be appreciated or critiqued on their merit, but that is not the issue in this chapter. Only three points articulate aims proper. This shows the understanding of education that goes into this policy framing. Now we will turn to the educational aims scattered in various places in the draft.

Aims of education

The Draft NEP 2016 makes a statement in its preamble, on page 5, that it envisions an education that produces graduates

> (a) '*equipped with the knowledge, skills, attitudes and values*'. These knowledge, skills, attitudes and values should be those that are

(b) 'required *to lead a productive life, participate in the country's development process, respond to the requirements of the fast-changing, ever-globalising, knowledge-based societies, and developing responsible citizens who respect the Indian tradition of acceptance of diversity of India's heritage, culture and history and promote social cohesion and religious amity.*'

(Italics added)

Undoubtedly qualities of character are developed through acquiring what is listed in (a), i.e. knowledge, skills, attitudes and values. Item (b), which lists qualities of character, includes leading a productive life; responding to requirements of the knowledge-based society; and creating responsible citizens who respect the Indian traditions of diversity, culture and history and who promote social cohesion and religious amity.

These sound like great and comprehensive aims of education until one notes that a responsible citizen is defined in a particular manner. It is someone who respects certain traditions and works for social cohesion and religious amity. What is the role of a 'responsible citizen' in a situation where the injustice and inequality are the order of the day in a society? Does this citizen criticise, protest, speaks out, resist? Or does she or he only work for cohesion and amity, and pleads with the government and the oppressive forces? In other words, the criticality of a democratic citizen seems to be missing.

That brings out a need to look at the whole picture that is being painted more closely. Items (a) and (b) actually mutually define each other's true character. What kind of qualities of character are envisaged can be gleaned from the kind of knowledge, etc., that is recommended, and what kind of knowledge is supposed to be imparted can be worked out from the elaboration upon the qualities of character. That is precisely what I will try to attempt in this section.

When one wants to create a coherent picture from all the statements scattered across the report concerned with aims of education, they can be grouped into a few categories. The most appropriate titles that I can give are *employable skills; cultural heritage; values, knowledge and critical ability; and social concerns*. I will try to analyse the kind of content in each of them that is envisaged, as well as the relative importance they are given in the draft.

Employable skills

The paramount concern of the policy seems to be teaching employable skills. Indian society is seen to be almost taken over by the ever-changing, globalising, knowledge-based economy, and the policy is striving to cope with the global trend thrust on India. It is primarily a policy to 'cope with the changes effected by others'. The earlier policies of education and commission reports were all aware of the changes taking place in the world economic and political order and role of technology in it. But there seem to be two crucial differences: one, they were also aware of the implications of these changes for politics, human values and human life. They saw it as necessary to deal with this change but were also aware of the debilitating effect it could cause, therefore, emphasising certain values and the capability to not surrender totally but to resist it where need be. The Draft NEP has no notion of resistance; it just wants to 'cope' with this. And the most important ways it sees to cope with it is to gear education towards employable skills.

And this thrust on skills is clear from elementary to higher education, as is evident in many statements; for example: *[S]kill development programmes in school and [the] higher education system will be reoriented not only for gainful employment of our students but also help them develop entrepreneurial skills'* (26). The document justifies this reorientation of education because according to it, a 'large proportion of the products of the education system are found to lack employable skills' (9).

This emphasis is everywhere in the policy document, for example, in goals and objectives in school education (15), in goals and objectives for higher education, in the mission statement (4), in curriculum renewal (21) and even in inclusive education and support (23).

The nature of these skills, however, is left to the curricular revision that is supposed to follow, perhaps a legitimate stand for a policy document. All that is mentioned is 'employable skills', 'entrepreneurship skills', 'life skills', 'human skills', etc. The idea seems to be that the market is the real master of the society, and it requires a certain kind of population to function; that population requires skills to produce goods and provide services; therefore, whatever is required by the market at a given time and place, education should supply that with efficacy and promptness.

Cultural heritage

The mission statement makes it clear that the policy is to

> [E]nsure that school and higher education as well as adult education programmes inculcate an awareness among children, youth and adults of India's rich heritage, glorious past, great traditions and heterogeneous culture.
>
> (14)

Similar statements are repeated at other places; for example

> [T]he aim of education is to inculcate awareness among learners of India's rich heritage, glorious past, great traditions and heterogeneous culture.

Again, it is recommended for higher education, especially technical education, that 'institutions, will provide opportunities to all students to learn about India's rich heritage, linguistic and cultural diversity and knowledge systems'.

Promoting the culture of the country through education is certainly a legitimate aim; our earlier policies have been emphasising it too. Therefore, an emphasis on culture as such can hardly be objected to. But here also there is a crucial difference: the earlier documents almost always note that culture changes with the time, and in any culture there is much that should be critically examined and weeded out. Second, earlier documents seem to have a desire to be Indians and being recognised as such but no noticeable desire for world domination. The present document hardly refers to any problems in Indian culture and only eulogises it.

The policy takes a quote from Sri Aurobindo: 'The sun of India's destiny would rise and fill all India with its light and overflow India and overflow Asia and overflow the world'. It concludes that the 'rest of the 21st century could then belong to India'. This seems to express the upbeat mood that the ruling BJP and RSS want to create in the middle class and will likely go very well with a section of the Indian population. In the opening paragraph it refers to the glory of intellectual achievements of ancient India. Then it jumps forward 1,000 years and comes to the freedom struggle as if nothing happened in India in that whole millennia. Therefore, the problem is not an emphasis on Indian culture, but attributing all the glory of Indian culture to ancient India, providing non-critical eulogisation of it and making it a tool for 'overflowing the world' with its light. When culture, which is dear to everyone's heart, is used in this manner, it becomes toxic indoctrination.

Values

The draft rightly notes the importance of values in education. It repeats a list of values at several places. If one goes by the list and its literal meaning, there seems to be a lot of importance on democratic values. For example, the mission statement, after emphasising the culture, continues: 'and promote acquisition by the learners at all levels of *values* that promote responsible citizenship, peace, tolerance, secularism, national integration, social cohesion and mutual respect for all religions, as well as universal values[1] that help develop global citizenship and sustainable development'.

This is an interesting paragraph. Here the values that are mentioned are deemed to contribute to 'responsible citizenship'. A responsible citizen is someone who is committed to peace, tolerance, secularism, national integration, social cohesion and respect for all religions.[2] This is a citizen who largely is amenable to the state and political power, who has full belief in the state's goodness and accepts the social structure. One wonders whether a responsible citizen should also be concerned if state and society perpetuate injustice to large sections of society. In such a case, should a *responsible citizen* raise her or his voice? Should they make noise, agitate and oppose the government actions and policies, or should she or he be more concerned with social cohesion and peace and be tolerant of the state injustice?

One can argue that this problem is taken care of, as the draft also says that

> [E]thics education will be integrated at all levels for inculcating values of equality and equity, social justice, fraternity, democracy, responsible freedom and liberty, spirit of fraternity and national integration.
>
> (31)

In addition, the draft shows sensitivity to social concerns; for example, it states:

> [I]ssues of gender, social, cultural and regional disparities, with an emphasis on diversity, will be properly addressed in the curriculum and its transaction. Curriculum will cover the issues of social justice and harmony and legal measures in order to avoid social discrimination.

However, the qualification of 'responsible' for freedom indicates a certain interpretation of action for social justice, democracy and liberty when read with 'responsible citizenship', peace and social cohesion. That indicates a certain unease or even fear of a free and critical citizen. References to 'instilling' in students 'discipline, punctuality, . . . good conduct', etc., also strengthen this point.

Overall reading of the values seems to be for a loyal, more working and less thinking citizenship. One often feels that the JNU and similar incidents in the recent past have been playing on the minds of the people who drafted this document. This is not unnatural, or even completely unjustified, seeing the disrespect for the society, nation, state and truth displayed in these incidents. A lot of academic, political and cultural irresponsibility was evident for a thinking person in these episodes. However, the remedy for that does not lie in blunting the critical edge of education. It lies elsewhere.

Knowledge

Knowledge is mentioned first in the oft-repeated (four times) phrase 'knowledge, skills, attitudes and values' with which the graduates are supposed to be equipped. However, knowledge and critical abilities are also the most neglected aspects of the educational aims in the draft. While reading the document, one often comes across the term 'knowledge', yet it never gives an insight into 'what kind of knowledge?' and 'for what purpose' it is intended.

In sheer frustration I used a trivia-generating and pedestrian methodology to get at least a tentative grasp on the issue. The term 'knowledge' occurs 42 times in the document. I tried to understand in what context and to what purpose the term serves. It was a surprise to find the term 'knowledge' occurs 11 out of 42 times as an adjective for 'economy' or 'society'; i.e., mostly as 'knowledge economy' and a few times as 'knowledge-based society'. That gives the first hint at the kind of knowledge with which the 'graduates' are to be 'equipped'. This is the knowledge that is useful in a 'knowledge economy'. Primarily the technical knowledge of immediate market value, the knowledge of providing services, management knowledge, marketing, etc. Knowledge-based society is simply a more palatable description of knowledge economy. It is continuously repeated that students should be equipped with the knowledge required to meet the challenges of a knowledge economy.

The second most frequent occurrence of 'knowledge' is in connection with the generation of new knowledge (ten times), and, unsurprisingly, it is closely connected with the 'knowledge society'. It is to generate new knowledge that has immediate applicability in the knowledge economy. There is no mention of any fundamental research at all. Of course, there is a lot of emphasis on generating new knowledge, but that is the same kind of knowledge as required in the first case.

The third most often occurrence of the term (five times) is in connection with equipping[3] students with knowledge that is required to deal with a 'changing skill environment' or 'entering [the] workforce'. It is really very logical: (1) knowledge is needed for the knowledge economy; (2) we lack that, so generate or import it; and (3) impart the same knowledge to students to enter into the knowledge economy.

The fourth most frequent occurrence is (1) in connection with Indian knowledge or Indian knowledge systems and (2) as part of the catchphrase that summarises educational aims 'knowledge, skills, attitudes and values'. Item (2) need not be discussed, as it is simply a summary of aims. The first – Indian knowledge – connects well with the cultural heritage aims. The rest of the occurrences are in connection with assessment or teachers' subject knowledge (only once) or body of research knowledge, which either don't give any hint at knowledge as an aim of education or give a very weak tentative hint. Knowledge, then, in this document is a tool for developing productive and employable skills. It is actually an extension of skills; there is no knowledge in the document in its true sense.

Of course, it could be argued that in the current globalising word where is the problem if knowledge is used for a better economy, for employability, for enhancing skills, for making skill learning a lifelong process and so on. Well, there is no problem, not at all. It is all very legitimate and should be there. The problem is with what is left out: knowledge is also to understand the word – natural and social, to understand human life, to appreciate human

104 Rohit Dhankar

achievements in the aesthetic field, for sheer intellectual flight. Knowledge is to gain insight into human existence, to enter into the complex ethical world, to make independent judgments and to decide what is worth living and dying for. To decide when to support and appreciate a state and the government and when to resist and fight it. In short, to become a rationally autonomous being and still be completely embedded into the whole of humanity. To expand one's intellectual, ethical and aesthetic horizon. And that knowledge is nowhere to be seen in this document. That is the problem.

Summary and conclusion: education for a pliable workforce

> Public policy is the making of governmental rules and regulations to benefit not one individual but society as a whole. It asks, what is the best way to conceive and evaluate policies aimed at the public as a whole and its various subgroups? Who benefits? How much does it cost?
>
> (Gomery, 2008)

Winch, as mentioned in one of the sections earlier, argues that if a public education system, which is governed by public policy, does not have clearly debated and articulated educational aims, it operates on covert aims. And that gives an opportunity to the powerful sections of society to direct the system for their own benefit. The less influential sections thus are marginalised in the system.

If we accept this claim, then a proper analysis of the aims of education in the Draft NEP 2016 becomes imperative. It does not only bring the purposes and directions that education is going to take clear, it also throws useful light on interpretation of particular recommendations and proposed initiatives in the policy document.

In this chapter I have attempted to understand the aims of education in the current draft in light of earlier two National Policies on Education (NPE 1968 and NPE 1986).

A quick analysis of the NPE 68 and NPE 86 reveals that the social purpose of education in both documents is closely connected with the national goals. The national goals are those of an economically prosperous nation that is democratic in character, culturally rooted but aware of the shortcomings of its own culture, well integrated internally and secure from outside aggression. They envision a pluralistic society in which equality, justice, liberty and dignity of all citizens are guaranteed. Social cohesion and fraternity among the citizens are seen as important goals. The policy and social ethos are based on secularism and a scientific temper.

Both the earlier policies, though, do not use the term 'aims of education' but under the role of education mention the social purposes noted earlier.

They are also very clear that to achieve these social purposes, education has to develop certain qualities and capabilities in the learners. Only citizens with those capabilities can achieve the defined social purposes. These capabilities of individuals, or aims of education, have democratic values, open-mindedness, appreciation of Indian culture, critical thinking and a sound base of knowledge that helps them become active and contributing citizens.

The new Draft NEP 2016 is substantially different in its vision of society, social purposes, understanding of aims of education and articulation of aims of education. It is neither overtly undemocratic nor overtly sectarian. It also mentions all the appropriate values, etc., but the complete reading and reading between the lines give a very different picture.

The first significant difference to note in this regard is the vision of society. The Draft NEP 2016 is almost obsessed with the 'fast-changing, ever-globalising, *knowledge-based economy and society*' (KBES). It sees these changes as God-given, and no critique of these changes in terms of impact on human life and wellbeing is attempted. This is a fact: the forces that bring this are unseen and unchallengeable; therefore, all that is left for India is to go with the flow and 'cope' with it. The document does mention social concerns, disparities, issues of social justice and democracy, etc., but its eyes are fixed on what it calls the 'knowledge economy' and a cohesive society with a certain cultural hue. That culture is not to reinterpret or challenge or search for alternatives to the KBES, but only to wave a flag of different colour to say that 'look we are here too'.

The authors of this document are conceptually confused about national goals (creation of a just and equitable society), the education department's or system's targets (to bring all children to school) and educational aims (inculcate values of justice and equality in the learners). They all are put in the same category of educational objectives. That, in national policy, gives a feeling of being directed by incompetent people, if nothing more. What the policy draft lists under the educational objectives are mostly the system's targets. Aims are scattered all over the document, and one has to cull them out.

I have analysed the aims under four categories, namely *employable skills, cultural heritage, values* and *knowledge*.

The thrust of the policy is clearly employable skills. Recommendations concerning skills dominate every section. It is also understandable that if the society is seen as KBES, then the most important task for education is only to prepare people who can be employed in it. The aims also make it amply clear that the skills are needed to cope in this system, not to challenge or modify it.

The cultural heritage is indicated as the culture of ancient India. Though there is mention of cultural pluralism, diversity and tolerance, etc., what is described at one place is only the ancient Indian contribution to the world of knowledge. With the authority of Sri Aurobindo, there is also a hope and desire that the rest of the 21st century will belong to India, whatever that might mean. There are no overt statements that might charge the document with sectarianism, but no indication of any culture is given, and the characteristics that are listed are ones claimed for the ancient Indian culture.

Almost everything is mentioned in terms of values, from democratic values of justice and equality to punctuality (a KBES value, perhaps). However, a close reading of the places where these values occur and qualifications that are put on citizenship, freedom, etc., give a very clear indication of a pliable kind of citizen. The education under this policy will endeavour to 'produce' 'responsible citizens' who use 'responsible freedom'. If one reads this in light of the overwhelming emphasis on employable skills, knowledge for KBES and complete absence of critical thinking (mentioned twice in passing), then the citizen that seems to be desired is one who largely is amenable to the state and political power, who has full belief in the state's goodness and accepts the social structure. There is no place for a citizen who feels responsible if the state and society perpetuate injustice to large sections of society. No place for a citizen who makes noise, agitate, and opposes the government actions and policies. It is a citizen who is more concerned with social cohesion and peace and is tolerant of the state's injustice.

The knowledge as envisaged in the policy draft is almost completely the one required for KBES. That is the knowledge to be imparted to deal with a changing skill environment and lifelong learning of skills, to prepare for the workforce and to be productive. The knowledge which is to be generated is that which is applicable in the employable skills. Indian traditional knowledge, however, is fine, as that is needed for the awareness of cultural heritage.

The knowledge which is required to understand the world – natural and social, to understand human life, to appreciate human achievements in the aesthetic field, for sheer intellectual flight, etc., is not indicated at all. Knowledge to gain insight into human existence, to enter into the complex ethical world, to make independent judgments and to decide what is worth living and dying for, has no place. The knowledge to decide when to support and appreciate a state and the government and when to resist and fight it does not seem to be part of it. In short, the knowledge to become a rationally autonomous being and still be completely embedded into the whole of humanity is absent.

In conclusion, one can say that it is a policy to gear education to producing pliable citizens who work as the government says, believe it, obey it, produce but do not think and do not question. It is a policy to craft an education system that is to dumb down the citizenry. It is time for India again to remember that a just and functioning democracy squarely depends on citizens who can think clearly and critically and who can act on their convictions in the face of risks. Democracies are not sustained by obedient productive units in so-called KBES.

Notes

1 One wonders what those 'universal values' are and whether 'peace', 'tolerance', 'secularism', etc., are seen as non-universal. But we will ignore this point.
2 One can (should) equally respect all human beings, who may be believers in different religions. But respecting 'equally' all religions in terms of their ideology and theology is tantamount to abandoning one's critical outlook. Actually, the ideologies and theologies of religions can be more or less justified and, therefore, more or less respectable. But that is not the issue in this chapter.
3 I am not commenting on this term here, which gives a feeling of saddling a beast of burden.

References

Dearden, R. F. (2012). *The philosophy of primary education*, (First published in 1968). Milton Park, Abingdon and Oxon, OX: Routledge.

Dewey, J. (1983). Report and Recommendation upon Turkish Education. The Collected Works of John Dewey, 1882–1953, The Middle Works of John Dewey, 1899–1924, vol. 15(1923–1924). Carbondale and Edwardsville: Southern Illinois University Press, p. 273.

———. (2004). *Democracy and education*. New Delhi: Aakar Books.

GoI. (1953). *Report of the secondary education commission*, Ministry of Education, Government of India. First Published September 1953.

———. (1962). *Report of the university education commission*. New Delhi: Ministry of Education Government of India 1950. Reprint 1962.

Gomery, D. (2008). *Public policy, entry in international encyclopedia of social sciences*. New York: Palgrave Macmillan.

MHRD. (1986). *National policy of education 1986*. New Delhi: Ministry of Human Resource Development, Government of India.

———. (1998). *National Policy on Education 1986 (as modified in 1992) with National Policy on Education, 1968*. Government of India, Department of Education, Ministry of Human Resource Development, New Delhi. Available at: http://mhrd.gov.in/sites/upload_files/mhrd/files/document-reports/NPE86-mod92.pdf (Accessed on 12 June 2017).

———. (2016a). *National policy on education, 2016: Report of the committee for evolution of the new education policy*. New Delhi: Ministry of Human Resource Development, Government of India.

———. (2016b). *Some Inputs for Draft National Policy on Education (Draft NPE)*, New Delhi: Ministry of Human Resource Development, Government of India, http://mhrd.gov.in/sites/upload_files/mhrd/files/Inputs_Draft_NEP_2016.pdf (Accessed on 18 June 2017).

Winch, C. (1996). Quality of education. *Journal of Philosophy of Education*, 30(1), p. 33.

Chapter 6

Bin bhay hoye na preet

Resilience of the fear-based examination-detention policy in the Indian education system

Disha Nawani

Introduction

Assessment systems or policies in India have rarely received such attention as in the past few years. Although several government policies and documents pointed out the ills of our public examination system, which was established during British rule, and made appropriate suggestions to address them, it was only after the enactment of the RTE Act in 2009 that concrete and, to some extent, radical steps were actually implemented across the country. Despite being progressive in both spirit and nature, they received public flak and were eventually withdrawn.

This chapter attempts to understand the historical and sociological reasons behind the reversal and near-unanimous support for these decisions. This chapter is divided into three sections. The first consists of an interview dated 1995 with Krishna Kumar, an educationist who is known for his scholarship on the Indian school system.[1] His interview explains the causes for the deep-seated entrenchment of the public examination in our education system and ensuing failure and rejection of a large number of students every year – a system, which by eliminating a huge majority of aspirants, effectively maintains and legitimises the social hierarchies existing in our society.

The second section briefly dwells on the origin and central features of the Indian school examination system, which in a way are also its defining characteristics explaining its resistance to change. The third section enunciates reforms proposed in existing assessment policies and the rationale behind, them highlighting reasons for discomfort with them leading to their eventual reversal. The three sections, despite seeming discontinuous in format and perhaps in the timing of their articulation, are integrally interlinked in helping one understand the resilience of the traditional public examinations system and its pass-fail or promotion-detention policy in which examinations unabashedly tested the child, held him singularly responsible and therefore rewarded or penalised him. For obvious reasons, such a system thrived on the perennial fear that the school students lived under and considered it the most vital ingredient for the successful functioning of our school education system. The views articulated in the first section were ratified even three decades later, thereby forming a relevant backdrop against which contemporary reforms in assessment and responses to it can be understood.

I Understanding the resilience of public examinations: a conversation with Krishna Kumar

D.N.: What role do public examinations serve in the Indian society?

K.K.: Indian society is very hierarchical and opportunities available to different sections of society are radically different. For some, education is not only an assumed right but a privilege. For others, education is a distant dream. In a society that is so iniquitous, the social order virtually demands that a mechanical system which would permit different sections of society to participate under common norms be maintained. The historical legacy of the Indian examination system is that it brings together the extremely privileged and extremely underprivileged on the same desk for the same period of time under completely impersonal conditions. Like instead of a name, you have a common roll number, instead of your school, you sit in someone else's school, instead of a teacher, you have an invigilator – an unknown examiner and paper setter.

By creating this system in the late 19th century, the colonial state was putting together a structure which conveyed its impartiality and fairness. The Hunter Commission had said in its report of 1885 that all sections of society will have the opportunity to participate in the system of education. Before that Queen Victoria's Proclamation had said that jobs and opportunities will be equally distributed not on the basis of caste, creed or birth but on the basis of merit. This message from the Queen carried a certain kind of authority and a system needed to be therefore built which would implement that kind of vision. Howsoever narrowly it was conceived, its symbolic message was of far greater significance.

Examination system, we must realise, is a perfectly legitimate symbol of fairness. It conveys that you may be the child of a huge landholder or you may be coming from a school where every room is in order or from a school where there is no teacher . . . but on this day, you will be given the same opportunity and nobody will know who you are. So this kind of impartiality and confidentiality is what keeps the examination system not only going but it makes the system virtually indispensable for a social structure which is extremely hierarchical.

D.N: This means that the primary function of the examination system is to block the entry of a large number of students either from the race to higher education institutions or lucrative jobs?

K.K: Yes, it is because it tries to eliminate the child. We know broadly speaking, that from classes I–X, about 10% of India's children will perhaps remain in the system and the others will gradually exit. An iniquitous social order and education system both demand that a legitimate way of reducing school population at different stages be found; otherwise, the system will collapse. If you consider the statistics just for classes X or XII for any given two years, an exercise which I have been engaged with for the last 20 years, you will find that between classes X and XII, our system manages to fail 80% of the children who come to class IX. Now that's a great service that the exam system does for you. And if it didn't do this service, you'd either have to face a society with millions of children who feel that they have a right to proceed further and a social order which can't cope with them and a higher education system which would simply have no way of handling the amount of numbers that it has to handle.

D.N: Are you then suggesting that their role of selection and elimination is justified?

K.K: Let me make this very clear. When you study the education system as a scientist or a sociologist, the question of motives should/does not arise. This is precisely why a school like structural functionalism in sociology is very important, for it tells you what function a certain system is serving without being charged of justifying it. So, now we are looking at the examination system in a very objective way and the proof for it can also be given in the fact that it enjoys a certain legitimacy and is accepted by those who fail, so that they begin to feel that they deserve to fail. What does that mean? As a social order, Indian socio-economic reality requires a system which eliminates, and this is a functional requisite as our economy is unable to generate enough jobs. On the other hand, you have a democracy which permits people to have equal dreams, so how do you match the two, and it's here that exams play an important role by addressing this mismatch.

Ronald Dore (1976) in his book, The *Diploma Disease: Education, Qualification and Development*, explains the 'diploma disease', which is that you make people hanker after certification. The hankering desire has to be so intense that failure to get certification should be perceived as a legitimate failure. Otherwise, the system cannot operate. This is a functional requisite of the system and the functional apparatus cannot be improved so long as it has a function to perform. The function is dependent upon economic development. If you have a fast-moving economy, a greater dynamism in the economy, which is generating jobs of various kinds, then surely a large number of people who are appearing with the fear that they are going to fail, will rather not appear in the examination. At the age of 17, they will do something else. However, if the economic development is sluggish, then naturally people are going to find ways which in the meanwhile are going to increase their certification so that someday, when opportunities are there, they are not found wanting as far as the certification is concerned. Now in the education system which otherwise makes people aspire for more and more, there is no system like the examination to cool off their aspirations.

This does not mean that I am advocating the utility of examination, but I am simply trying to understand and explain its overwhelming presence and continuity in an unequal society. This is simply one aspect of the examination. We should also see a proof of this theoretical observation. In the last 100 years the system has been in place and there is not a single Commission appointed either by the British or Indian government which has not criticised the examination system, yet the system has survived. It has remained so resilient that even when there are certain things to marginally improve it, after a few years it comes back to its old colours. Now why is marks orientation so important because numbers involved for any selection in any economy are very large. In such a case, cooling off people around grades will not work. If it is important to let's say, eliminate 18,000 people in our own entrance test in which only 300 people will succeed, then surely we will have to have marks. Then we can tell somebody that you have got 84 out of 100 – too bad, we have somebody with 85, then that person knows that there is an objective explanation of his performance and if the selection is based on this objective indicator, he will have no complaints.

So, this improvement from marks to grades can't be implemented so long as we have limited opportunities. Grade system works in societies, where competition is not hard, where the premium attached to particular opportunities is not so substantial that your life is a preparation for success in that exam. This is just an example to show the resilience of the system. So, despite Hunter, Kothari, Yashpal, and various other Commissions having recommended that the system be improved, the system has still refused to improve.

D.N: So, what you are suggesting is that both psychologically in terms of justifying one's performance in examinations and sociologically in terms of curbing possible social discontent, examinations have an almost indispensable role to perform in unequal societies such as ours?

K.K: Yes, it has a function which is rooted in the material conditions of society and so therefore, it has a firm place in society. It is not someone's will or sluggishness but in fact, the most dynamic part of the system. If you consider the regularity with which it takes place, the cooperation that it involves from different sections of society. . . . Consider for example, the police are said to have a very inefficient workforce in the country but in exams they are so efficient. They help in the movement of confidential exam papers to remote distant villages in a way that leakages become news. Consider how big and well recognised this institution of examination is. I am calling it an institution because it's a set of roles and those serving very specific roles across an extremely diversified structure of society, from richest to poorest, everybody knows what it means to fail in an exam. The failure may be unjustified. If you say that a child who has no opportunity to prepare, whose house has no electricity, whose school was barely a school, whose school had no map, no teacher or teachers hardly ever came to school, has been placed against a child from a public school who has everything working for him – upper-middle-class background and adequately resourced school, etc. – and despite this, if you say that you'll judge both of them by the same yardstick then, morally speaking, this is the most unjust system of the world. However, socially this system is working for a society which is divided hierarchically. Unless this society does something about that hierarchical order, it's very unlikely that it can do something specifically about improving the exam system.

D.N: Does this mean that examination reform will have to wait to be effective for larger social processes?

K.K: You can read the preface of Yashpal Committee Report in which Prof Yashpal, in his letter to the Minister says, 'we had lots of differences among ourselves, or even developing a conviction that something has to be done. The difficulty for me personally has come from my inability to persuade myself that the state of our school education is not an independent variable that it could be altered without altering a lot of things in our social set up. Indeed, it's not only the set up in the country but also the defective interpretation of the external scenario that finally impacts our young students, etc'.

The point that he is making is that he himself is perplexed. It is difficult to say whether social reality will change first or whether schools will change first. Both must change in order for an education system to function differently. That's the message we learnt from virtually any education system in the world. I think when it comes to examination, we are looking at a very specific organ of the overall system, an organ which has a specially hard role to perform and that role is of telling somebody, that you are not supposed to come from tomorrow at a great moral/cultural cost. However, as long as the conditions which make their failure necessary, the system will remain in place, irrespective of the hue and cry we may make. But that doesn't mean that we shouldn't make a hue and cry. Our struggle to point out the unjust aspects of the system must continue, but at the same time, we must extend the scope of our struggle to other unjust aspects of society affecting its different sections. If we are looking at this kind of a thing, we are talking about social change in the larger sense of the term – anything which mitigates the hierarchical order, as it operates in the caste system or in the gender context, or in the purely economic class context, will ultimately make it possible for us to improve the exam and education system . . . so in that sense, the struggle is much larger.

D.N: What are your views on the open-book examination system?

K.K: The open-book exam is very good idea, but on a limited scale. I am a great proponent of the idea and use it in some of my classes. However, the idea requires a tremendous amount of theoretical awareness on part of the teacher. It can't operate in a system when even the teacher is in complete dark about even the objectives of education. In such a scenario, how do we today convey the objectives of an open-book examination, which is a very sophisticated procedure for her to adopt? The intensity of interaction between teachers and other shareholders/ aspects of the system is what you require for that kind of a thing to work. For individual teachers to take open examination in their own classroom, it is okay. However, as a systemic change or proposal, it will take time.

D.N: While I understand your point, I feel that you are being very kind to the exam system. What about the children, who in this process get smothered by its oppressive nature?

K.K: That's right! To throw this attitude back, you are now taking a very romantic view of the child. It's not just the examination system that smothers the child. So much else smothers the child, this is just one nail; there are many more.

D.N: In all your work, you have always taken the child's perspective. Somewhere one gets the feeling that when you are talking about [the] examination; you seem to have forgotten the child. In your effort at being objective, you seem to be presenting [examinations] as a fair institution in serving an important social objective.

K.K: I think the word fair is a moral category. I am being very objective, emotionally detached in that sense. Okay, let me be emotionally detached to say that [the] examination system costs the country the frustration of millions of younger people. Imagine a country which fails 1% of its total population every year, amounting to millions of young students. We have a depressive social ethos in which everybody has to fail at one point or another. This is a system which stigmatises people, gives motivation, creates a social ethos in which any kind of fairness/opportunity/ freedom, etc., are looked at very suspiciously in an unconvinced sort of way. This is the cost we pay for maintaining the system and I am deeply sorry for this, but I will be failing as a student of this field if I spoke the language of Kothari Commission or some other Commission and simply say that the system must improve.

The next section systematically explains the resilience of the public examination system by tracing its roots in a colonial past, highlights its chief features, especially the grounding of fear, and in the third section links the resilience to explain the resistance to recent reforms in assessment policies.

The views presented here were gathered more than 30 years ago, and one can still see their relevance even today, where the external public examination system continues to hold its own as an invincible pillar of the Indian school system.

II The examination system: origin and basic features

The examination system was institutionalised under the colonial system of administration, which formalised the existing but disparate education systems in India. Under this system, textbooks began to be prescribed, a syllabus needed to be completed within an academic year and, most importantly, examinations were removed from the purview of the individual schools. To give a semblance of impartiality, uniform exams began to be conducted by external bodies which were not known to either the teacher or the students.

Interestingly, performance in these exams began to be linked to financial aid given to schools, which meant that aid was granted only if a certain number of their students passed these examinations. Gradually, recruitment to service was related to an exam result, and the concept of a minimum standard of proficiency and hence the concept of pass and fail automatically crept in. In all these examinations, the stress was on memory, and this was accentuated by the general background of our own teachers, traceable to the old pathshala technique (NCERT, 1971: 12), where teachers taught orally and students, in the absence of too much written text, rote-learned the knowledge thus communicated to them. Another reason for this mechanical selection was the sheer number of candidates, which made it difficult to give any importance to other aspects of students' personality, and the percentage of marks scored in such exams became the sole criteria for their selection (NCERT, 1971: 13).

Such a system acquired legitimacy both among the privileged classes and even among the dispossessed. This was because in the colonial perception, Indian society was divided along caste and religious lines. The colonial state claimed that by virtue of its foreignness, it stood above these different groups, mediating between them, and was neutral in its approach towards them. The setting up of question papers and evaluation of students by people other than teachers who taught them was one such measure of expressing its neutrality.

This system continued after India acquired independence, when separate and autonomous Boards of Secondary Education were set up in most states. As the number of students increased at a phenomenal rate, the school boards became more important and continue to be so, especially in the conduct of examinations and declaration of results on time. The practice of screening large masses of students and selecting only a small number to match the number of seats available is followed in most states (Singh, 1997). One can see a continuity in examination results serving as a criterion for limited opportunities (both admission to institutions of higher learning and employment) in colonial as well as independent India.

The central features of this examination system thus established were:

- Externality, given the public nature of these exams
- Formality – essentially written
- Objectivity – the identities of the teacher and those taught remained hidden from each other, which also indicated a complete distrust of the teacher
- Uniformity in treatment of students with no concession for individual differences among learners
- Introduction of bureaucratic processes laced with formal rituals and infrastructural paraphernalia
- Unilateral dependence on prescribed textbooks
- Non-transparency in the process of evaluation
- Regulatory role and public use of its results
- Attaching of rewards and sanctions to performance in exams

Central to the pervasiveness and ubiquitousness of board examinations in students' lives was the grounding of fear as being integral to school learning. The fear associated with non-learning was unique to colonial times, as it began to be associated with denial of several rewards which the Western education brought along with it. There was only one roadblock in the way to people's aspirations getting fulfilled, and that was failure in those examinations. Entrance to school meant being gradually initiated into a world of fear, where all that mattered was success in examinations, which was especially terminal. The fear of failure and associated shame and humiliation became part of the lore of childhood and adolescence (Kumar, 1991). Munshi Premchand's *Bade Bhai Saheb* (My Elder Brother), written in 1910 (Stories from Premchand, 1986), is a classic story which conveys the anguish of a student who repeatedly fails in exams.

The feeling of fear associated with school learning did not dissipate with the attainment of independence, but was further strengthened. That is the reason why students are often found flocking the temples especially during exam time, seeking divine interventions, wearing religious markers and making religious symbols on their answer scripts. Reminiscing about his childhood days, the famous sociologist T. N. Madan, born in 1933, writes about the fear he experienced when after five years of home-based education, he was to join a school in Class VIII. As he was presented before the inspector of schools in his big office, he sweated and trembled with fear.

> I was however, oppressed by the fear of the upcoming examinations . . . the entry into school ended my childhood, bringing with it many

anticipated joys, but also unknown fears, including the examination blues.

(Madan in Karlekar and Mukherjee, 2010: 192–93)

The feeling of fear was particularly associated with board exams, which performed the important role of filters. A system which was marked by uniformity, secrecy and impartiality could hardly be faulted, and students' success and failure in examinations was justified as the presence or absence of individual effort and talent. Thus, the structural inadequacies of the system in being unable to either provide seats in institutions of higher learning or employment in the market were masked behind the superbly efficient system of examination in successfully eliminating a large number of job seekers/aspirants. Teachers and students both became pegs in such a system which was dictated by fear and desperation to do well, and the bitter pill of failure was swallowed unquestioningly as being caused by one's own inability and incompetence (Nawani, 2017).

It is interesting to note that no sooner was the system of external examinations introduced in India, that educationists and policymakers began to recognise its limitations. Commission after commission pointed out the malaise afflicting the Indian education system, particularly examinations, and the deleterious impact that they were having on the meaning of education at large and school education in particular. This kind of a written examination system has been subject to intense critique in various government of India reports (Ministry of Education, 1966; GoI, 1986, 1992; MHRD, 1993). The specific problems associated with this form of assessment are that they create enormous stress for students; they mostly test students' ability to memorise and fail to test higher-order skills; they are inflexible, as they are based on a 'one size fits all' principle and make no allowance for different types of learners and learning environments; they and do not serve the needs of social justice (NCERT, 2006).

Despite meaningful suggestions made repeatedly by various commissions set up for the purpose of reviewing the examination system in India, precious little was done until 2009 to ameliorate the ills plaguing it.

III Situating the reforms in a contemporary context

Over the past decade India has witnessed some important developments in the area of school education, the most important of which is the enactment of the historic RTE in 2009, which gave elementary education the status of a fundamental right. Prior to this, the National Curriculum Framework (NCF) was re-constituted in 2005, which had its roots in the 'Learning Without Burden' report (MHRD, 1993). This report aptly located the load of students' learning on 'incomprehensibility, where a lot was taught but little was learnt or understood' (Ibid, p. 8) and observed that in such a system, very little understanding was required on the part of a child to pass an examination.

Therefore, besides several other curricular, pedagogic, infrastructure and teacher-related measures, both the NCF 2005 and RTE 2009 proposed meaningful shifts in the assessment system.

Specifically with regard to assessment, the RTE, 2009 mandated:

1   No child admitted in a school shall be held back in any class or expelled from school until completion of elementary education.
2   No child shall be required to pass any board examination until completion of elementary education.
3   Continuous and comprehensive evaluation of a child's understanding of knowledge and his or her ability to apply the same.

The rationale underlying these reforms was to make assessment an integral part of learning, to challenge the legitimacy of one-off board examinations in the elementary school years, to dissociate learning from fear and ultimately provide a non-threatening learning environment for all children. These children, despite their inability to cope with the demands of a formal system, were never made to feel inadequate/unsuitable and pushed out of the school. In a way these provisions respected the diversity in children's backgrounds and also recognised the limitations in learning environments and did not hold the child singularly responsible for his or her failure. They also recognised that just like learning is a continuous affair, assessment could not be reduced to a single mega-event in which all children's learning could be manifested. Similarly, these changes reiterated the need to re-imagine assessments so that they contributed meaningfully towards the growth of every single child, especially the one from a disadvantaged environment.

Resistance expressed

The examination system, thus established, was fairly resilient and withstood the onslaught of general public and various commissions which critiqued it. Even now, voices of dissent came from all quarters and were almost condescending of these new provisions mentioned above as being detrimental to all learning in schools.

With several states registering their discontent, the MHRD in 2012 set up the Central Advisory Board of Education (CABE) Sub-Committee to examine the efficacy of these measures. Two central concerns that informed this committee's analysis of the provisions under study were (1) declining learning level outcomes (LLOs) of government school children and (2) migration of children from government schools to private schools, as reported by Annual Status of Education Report (ASER, 2012) reports, which clearly point out that the no-detention policy (NDP) of the public schools proved to be a major deterrent in providing meaningful support to children in their education. This was because of the commonly misunderstood interpretation of the NDP as implying absence of assessment. It also pointed out that the CCE was also being misconstrued by schools in two diametrically opposite ways – either no examination or a spate of constant tests. The committee also asserted that the popular perceptions among most teachers, parents and administrators of the government schools was that both these provisions have jointly played havoc with the child's actual learning in school. Because an annual exam system was a well-understood system, even by parents, where the declaration of results certified a child's progress to the next level, this new scheme of assessment and unconditional promotion of the child to the next level is a bit ambiguous and puts neither any responsibility on the child to learn nor on the teacher to ensure that the child learns.

In effect, the main anxiety against these provisions was that they eradicated fear from the school system, from the minds of students and teachers. Bin bhay na hoye preet, the phrase from which the title of this chapter is drawn, is a famous verse from Tulasidas's work, who wrote that 'even love is not possible without fear'. This is when Ram requests the mighty sea for its permission to build a bridge across it to be able to reach Lanka with his fleet of monkeys. On being ignored by the sea for three days, when Ram threatens to pierce it with his bow and arrow, the mighty sea appears and humbly apologises. This anecdote pertains to the idea that even the mighty Ram had to use force to get the sea to respond to him. The idea of 'fear' occupies a fairly central place in both mythology and real life in India – fear of God, fear of bad karmas, fear of evil spirits, etc. This fear is related to the consequences of either doing/not doing something – for example, ignoring popular superstitions, like going ahead even when a cat crosses the road and not performing established rituals in accordance with one's own culture/ religion, etc., can lead to impending doom. Interestingly, more so in the Indian education system, the idea of 'fear' associated with consequences of not-learning takes precedence over the 'joy of learning' and use of danda for facilitating learning is justified, as exemplified in a Marathi Balgeet – 'chadi laage cham, vidya yeyi gham' (the harder the stick beats, the faster the flow of knowledge) and also in Hindi, 'laaton ke bhoot, baton se nahin maantey'.

If one were to examine all the charges against these provisions, one would realise that they all had one thing in common – they would lead to a total eradication of any fear from the education system, and both teachers and students, in the absence of fear, would become disinclined towards performing their job. With fear gone from the lives of important stakeholders, the system would collapse. Therefore, it was considered important to bring back the fear into the formal education system which celebrated it right from its inception.

Latest policy decisions

In 2017, the Union Cabinet finally approved the scrapping of the no-detention policy in schools until Class VIII. There was an amendment in Section 16 of the RTE Act 2009 which provided that no child admitted in a school shall be held back in any class or expelled from school until the completion of elementary education. The change was that there now would be regular examination in Classes 5 and 8, and if the child failed, he or she would be given additional opportunity for re-examination in two months' time, and if the child still failed, he or she would be held back. The amendment empowers the state/union territory governments to hold a child in Class 5 and 8, or either of them, or not to hold in any class until elementary education is completed.

Concluding insights

If one ties the insights from all the sections, it becomes fairly evident why the progressive reforms in assessment faced stiff resistance and were eventually pulled back.

1   Public examinations right from their inception have played a significant social role in India in justifying and redressing probable grievances emerging from an unjust social order in both colonial and independent India.
2   A system which thrives on individualising structural failures by finding easy scapegoats in children will continue to be resilient to change so long as one finds solutions to structural gaps.
3   A system which celebrates fear and works on the principle of intimidation and penalising failure, irrespective of the causes for it, will fight tooth and nail any attempt to discard fear and make learning fear-free.

Added to all this is the neoliberal influence on public policy which cherishes free enterprise, profit making and competition in education. It believes in the professed superiority of the private initiative in the name of efficiency, quality and accountability. It juxtaposes these with lethargy, smugness and poor quality in the free public institutions. Linked to this mass hysteria created around public versus private is the newfound obsession with learning outcomes – definite numerical expressions of learning. This is largely driven by organisations keen to prove their worth and assessment agencies trying to establish the superiority of learning in private institutions vis-a-vis learning in public schools. The neoliberal discourse, with its emphasis on LOs, challenges the assumptions on which these progressive provisions are based.

An ideology which believes in measuring and objectifying learning will oppose an understanding of learning which is nebulous and where the purpose of assessment is not to only to test the child. Most importantly, formal external public examinations established to perform a select social role of elimination are unlikely to wither unless social inequalities are diminished. The improbability of this happening also means the improbability of examinations losing its hold on the Indian school system.

Note

1 I interviewed Krishna Kumar in 1995–96, when I was a young research scholar at Jawaharlal Nehru University, New Delhi. The interview covered a range of questions based on his scholarship in both Hindi and English. Some of the questions pertaining to his understanding of the significance and resilience of the public examination system in India are being presented here because they help us situate our prevailing resistance to the assessment-related provisions in RTE 2009.

References

A S E R (Rural). (2012). *Annual status of education report.* New Delhi: Pratham Resource Centre.

Dore, R. (1976). *The diploma disease.* London: Allen & Unwin.

GoI. (1986). *National policy on education, 1986.* New Delhi: MHRD, Department of Education, Government of India.

———. (1992). *Report of the committee for review of NPE: Towards an enlightened and humane society.* New Delhi: MHRD, Department of Education.

———. (2009). *The right of children to free and compulsory education act.* New Delhi: Ministry of Law and Justice, Legislative Department, Government of India, Available at: http://mhrd.gov.in/sites/upload_files/mhrd/files/rte.pdf (Accessed on 24 June 2017).

Kumar, K. (1991). *Political agenda of education: A study of colonialist and nationalist ideas,* 2nd ed. New Delhi: Sage Publications.

Madan, T. N. (2010). Between the braying pestles and the examination blues: The childhood years. In: M. Karlekar and R. Mukherjee eds., *Remembered childhood: Essays in honour of Andre Beteille.* New Delhi: Oxford University Press.

MHRD. (1993). *Learning without burden- Report of the national advisory committee* appointed by. MHRD: New Delhi.

———. (2014). *Report of CABE Sub-committee on assessment and implementation of CCE and NDP (under the RtE Act, 2009).* New Delhi: MHRD.

Ministry of Education. (1966). *Education and national development, report of education commission (1964–66).* New Delhi: Government of India.

National Council of Educational Research and Training (NCERT). (2005). *National Curriculum Framework 2005.* New Delhi: NCERT.

Nawani, D. (2017). Examination for elimination: Celebrating fear and penalizing failure. In: *Handbook of Education in India: Debates, Policies and Practices.* London and New York: Routledge Taylor & Francis Group.

NCERT. (1971). Report of the committee on examinations, CABE, ministry of education and social welfare, India, New Delhi: NCERT.

———. (2006). *Position paper: National focus group on examination reforms.* New Delhi: NCERT.

Report of Indian Education Commission, 1882–83. (1884). Calcutta: Government Printing Press.

Singh, A. (1997). *Remodelling of school education boards: Report of the task force on the role and status of boards of secondary education.* New Delhi: MHRD.

Stories from Premchand. (1986). *Madhuban educational books.* New Delhi: Vikas Publishing House Private Ltd.

Chapter 7

Indian modernity as the problem of Indian education

Nita Kumar

As an ethnographer and historian who worked primarily with artisans in the beginning of my career (Kumar, 1988), I was able to follow the fate of my informants for the next thirty years, well into the time when I had been doing research into various aspects of education. In an unplanned way, it turned out that the artisans taught me to a large extent how to understand the changing scenario of education in India. I will abbreviate my larger findings into two simple points.

One, all the artisans I had studied had been, sans exception, unschooled. At the same time, they were very 'educated'. They knew histories, literatures, sciences and philosophies, and could align them with their lives to come across as extremely rooted, holistic people. Though poor, they liked their profession and lifestyle, and could articulate its virtues as lying in the achievement of *balance*, between work and play, calculation and carefreeness, the spiritual and the mundane.

But two, in each generation of the approximately three I got to know of each artisan family, they demonstrated increasing faith in the promise of the constitution. They trusted the state. If the state said, 'Your children must go to school. Thus, shall they progress,' they did send the children to school. When the government school failed to impress, they spent their hard-earned money on a private school. When needed, as they read the writing on the wall, they got private tutors to supplement the schooling.

The children did not progress. They remained, at the end of their schooling, incapable of any mobility from their ancestral professions. The professions of brass and copper manufacture faded, and more alienating and equally ill-paid ones such as metal lathe work, took over. Silk hand loom weaving was replaced by the jarring power loom. In comparative terms, workers had the fate of earning less than their fathers *and* of having a poorer quality of life, *because* they had had faith in an education to change their lives and their schools had belied that faith. As the results of their trusting naiveté became apparent, the answer regarding the failure of their schools stared us in the face. It was the *technology* of schooling. And not only the poor technology of the schools artisan children went to but also the poor technology of elite schools such as Indian leaders and intellectuals had gone, which kept the very importance of technology hidden and which disguised educational difference as some other kind of social difference.

Let me explain. If after years of attending school, you cannot read or write well, have not mastered the basics of mathematics, social studies or science, cannot debate or enquire, are not intellectually curious – this is a technical failure of the school, to do with curriculum and teachers, resources, systems and processes. These things are what I call technology. If in elite schools, after years of attending school, you *can* do these things – why, then, we have a model of the technology we need. But these elite schools in fact fail to reveal it to us. Their technology remains opaque. Their reliance on children's families remains hidden. Their successful students take away a sense of mysterious privilege or of a simplistic ideology of the virtue of 'education', not a practical sense of how the machinery works. The more the elite children succeed, the more self-willed the failure of poor children and families comes to seem. If we look at the history of mass education in India, it is remarkable to note how those who started schools were full of idealism but lacked a practical understanding of the kinds of schools that were needed. Their own education had been successful, but they seemed to have no idea how it worked (Kumar, 2012).

This realisation underscores the two clear problems of education. One is the problem of technology – of curriculum and teaching methods. The other is the problem with our politics. It is a politics of difference: poor children, such as artisans' children, go to cheap and poor schools, or to no schools at all. Rich children go to expensive schools. Those who go to poor schools or no schools are guaranteed 'backwardness' as their defining characteristic. Those who go to rich schools are guaranteed a feeling of superiority in being different from the masses, accompanied by an unacknowledged failure of skills to practice leadership. The uneven quality of formal education results in the reproduction of backwardness *and* an ignorance about it. Instead of blaming our resources or processes, we blame the people victimised by them. This is the *political* problem. Our politics of democracy are weak and reproduce inequality constantly. This has a long history in India, dating from the very introduction of colonial education in the mid-nineteenth century. There were state schools and private schools, mostly set up by missionaries, which were free. But they were always poorer in quality than the private schools that were expensive and gave very few scholarships to those who could not pay.

As this volume emphasises, there has been a progressive retreat, particularly in the last two to three decades, from a position that pushed free, public education as desirable to one that sees privatisation of schooling as unproblematic. This betrayal by the state has been sought to be explained and understood in several ways. On my part, I find a continuity with the past. The problem is enshrined in our very discourse of education.

The discourse of education and of children in India has been, from the outset, 'modernist', which means 'aiming to be modern'. This discourse presumes that formal education, measured by literacy and success in schools, is of central importance. Children who do not get this education are 'failed' or 'backward'. Adults who do not have it are a huge problem. Government and private reports, such as the 'Public Report on Basic Education in India' (PROBE Team and Centre for Development Economics, 1999), or the ASER (various years), document the various failures of formal education in India. However, this discourse of the superiority of formally educated adults and children is not a natural one – or the only one possible. It is belittling to many people and is not shared by all. But let us presume that we, the author and readers, share the premises of modernity and believe in the constitution of India, which, in 1950, stated the bold, brave idea that the people of India constitute for themselves a sovereign, democratic, secular republic, including the goal of imminent equal access to education for everyone. The goal was re-stated in succeeding years and, some subversion and compromise notwithstanding, remained firm. My referring to the constitution echoes the thought of Bhim Rao Ambedkar, the leader of the constituent assembly, when in 1950 at the time of its completion, he talked of 'constitutional morality', or faith in the constitution, and the worry that a constitution's value lies not in its making but in its application, and that its successful application necessarily rests partly on faith (Guha, 2010). These were loyalties and worries shared by most nation-builders of India and many elite, educated people today. Obviously, it is this 'constitutional morality' that is lost. Otherwise, why would *today* Indians be divided into some people considered to be intellectually poor and even incapable of learning and others to be normal?

In what follows, I discuss the meanings of Indian modernity through four ethnographic case studies. My argument is to demonstrate that our present location in a neoliberal matrix, where education has become an extension of the market and of commodification, is in continuity with the past. There is an intensification of a politics of difference, but the politics itself were already there.

Vinod, or modernity as development

Modernity may be judged along four axes: as development, consumerism, discipline and performance. First, as 'development', I will give the example of Vinod, to do which I have to cite from *The Journal of Indian Education*.

> There is no doubt that the majority of students studying in government primary schools belong to poorer sections of the society. Many a time, the parents are unable to provide them with uniform and necessary stationery items. Moreover, due to the illiteracy of the family they

do not get any academic support, proper guidance or encouragement. On the other hand, they are supposed to help the family in household tasks, such as kitchen work, looking after younger siblings or taking care of animals, etc. Parents are too busy with economic and domestic problems to take any interest in the performance of their children at school. The atmosphere at home is one of frustration compounded by use of abusive language, alcoholism, and above all, lack of love which are harmful for students' psyche.

(Kaul et al., 1996)

Vinod, eight years old when I studied them, the son of a housemaid mother and a rickshawalla father, a student of their local municipal school for three years, is *fully* described in the quote here. He has no history or story – he and his family are only 'problems'. His family is too poor to afford what the school considers necessary and too unaware of the discourse of modernity to guess at everything that is considered necessary. Vinod was constantly running around on domestic errands as a child, and as a teenager became an apprentice to a carpenter, like his older brother was. His father was largely unemployed, and his mother absolutely too busy making her meagre wages to 'take any interest in the performance' of her child. Only the last sentence of the quote is incorrect: there is no lack of love in the home. But the confident generalisation that a lack of love follows on ignorance about school culture is symptomatic of the myriad of ways that the municipal school looks down upon the families of its students and imbues its space and culture with this message.

Thus, even while possessing many of the structural features of the modern school, the municipal school is a weak adherent of modernity. The distinction made by teachers in municipal schools between 'us' and 'them' is based on class and knowledge, but is not mutable, as class and knowledge can be. There is no perceived one-ness of the two parties, educators and guardians, by virtue of their sharing the same nation, the same constitution or the same history. It follows that there is no real effort by the school towards change. The efforts towards change are always defeated by the prior knowledge of how the children of certain families cannot change. The municipal school does not treat parents as customers who need to be gratified and does not provide them with what they seek. It fails to perform modernity except by performing its lack and giving the moderns an 'other' to contrast themselves to. As an arm of the state, it is antagonistic to the community and family to the point that they can never do anything right. In its alienating and intolerant atmosphere, parents and children find themselves stigmatised in advance and predictably fail. The school *makes* them fail. It starts with the proposition 'These families cannot produce educated children'. Then it dedicates itself to proving it. Its formula is a simple one: to counterpose the qualities of 'culture' such as time management, thrift, cleanliness and literacy, with those of 'backwardness' such as poverty, illiteracy and seemingly unstructured lifestyles; to demand the former set of qualities; and then to fail the family for not possessing them.

The discourse of modernity as development poses a test which, by its very nature, constructs the municipal or village government school, and the child who goes to it, as a failure. In education, the idea of modernity has been a set of rules and norms that were put in place in the eighteenth century as exemplars of the school-as-factory model. When introduced into India, they did not touch a familiar chord with a population that was in fact not going through an industrial revolution in which all the concepts of space, time, discipline and rule would become transformed. So, a huge chasm opened up. The government's affiliating boards have certain requirements of schools. The majority of schools, through a combination of middlemen's efforts, bribery, fraud and performance, succeed in meeting these requirements. Schools demonstrate that they do not understand the *meaning* of these requirements, just that 'modernity' requires these conditions. They see nothing problematical in taking an observer around to show them a 'library' that is nothing but half-filled, with never-opened cupboard, or a 'library class' which is simply a group of children studying from their textbooks, none of them aware of the magic of books, the rich stores of reading materials a library could potentially offer them and the pleasure of reading. Almost all private schools fail this test of modernity as well. Still, the schools for the rich have been always closer to the development model. Today, there is a black-and-white situation. You can *buy* school facilities with the fees you pay. That you get almost nothing, or very little, in a free school, goes without saying.

The pity is that the achievement of our development model could have been the development of our schools for the masses.

Ruksana, Faiz and modernity as freedom

The other way in which education is seen as a form of development is as personal development, a cross between the rights of citizenship and the freedom of choice in the market. Indeed, education, in Amartya Sen's famous phrase, *is* development, and 'development is freedom' (Sen, 2010). Through 'education' a person becomes a subject and agent and can make choices and fulfil his destiny. He becomes a legitimate member of the modern world. Here I give the example of Ruksana. She will not put her three children and, most vociferously, her son, Faiz, in the free government school where they would also get free lunches and books, but puts them in a private school because she realises its promise even though it requires tuition and the books and uniforms are, of course, not free. She works long hours and now does every kind of work that she earlier resisted (being high school educated herself): sweeping, dusting, washing, ironing, cooking and doing dishes. The question is: How long can she do this and how far will it take her? As the children grow, the cost of their schooling will only increase, as will the cost of their books and clothes, their food and pocket money. Ruksana may be educated, but it is the same level of education as in other cases, that is to say so low-level that it has not left her qualified for any work but housework. Even at that she underperforms. She has the personality to wheedle advances, loans, favours and can beg or borrow a lot in order to live simply and survive. But for how long? When she comes to me for a loan for the umpteenth time, I have to admit to anger. I already work hard to do the research towards an excellent education and help children in several ways. In how many other ways can I work for her? All around there are scores of people like her, some gentler and more likable, some simply more hard-working and efficient. I can cheer for her recognition of 'education as freedom'. But what her plight moves me to do is to want *not* to help her personally or influence her in any way, but to work to improve the quality of education in the municipal school that her children *should* go to but that she refuses out of the very consciousness of the power of education.

It is not that people do not understand the power of education. It is not that education is not a good idea. It is the riddle: *How do we elevate the quality of education overall to actually give power to those seeking it?* The Ruksanas of the country are already modern people. Their schools are not. The recent Right to Education Act seems ostensibly to have opened the door to personal development for some underprivileged children. But as an over-all strategy of equalisation, it is a dismal failure because it continues to be based on the politics of difference. Schools are seen as necessarily separate for the rich and the poor; only now the largesse of the rich extends to a few more poor permitted into their territory.

Aditi and modernity as consumerism

Let us look quickly at the panorama of an average Indian city, not a metro. In any city in India, there is construction every few yards. Skylines are chang-ing rapidly, with high-rise apartment buildings coming up in all directions. New private schools are equally coming up, from the outside in. First a shell is constructed, with a grand façade and a hollow inside. A few rooms suffice for a school to declare itself open. Then classrooms, walls, etc., are gradu-ally built. Hoardings that promise utopian enclaves in the new apartment buildings bristle all over the city. These advertisements for apartments have frolicking families of four advertising the happy life, set against the apart-ment complex and equally the *insides* of apartments: the refrigerators, air conditioners, almirahs, sofa sets, furnishings and foods that a happy family must have. Similarly, some of the largest hoardings in the most prominent places are the advertisements of private schools. They compete for the con-sumer on an equal footing with refrigerators, cell phones, jewellery, creams and shampoos. Their messages are similar as well: this school is a high-quality product leading to a guaranteed future of happiness and success. 'Savour it!' they are saying, just as in the advertisements for other products. 'Trust it! Surrender yourself to it!' Schools are openly and exuberantly proclaimed as an important part of modernity. There can be no development, no increased wealth and therefore no consumerism – no means to fan the flames of desire – without education. There are no hoardings, of course, advertising government schools.

The connections of modernity as consumerism to education are several and profound. Consider the following example. Aditi, as small as four years old, is learning in a holistic way in her nursery class. Her mother can see that Aditi loves to go to school, enjoys learning and is growing and developing every day. But she comes to me and complains. 'My daughter cannot recite the tables. The neighbour's daughter can. My daughter prefers to colour than to write. Why does her school have so much colouring?' The mother goes on to complain that it is all very nice to talk about the growth of children and their age-appropriate phases – but the world, after all, is competitive.

Aditi's mother might as well buy the latest gadget and display it to her neighbours. What her worry about her daughter translates into is a concept of the child not as an individual in her own right, but as a status symbol for her parents. The child in India has not emerged as a product of modernity a la Phillippe Aries, but as a *producer* of modernity. The school is a status symbol, and the schooling received is a valued commodity consumed by the parents. Together with consuming new products and services and thus establishing an image of themselves, adults use the child as an aid to further establish their image as modern. This also explains to some degree the difference between schools. Upwardly mobile middle-class parents seek certain things from schools, and private schools are anxious to supply that. Working-class and poor parents have the simplest expectations from schools and get, according to their poor schools, the kind of poor services they expect and deserve.

So, a 'modern' school for its clientele must show the physical signs of modernity: a solid building, a large metal gate, certain letters and pictures, a signboard in English. It must proclaim itself as being English medium through these images and signs. The bottom line for parents is development: their child must learn good English and mathematics and compete successfully in the language and mathematical competitive tests that follow schooling. There is nothing they want more than that. But they don't know how to measure the existence or availability of that and confuse the two kinds of development. They go by the physical signs in the school: the approach, the walls, the gates, the reception, the signboards, the notice boards, the flowerpots, the first people to meet you. The hoardings and other advertising techniques of schools show an understanding of what the parents want to consume.

The tragedy is that the poorest of parents, as in the case of the artisans with whom I began my chapter, fall victim to the same advertising. I have the example of Kanti, the mother of Vinod, discussed in an earlier section. Her older son, Pramod, a mason, has been persuaded by the discourse of the market and the family's understanding of changing times to keep a tutor for their preschool daughter. He pays for the tuition out of his meagre earnings double what the little girl's private school fees cost. Kanti, my informant, expresses an undiluted satisfaction that everything is going on the right path.

Modernity as discipline

Now, there is another meaning of modernity that seems to be out of fashion, now denigrated as Nehruvian. It is astounding how out of fashion a nationalist ethics has become: the love for other Indians, the sacrifice for the nation, the pledge for justice, equality, peace. Schools are by far the most important socialising and acculturating agencies in the child's life. They have historically everywhere in the world performed the task of creating a modern citizen and of unifying diverse communities, identities and regions under a central, normative ideology. In India, they had barely started doing that when the *desh ka sipahi* and *insaf ki dagar* ('the soldier of the nation' and 'the path of justice' – two popular film songs featuring school children) got lost. They have been lost for a few decades now, and today's schools would deliberately abstain from this non-appropriate, irrelevant role. They have to satisfy the consumer, and the consumer wants success in examinations, followed by a transformation into a modern, 'cool' person. Educators might privately complain at the loss of their leadership roles, but they are not inventive or skilled with the curriculum and throw up their hands in helplessness when confronted by market forces.

Schools play a role in the absence of citizenship values in the country by failing to be the modernising agencies they should be. Schools should be key to the production of the discipline that characterises the modernity described by Michel Foucault. This is an internalised discipline that produces pleasure, that makes the subject feel empowered, instead of, as in the past, controlled overtly from the outside. A study of schools in Europe or North America would show that from kindergarten onwards, children are taught to follow the rules that make the society depend on its adults to believe in rules and exercise a self-discipline that exceeds in its effectiveness any overt, external product of control. In India, schools exercise only external, contextualised discipline. Children do not necessarily leave school transformed into adults who have internalised the disciplines of citizenship, democracy and secularism.

There is no value to parents of the discipline of civic modernity that would teach children to be rule-abiding citizens. It would make parents nervous if a school were to publicise that as part of its agenda, and they would suspect the school of shirking its real purpose. By contrast, people are very proud of a quite different kind of disciplining, an authoritarianism in school practice. The better a school's ritualised performance of modernity through authoritarian rules, not through any pursuit of lessons in citizenship, the more admired it is.

Modernity as performance: the rituals of the tie and the PTA meeting

Two examples can illustrate what I mean by ritualised performance. A Hindi-medium school like Anglo-Bengali has parents who are waiting for a new, more progressive principal to introduce the tie into the school uniform, because a tie worn with pants and shirt announces modernity. On a bigger scale, a public school like Angel Hall performs many scenarios clearly put together to gratify parents regarding their complicity in modernity. One such scenario was reported to me by a thrilled parent when he described how, at the annual parents–teachers meeting, the event was so terrifically orchestrated that the light flashed on to the podium *just* as the director appeared for his speech, and the light flashed on at the opposite end of the stage *just* as something else was to happen there.

Schools vary in the store they set on impressing the customer, depending on the business acumen of their managers. But in all cases, it is a performance. Their identity comes from their market savviness, such as in their logo and their self-presentation. None of the devices they use, such as creating a room for media use, or having students wear a special sports outfit one day of the week, is based on appreciation for children's needs or a discourse of learning. As the principal of Shining Academy told me in response to my question about the huge success of his young, but large, school, 'I did my home-work. I studied the market'.

The performance starts with the name and choice of image in the advertising itself. A school called Malaviya Shishu Vihar or Tulsi Vidya Niketan has less cache in the market as an English-medium modern school than one called Kiddy Convent or Glorious Academy.

Elite schools, families and relative success

One question that arises is this: If elite schools know how to teach well and excellent teaching is not unknown in India, why don't the other schools simply learn these techniques and use them? Obviously, the problem is not cultural or of manpower or ignorance or even political.

The answer is twofold. One, the elite schools actually do *not* know their own technique. Because their technique is to rely on the social capital and support structure of the family and have the family do the significant part of the educational work of the school. This is never articulated or admitted, and in either case the technique cannot be replicated. A new discursive cycle is created, beginning with the very process of admission.

Because these top-ranking schools depend so heavily on the labour of the family, it becomes the norm for the family to labour in this way. The majority of families in India simply *cannot* thus labour. They do not have the intellectual or the economic means. They are thus predefined, even before the child or the guardians attempt education, as failures in a spectrum from the utter failures at the bottom to the near failures in the middle. They acknowledge themselves as different degrees of failures and are thus referred to by the state, by educators, by public opinion and by the market.

As Mr Saxena, principal of Kendriya Vidyalaya, had disclosed with envy, the schools admitted only those who had English-speaking parents, thus guaranteeing success in their educational efforts. The schools are important to me, and I allude to them in my study, because they are on everyone's minds as the model of how a school should be. The model, however, includes a *model of the family* as much as a model of the school. No one could describe, and in fact no one seems to be interested in, how the school conducts its classroom practices – except that it is authoritarian and makes strict demands on the family. Everyone is in awe of the fact that the family has to submit to all these demands, and if it cannot cope, they get as much extra help from tutors as needed. It is the family–school relationship which seals the fate of such schools' exclusivity.

The discourse of the child

The teachers in modern-day India are trained to respond that the child is an individual. An observation of practices in the classroom and throughout the school day reveals how this is the *performance* of a belief rather than its practice. Elsewhere, I have focused on the split between the idea of the child as malleable and formable, and the child as fixed in essence. Hindu mythology suggests that a child does *not* have a fixed nature, that 'anything is possible' to achieve through certain technical procedures, predominantly self-discipline and obedience to the teacher. A child could learn and conquer the world; all he needed was the teacher and/or his dedication. Again and again we are told how hard work and single-mindedness led to power. Of course, some are more capable than others of conducting a struggle successfully. It is a narrative of empowerment through dedicated teaching and labour that also acknowledges the vicissitudes of power.

The question that I find compelling for education in the present is, how does this older narrative survive in the present time? The older, 'caste' discourse ascribed different trajectories in life to different groups, so the all-empowering effect of education was necessarily very context specific. But the discourse of modern education is not context specific, that is, modern education is theoretically available on a par to everyone. However, there is no discourse of the teacher and the student in modern education to match the older ones of the guru and his students and of knowledge as power. With the new education, the *technicality* of learning through discipline and the teacher's guidance becomes transformed into an alchemy and a mystery. If India's caste system produced inequality and caste was partly reproduced through education and socialisation, there was no illusion hiding this reality and no calls for mass education (Bayly, 1999; Conlon, 1977). In the modern system, there is mass education. Everyone can get an education, but no adult wants to acknowledge that theirs is the responsibility for teaching; that what children are *taught* is what they know. With modern education, more become underachievers and can be labelled such than ever before. There are now only *some* children who can learn. The rest, goes the unchallenged claim, fail due to some unnamed inner incapacity, the fault lying now in the family and now in the individual child. When it is the child's fault, the solution is, at its simplest, to hire a tutor. When it is the family's fault, almost all schools and educators throw up their hands and declare their helplessness.

This leads seamlessly to a different split as well. India's is not a premodern society where some Indians have yet to develop an idea of the child as a discrete individual with her own rights and needs, and others have developed the idea already (Aries, 1962). Rather, India's citizen body is split up between those who *claim* to give time, interest and money to the care of the child and those who are *supposed* to be 'neglecting' the child. There are the 'good' families who co-operate with the school in fulfilling its mission of educating the child. And there are the 'bad' families who will not listen. What people believe, I argue, is less significant than how one group uses their ideas to further practise the hierarchy that is inherent in the performance of modernity.

In fact, even while most trained and experienced teachers pay lip service to the idea of the child as an individual in his or her own right, this is not demonstrated in their classroom practices in schools ranging from the top to the bottom. In India, 'freedom', 'individual', 'choice' and related terms come to be just words, linguistic conveniences for ideas that have little bearing on reality. They are used comfortably with private reservations amounting to 'This is not how real life is'.

The plot of the story of Indian education becomes clear. We have a huge colonial legacy in India which continues into a self-colonisation today: Indians believe that children are not all equal and that is mostly the fault of certain kinds of families. It is a colonial legacy because the rationale of the colonial state was its superiority to the Indian family. It was there to teach and reform Indians. But not all Indians, as colonial government reports made clear from the very beginning, could be taught and reformed. Some kinds of people, castes, sub-castes, communities, families, could never be.

This legacy continues today. The particular track of Indian modernity continues the story from there. To simply perform the modern notions of individualism and free choice is enough and can replace the reality that, most would claim, exists nowhere. By emphasising these discourses of the child, I want to underscore how the discourses support and legitimize, if not actually produce, a politics of education that is largely at the heart of the failure of Indian education.

Conclusion

I will end with an ethnographic note. I was sitting in the office of the most venerable school in my research city, called, as such schools would be, St John's. St John's was a fortress to crack. You had to swear an oath that you were not there to plead for admissions, so besieged were they by petitioners with begging bowls in hand, and then with great suspicion by the staff, you could be led in to meet the principal. As I waited, in front of me, behind the padre's chair, was a framed picture that read, 'Are you part of the problem? Or are you part of the solution?' Extremely moving and motivational as the message was, it was also disturbing. To be a member of a population categorically divided into 'problems' and 'solutions,' to be obliged to separate oneself from one body of people and belong strictly to another, was a troubling choice. It indicted the educational enterprise in India and based it on a false, presumably invincible, division of work. It sets the theme for my chapter, with which I would like to conclude. We need to problematise the role of civil society and the discourse of modernity that *everyone* is ruled by. We need to look closer at our understanding of 'the modern' in India and then see how education is indicted by the very ways in which we have boxed ourselves in with our modernity.

References

Aries, P. (1962). *Centuries of childhood: A social history of family life* (Translated by Robert Baldick). New York: Vintage Books.
ASER. (various years). *Annual status of education report*. New Delhi: ASER Centre, Pratham.
Bayly, S. (1999). *Caste, society and politics in India from the eighteenth century to the modern age*. Cambridge: Cambridge University Press.
Conlon, F. (1977). *A caste in a changing world: The Saraswat Brahmans*. Berkeley: University of California Press.
Guha, R. (2010). *Makers of modern India*. New Delhi: Penguin Books.
Kaul, M., Sukhdev, S. and Gill, S. S. (1996). Facets of primary education in rural Punjab. *Journal of Indian Education*, XXII(3), Nov. 1996, pp. 1–14.
Kumar, N. (1988). *The artisans of Banaras: Popular culture and identity, 1880–1986*. Princeton: Princeton University Press.

———. (2012). India's Trials with Citizenship, Modernisation and Nationhood. In: L. Brockliss and N. Sheldon eds., *Mass education and the limits of state building, 1870–1930*. New York: Palgrave Macmillan.

PROBE Team and Centre for Development Economics. (1999). *Public report on basic education in India*. New Delhi: CDE.

Sen, A. (2000). *Development as freedom*. New York: Anchor, Reprint Edition.

Part III

Schooling, social justice and critical pedagogy

Chapter 8

Sanskara[1]

The notion of hereditary educability and changing behaviour of the teachers

Sanjay Kumar

Introduction

The school in India has remained silent in initiating and developing a perspective and methodology to change the teacher's belief and notion of educability towards children, especially those who come from marginalised and oppressed communities. As a consequence, there is negligible literature in the form of research in both policy and academics, case studies and even policy guidelines for teachers, headmasters, teacher educators and educational practitioners in order to let them have insight into and reflection on the methodology for ensuring equal participation, cognitive development and joyful learning for all children.

It is significant that in the arena of grassroots practices in the recent past, civil society organisations have not only been confronting the teacher's belief and notion of educability across India, but they have been playing a significant role in creating dialogues with the teachers and the headmasters in order to make them aware of the problems in the schools in order to make the classroom participatory for the children, especially those who come from Dalit communities.

However, in the last two decades, there have been a number of research studies, case studies and evaluation reports – both quantitative and qualitative – on alienation, traumatic experiences and caste-based violence as part of the problem areas in the schools and the classrooms, which function as a barrier in the cognitive development, retention and learning output of the children. Some of these are (Probe Report, 1999; Nambissan, 2001; Govinda, 2002; Ojha, 2003; Velaskar, 2005; Singh and Kumar, 2010; Krishna, 2012, Naorem and Ramachandran, 2013; Tiwary et al., 2017). It is also notable that a number of Dalit writers have not only referred to their alienation from the schools in general and classrooms in particular in their autobiographies but they have also vividly described the negative attitudes and violent expressions of their teachers and headmasters which they suffered severely (Valmiki, 2003; Biswas, 2015; Bechain, 2017; Byapari, 2018).

It is worth noting that a large number of the enrolled children in the elementary schools (primary and upper primary) belong to SCs, STs, OBCs and Muslim social backgrounds. In the action research year of 2013–14, the primary schools of Bihar consisted of 19.9 per cent SCs, 1.9 per cent from STs, 65.1 per cent from OBCs and 15.6 per cent from the Muslim communities and in the upper primary schools consisted of 17.2 per cent SCs, 1.6 per cent STs, 66.1 per cent OBCs and 13.3 per cent from the Muslim (NUEPA and MHRD, 2014). It is noteworthy that the social category–wise population ratio of Bihar for the marginalised social groups is reflected in the same ratio in the enrolment profile of the children from the marginalised communities. These data show that the nature and social composition of schools have not only changed rapidly, but these also indicate that the social context of the children has become a key factor in dealing with the questions and challenges in the contemporary schools in general and classrooms in particular.

In the midst of this scanty research and grassroots practices, this study deals with the following questions: How can the teachers be made aware of the problem areas around the notion of heredity-based educability and *sanskara*? In what ways can we enable the teachers to reflect on their own belief and assumptions about the key concepts of education, learning and the notion of caste during the action research study?

This question emerged from the pilot study of the two schools which was conducted by Deshkal Society in Wazirganj block of Gaya district of Bihar. This study was conducted from an ethnographic approach, which was primarily based on the observations, FGDs and interviews from the teachers and the headmasters of these schools. Key findings of the study are given below.

'*Sanskara*' is thus considered by many teachers to be a hereditary attribute which is transferred from parents to children from generation to generation. If parents have 'good *sanskara*', their children will also have 'good *sanskara*'. Further, teachers related the 'good *sanskara*' with the learning ability and the interest of children. A cyclical argument is presented in this regard, as indicated in the introduction: 'good *sanskara*' comes from education, and education is not possible without 'good *sanskara*'.

Because parents from marginalised communities are illiterate, they do not have 'good *sanskara*'. As they themselves do not have 'good *sanskara*', they cannot inculcate the same in their children. Since these children do not have 'good *sanskara*', they cannot study and learn. Finally because '*sanskara*' is hereditary these children are hereditarily 'uneducable'. Through these cyclical arguments, the teachers construct their perception of children from the marginalised communities as being 'learning deficient' or 'uneducable' (Singh and Kumar, 2010, p. 36–37).

The vicious circle of exclusion of children from the marginalised communities is revealed in Figure 8.1.

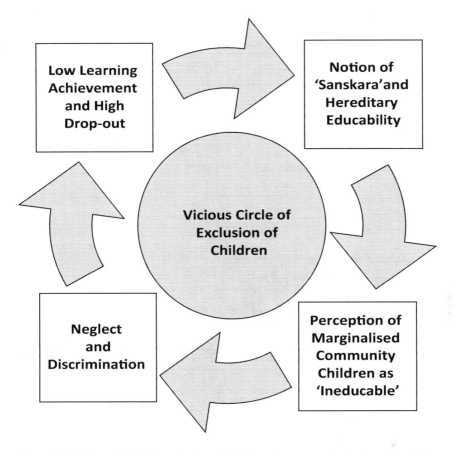

Figure 8.1 Vicious circle of exclusion of children from marginalised communities

The social and educational context of children and their location

The problems identified in the pilot study created the grounds for conducting an action research project in 2013–15 to probe and explain the key question through engaging 858 teachers consisting of 541 males and 317 females at 13 cluster resource centres (CRCs) covering 166 schools in the Wazirganj block.

According to the Census 2011, the Wazirganj block has a population of 2,21,731 (male: 1,13,601; female: 1,08,130). The number of Scheduled Castes inhabitants is 74,859 (male: 38,270; female: 36,589), which is 33.76 per cent of the total population. The share of SC population in the block is more than twice the state average. Wazirganj block counts 95 primary (I to V), 68 upper

140 Sanjay Kumar

primary (I to VIII) and 3 middle schools (V to VIII). In Classes I to V, there were 55,630 enrolled students. The number of SC students in these grades was 26,418, which was more than 47 per cent (BRC, 2013). It was notable that in these schools, among the sizeable number of enrolled SCs children, 77.2 per cent of them belonged to Musahar community,[2] often referred to as Dalits, at the bottom rung of the society in this region.

In the upper primary grades (VI to VIII), on the other hand, 22,523 students had been enrolled, and the share of the SC students was 8,404 (approximately 37 per cent). These data underline the fact that elementary education in the block was most extensively availed by SC students. The average number of teachers per school was 5.1.

In the social context of enrolled children, it is noteworthy that the percentage of out-of-school children in the 6 to 13 age group in the state of Bihar was 4.95 per cent and 2.95 per cent for the country as a whole (SRRI, 2014); another Deshkal Society and UNICEF baseline study suggests that as much as 29 per cent of children in Wazirganj block were out of school (Deshkal Society, 2013a).

This substantial number of out-of-school children reinforced the assumption of the action research study that children in schools with a large number of children from marginalised communities, especially those from Dalit communities, were compelled to be pushed out of schools. A number of factors were responsible for their being pushed out of schools, but one of the key factors was the discriminatory attitudes and practices in schools which underlie caste hierarchies and relations in the larger society.

The focal location of the action research project was the 13 CRCs in the block. In the state of Bihar, CRC activities include, among others, organising teacher education programmes under the direction of DIET and BRC, a monthly orientation workshop based on grade and subject requirements and support for headmasters and teachers (SCERT, Bihar).

Methodology: processes and practices

The parameters which determined the method of the action research project are presented in Figure 8.2 (Palshaugen 2006).

In the beginning of the first phase of the action research project, the project team, along with the teacher educators, developed multiple strategies for creating an engagement/dialogues with teachers, headmasters and teacher educators at CRCs.

These strategies included (1) orientation workshop at CRCs through the tool; (2) studying cognition and learning, the social constructivism of learning and the notion of educability; (3) reading a Dalit autobiography and engaging with the teachers; and (4) observing the teachers in their classrooms.

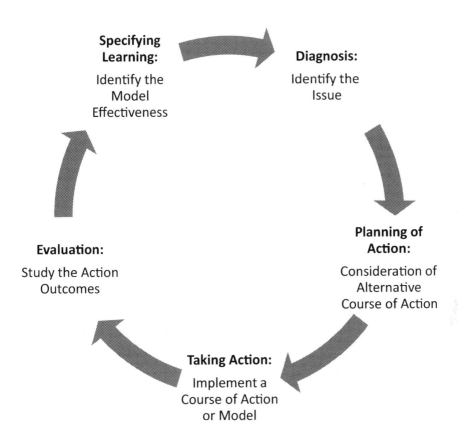

Figure 8.2 Parameters of action research

Orientation workshop at CRCs through the tool

The tool, titled *Hashiye per Bacche* (Children on the Margins), was developed from the perspective of critical pedagogy and contains chapters on mapping the habitat, forgiveness and non-violence, from school to community and community to school, the notion of educability and caste, dare to change, how full is your cup, society and work, the boy of Ramdev Manjhi, child labour, etc. (Deshkal Society, 2011). The basic purpose of the tool was to create awareness among teachers and trainers and acquaint them with the action research objectives, questions and processes at the CRC level. The tool was shared in an orientation workshop for teachers, headmasters and trainers, with an assumption that they would understand the salient features of the action research project. The project team starkly observed that teachers both from Dalit and non-Dalit social backgrounds received the tool in a routine and symbolic way and on their own neither showed interest nor shared their review feedback.

Studying cognition and learning, social constructivism of learning and notion of educability

In order to initiate the processes to develop an understanding of cognition and learning, the social constructivism of learning, the notion of educability and child-centred learning, a selection of articles, reports and training materials representing multiple approaches were distributed amongst the teachers as part of their study material. This initiative which took the form of a small workshop with the teachers, was divided into three stages in which they were encouraged to read and analyse the materials, particularly the concepts and the terminologies in the first stage, and following this they were asked to write short passages on distributed training materials in the second stage.

It is noteworthy that the reflections and opinions generated by the teachers on the concepts were diverse and contradictory. Some teachers expressed that learning and reasoning is an individual mental process which is primarily dependent on the cognitive ability of the children. Another sizeable section of the teachers expressed their belief that educability is hereditary and has biological foundations. Analysing the reflections and opinions shared in the writings indicated that teachers were not aware of the ideological vantage point for their reflections. It is important to note that they were never acquainted with these concepts and terminologies, either in their own educational career or in pre-service and in-service teacher training courses.

Against this background, the third stage of the workshop focused on sharing the micro-level empirical data, which included parents' educational background and land ownership, so that teachers could be sensitised to the social and economic backgrounds of the children in their classroom. The data are presented in Tables 8.1 to 8.4.

During the sharing of the data and discussions on the same with the teachers, we adopted a specific strategy; we gave an assignment to them – a question asking them to share their understanding of the home background of the children instead of simply writing their reflections on the empirical data. It was significant that the teachers understood the home backgrounds of the children and could informatively reflect on the differentiation amongst the children in terms of their socio-economic indicators and its implications. Not only did they realise why they had not confronted such data and questions earlier, but this realisation also became the basis for self-critique and contemplation. The three-stage process of the workshop thus

Table 8.1 Percentage of children by social category and education of father

| Social category | Educational status of father | | | | | | | | | | | | |
| | Never enrolled in school | | Enrolled but did not complete primary level | | Primary | | Matric | | Intermediate | | Graduate and above | | Total | |
	No.	Per cent	No.	Per cent	No.	Per cent	No.	Per cent	No.	Per cent	No.	Per cent	No.	Per cent
SC	728	45.25	201	12.49	356	22.13	202	12.55	62	3.85	60	3.73	1609	100.00
ST	18	54.55	4	12.12	4	12.12	6	18.18	1	3.03	0	0.00	33	100.00
OBC	262	20.74	151	11.96	383	30.32	284	22.49	98	7.76	85	6.73	1263	100.00
MBC	116	21.05	69	12.52	172	31.22	127	23.05	33	5.99	34	6.17	551	100.00
Muslim	17	4.93	7	2.03	71	20.58	116	33.62	73	21.16	61	17.68	345	100.00
Upper Caste	65	25.29	56	21.79	98	38.13	29	11.28	5	1.95	4	1.56	257	100.00
Total	1206	29.72	488	12.03	1084	26.71	764	18.83	272	6.70	244	6.01	4058	100.00

Source: Deshkal Society (2013b).

Table 8.2 Percentage of children by social category and education of mother

Social category	Educational status of mother												
	Never enrolled in school		Enrolled but did not complete primary level		Primary		Matric		Intermediate		Graduate and above		Total	
	No.	Per cent	No.	Per cent	No.	Per cent	No.	Per cent	No.	Per cent	No.	Per cent	No.	Per cent
SC	1201	74.64	261	16.22	90	5.59	27	1.68	6	0.37	24	1.49	1609	100.00
ST	27	81.82	6	18.18	0	0.00	0	0.00	0	0.00	0	0.00	33	100.00
OBC	807	63.90	224	17.74	144	11.40	60	4.75	18	1.43	10	0.79	1263	100.00
MBC	311	56.44	118	21.42	90	16.33	22	3.99	9	1.63	1	0.18	551	100.00
Muslim	92	26.67	55	15.94	103	29.86	73	21.16	11	3.19	11	3.19	345	100.00
Upper Caste	135	52.53	93	36.19	23	8.95	3	1.17	3	1.17			257	100.00
Total	2573	63.41	757	18.65	450	11.09	185	4.56	47	1.16	46	1.13	4058	100.00

Source: Deshkal Society (2013b).

Table 8.3 Percentage of children by social category and household landownership

Social category	Land ownership												
	Landless		Up to 1 bigha		> 1–3 bigha		> 3–5 bigha		> 5–10 bigha		More than 10 bigha		Total	
	No.	Per cent	No.	Per cent	No.	Per cent	No.	Per cent	No.	Per cent	No.	Per cent	No.	Per cent
SC	1354	84.15	204	12.68	48	2.98	3	0.19	0	0.00	0	0.00	1609	100.00
ST	28	84.85	5	15.15	0	0.00	0	0.00	0	0.00	0	0.00	33	100.00
OBC	311	24.62	491	38.88	313	24.78	135	10.69	7	0.55	6	0.48	1263	100.00
MBC	335	60.80	157	28.49	53	9.62	6	1.09	0	0.00	0	0.00	551	100.00
Upper Caste	53	15.36	110	31.88	100	28.99	68	19.71	11	3.19	3	0.87	345	100.00
Muslim	197	76.65	39	15.18	13	5.06	5	1.95	1	0.39	2	0.78	257	100.00
Total	2278	56.14	1006	24.79	527	12.99	217	5.35	19	0.47	11	0.27	4058	100.00

Source: Deshkal Society (2013b).

Table 8.4 Percentage of children by social category and occupation of father

Social category	Occupation of father												
	Casual labour (code 1 + 2)		Cultivator (code 3)		Artisan (code 4)		Service (code 5 + 6)		Business/Trade (code 7 + 8)		Other (code 9 + 10)		Total
	No.	Per cent	No.	Per cent	No.	Per cent	No.	Per cent	No.	Per cent	No.	Per cent	No.	Per cent
SC	1073	66.69	86	5.34	43	2.67	196	12.18	148	9.20	63	3.92	1609	100.00
ST	23	69.70	3	9.09			1	3.03	5	15.15	1	3.03	33	100.00
OBC	273	21.62	601	47.59	26	2.06	201	15.91	126	9.98	36	2.85	1263	100.00
MBC	136	24.68	76	13.79	81	14.70	103	18.69	132	23.96	23	4.17	551	100.00
Muslim	21	6.09	151	43.77	3	0.87	110	31.88	43	12.46	17	4.93	345	100.00
Upper Caste	92	35.80	30	11.67	8	3.11	57	22.18	65	25.29	5	1.95	257	100.00
Total	1618	39.87	947	23.34	161	3.97	668	16.46	519	12.79	145	3.57	4058	100.00

Source: Deshkal Society (2013b).

set the stage to take the dialogue forward, with the teachers as co-partners, with the purpose of building a broad understanding around the topics of cognition and learning, social constructivism of learning and the notion of educability.

Reading a Dalit autobiography and engaging with the teachers

In the second part, the most difficult aspect of engaging with the teachers was finding a way to understand the operation of caste in the schools. In order to make the teachers aware of this issue, part of the autobiography of the Dalit writer Om Prakash Balmiki, titled *Joothan*, was introduced to the teachers for reading and reflection; this was intended to enable them to have a vivid sense of the experiences of a Dalit child in the school. In his autobiography the author describes the humiliation and violence he suffered in the school due to his caste status. A short passage from the autobiography which was introduced to the teachers is presented here:

> One day Headmaster Kaliram called me to his room and asked: Hey, what is your name? Omprakash, I answered, slowly and fearfully. Children used to feel scared just encountering Headmaster. The entire school was terrified of him.
>
> "You are a Churah?" Headmaster threw his second question at me.
> "Ji."
> "All right. . . . That teak tree there. Go climb that tree, break some branches and make a broom. And sweep the whole school clean as a mirror. It is family occupation. Go . . . do it pronto."
>
> The third day I went to the class and quietly sat down. After few minutes, his loud thundering was heard: "O . . . ing Chaurah, where are you hiding. . . . Your mother."
>
> (Joothan, 2003, p. 53)

On one hand, reading, discussion and reflection based on the lesson created a ground for intense engagement with the teachers on the issues of caste, education and the school environment, and on the other hand, a discursive and reflective space was created in which the teachers could deeply reflect on their own past so that they could relate the school experiences of their childhood with the mistreatment suffered by Dalit children like Balmiki in school.

A section of the teachers who were from a Dalit background shared anecdotes about the behaviour of their teachers in their school days, which according to them was always discouraging, unpleasant and insulting. One of the teachers shared an example of the school days of Dr Ambedkar, who had to suffer humiliation and violence because he belonged to the Mahar caste. With this example, the teacher pointed out that the alienation and violence suffered by Dalit children in school are not current phenomena, but have existed for a long time. In contrast to these tales of discriminatory treatment, the teachers who belonged to upper castes shared their childhood memories of receiving encouragement to perform well in school, which motivated them to learn more in class The common ground which emerged through these narratives is that the teacher is the key agent who ensures the effectiveness of learning practices in the school in general and that he or she plays a significant role in ensuring participation and learning of all children in the classroom. In the discussions with the teachers during the workshop, it also became clear that the notion of caste-based educability deeply influences the attitudes and behaviours of the teachers, which in turn creates a greater negative impact amongst Dalit children; it undermines the self-belief of the Dalit children in their cognitive abilities, and this eventually leads to their being pushed out of the school. Apart from this, the exchange of different viewpoints and narratives prompted by the reading of the autobiography and the narration of the teacher's own school learning experience offered a common ground for teachers to reflect on their assumptions regarding caste-based educability and how this functions as a factor for the humiliation and alienation of Dalit children in the school, thereby leading to low learning levels and higher school dropout rates for Dalit children.

Observing teachers in the classrooms

The third stage of the process dealt with evaluating the cognitive change amongst the teachers in the classrooms towards children belonging to Dalit communities after the session on reading, writing and reflection based on the study materials and the self-narratives. In light of this question, the teachers were encouraged to ask the children to write an essay on their favourite animal during language class by giving them examples of two types of animals. Before initiating this exercise in the classroom, the teachers intensely discussed the types of animals to suggest to the children, and they collectively decided on the cow and the pig as the essay topics.

First, all the students who participated in the essay writing exercise had an option for an essay on the pig. The experiential knowledge narrated by a sizable section of the children who had written their essay on the pig stunned their teachers. The children not only eloquently described the features of the pig but also narrated in detail the benefits that accrue to their parents from pig rearing. The children explained that the sale of pigs is instrumental in fulfilling the financial needs of the family during periods of economic crisis. The teachers quickly grasped that the essays on the pig were written by the children primarily belonging to the Musahar community.

It is worth noting that across schools in northern India when children are required to write an essay on their favourite animal, it is expected that they will most likely write their essay on the cow. This excludes children from Dalit communities, whose parents mostly raise pigs and not cows. The most disturbing aspect of this practice is the fact that the teachers believe that this is a straightforward choice for an essay topic; they are not even aware of their own ideological vantage point which is reproduced in the classrooms on a day-to-day basis.

The unexpectedly detailed essays written by the Dalit children prompted reflection amidst the non-Dalit as well as Dalit teachers on their own opinions about the cognitive ability of the children. Not just that, they also critically reflected on their own implicit assumptions about the learning and cognitive ability of the Dalit children, and this critical play of reflections changed their perceptions on their past notions of educability and learning amongst Dalit children in general and the children belonging to the Musahar community in particular. They also realised that information and knowledge have a social and cultural context against which they are propagated, rather than having its origin in individual mental activity or heredity-based educability.

The way forward: practice and policy implications

How to radically transform the conventional methodology is a major implication of the action research for enabling the teachers to reflect on their own beliefs and assumptions on the notion of educability and create a democratic space at CRCs in general and schools in particular. A prerequisite condition in this would be to urgently employ an appropriate approach in order to engage the teachers, headmasters and teacher trainers through conversation, one-on-one discussions, small-group meetings and workshops adhering to the basic principles of the egalitarian dialogue.[3] It is a concept in dialogic learning. It may be defined as a dialogue in which contributions are considered according to the validity of their reasoning, instead of according to the status or position of power of those who make them. A new kind of methodology represents a class of dialogue practices developed as a means of orienting the dialogic discourse towards understanding problems and consensual action. A critical analysis of the change processes in the teachers' belief in hereditary educability during the action research project showed that the conventional methodology of the teacher training programmes is based on the principle of a hierarchical and unidirectional transmission of information in which teachers are passive recipients of the instruction from the teacher educators and the administrators.

Similarly, how teachers form the groups, how they plan the lessons, what form the relationship between the trainees and the trainers should take and how trainees present their learning would be leading questions for the development of techniques and methods of a participatory teacher training programme.

In this context of building perspectives and techniques of the methodology for social behaviour change among the teachers based on egalitarian dialogues, it is important to keep in mind that the teachers and the headmasters of the rural schools generally come from peasant and low- and middle-rural-income backgrounds. Their primary method of expression and learning has been largely oral and dialogical in nature, rather than written and formal since childhood, and as a consequence, their cognitive thinking is better attuned to the narrative verbal mode rather than a rigidly structured, written mode.

The preparation and the content development and its design are one of the practice and policy implications which emerged through the processes of the action research. In this context, the social, economic, educational and cultural background of the children, their parents and the communities constitute the basic parameters of content development. It is essential that both quantitative and qualitative reading materials like empirical research, case studies, innovative practices, etc., are made available for the teachers and their educators that orient them to not only understand the social, economic and educational context of the children but also realise that key factors of the educational failure of the children emanate from the deeply ingrained social and structural inequality in society. It is equally important that teachers and teacher educators discern the nature of the learning needs and constraints of the children from diverse backgrounds from a critical perspective in order to facilitate and guide them in the classrooms on a day-to-day basis.

There is an urgent need to create a mandatory space in the content of teacher education and training in order to understand key concepts in education, pedagogy and learning. Concepts such as cognition and learning, social constructivism of learning, inclusive classrooms and social diversity, notion of educability and child-centred learning, etc., not only would contribute to building the perspectives of the teachers and the teacher educators but would also provide the context for dealing the questions and challenges faced in the classrooms today.

Rather than introducing a pre-determined content and design of the training, the practice and processes of the action show that understanding the content design is a prerequisite condition for the policymakers, educationists, development practitioners, teachers and headmasters, who would be indispensable partners in the content development. It appears very appropriate that the basic processes involved in content design would be semi-structured and flexible in order to let the training team and educators assimilate the critical learnings and experiences emerging during the course of the training and ensure their preparedness for integrating new concepts, issues and questions into the content design.

Certainly, a tool in an integrated form, bringing together the content and the design of the training, is urgently needed for teachers and teacher educators.

Against this background, it is worth considering that the training manuals and tools that have been prepared and developed by the Department of Education and the government of Bihar in coordination with the State Council for Educational Research and Training have failed to address the cognitive development, learning constraints and educational failure of children, especially those who belong to the marginalised communities, from the perspectives of critical pedagogy. This failure of the government is institutional, and the teachers and teacher educators have remained unsuccessful in building a critical understanding which would equip them to resolve the problems and challenges of the contemporary schools and classrooms and orient them to engage with the same constructively and meaningfully.

An initiation of the in-service training at the CRC level informed by the findings of the action research project and its suggested implications for the policies and practices would be a modest beginning, and the journey undertaken by a civil society organisation would have a larger impact, reaching 4,500 CRCs in Bihar, where approximately half a million teachers are participating in the in-service training programme.

Undoubtedly, Bihar, which is well known as a state for the politics of social justice, would be the first state in India to initiate a teacher education and training programme informed by the *perspective from below*.

Notes

1 In the context of karma theory, *sanskara* are dispositions, character or behavioral traits, that exist as default from birth or prepared and perfected by a person over one's lifetime, that exist as imprints on the subconscious according to various schools of Hindu philosophysuch as the Yoga school. These perfected or default imprints of karma within a person, influences that person's nature, response and states of mind. https://en.wikipedia.org/wiki/*Sanskara*_(rite_of_passage). In common parlance, *sanskara* is popularly referred as attributes of hereditary, hierarchy and status in the context of caste which determines that lower castes have absence of the *sanskara* and higher castes are endowed with the *sanskara*.
2 The origin of Musahars, which are known by different names in Bihar and its adjoining states, has still remained debatable. In colonial ethnographic works they have been related to different tribes both within and outside the region. While Nesfield (1888) linked their origin to the Kol and Cheru tribes of Chotanagpur based on legendary myths of 'Deosi,' Risley's (1891) hypothesis based on the etymological explanation of the word Musahar (rat-eater or 'rat-catcher') traces their origin to the equally Dravidian Bhuiyas of southern Chotanagpur. Indian ethnologist S.C. Roy (1935a, 1935b) links their origin to the independent section of the old 'Desh Bhuiyas' or 'Pauri Bhuiyas' in the tributary state of Orissa. For a detailed discussion on this see Prakash (1990).
3 For details about the basic principles of the dialogue, refer to https://en.wikipedia.org/wiki/Dialogue

References

Biswas, M. M. (2015). *Surviving in my world growing up Dalit in Bengal.* Kolkata: Stree.

Byapari, M. (2018). *Interrogating my Chandal life: An autobiography of a Dalit.* New Delhi: Sage.

Bechain, S. S. (2017). *My childhood on my shoulders.* New Delhi: Oxford University Press.

BRC. (2013). *Annual enrolment register of school children in block Wazirgaj, 2013–14.* Gaya: BRC.

Census of India. (2011). *Primary census abstracts.* New Delhi: Census of India.

Deshkal Society. (2011). *Toolkitforteachers_Hindi_DFID.* Available at: www. deshkalindia.com/img/reports/1.%20Toolkit%20for%20teachers_Hindi_%20 DFID-%2026–8–2011.pdf (Accessed on 12 June 2018).

———. (2013a). *Baseline survey report on out of school children in block Wazirganj (Gaya).* Delhi: Deshkal Society.

———. (2013b). *Survey on social diversity and learning achievement. The status of primary education in rural Bihar.* Delhi: Deshkal Society.

Govinda, R. ed. (2002). *India education report.* New Delhi: Oxford University Press.

Krishna, M. M. (2012). Pedagogic practice and the violence against Dalits in schooling. In: C. Sleeter, et al. eds., *School education, pluralism and marginality: Comparative perspectives.* New Delhi: Orient BlackSwan.

Nambissan, Geetha B. (2001). Social diversity and regional disparities in schooling: A Study of Rural Rajasthan. In: A. Vidyanathan and P. R. Gopinathan Nair eds., *Elementary education in rural India: A grassroots view.* New Delhi: Sage.

Naorem, T. and Ramachandran, V. (2013). A synthesis of a six-state qualitative study: What it means to be a Dalit or tribal child in our schools. *Economic and Political Weekly,* 48(44), 02 Nov., 2013.

Nesfield, J. C. (1888). The Musheras of central and upper India. *The Calcutta Review,* 171.

NUEPA and MHRD. (2014). *State Report Cards 2013–14,* New Delhi: NUEPA and MHRD, Department of School Education and Literacy, p. 13.

Ojha, L. B. ed. (2003). *Dalit, adivasi and school.* Bhopal: Samavesh.

Palshaugen, O. (2006). Dilemmas of action research-an introduction. *International Journal of Action Research,* 2(2), pp. 149–162.

Prakash, G. (1990). *Bonded histories: Genealogies of labour servitude in colonial India.* Cambridge: Cambridge University Press.

PROBE Report. (1999). *Public report on basic education in India.* New Delhi: Oxford University Press.

Risley, H. H. (1891). *Tribes and castes of Bengal,* 2 vols. Calcutta: Bengal Secretariat Press.

Roy, S. C. (1935a). *Hill Bhuiyas of Orissa.* Ranchi: Man in India Office.

———. (1935b). Report of anthropological work in 1930–31: Chotanagpur, the Chutias and Bhuiyas. *Journal of the Bihar and Orissa Society,* 18.

SCERT. (2008). *Prakhand Sansaadhan Kendra evam Sankul Sansadhan Kendra Samanyavak: Margdarshika.* Patna: SCERT.

Singh, P. D. and Kumar, S. (2010). *Social hierarchy and notion of educability*. Delhi: Deshkal Publication, pp. 36–37.

SRRI. (2014). Social and Rural Research Institute, *National Sample Survey of Estimation of Out-of-School Children in the Age 6–13 in India*, Available at: https://mhrd.gov.in/sites/upload_files/mhrd/files/upload_document/National-Survey-Estimation-School-Children-Draft-Report.pdf (Accessed on 20 June 2018).

Tiwary, M., Kumar, S. and Mishra, A. K. (2017). *Dynamics of inclusive classroom social diversity, inequality and school education in India*. New Delhi: Orient Blackswan.

Valmiki, O. P. (2003). *Joothan*. Delhi: Rajkamal Prakashan, p. 53.

Velaskar, P. (2005). Education, caste, Gender'. Dalit girls. Access to schooling. *Maharashtra. Journal of Educational Planning and Administration*, 19(4), pp. 459–482.

Chapter 9

Consensualised reproduction and the fascised rule of capital

The responsibility of critical pedagogy[1]

Ravi Kumar

Consensualisation as a process is not one way in which the masses are passive recipients and the hegemonic interests work overtime to establish their ideas as the dominant ones. It is rather a more complicated process in which the hegemonic class interests work their way through ideas, which might *appear* inimical to them and through agencies (of masses) that might *appear* opposed to it. For instance, the pedagogical defeat of the radical critical political masses lies in the fact that they have not been able to understand the significance of *processes* and have failed to conceptualise the idea of subversion as going beyond moments in which they are born. In fact, subversion's radical potential embedded in the moment might turn out to reflect the status quo in long run when it gets co-opted within the system. Hence, the defeat also lies in a failure to recognise the fact that one loses sight of the designs of the system. The teacher in the classroom contributes to consensualisation in favour of the ruling class by not only ignoring the illustrations from the lives of the majority of the exploited and oppressed but also by not bringing the anti–status quo within the classroom. (One can debate how to bring those aspects into the classroom.) In this sense, consensualisation is more an act of the reactionary hegemon. It is implemented by the workers as well by not knowing that their actions will affect their own individual interests in the long run. This is also ensured by the unrelenting effort of capital to individualise, thereby not only fragmenting resistance against capital but also ensuring that it flourishes. It is also not an individual human being but a constitution of individual identities. So, the teachers do not struggle along with other workers within the given institutions, despite the same oppressive institution reducing them to paupers. They are fragmented not only as different types of workers but also as workers with different social affiliations, as if their being a worker is determined primarily by their 'social' affiliation, which is, undeniably, a significant element that constitutes the *being* of the worker (but not the only one). In other words, there is a fragmentation of the *being*, as social, political and cultural, without any sense of a dialectical connection constituting the being (as an individual human or the individual collective identity). Teacher as worker is therefore not a subject without any social or cultural complexities.

The teacher is constituted through this complex process wherein its labour power is up for sale, and therefore it also surrenders itself to the rule of capital in the absence of any collective resistance, as well as due to its compulsion to survive. Because the struggle is to survive and it enforces an *apparent* willingness, this act of surrender appears willing. Capitalism, through processes of commodification, intensifies this process as it brings everything gradually into the realm of exchange. Teachers held a prestigious position at one stage in the development of capitalism; however, that position no longer exists as digitised forms of knowledge replace the need for human teachers. Along with digitisation the student realises that she has paid a sum of money to get into the school and stay there. Hence, the teacher is a mere service provider, not an agent involved in a dialogic education. This was illustrated recently when I encountered this reality in the field.

In a parent–teacher meeting (PTM) in a private school, the teacher asked the parents how should the students or their parents be punished when they did not do their homework. She felt that taking away the 'games period' was a good way to punish the students because that is the class they love the most. (Obviously, the question would be why do they dislike the other classes.) But how should parents be punished? The crowd dispersed without any conclusion. In a group of parents, who are also teachers in private schools, we discovered that the students in Classes IX onwards hardly do their homework, and the teachers have stopped castigating them for this because they realised it is safer not to confront them due to fear of losing 'respect'. One of the teachers said that these students do not think of teachers as anything more than a service provider. From their behaviour towards teachers, one can make out that they are aware of their position as consumers who pay to get the services they want from teachers. This can be understood as a logical trajectory of mindless privatisation of school education, from the philanthropic organisations running schools to business houses doing it. The moment education is brought within the realm of the market, it works like any other commodity, assuming a life of its own. This is only aggravated when the idea of teaching-learning is taken away from the human realm to that of machines – when mobile applications assume the role of teachers. It not only demeans the significance of the teacher in the process of learning but also creates a situation of extreme pauperisation for teachers as a group, which is dependent on the logic of market.

At the level of pedagogy, this takes an interesting form. The pedagogical apparatuses are more and more found in the realm of the digitised world, where the humans are being taught through different forms of 'social' media. This dependence has taken away the possibility of a critical engagement embedded in the idea of dialogue. The teacher-worker's role has become crucial, as well as much more difficult. She needs to work overtime to engage a student who is not only learning mathematics from a mobile application but is also absorbing an uncritical understanding of nation, nationalism, economy and social relations in general.

The teacher and the students and their relationship need to be understood in the larger context of the economy and politics of capital. The imagination of an education system – whether a school or higher education institution – for capitalism is nothing beyond producing a skilled labour force for the kind of work that it requires. Hence, it develops an education system wherein students are evaluated as per numerical marks that they get in examinations, and those marks are manipulated to such an extent that a student easily manages to get 100 out of 100 in social sciences and humanities. These are the same students who are not required to develop a critical understanding of the world around them. In other words, the design is to mould education in such a way that it remains a tool of skill building that suits the needs of the market. It ceases to be a playground of harnessing creative and critical potential. This is effective for capital in times of crisis as well because it contains the possibilities of resistance and allows consensualisation of different kinds to take place to sustain and further the rule of capital. The teacher-worker becomes a party to this, given its location and given the absence of a political alternative that imagines pedagogy differently.

The attack of capital on the labour in general to labour in particular

On 7 November 2014, the president of India approved three labour law amendment bills sent by the government of Rajasthan after getting them passed in the assembly (Jha, 2014). These amended labour laws (namely the Industrial Disputes Act 1947, the Contract Labour Act 1970 and the Factories Act 1947) have become more business friendly. It would also mean that they are more anti-labour. The Indian government is interested in changing the labour laws as part of its central legislations, and among other pending bills it wants to get through the Parliament are the Industrial Relations Code Bill 2016 and the Wage Code Bill 2016.[2] Once passed, these will facilitate easier hiring and firing in factories. The Indian state wants this change because it would boost economic growth (Nanda, 2017) (and I always wonder at whose cost!). The same governments who want to withdraw whatever benefits of labour laws that the workers have also create high unemployment by taking away their jobs, as the whole employment scenario becomes precarious. On the other hand, the nature of capitalism, which would inevitably get stuck in one kind of crisis or the other, has led to the creation of jobs (which are counted by census as employment), which are 'momentary' in nature (and I am not even inclined to use the word 'temporary' here), what in the UK are called 'precarious' jobs. McDonald's shuts down shops in many Indian cities until further notice due to various reasons (Montgomery and Iyengar, 2017); there have been massive layoffs in the IT sector (which will continue the in days to come, as argued by many economic analysts);[3] the job loss in general has been there as well.[4] All these developments, if combined with the worsening labour conditions, do not paint a good picture for India's working class. Pauperisation would grow along with a very skewed income/wealth inequality, as statistics also seem to be indicating.

This was a general question of labour, but if one turns towards the teachers, one finds that 13.18% of teachers at the primary and secondary schools are contractual (non-permanent) and the forms of the contracts vary. This would come to a whopping 1,064,434 in absolute numbers. There are states with as high as 54% (Mizoram, in northeast India) of the teachers being contractual (Mehta, 2016). This trend looks likely to worsen. It is in this situation that one finds a state like Bihar announcing that it will 'compulsorily' retire 'non-performing' teachers above the age of 50 years (A. Kumar, 2017). On the other hand, the Rajasthan government has decided to give away the government schools to the private sector.

> As per the policy, 75% schools in rural areas and 25% schools in urban areas will be identified on the basis of their recent results and will be given to private players who have to pay Rs. 7.5 million for operating each school. The state government will reimburse the amount over a seven-year period time at Rs 1.6 million per annum. Another Rs 20,000 would be reimbursed to the private parties as expenses per student.
>
> (Rawal, 2017)

One cannot have a better example of throwing open the schooling system to the forces of the market and therefore an inevitable shutting down of the government schooling system. This would also imply that the workers teaching in schools will be as much at the mercy of capital as those working in the soap factories. Marx sounds so true here when trying to make sense of productive labour, he gives the example of the schoolteacher. He writes:

> Capitalist production is not merely the production of commodities, it is essentially the production of surplus-value. The labourer produces, not for himself, but for capital. It no longer suffices, therefore, that he should simply produce. He must produce surplus-value. That labourer alone is productive, who produces surplus-value for the capitalist, and thus works for the self-expansion of capital. If we may take an example from outside the sphere of production of material objects, a schoolmaster is a productive labourer when, in addition to belabouring the heads

of his scholars, he works like a horse to enrich the school proprietor. That the latter has laid out his capital in a teaching factory, instead of in a sausage factory, does not alter the relation. Hence the notion of a productive labourer implies not merely a relation between work and useful effect, between labourer and product of labour, but also a specific, social relation of production, a relation that has sprung up historically and stamps the labourer as the direct means of creating surplus-value. To be a productive labourer is, therefore, not a piece of luck, but a misfortune.

(Marx, 1887)

The number of private schools is increasing, which inevitably has worsened working conditions due to its direct effort at surplus maximisation. There can be different ways to understand the growing privatisation of the school, as well as higher education. One way to look at it is by studying the enrolment figures in the government as well as private schools, and the other way to understand privatisation is by looking at the number of institutions. National Sample Survey Organisation (NSSO) data show that between 2007–08 and 2014 the percentage distribution of students in government primary schools has come down to 62% compared to the earlier figure of 72.6%. On the other hand, the same figures have gone up for the private aided schools (private schools who also get government support), from 6.5% in 2007–08 to 8.1% in 201,4 and the increase in the share for the private unaided schools (schools not financially supported by government) has gone to 29.7% from 20.3% (NSSO, 2014: 69). In terms of the number of private schools, between 2010–11 and 2015–16 a total of 77,063 private schools have appeared in India as opposed to 12,297 government schools (Kingdon, 2017). One can see similar trends for private unaided upper primary and secondary schools as well. The same is true for technical/professional institutions in the higher education sphere, where most students study in private unaided institutions. Even the government schools have adopted contractualisation as a policy decision to hire teachers. There are federal states which have not hired regular teachers for decades. Now federal states like Rajasthan have been handing over the state-run schools to private players (Rawal, 2017).

Higher education is not better off. The number of private institutions has gone up, and the 'normalisation' of informalisation of the labour force has led to worse working conditions. Although the number of private universities in March 2012 was 111, it went up to 235 in March 2016, that is, it more than doubled in four years (UGC, 2016: 88). The number of colleges run/managed by private entities is much more when compared to government-run colleges. The number of private unaided colleges is 22,755, and private aided is 4,924 (the total number of private colleges is 27,679), whereas the number of government colleges is only 7,988 (GoI, 2016). Along with this, and as a natural corollary, one finds informalisation of the workforce in universities and schools. So, one finds a huge number of teachers in schools, faculty members in colleges and universities and the non-teaching workers being employed on a temporary, contractual basis. Their salaries are lower than what a regular, permanent worker would get, and they can be fired anytime. This allows for a cheap labour workforce and curtails possibilities of unionisation due to the extreme insecurities imposed on them.

So, something like this also happens:

An institution gets someone from a well-known university to teach some professional courses, such as Bachelor of Education. It calls for applications for jobs as per the UGC norms, which is not a bad salary compared to most of India's working population. People apply and get jobs as well. Because the Indian state is committed to rooting out corruption, fund leakages, etc., a bank account with Aadhar[5] has to be opened and so on and so forth. Being a staff member of a faculty seems a good enough job. But what happens when the salary gets transferred to your account? One finds that all documents of the faculty are with management. They transfer money as per the UGC scale into your account but then also force you to issue them some cheques to pay back what they have been given to show the authorities. This and many more innovative mechanisms are developed, not exceptionally, but on a large scale.

Although these issues are related to income and economics, there is an increasing surveillance, non-involvement of faculty in designing the courses or indirectly, etc., making life much more difficult in the higher education system. Therefore, the teacher as a worker and the school as the institution, with all its dimensions such as curriculum and pedagogy, must be located within the labour–capital dialectic.

The lurking danger: fascism and fascisation?

Why talk about fascisation? Are we living in a fascist state? These are tough questions to answer because of the complex situations that we encounter today. One can immediately get back to history and look at the fascism of the Auschwitz variety and immediately conclude that India is still far from it. But on the other hand, one finds oneself trapped in a dilemma when one after another dissenting voice is murdered along the likes of what the Nazi SS or the Gestapo would do. There is a clear similarity between the global assertion of the Right (Hill, 2018) and what is happening in India. This has led to debates about whether India can be called a fascist state. Ever since the right-wing Bharatiya Janata Party (BJP) came to power, quite a few intellectuals have been targeted. Govind Pansare, a communist leader, was killed in 2015; M. M. Kalburgi, the noted Kannadiga writer and a rationalist, was also killed the same year. Then in 2017, the anti-right journalist Gauri Lankesh was gunned down. Now the renowned intellectual and a staunch critique of the Brahmanical order, Kancha Illaih, has been getting death threats. Apart from these, a new trend of public mob lynching, primarily of Muslims, has emerged.

> Muslims were the target of 51% of violence centred on bovine issues over nearly eight years (2010 to 2017) and comprised 86% of 28 Indians killed in 63 incidents, according to an India Spend content analysis of the English media.
>
> As many of 97% of these attacks were reported after Prime Minister Narendra Modi's government came to power in May 2014, and about half the cow-related violence – 32 of 63 cases – were from states governed by the Bharatiya Janata Party (BJP) when the attacks were reported, revealed our analysis of violence recorded until June 25, 2017.
>
> (Abraham and Rao, 2017)

There has been a virtual erasure of any autonomy of the judiciary and executive, with some exceptions. Government has openly voiced its opinion to have say in the appointment of judges to the highest courts, and the right-wing leaders have been made into Indian state icons, ending the era of liberal capitalist iconography, examples being Deen Dayal Upadhyay, Nanaji Deshmukh (who was closely associated with the right-wing Rashtriya Swayamsevak Sangh) and so on. The party in power hounds any dissenter, even of the liberal variety, with active support from instruments of the state. Universities have been under great attack, with vice-chancellors dictating the terms of running it, centralising all powers. Any academic who works from a left perspective, specialises in gender studies and is vocal about her beliefs and analysis, or even if anyone does a negative analysis of the current government, has been hounded (R. Kumar, 2017). In debates scholars have called this a neo-conservative tendency, which for them works at three levels: first, as 'the circumscription, the attempt to straightjacket students', teachers' and professors' practices'; second, as centralised enforcement by state apparatuses; and third, as 'cultural wars' through use of ideological apparatuses (Hill, 2006). So, it might appear that India's situation today is not fascistic but authoritarian. It is in this context that there have been debates of whether to call this situation fascist.

Karat writes that

> Fascism as an ideology and as a form of political rule emerged in between the two World Wars in the 20th century. When the capitalist system was engulfed in deep crisis and faced with the threat from a revolutionary movement of the working class, the ruling classes in Germany opted for an extreme form of rule that abolished bourgeois democracy.
>
> (Karat, 2016)

Consensualised reproduction   161

When in power, fascism becomes 'the open terrorist dictatorship of the most reactionary, most chauvinistic and most imperialist elements of finance capital'. Based on the fact the conditions for the emergence of fascism – 'in political, economic and class terms' – are not present because the ruling class is not confronted with any imminent danger of its collapse, neither is Indian capitalism facing a crisis, and no section of the ruling class is working for the overthrow of the bourgeois parliamentary system. It would therefore be difficult to call the current state of affairs as fascist. Rather, 'what the ruling classes seek to do is to use forms of authoritarianism to serve their class interests' (Karat, 2016). All the restrictions that we encounter today are the ones imposed by the neoliberal order, Karat argues. He goes on to say that under fascism, elections are redundant, but in India they are very important.

He is confronted by Jairus Banaji (2016), who argues that treating fascism as entirely about 'finance capital' ignores the formation of culture and looks simply at the economy as a force that affects politics without mediations of any sort. He goes on to say that

> Anti-Semitism, racism, xenophobia, Islamophobia, Islamism, Hindutva, patriarchy, male violence, caste oppression, militarism, and (not least!) nationalism then become basically irrelevant; window-dressing on a beast (capitalism) that works in some purely economic way, as if the 'formation of the authoritarian structure' (Reich, 1946) which has everything to do with how reactionary ideologies come about in the wider reaches of civil society is not a process every bit as material as the economy.
>
> (Banaji, 2016)

He argues how would one understand the mass violence against Muslims, the compromised justice system, the corporate support for a 'decisive leader' or use of nation and nationalism as instruments to whip up frenzy. He writes

> While all authoritarianisms are not fascist, all fascisms are a form of authoritarianism. What is distinctive about fascist authoritarianism is its appeal to forms of mass mobilisation and attempt to create sources of legitimacy among 'the masses' – through cultural (e.g. pseudo-religious) and ideological domination.
>
> (Banaji, 2016)

A significant question is also posed when Banaji asks whether fascism comes all of a sudden or if there are processes which go into the making of this final culmination of the fascist state. There is a mass mobilisation which fascism is able to generate, and this happens through a variety of mechanisms – from the use of cultural symbols, playing with ideas of 'nation' and 'nationalism', etc. Wilhem Reich writes that

> Since fascism, always and everywhere, appears as a movement which is supported by the masses of people, it also displays all the traits and contradictions present in the average character structure: Fascism is not, as is generally believed, a purely reactionary movement; rather, it is a mixture of rebellious emotions and reactionary social ideas.
>
> (Reich, 1946: 5)

Even within Marxism there have been at least three theories of fascism. The first one, which Renton calls the 'the left theory of fascism', looked at 'the conditions of its growth'. This theory considered 'the purpose and function of fascism, as a form of counter-revolution acting in the interests of capital' important. Renton's critique of this theoretical strand has been that it failed to talk about the specifics 'about fascist counter-revolution', which did not allow the Italian or the German Communist parties to take it as a serious threat. 'The second, or right theory of fascism' took the opposite approach of 'ignoring the rise and function of fascism, and examining instead its ideology, and the mass, radical character' of the movement (Renton, 1999: 3). So, for Marxists looking at it, fascism became 'radical and exotic, outside and threatening to capital'. Consequently, 'the Italian and German Socialist Parties in the 1920s and 1930s, and the Communist Parties after 1934, described capitalism itself as a bulwark against fascism, and stood paralysed and unable to act when members of the ruling class allied with fascism' (Renton, 1999: 3). Renton goes for the third theory, which he calls the 'dialectical theory of fascism', developed by Leon Trotsky. This theory treated fascism as both a reactionary ideology and a mass movement (Renton, 1999: 4). He accepts that there is a resurgence of fascism today (and he is writing in the European context) and that this would grow. The features that he highlights can be found in India as well, and this grows out of the crisis that capitalism faces in its smoothly functioning. In other words, the fascist possibilities might be latent and become manifest when the survival question for capital becomes important. Renton writes

> Fascism thrives on bitterness and alienation, both of which capitalism nourishes with regular doses of unemployment and crisis. This fuels despair, which further stimulates fascism to grow. Fascism lives off racism, sexism and elitism, while capitalism promotes its own prejudices, guised as common-sense beliefs, which seem to fit people's experiences, while effectively holding them back from challenging the system. Capitalism generates the myths of racism and elitism, which fascists use for themselves.
>
> (Renton, 1999: 16)

Ghosh (2016) argues that fascism becomes a political regime

> constitutive of the mobilisation of objective revolutionary possibilities, which inhere in increasing subalternisation of the masses, against the liberal form of the capitalist state precisely in order to reproduce that state by recomposing the political form of its embodiment. (The state, we would do well to realise here, is nothing but the institutionalised congealment of the value-relational grammar of social relations.) In this process, it cannibalises the earlier liberal-institutional form of the state. This unambiguously reveals why Fascism is a mystification of revolution and is, therefore, a counter-revolution.

It is in this sense that fascism, as an expression of unrest/discontent among the masses, can be understood. Reich traces it to the individual and his cravings, which would lead him to be part of the collective mobilisations that fascism creates. He writes

> Fascist mentality is the mentality of the subjugated 'little man' who craves authority and rebels against it at the same time. It is not by accident that all fascist dictators stem from the milieu of the little reactionary man. The captains of industry and the feudal militarist make use of this social fact for their own purposes. A mechanistic authoritarian civilization only reaps, in the form of fascism, from the little, suppressed man what for hundreds of years it has sown in the masses of little, suppressed individuals in the form of mysticism, top-sergeant mentality and automatism.
>
> (Reich, 1946: 6)

Riley (2016) works on Gramsci and believes that fascism, for him,

> represented for Italy and Germany their belated and terribly distorted version of the French Revolution. There was an undeniably 'modernizing' element to these regimes that was fused with their attack on the Left, and with their racist imperialism.
>
> (Riley, 2016)

Posing his understanding of the contemporary right wing, he remarks that 'increasingly, profitability requires direct political support (bailouts, austerity programs, and so on). This undermines the operation of "liberal democracy," which has been the 'central political and ideological cement of the capitalist class across the advanced world since 1945' (Riley, 2016). If this has been the case, then does it also not imply that the capital seeks to connect more and more to the masses directly now for a variety of reasons? There ought not be too many mediating agencies between the state and the people. The presence of mediating agencies raises questions about the conduct of the state and its relationship with the corporate capital, so that the processes of accumulation can work unhindered and when crisis emerges it can tackle them directly. An authoritarian, fascist regime can create this simple-looking, straightforward, uncomplicated relationship to have the autocracy of capital.

However, this fascism is also not of the same form as we saw in early 20th century because it lacks the energy of the earlier avatars. Riley attributes this to the absence of an opponent such as the Soviet Union. But can one say that it creates new oppositions such as the Muslims, the communists, so-called anti-nationalists and the dissenters? Within nation-states, there is a weak or absent opposition to capital, which can mobilise the masses, and that is also the reason why the right does not have similar energy. But this right continues to proceed conquering the popular imagination.

Obviously, the question that comes to one's mind is how does one understand the India of today? Despite the talks of a country unhurt by the economic recession that affected the United States, is it a country where, if one goes by the accounts of bourgeois/liberal intellectuals, everything is fine? It doesn't seem so. In an age of unreality, despite the spectacle of governance aided by the untruth-spinning doctors of diverse disciplinary backgrounds, the crisis seems to be looming large. This crisis experienced by the people beneath the spectacle must be tackled as soon as possible. It could burst into an upheaval anytime, as shown by the ILO study (ILO, 2011). There has always been an impending crisis – generated by the asymmetry between aspirations and income due to alienation of the worker from the product created through the processes of surplus accumulation. The new labour processes, which brought about newer techniques of appropriating surplus under different idioms such as 'opening up', 'liberalising', 'competition', 'efficiency', etc., also created a crisis in the individual lives of workers. We are still realising on a mass scale the manifestations of this crisis which have established linkages between the household and work place at an unprecedented scale and brought the tension, alienation and repression of the workplace into the very 'private' lives of the workers and their families. This impending manifestation can take different forms – from a rebellion against capital to a rebellion/diversion of energy towards a violent state of being, resulting in support for a sectarian, fascist political force. It is the corporate capital understanding the fragility of situation that wants a 'decisive' leader and government, somebody who does not listen to anybody but himself, not even his party and his associates, thus setting into motion a process of the fascisation of society – individuals and institutions alike. The similarities between the way Indian state today functions and the way university vice-chancellors work are quite similar. The tragedy is that they do it with the support of the masses. The online world of concern that we encounter seems disconnected in their thought from that of the masses. The online anti-right

Consensualised reproduction 165

presence does not seem to reflect a similar sensibility on the ground. This is reflected in the absence of mass mobilisations even when something like demonetisation happens or when Muslims are repeatedly lynched. It would be worth understanding from where the consensualised popular support for the Right emerges. It is this consensualisation that is allowing capitalism in its present form to be reproduced.

Consensualisation to reproduce the rule of capital

How and why does consensus get created? There are many ways in which this happens. It is relevant to bring in Althusser (1971) here, who argued that capitalism, in order to survive, must reproduce the conditions of production. What does this mean? It simply means at one level that in order to live longer, every social formation must reproduce (1) the productive forces and (2) the existing relations of production. Hence, the system must reproduce the labour power through payment of wages, which is necessary for the survival of labour. However, because the society is not static and is constantly progressing, this labour power cannot remain static. It has to be 'competent'. The teacher of yesteryears is useless today. She or he cannot teach today because of a lack of competence. The skills need to be constantly updated and enhanced. But then the question arises as to how this labour skill gets reproduced.

> Unlike social formations characterized by slavery or serfdom, this reproduction of the skills of labour power tends (this is a tendential law) decreasingly to be provided for 'on the spot' (apprenticeship within production itself), but is achieved more and more outside production: by the capitalist education system, and by other instances and institutions.
> (Althusser, 1971: 132)

These institutions which reproduce skills also simultaneously ensure the reproduction

> of submission to the ruling ideology for the workers, and a reproduction of the ability to manipulate the ruling ideology correctly for the agents of exploitation and repression, so that they, too, will provide for the domination of the ruling class 'in words',
> (Althusser, 1971: 132–33)

Children learn what is 'good behaviour' (which is defined as 'the attitude that should be observed by every agent in the division of labour, according to the job he is "destined" for: rules of morality, civic and professional conscience, which actually means rules of respect for the socio-technical division of labour and ultimately the rules of the order established by class domination' (Althusser, 1971: 132), and this 'goodness' is defined as per the requirements of the larger system.

The education system is nothing but an instrument which seeks to create propitious conditions for capital to exist and expand. It is in these terms that it is important to locate education as 'an aspect of the class relation', which is involved 'in generating the living commodity, labour-power whose consumption in the labour process is a necessary condition for the social existence of the class relation between labour and capital in contemporary capitalism' (Allman et al., undated). If one recognises this aspect, the conceptualisation of the education and critical education would also be different and, hence, it has a lasting impact on our vision of how education is to be located.

The consensus, which is being created by capital right now, is based on this logic of reproduction. The schooling system, as well the higher education system, is dedicated towards this consensus-building exercise. This consensualisation process becomes even more complex when one looks at how the technology is used to exercise control and domination over our minds. Marcuse had amply shown how the techno-bureaucratic system exercises this control, which does not lead us to think the way we should have thought, but rather we think the way capitalism wants us to think. This use of technology reflects how social relationships are designed. He writes that

> Technology, as a mode of production, as the totality of instruments, devices and contrivances which characterize the machine age is thus at the same time a mode of organizing and perpetuating (or changing) social relationships, a manifestation of prevalent thought and behavior patterns, an instrument for control and domination.
>
> (Marcuse, 1998: 41)

He goes on to elaborate on the consensualising efforts of the system, which makes us a one-dimensional man, an entity bereft of any independent mind, a representation of the state, with a loss of criticality. This is achieved through elements of fear that the system generates amongst us – fear of different kinds ranging from our own neighbour who is a Muslim to a neighbouring country or the fear of our livelihood being taken over by communists. And technology is woven into this to such an extent that it makes us support authoritarianism, corporate sharks and the mindless race for nuclear warfare. We become part of the designs of the capitalist state, even the fascist state, when there is no place for fear to exist.

> In National Socialist Germany, the reign of terror is sustained not only by brute force which is foreign to technology but also by the ingenious manipulation of the power inherent in technology: the intensification of

Consensualised reproduction 167

labor, propaganda, the training of youths and workers, the organization of the governmental, industrial and party bureaucracy – all of which constitute the daily implements of terror – follow the lines of greatest technological efficiency. This terroristic technocracy cannot be attributed to the exceptional requirements of 'war economy'; war economy is rather the normal state of the National Socialist ordering of the social and economic process, and technology is one of the chief stimuli of this ordering.

(Marcuse, 1998: 41–42)

This situation of a relentless war against teaching-learning, against the workers involved in this process, necessitates the need to imagine and re-imagine the educational processes in such a way that we begin destroying this system. And the role of critical pedagogy becomes significant here.

The working class must enter the pedagogical war

The process of consensualisation and the process of reproduction are also pedagogical processes unleashed on the masses to ensure that capitalism, the rule based on inequality and exploitation, thrives. Pedagogy is used to ensure that all children not only become part of this process but accept the fact of surplus accumulation as given, inevitable and the best possible framework to live in and survive. It is in this context that it prepares either so-called neutral masses or those who believe that there is no alternative to the way things are conducted. The task of this pedagogy is to demonstrate the beauty of exploitation, the absence of hope and the impossibility of an alternative. But Shaull says that

There is no such thing as a neutral educational process. Education either functions as an instrument that is used to facilitate the integration of the younger generation into the logic of the present system and bring about conformity to it, or it becomes 'the practice of freedom,' the means by which men and women deal critically and creatively with reality and discover how to participate in the transformation of their world. The development of an educational methodology that facilitates this process will inevitably lead to tension and conflict within our society. But it could also contribute to the formation of a new man and mark the beginning of a new era in Western history.

(Shaull, 2005: 34)

Hence, there has to be a counter-position of how the critical pedagogy looks at education and of its practices vis-à-vis that of capitalism (which is fascising today). That alternative imagination of education must be formed with rigour and vigour to counter the educational blasphemy of the ruling classes. But the challenge also is that there are too many alternative pedagogies in front of us and whether they (1) root themselves in the processes of production and recognise the linkage between educational processes and the exploitative social relations and (2) whether they confront the exploitative system with a pedagogy which also talks of altering the existing social relations based on and emanating out of the processes of accumulation. These pedagogies/visions must be used to demonstrate the cracks in the existing system as well. bell hooks argues that the school must reveal to the students what the social realities are, and how those realities come into existence must constitute a fundamental part of the teaching-learning process. However, the schooling system is not designed to be like that. It hides those realities because they might produce subversive humans who would challenge the status quo. Hence, the school as an institution must produce obedient humans. She writes:

> School changed utterly with racial integration. Gone was the messianic zeal to transform our minds and beings that had characterised teachers and their pedagogical practices in our all-black school. Knowledge was suddenly about information only. It had no relation to how one lived, behaved. It was no longer connected to antiracist struggle. Bussed to white schools, we soon learned that obedience, and not a zealous will to learn, was what was expected of us. Too much eagerness to learn, was what was expected of us. Too much eagerness to learn could easily be seen as a threat to white authority.
>
> (hooks, 1994: 3)

This would seem so true of the oppressed groups in any part of the world – the marginalised castes, ethnicities and gender, as well as classes in any part of the world. She goes to the extent of drawing the linkages between the production process and the hegemonic schooling/education system, but argues against the existing framework based on her experience as a black student how the schooling system made even the blacks reinforce the domination of the white hegemony. She brings in the element of *excitement* as a subversive category when she argues that excitement is

> viewed as potentially disruptive of the atmosphere of seriousness assumed to be essential to the learning process. To enter classroom settings in colleges and universities with the will to share the desire to encourage excitement, was to transgress. Not only did it require movement beyond accepted boundaries, but excitement could not be generated without a full recognition of the fact that there could never be an absolute set agenda governing teaching practices. Agendas had to be flexible, had to allow for spontaneous shifts in direction. Students had

Consensualised reproduction 169

to be seen in their particularity as individuals . . . and interacted with according to their needs.

(hooks, 1994: 7)

Because of its hegemonic ideas, the education system ensures that everyone gets drawn into its project of shaping the world, and it does not acknowledge the presence of marginalised students in the class. This can be seen in the case of EWS students in the schools, or the Dalits, or even girls. hooks argues that

> any radical pedagogy must insist that everyone's presence is acknowledged' and this insistence 'has to be demonstrated through pedagogical practices'. In a critical pedagogical practice 'there must be an ongoing recognition that everyone influences the classroom dynamic, that everyone contributes. These contributions are resources. Used constructively they enhance the capacity of any class to create an open learning community.
>
> (hooks, 1994: 8)

For scholars like Henry Giroux, the critical pedagogy develops out of

> a recognition that education was important not only for gainful employment but also for creating the formative culture of beliefs, practices, and social relations that enable individuals to wield power, learn how to govern, and nurture a democratic society that takes equality, justice, shared values, and freedom seriously.
>
> (2011: 4)

Critical pedagogy is about transforming knowledge and therefore becoming active agents in the process of this transformation, which is much more than merely consuming it.

There are scholars who would state that from the way education is to be understood as located within the universe of capital–labour relations and therefore the idea of an alternative, critical pedagogy also has to emanate from there. Because the system is mechanical, because it is dehumanising, because it is teaching hatred, because it is making children averse to having a sense of history that locates them and their previous generations in a context of strife and struggle for survival, there has to be a critical pedagogy that questions these dangerous trends by reconstituting its own vision – by bringing forth the idea that dreams are essential for envisioning, that daydreaming, as Ernst Bloch taught us, can be a way to ascertain imaginations to work on. He says

> It is a question of learning hope. Its work does not renounce, it is in love with success rather than failure. Hope, superior to fear, is neither

170 Ravi Kumar

passive like the latter, nor locked into nothingness. The emotion of hope goes out of itself, makes people broad instead of confining them, cannot know nearly enough of what it is that makes them inwardly aimed, of what may be allied to them outwardly.

(Bloch, 1996: 3)

The daydreams can be 'provocative, is not content just to accept the bad which exists, does not accept renunciation', and it is 'has hoping at its core, and is teachable'. It is this hope that the relations of production that have brought them into this state of being can be altered, that the world of misery and exploitation can change and that this process of change does not stop anywhere, as many 'leftists' in past believed, but it is a continuous process.

If critical pedagogy is imagined as hoping and imagining, against a mechanical process that simply prepares an individual to be subservient to the system, then it is for a radical social transformation as well. McLaren (1999: 32–33) argues that critical pedagogy must have the 'capacity to foster the principle of social justice and to propel this principle into the realm of hope, so that it might arch towards the future in a continuing orbit of possibility' will not be achieved. McLaren and Farahmandpur go on to say that in the process of doing this critical pedagogy it

> offers a historical challenge to helplessness and despair. Its strength also resides in its singular ability to make resignation implausible and defeat untenable, despite the criticism launched by some that would immobilize critical pedagogy by dismissing it as 'always already' trapped within a modernist voice of sovereign authority and totalizing certitude. Critical pedagogy functions as a form of critical utopianism that reveals the birth of tomorrow out of the struggle of today. . . . Yet it needs to recognize its own provisionality, and to caution itself against prematurely bringing closure to the narrative of emancipation. The politics of the imagination upon which critical pedagogy is based also requires that we imprint our collective will on the workings of history. What the left needs is not a republic of dreamers isolated from class struggle but a contraband pedagogy, a profane pedagogy and educational brigandism for the next century, one capable of forging new tactical possibilities for pressing forward the project of social democracy and setting limits to the reign of capital. It is this unalloyed commitment to critical agency.
>
> (McLaren and Farahmandpur, 2005: 32–33)

[C]ritical pedagogy needs to establish a project of emancipation that moves beyond simply wringing concessions from existing capitalist structures and institutions. Rather, it must be centred on the transformation of property relations and the creation of a just system of appropriation and distribution of social wealth. It is not enough to

Consensualised reproduction 171

adjust the foundational level of school funding to account for levels of student poverty, to propose supplemental funding for poverty and limited English proficiency, to raise local taxes to benefit schools, to demand that state governments partly subsidize low-property-value communities, or to fight for the equalization of funding generated by low-property-value districts (although these efforts surely would be a step in the right direction). I am arguing for a fundamentally broader vision based on a transformation of global economic relations – on a different economic logic, if you will – that transcends a mere reformism within existing social relations of production and international division of labor. But challenging the swaggering, gunslinging, frontier-style economic practices of the tycoon capitalism that we are witnessing today must also be accompanied (as Giroux argues) by a powerful cultural critique that can speak forcefully to the creation of antiracist, antisexist, and antihomophobic pedagogies of liberation.

(McLaren and Farahmandpur, 2005: 31)

This understanding of critical pedagogy also emanates from an understanding that education makes capitalism possible. It is not only a cultural handiwork to teach hatred to children, but it is located in a context of labour–capital relations where teaching hatred is required by capital because it feels threatened by the possible eruptions against its misdeeds. It is precisely because of this that pedagogy within classrooms is asking us to read texts of a particular kind, why teachers of a particular kind are being appointed in universities and schools and why refresher courses are being redesigned as well. Outside these institutions the pedagogical significance of advertisement lies spread through social media and technological advancement used to dislocate and relocate the figures of leaders, which is another of pedagogy. But to ensure that this is carried out in the most effective way, the education system is proving dangerous to them, because sitting here we all are also talking about critical pedagogy and something called neoliberalism. There is a need to change this body of people called teachers because they can be dangerous as well.

[B]ecause education and training socially produce labour-power, and there are real limits to this process, this is a source of labour's strength as well as its tragic predicament. On the latter, the tragedy of labour results from the fact that labour creates its own opposite (capital) that comes to dominate it. . . . Indeed, it creates something that permeates its own soul in the form of human capital. On the other hand, teachers and trainers are implicated in socially producing the single commodity – labour-power – on which the whole capitalist system rests. This gives them a special sort of social power. They work at the chalkface of capital's weakest link: labour-power. Hence, they have the capacity to work with Red Chalk . . . to open up visions of alternatives to capitalism in the classroom, or at least provide vital critiques of its violent class relation and market inequalities. Teachers are in a special position regarding their capacity to disrupt and to call into question the capitalist class relation. Furthermore, teachers can also insert principles of social justice into their pedagogy, principles that are antithetical to the generation of the class divide and also market and social inequalities.

(Allman et al., undated)

The war is on – those with access to resources, technologies and all kinds of weaponry are out there to fight. The counter-offensive is weak because the understanding of the situation itself is very superficial. To fight fascism, we go back to the liberals, as Gramsci puts it,

The worker, the peasant, who for years has hated the fascism that oppresses him believes it necessary, in order to bring it down, to ally himself with the liberal bourgeoisie, to support those who in the past, when they were in power, supported and armed fascism against the workers and peasants, and who just a few months ago formed a sole bloc with fascism and shared in the responsibility for its crimes. And this is how the question of the liquidation of fascism is posed? No! The liquidation of fascism must be the liquidation of the bourgeoisie that created it.

(Gramsci, 1924)

Hill (2017) intervenes in this whole debate in an extremely sharp manner, when he succinctly points out that being critical means 'teachers should be actively involved in the fights for economic and social justice, that they should be critical, organic, public, socialist, transformative intellectuals, who are activists'. He goes on to define each of these concepts:

Critical means just that – being suspicious, questioning, interrogating, not accepting prima facie evidence, digging deeper, with a commitment to social and economic justice.
Organic is being part of, knowing about, living, and representing the class/section of the class we are representing.
Public means going public, speaking out, and defying intimidation.
Socialist means being egalitarian, working for an egalitarian, and non-capitalist society, where the wealth (such as 'the commanding heights of the economy' – banks, industry, and public utilities) of the country is owned collectively.
Transformative means using out abilities, teaching, membership, and leadership to critique and work towards reconstruction.

Then he says that we are not merely intellectuals, but we are 'socialist critical transformative intellectuals whose responsibility is 'to offer intellectual stimulus, analysis, utopianism, hope, vision – and an analysis of how to get there – organization.' Located within the labour–capital dialectic is the position of the teacher and the task of critical pedagogy. However, this location remains non-effective unless there is a conscious responsibility taken upon the self by the critical educators to act towards the goal of a non-exploitative, non-oppressive social and economic order. Unfortunately, that is where the left educators fail in their own different ways. Being an organised Left, they have not created a well-thought-out critical pedagogy as per the debates outlines earlier and developed critical voices that become participants in the anti-systemic struggles. Or they have confined their analysis to how the powerful space of education – classroom or institutions – is not leading to the logical culmination of how those spaces become part of street struggles. This inability to *go beyond* has also led to making universities into a separate set of battlegrounds, and India is a good example of how over the last decade or so universities have lost most of their battles against the system, because the support base of those struggles always remains confined within the boundaries of intellectuals and does not spill onto the streets and societies outside of it. If fascism or any form of authoritarianism is to be fought, the correct measure of the battleground has to be made – it is more than the universities. It is everywhere, and as critical educators, this understanding would lead to better strategisation of fights against the system that has created a complex web of consensualising mechanisms – within as well as outside the educational institutions.

Notes

1 I am thankful to Dave Hill and Jyoti Raina for their comments. It has helped me to reflect on certain aspects, which were completely left out. This chapter is an expanded version of an article titled 'Consensualised Reproduction and the Fascisation of Society: Critical Pedagogy in Times of Despair' that appeared in the *Journal of Critical Education Policy Studies*, Vol. 15, No. 3.
2 The labour laws can be changed at both levels. In the federal structure, different federal governments have the right to change the labour laws within their own territories and for the industrial units that come under their purview, whereas the central/national government has to change the laws for the units that come under its purview.
3 For related information see: http://economictimes.indiatimes.com/tech/ites/it-to-layoff-up-to-2-lakh-engineers-annually-for-next-3-years-head-hunters-india/articleshow/58670563.cms; https://thewire.in/157093/1-5-million-jobs-lost-2017-demonetisation/; www.livemint.com/Industry/4CXsLIIZXf8uVQLs6uFQvK/Top-7-IT-firms-including-Infosys-Wipro-to-lay-off-at-least.html
4 www.bloombergquint.com/business/2017/06/27/india-may-see-more-job-losses-over-next-decade-low-skill-jobs-skill-development
5 Aadhar is a national identification number allotted to each individual to which there are massive oppositions, but the government is forcing it upon people. Some

of these views can be found at https://scroll.in/article/832595/privacy-security-and-egality-are-not-the-only-serious-problems-with-aadhaar-here-are-four-more; https://thewire.in/119323/real-problem-aadhaar-lies-biometrics/; https://thewire.in/136102/coercion-aadhaar-project-ushar/

References

Abraham, D. and Rao, O. (16 July 2017). 86% killed in cow-related violence since 2010 are Muslim, 97% attacks after Modi govt came to power. *Hindustan Times*, Available at: www.hindustantimes.com/india-news/86-killed-in-cow-related-vio lence-since-2010-are-muslims-97-attacks-after-modi-govt-came-to-power/story-w9CYOksvgk9joGSSaXgpLO.html (Accessed on 13 September 2017).

Allman, P., McLaren, P. and Glenn, R. (undated). *After the box people: The labour-capital relation as class constitution – and its consequences for Marxist educational theory and human resistance*. Available at: http://citeseerx.ist.psu.edu/viewdoc/download;jsessionid=BFDEFE6FFB000D946CB816F6B4B0BC0A?doi=10.1.1.202.59&rep=rep1&type=pdf (Accessed on 12 May 2017).

Althusser, L. (1971). *Lenin and philosophy and other essays*. New York and London: Monthly Review Press.

Banaji, J. (12 September 2016). Stalin's Ghost Won't Save Us from the Spectre of Fascism: A Response to Prakash Karat. *Sabrang*. Available at: www.sabrang india.in/article/stalin's-ghost-won't-save-us-spectre-fascism-response-prakash-karat (Accessed on 15 September 2016).

Bloch, Ernst. (1996). *The Principle of Hope* (Translated by Neville Plaice, Stephen Plaice and Paul Knight) Vol. I. Massachusetts: MIT Press.

Ghosh, P. (23 February 2016). Fascism or Dictatorship of Neoliberal Capital? The Need for a Correct Line. *Radical Notes*, Available at: https://radicalnotes.org/2016/02/23/fascism-or-dictatorship-of-neoliberal-capital-the-need-for-a-correct-line/ (Accessed on 10 May 2017).

Government of India. (2016). *All India survey on higher education (2015–16)*. New Delhi: Department of Higher Education, Ministry of Human Resource Development, Government of India.

Gramsci, A. (1924). *Neither fascism nor liberalism: Sovietism!*. Available at: www.marxists.org/archive/gramsci/1924/10/fascism-liberalism.htm (Accessed on 16 June 2016).

Hill, D. (2006). Class, Capital and Education in this Neoliberal/Neoconservative Period. *Information for Social Change*, 23. Available at: http://libr.org/isc/issues/ISC23/B1%20 Dave%20Hill.pdf (Accessed on 15 May 2017).

———. (5 January 2017). The Role of Marxist Educators Against and Within Neoliberal Capitalism, *Insurgent Scripts*, Available at: http://insurgentscripts.org/the-role-of-marxist-educators-against-and-within-neoliberal-capitalism/ (Accessed on 20 March 2017).

———. (2018). Marxist education against capitalism in neoliberal/neoconservative times. In: L. Rasinski, D. Hill and K. Skordoulis eds., *Marxism and education: International perspectives on theory and action*. New York and London: Routledge.

Consensualised reproduction 175

hooks, b. (1994). *Teaching to transgress: Education as the practice of freedom.* New York and London: Routledge.

International Labour Organisation. (2011). *World of work report 2011: Making markets work for jobs.* Geneva: International Labour Organisation.

Jha, S. (9 November 2014). President okays Rajasthan labour reforms: Firms with 300 workers need no govt nod to sack (State expects more investment as industry cheers move). *Business Standard.* Available at: www.business-standard.com/article/economy-policy/president-okays-rajasthan-labour-reforms-firms-with-300-workers-need-no-govt-nod-to-sack-114110801356_1.html (Accessed on 10 May 2017).

Karat, P. (6 September 2016). Fight against BJP cannot be conducted in alliance with the other major party of the ruling classes. *Indian Express.* Available at: http://indianexpress.com/article/opinion/columns/india-nda-government-narendra-modi-bjp-right-wing-hindutva-3015383/ (Accessed on 8 September 2016).

Kingdon, G. G. (March 2017). *The private schooling phenomenon in India: A review.* Discussion Paper Series, IZA-Institute of Labor Economics: Bonn.

Kumar, A. (3 August 2017). Bihar government to compulsorily retire non-performing teachers, officials above age of 50 years. *The Hindustan Times,* Available at: www.hindustantimes.com/india-news/bihar-govt-to-compulsorily-retire-non-per forming-teachers-officials-above-age-of-50-years/story-uDSKFNw2lZuc2cnHN0 jT1J.html (Accessed on 4 August 2017).

Kumar, R. (10 September 2017). Victory of Left Reflects JNU's Resistance to BJP's Campaign to Alter the DNA of Indian Varsities. *The Wire.* Available at: https://thewire.in/175931/victory-left-reflects-jnus-resistance-bjps-campaign-alter-dna-indian-varsities/ (Accessed on 10 September 2017).

Marcuse, H. (1998). Some implications of modern technology. In: K. Douglas, ed., *Technology, war and fascism (collected papers of Herbert Marcuse).* New York: Routledge.

Marx, K. (1887). *Capital: A critique of political economy,* Vol I. Available at: www.marxists.org/archive/marx/works/1867-c1/ch16.htm (Accessed on 12 June 2017).

McLaren, P. (1999). Traumatising capital: Oppositional pedagogies in the age of consent. In: P. McLaren, ed., *Critical education in the new information age.* Lanham: Rowman & Littlefield, pp. 1–37.

McLaren, P. and Farahmandpur, R. (2005). *Teaching against global capitalism and the new imperialism: A critical pedagogy.* Lanham: Rowman & Littlefield Publishers, Inc.

Mehta, A. C. (2016). *Analytical tables 2015–16: Progress towards UEE.* New Delhi: NUEPA.

Montgomery, M. and Iyengar, R. (22 August 2017). Closed until further notice: Most McDonald's restaurants in India's capital. *CNN Money.* Available at: http://money.cnn.com/2017/06/29/news/india/mcdonalds-india-delhi-stores-closed/index.html (Accessed on 22 August 2017).

Nanda, Prashant K. (12 September 2017). NDA plans new push for labour reforms. *Live Mint,* Available at: www.livemint.com/Home-Page/nnOHLRpsWxkGk80 J2sHW 2L/NDA-plans-new-push-for-labour-reforms.html (Accessed on 12 June 2017).

NSSO. (2016). *Education in India, NSSO, 71st Round (January–June 2014)*. New Delhi: Ministry of Statistics and Programme Implementation.

Rawal, Urvashi Dev. (Sep 08, 2017). Rajasthan government's move to privatise school education draws flak. *The Hindustan Times*, Available at: www.hindustan times.com/education/rajasthan-govt-s-move-to-privatise-school-education-draws-flak/story-Xgn0kcAElbfH9eefJ8U8IK.html (Accessed on 8 September 2017).

Reich, W. (1946). *The mass psychology of fascism* (English translation by Theodore P. Wolfe). New York: Orgone Institute Press, Inc.

Renton, D. (1999). *Fascism: Theory and practice*. London: Pluto Press.

Riley, D. (19/08/2016). Fascism and Democracy. *Jacobin*, Available at: www.jacobin mag.com/2016/08/trump-clinton-fascism-authoritarian-democracy/ (Accessed on 12 February 2017).

Shaull, R. (2005). Preface. In: P. Freire, eds., *Pedagogy of the oppressed*, 30th ed. New York: Continuum.

University Grants Commission. (2016). *Annual Report 2015–2016*. Delhi: University Grants Commission.

Chapter 10

A strategy for exclusion

How equality and social justice have been derailed in Indian elementary education

Madhu Prasad

The GoI has been claiming over 98% enrolment at the elementary level as a great achievement following the implementation in April 2010 of the RTE Act 2009. Several state governments have made similar declarations. However, before these claims are accepted as constituting some kind of significant milestone in the Universalisation of Elementary Education, it is necessary to clarify certain core conceptual features.

The universalisation of school education (even if currently limited at the elementary level, i.e. up to Class VIII) is not primarily a question of reaching a *numerical* target, whether as a pre-determined goal or as an objective that is practically achieved. It is in fact a fundamental component of *a conception of society in which all sections of the population, including children, have equal rights and claims on the state, not merely to protect those rights but also to ensure that they are realized in ways that comply with the principles of equality and justice.*

In contemporary neoliberal conditions where all aspects of social and personal life are rapidly becoming commoditised and subjected to evaluation and control only by their 'worth' as market values, this may sound like a rather grandiose overstatement inflating both the nature of rights and the role of the state. However, historically it can be shown to be the basis of intellectual, social and productive developments that have shaped society for over 200 years.

The opening sentence of Descartes's *Discourse on Method* (1638) states 'Reason is of all things the most evenly distributed by Nature among all men', which lies between the earlier notion of 'privilege' and the *modern* conception of 'right', which is both universal and plural – that is, it applies universally *across all differences between individuals*. Descartes asserts the species-specific ability to reason, and hence to choose, as the basis for the integrity and authenticity of human action. He does not privilege particular forms of reasoning – although he does state that his personal experience and the history of his times led him to adopt and further evolve the empirical-experimental scientific method for acquiring knowledge – but sees the ability itself as determining the character and quality of all *specifically* human action. When all humans are naturally capable of choosing, and hence attaching value to their actions, then the *theoretical* dependence on status or wealth, religious dogma or political power diminishes and the possibility arises of envisaging individual freedom, agency and hence rights.

This fundamental idea evolved in the philosophy of social contract theorists like Thomas Hobbes and John Locke into the conception that all citizens are free by virtue of being *naturally* in possession of their own capabilities and hence have the right to pursue their own goals and satisfactions. Freedom is knowledge of and control over things, the objects of satisfaction, and not control or domination over others. Society is therefore not conceived as a pre-destined hierarchical structure, but as the product of a contract amongst free and equal individuals. Locke, however, extended this *freedom* to an individual's right to 'alienate' any of her capacities by selling them to another. This brings the concept of the market into a central role, both as the site of the creation of inequalities and as the cause of one's being deprived of one's right to the 'fruits of one's labour'. It also makes this market transaction the basis for justifying the accumulation of capital in the hands of a class that could now use its 'domination over things' for acquiring 'domination over others' who, once deprived of the right to the product of their labour, become dependent on the owners of capital for exercising their productive capacities.

By the nineteenth century, support for the right to private ownership of capital justified the inequality inherent in the capitalist mode of production and the dominance of the market in determining the exchange value of *commodities*, rather than the intrinsic value of objects for the satisfaction of human wants.

The progress towards the formation of the modern state was an outcome of the growing primacy of the market which necessitated the 'secularizing' of the economic, social and political functions that had frequently evolved and remained within the ambit of powerful religious institutions. The hegemony of the church was also weakened by the pre-eminence of reason and the growth of scientific knowledge as an instrument furthering productivity and trade. Eventually, the secular state would emerge as the provider for, and defender of, the rights of its citizens.

From the mid-nineteenth century onwards, industrialising nations placed the responsibility for providing education on the modern states that developed with the rise and consolidation of capitalism in order to fulfil both the productive and democratic requirement not only for a better educated labour force but also one that was freed from the bondage of landlord–serf relations. From these prerequisites of the conditions of production under capitalism, there arose the possibility of the socio-historical actualisation of the idea of individual freedom, articulated during the Enlightenment.

However, the contradiction inherent between the objective interests of the capitalist ruling class and the dispossessed working class exposed the supposedly harmonious and 'contractual' nature of the organisation of society. The concepts of right, equality and justice became problematised.

Fredrick Engels (1845), who upheld the rationale of the demand that the state make educational provisions for a democratic, better educated working class – a view embedded in the modern rights-based perspective – also indicated the conflicting contours of the now-problematised concepts of liberty and equality:

> [The] general education of all children without exception at the expense of the state – an education which is equal for all and continues until the individual is capable of emerging as an independent member of society . . . would be only *an act of justice* . . . for clearly, *every man has the right to the fullest development of his abilities and society wrongs individuals twice over when it makes ignorance a necessary consequence of poverty.*
>
> (253, emphasis added)

More than 170 years later, this idea appears to have lost none of its force. There can be no universalisation of education without prioritising equality. Without the conception that every child has a right to receive an education, the impetus for universalising education is no longer there.

Emphasising that no country had successfully ended child labour without first making education compulsory, Myron Weiner noted in the 1990s that the development of Asian states that had made education compulsory – Japan in 1872, the two Koreas, Taiwan and China after WWII – was founded on successfully taking up

> the legal obligation of the state to provide an adequate number of schools, appropriately situated and to ensure that no child fails to attend school.
>
> (Weiner, 1994: 87)

All were poor states when they undertook the task, and their future development was based on this firm foundation. Modern states have a serious regard for every child's right to education, treating it as a legal duty devolving upon the state: 'parents are required to send their children to school, children are required to attend school and the state is required to enforce compulsory education'. The state is bound to protect children from the compulsions on impoverished parents and from would-be exploiters (Weiner, 1991, 1994).

For countries like India, the attempt to *leap-frog* over the democratising phase of ascendant capitalism, with its concomitant increased employment and mass provision of essential social services such as education, health, public utilities, etc., and to adopt the contemporary phase of neoliberal jobless growth with the accompanying privatisation and corporatisation of all essential services based on user-paid principles of efficiency, has resulted in a massive exclusion of those who *simply cannot afford to pay*.

This exclusionary phase of neoliberalisation constitutes a qualitatively distinct form of intensification of the exploitation and deprivation of the people, one that does not carry even the fig leaf of a justification and harshly exposes the *social irrationality of bare market transactions*.

This chapter seeks to plot the phases and repercussions of this fundamentally contemporary sense of 'exclusion' which has not only excluded the disadvantaged persons from access but also conceptually and politically *de-legitimized* and *shrunk*

1 existing sites of debate, dissent and resistance against a *perceived* oppression and discrimination;
2 the autonomy and self-governing capacity of the people; and
3 the democratic unity of society constituted as a nation.

This de-legitimisation raises several questions. How has it distorted the constitutional right to equality and justice that the Indian people had 'given unto themselves' when they constituted themselves into a republic in 1950? We need to explore and uncover the relation between this process and the attacks on constitutional rights and values launched by the present regime and its Hindutva supremacist ideological and organisational leadership in the Rashtriya Swayamsewak Sangh (RSS). We also need to examine and comprehend the convergence of the deeply anti-democratic and retrogressive idea of a *Hindu Rashtra* (Hindu state), with the predatory needs of international and national finance capital in their contemporary neoliberal phase.

Pre-colonial exclusions and colonial subjugation

Traditional hierarchies of caste and status severely restricted the aspiration and opportunity for the majority of people to educate themselves. Within the dominant Brahmanical system, caste determined access to education, as its purpose was the inculcation of such norms and practices as were appropriate to a pre-determined upper-caste station in society. The presently much eulogised traditional 'guru-shisya' relation between a teacher and his students was a pedagogical system imminently suited to its caste orientation, but is completely out of place, and even undesirable, within a democratic conception of society and education. At best, it could be dismissed as a piece of traditional sentimentality; at worst, it signals the persistent failure to break with hierarchical and highly discriminatory caste stratifications typical of a feudal social order. Although Muslim elites and British colonizers had no cultural affinity or religious empathy with the system, the stability of the caste system, even under the medieval and colonial regimes, has been attributed to the ease with which surplus could be extracted as tax from 'isolated' village communities constituted through caste divisions.

In India, the role of British colonialism has frequently been lauded as the engine of modernisation with little understanding of the impact of the predatory nature of imperialism:

> It is a startling but too notorious a fact, that, though loaded with a vastly greater absolute amount of taxation, and harassed by various severe acts of tyranny and oppression, yet the country was in a state of prosperity under the native rule, when compared with that into which it has fallen under the avowedly mild sway of British administration . . . it is, I believe, ability which has diminished . . . of late years a large portion of the public revenue has been paid by encroachment upon the capital of the country, small though that capital is in itself. I allude to the property of the peasantry. . . . In short, almost everything forces the conviction that we have before us a narrowing progress to utter pauperism. . . . Most of the evils of our rule in India arise directly from, or may be traced to, the heavy tribute which that country pays to England.
> (Marriot, 1846)

Under such circumstances, the lag between the technological modernity required by colonial economic interests and the spread of modern consciousness and practices in society was only to be expected. Undeniably, the introduction of the railways in April 1853 represented a significant step towards the technological 'modernization' of the country, but we ignore or forget at our own peril that Dalits and the 'lowered castes', to use B. R. Ambedkar's extremely perceptive terminology, were prohibited from drinking water from the 'common' facilities provided for the public at railway stations.

The East India Company's (EIC's) early educational initiatives at the level of higher education followed both caste strictures and religious divisions. The Calcutta Madrasa (1781) for Muslims and Benaras Sanskrit College (1791) for Brahmins were established by Warren Hastings and John Duncan, respectively, and followed the traditional Islamic and Vedic curricula. It was only with the establishment of the Delhi and Agra Colleges (1823–24) that 'open' admissions were allowed and that Oriental literature, science, history and jurisprudence were taught, along with mathematics and modern science. These apparently 'modern' features, for the introduction of which colonial rule is usually credited, in fact continued a practice prevalent in the madrasas of the region, which was still under the cultural influence of the Mughal court. Large numbers of Hindus, in particular from the Khatri and Kayastha upper castes, who were denied higher education as it was traditionally restricted to the Brahmins, were drawn to these schools of Persian literature, science and jurisprudence and went on to serve the Mughal and other native courts with distinction.

> The Persian schools are the most genuine educational institutions in the country. They are attended largely by the Khatris, the Hindus forming a greater proportion than the Muhammadans.
>
> (Arnold, 1922: 290)

The colonial policy for education, the first in the sub-continent to be determined by a trading corporation, was communicated through a despatch (29 September 1830) of the EIC's court of directors. It contained the exclusionary policy that would be advocated in its entirety in Macaulay's infamous Minute of 1835. Promotion of English as the principal medium of instruction was aimed at creating 'an elite class of learned natives' trained in European science and literature, who would 'communicate *a portion* of this improved learning to the Asiatic wider classes'. The government in India was instructed to 'use every assistance and encouragement, pecuniary or otherwise', including a declared preference in government employment, to further this goal.

> We wish you to consider this as our deliberate view of the scope and end to which all your endeavours with respect to the education of the Natives should refer.
>
> (Howell, 1872: 20–21)

The political strategy motivating this policy had extremely negative intellectual consequences. It cut the links of those who received this new 'education', with English medium and curriculum, from classical Oriental learning and not just from the traditional feudal elites who had patronised it. The attitude of the traditional cultured classes, particularly at Delhi where the learning, aesthetic and tastes of the Mughal court remained vibrant well into the twentieth century, was evident in the comment of Urdu poet and writer Altaf Hussain Hali[1]:

> [I]n the society in which I was raised . . . English education was not seriously regarded as learning . . . we regarded English as a means of getting a job, not an education.
>
> (Gupta, 1981: 7)

The promise of jobs in the government as a means of promoting the new education succeeded primarily in promoting 'baboo', i.e. clerical, culture. The term, a derogatory distortion of the word 'baboon', reveals the attitude of EIC officials towards the education and opportunities provided for Indians, as these were the only jobs open to 'natives'. The comparison between mimicking monkeys and native 'imitations' of colonial masters extended across South Asia and Africa.

> Dickens once said that he could never write the word (baboo) lest he should make it baboon. . . . That he (the baboo) should be created and then ridiculed is of a piece with the ideology of the cultural subjugation of colonial rule.
>
> (Chaudhary, 2002: 86)

Not surprisingly, one of the principal 'weaknesses of the native student' was identified as

> the strong temptation to lay aside his studies as soon as employment supplies his moderate necessities; the scanty inducement to fit himself for higher duties, – all help to dwarf the moral and intellectual growth. . . . His ambition waits upon his daily wants.
>
> (Education Commission, 1882: 300–4)

The company's policy that the common madrasa practice of providing stipends – to encourage education amongst those who could not afford private education at home – be abolished and that students pay fees undoubtedly aggravated this tendency. The gap between India and early leaders in years of schooling, such as the United States and Germany, increased from less than 2 years in 1870 to 7.8 years in 1950 (Lee and Lee, 2016). The resulting constraints and limitations of both content and access remained embedded in later colonial educational policy, ensuring that as late as 1921 only 11% of India's population was even literate.[2]

Education for all and the struggle for national independence

The demand for universalising four years of elementary education had been raised in an Appeal to the Education Commission (1881) by the nationalist economist Dadabhai Naoroji to substantially lessen the poverty resulting from colonial policy. In an extract from his influential pamphlet, *The Poverty of India* (1878), comprising papers read before the Bombay Branch of the East India Association in April and July 1876, he argued that British colonialism was leading to the general impoverishment of India's labouring masses: 'The EIC, on finding the provinces of Bengal and Behar continuously deteriorating', caused a long and minute survey of the condition of the people. This survey extended over nine years, from 1807 to 1816. The reports, however, lay buried in the archives of the India House, until Mr. Montgomery Martin (1834) brought them to light. He sums up the result of these official minute researches in the following remarkable words (vol. I:11):

> It is impossible to avoid remarking two facts as peculiarly striking – first, the richness of the country surveyed; and, second, the poverty of its inhabitants.

Before proceeding further, I must first say that the drain to which these great men have referred was much less than at present. I give the figures in Mr. Martin's words (12):

> The annual drain of £3,000,000 on British India has amounted in 30 years, at 12 per cent, (the usual Indian rate) compound interest, to the enormous sum of; £723,900,000 sterling. . . . So constant and accumulating a drain, even in England, would soon impoverish her. How severe, then, must be its effects on India, where the wage of a labourer is from two-pence to three-pence a day.

Naoroji drew further support for his position from Frederick John Shore, judge of the Civil Court and Criminal Sessions, Dist. Farrukhabad, who left the following account of the condition of the people:

> But the halcyon days of India are over; she has been drained of a large proportion of the wealth she once possessed, and her energies have been cramped by a sordid system of misrule to which the interests of millions have been sacrificed for the benefit of the few. . . . The grinding extortions of the English Government have effected the impoverishment of the country and people to an extent almost unparalleled.[3]

Jyotiba Phule's deposition before the Education Commission (1884: 140) also criticised the colonial government for financing education for the Brahmans and the children of the rich when the source of their revenue was the ryot.

> I wrote some years ago a Marathi pamphlet exposing the religious practices of the Brahmins and incidentally among other matters, adverted therein to the present system of education, which by providing ampler funds for higher education tended to educate Brahmins and the higher classes only, and to leave the masses wallowing in ignorance and poverty. . . . Perhaps a part of the blame in bringing matters to this crisis maybe justly laid to the credit of the Government. Whatever may have been their motives in providing ampler funds and greater facilities for higher education, and neglecting that of the masses, it will be acknowledged by all that injustice to the latter, this is not as it should be.

It is an admitted fact that the greater portion of the revenues of the Indian Empire are derived from the ryot's labour from the sweat of his brow. . . . A well informed English writer states that our income is derived, not from surplus profits, but from capital; not from luxuries, but from the poorest necessaries. It is the product of sin and tears.

In stark contrast, during the latter half of the nineteenth century and in the early twentieth century, rulers of Indian states spent twice as much per capita on education than British India, which had the lowest public expenditure in the world between 1860 and 1912 (Davis and Huttenback, 1986). The Maharajas of Kohlapur[4] and Baroda,[5] the Begums of Bhopal[6] and individuals like Savitribai Phule and Fatima Sheikh were engaged in radical endeavours opening up education for all, including lower castes and girls.

Education and the politics of an independent citizenry

A qualitative leap forward was taken at the Nagpur session of the Indian National Congress (INC) in 1920, which called upon students to withdraw from existing colonial schools and colleges to join the freedom struggle. It also called for the setting up of nationalist educational institutions. The idea that a system of education providing equality of opportunity and propagating values of patriotism, rather than encouraging empire worship, could become an instrument of social transformation became an integral part of nationalist thinking. The proceedings of the Wardha Conference (1937) on *Nai Talim* (New Education) were formulated in the Zakir Husain Committee Report, which recommended a system of free and compulsory education in the mother tongue based on practical work as the pedagogical means to enhancing comprehension and generating knowledge. Accessible to *all* children for eight years and up to fourteen years of age, it was defined as 'equivalent to matriculation *minus* English *plus* craft' (Naik, 1975). Gandhi's 'plan to impart primary education through the medium of village handicrafts. . . (was conceived) as a silent revolution fraught with the most far-reaching consequences' (Acharya, 1997). Opposing the inherently elitist character of colonial education 'through craft, Gandhi wanted to impart knowledge on all important branches of knowledge' (Biswas and Aggarwal, 1994: 90).

At the Haripura session of the INC in 1938 it was resolved that the national system of education would be built on a 'wholly new foundation'.

The colonial administration was compelled to respond to this growing radicalisation with a fundamental reversal of what had in fact been a continuation of the EIC's policy perspective of restricting education to an Anglicised set of 'native' collaborators. The Report of the Central Advisory Board of Education (CABE), *Post-War Plan of Educational Development in India,* released in 1944 now declared that 'the minimum provision which could be accepted as constituting a national system postulates that all children must receive enough education to prepare them to earn a living as well as to fulfil themselves as individuals and discharge their duties as citizens'. Further, it argued that

> if there is to be anything like equality of opportunity, it is impossible to justify providing facilities for some of the nation's children and not for others . . . a national system can hardly be other than universal. Secondly, it must be compulsory, if the grave wastage which exists today under a voluntary system is not to be perpetrated and even aggravated. And thirdly, if education is to be universal and compulsory, equity requires that it should be free and common sense demands that it should last long enough to secure its fundamental objective.
>
> (Government of India, 1944: 3)

The Report of the B. G. Kher Committee on the *Ways and Means of Financing Educational Development in India* (1950) stated that universal compulsory education for the age group six to eleven years be provided in two Five-Year Plans, i.e. by 1960, and that for the age group eleven to fourteen years in the Third Five-Year Plan, i.e. by 1965. This recommendation shaped Article 45 under the Directive Principles of the Constitution (1950), mandating that the 'State shall endeavour to provide within a period of ten years from the commencement of this constitution for free and compulsory education for all children until they complete the age of 14 years'.

The demand for universalising free and compulsory education was taken up as an essential component of the Indian people's right to constitute themselves as an independent nation by repudiating traditional and colonial hierarchies of caste/class and race. Incorporating the notions of both selfhood and nationhood, it brought to the forefront the idea of the democratic rights of all citizens. Movements of workers, peasants, Dalits, tribals and women gained in strength and articulation. The constitution of the newly independent republic was itself the culmination of the struggle and set the standard for evaluating current policies, distinguishing between those that would strengthen and advance the freedoms it promised and those that undermined its potential by compromise, infringement or direct violation. Therefore, the very idea of a national system of education was a matter of great national significance and a major democratic advance.

Independent India's first Education Commission (1964–66), the D. S. Kothari Commission, which examined the failure to achieve the constitutional goal of education for all up to the age of fourteen years by 1960, recommended far-reaching structural changes for setting up a national system of free and compulsory education. This could not be left to private institutions like the elite schools

> transplanted in India by British administrators and we have clung to it so long because it happened to be in tune with the traditional hierarchical structure of our society. Whatever its place in past history maybe, such a system has no valid place in the new democratic and socialistic society we desire to create.
>
> (GoI, 1966: 138)

The report strongly advocated the establishment of state-funded common neighbourhood schools with a socially, culturally and economically diverse student body as the authentic institution of a pedagogically sound and egalitarian national system of education which would 'provide "good" education to all children because sharing life with the common people is, in our opinion, an essential ingredient of good education' (10.19). Echoing its logic, *The Report of the Committee of Members of Parliament on Education* (1967) asserted that

> the unhealthy social segregation that now takes place between the schools for the rich and those for the poor should be ended; and the primary schools should be the common schools of the nation by making it obligatory on all children, irrespective of caste, creed, community, religion, economic conditions or social status, to attend the primary school in their neighbourhood. This sharing of life among the children of all social strata will strengthen the sense of being one nation which is an essential ingredient of good education.
>
> (GoI, 1967)

This principle has recently been reiterated in a landmark ruling by the single-judge bench of Justice Sudhir Aggarwal of the Allahabad High Court (AHC), 18 August 2015. It underlines the fact that universal access to education has been consistently acknowledged for its democratic content and purpose. The judgment bases its conclusions on egalitarian principles and the pedagogical importance of *shared* schooling for children from all sections of society:

> It will also boost social equation. It will give an opportunity to children of common men to interact and mix-up with children of so-called high or semi high society. . . . *The initial level mixing among all children will have a different consequence.*
>
> (italics added)

It notes that the failure of the state to fulfil its constitutional and political obligation by not implementing the policy recommendations outlined decades ago has led to an unhealthy division of schools into 'elite', 'semi-elite' and 'common man's schools'. The division is based solely on privilege and wealth. It has no educational basis or social value in a democratic society, as it excludes 'almost 90% [of] children' from the so-called good 'public' schools which are in fact private enclaves of the rich and powerful. The judgment clearly states that if the process is reversed and government schools are strengthened and properly run, the private schools will become irrelevant.

The judgment identifies the increasing gap between the interests of the political and administrative powers-that-be (the governing elite) and the lives and concerns of the ordinary citizens of the country as the source of the problem.

> After more than 65 years of independence, these Schools are still struggling to have basic amenities for children, coming thereat, like drinking water, space for natural calls etc. . . . It is not difficult to understand, why conditions of these Schools has not improved. The reason is quite obvious and simple, though the State Government is not able to see. There is no real involvement of administration with these Schools. Any person who has some capacity and adequate finances, sends his child/children in Elite and Semi-Elite Primary School. They do not even think of sending their wards for primary education to . . . third category Schools, i.e. Common-men's Schools. The public administration therefore has no actual indulgence to see functioning and requirements of these schools.

The solution of enforced integration ordered by the directive of the court makes sense only when it is seen in this context. It cannot be seen as a denial of a democratic 'choice' available to powerful and affluent elites. The judgment argues that *this so-called 'choice' is the reason for the vast majority of India's children being denied their fundamental right to education and therefore it cannot be democratically defended.*[7] Hence, the Uttar Pradesh chief secretary was directed to ensure that 'the children/wards of Government servants, semi-Government servants, local bodies, representatives of people, judiciary and all such persons who receive any perk, benefit or salary etc. from State exchequer or public fund, send their child/children/wards who are in age of receiving primary education, to Primary Schools run by Board . . . and ensure to make penal provisions for those who violate this condition'.

The complete failure to make any progress towards achieving the constitutional goal even after the order of the AHC to implement it 'within a period of six months' i.e. from the next academic session, requires some accounting for.

Subversion of the radical goals of the freedom movement

The Indian capitalist class had begun to align itself with sections of the feudal landowning elite as the struggle for independence advanced and a future less dependent on British capital appeared on the horizon. The growing militancy of the working class and the peasantry in the 1920s, 1930s and 1940s did expand the foundations of the movement, but it also posed a threat to the consolidation of the Indian capitalist class as the ruling class after independence. The impact of the October Revolution in Russia in 1917 had an important political and intellectual influence in India. The Communist Party of India (CPI) was established in the 1920s, trade unionism grew rapidly and in 1936 the INC had to incorporate a programme for agrarian growth based on peasant cultivators and an end to landlordism to bring an impatient peasantry firmly within the ranks of the movement. The student and youth movements also exerted an important influence – the Bharat Naujawan Sabha (a left-wing movement to arouse worker and peasant youth in rebellion against the British Raj) was founded by Bhagat Singh and his comrades in March 1926, and the CPI's All India Students Federation (AISF) was established ten years later. Growing anti-fascist and pro-democracy ideologies gained in stature and strength through the late 1930s and 1940s.

The alliance with the landlord classes meant that the Indian bourgeoisie was 'open' – just as we find it currently 'opening up' to international finance capital at the cost of the people's interests – to compromising on the egalitarian goals of the freedom movement, particularly in two major areas. Land reforms were not implemented effectively across the country and hence accommodation with the Brahmanical ideology (despite powerful social justice movements in southern and western India), which sanctioned harshly exploitative caste divisions among the toiling masses, was a foregone conclusion. This uneasy partnership allowed both classes to enrich themselves economically and politically, but it was at the expense and ruin of the majority of peasants, artisans, tribals and working people.

Having failed to break out of the vicious cycle of caste/class oppression by its retreat from modern social ideals, the democratic goal of universalising school education that was at the core of the freedom movement's conception of a *modern* republican nation could never be achieved by India's bourgeois-landlord ruling elite. The egalitarian socialist ideals and powerful principles of social justice that inspired the freedom movement evaporated into mere slogans. Caste and class prejudices remained intractable, leading to a failure to break the linkage of 'privilege' with 'quality' inherited from the past and cast into a distorted elitism through colonial policy and practice. The attempt at the elementary level

> to extend to the poor people an education system basically meant for the well-to-do middle classes did not succeed and the rates of stagnation and wastage became disturbingly high.
>
> (Naik, 1975: 47)

The poor and the marginalised lacked not only the economic but also the socio-cultural wherewithal to take advantage of such a system. The diversity of the life experience of India's children became a stumbling block because of the failure of an elitist system of education to meet the challenge of this diversity.

Innovative policies, generously supported by the state and endorsed by society, were required to effect a transformation of the structure and content of the education system. Unfortunately, no pioneering attempts were made to engage creatively with the ideas thrown up by the *Nai Talim*. It was side-lined as an 'alternative model' exerting no influence on the dominant colonial structure of education. The education system inevitably sank into deep crisis. This was aggravated as state funding contracted and policy decisions continued to narrow access with multi-track discriminatory arrangements – alternative schools, multi-grade teaching, education guarantee centres, use of contractual and para-teachers – all of which served to exclude larger and larger sections of children from accessing an increasingly dysfunctional system of formal education.

Neoliberal reforms policy and the crisis in education

The 1993 judgment (*Unnikrishnan v. the State of Andhra Pradesh*) of the Supreme Court was the last significant attempt to force the central government to correct course and defend the right of India's children to receive quality education through a state-funded system for the proper maintenance of which the state would be accountable. It stated that the constitutional Directive Principle 45 (free and compulsory education for all children up to fourteen years of age), supported by Directive Principles 41 (the state is to provide essentials, including education, if economic, physical or mental inabilities exist as impediments) and 46 (the state is to ensure education of Schedule Castes and Tribes), had to be read in conjunction with Article 21.

Embodying the right to life and personal liberty, Article 21 is an essential value in a democratic society. All other rights are interpreted as adding quality to the life in question and can be claimed when a person is deprived of his 'life' or 'personal liberty' even by the 'state'. Many rights find shelter under the wide canopy of Article 21.

In the *Bandhua Mukti Morcha v. Union of India* case (February 1997), which focused on bonded labour, including rampant bonded child labour, Justice P. N. Bhagwati observed:

> It is the fundamental right of everyone in this country . . . to live with human dignity free from exploitation . . . it must include protection of the health and strength of workers, men and women, and of the tender age of children against abuse, opportunities and facilities for children to develop in a healthy manner and in conditions of freedom and dignity, educational facilities. . . . These are the minimum requirements which

must exist in order to enable a person to live with human dignity and no State neither the Central Government nor any State Government-has the right to take any action which will deprive a person of the enjoyment of these basic essentials.

(emphasis added)

By interpreting the right to education as arising from the fundamental right to life, the court order converted 'the obligation created by the article (45) into an enforceable right'. This demanded not merely pious statements but a constitutional amendment. However, in 1991 the GoI had already formally adopted and embarked on the neoliberal economic reforms program. Consequently the 86th Amendment, 2002, was tailor-made to coincide with neoliberal dictates to reduce public spending on education. Two significant limitations to the 'enforceable right' restricted it, first, to children between six and fourteen years of age and, second, provided for education only 'as the State may, by law, determine'. The first condition continues to exclude crores of children up to the age of six years,[8] and the second limitation allows a retreat by the state from its original constitutional responsibility to provide access to *quality* education for all children.

Crafted in the context of the 86th Amendment, the RTE Act 2009 succeeded in legalising the inequity of a bewildering variety of parallel, discriminatory streams of 'education' through formal/non-formal, governmental/private and aided/unaided institutions which had sprung up over the decades in response to circumstantial pressures because of the political failure to realize the constitutional directive to universalize elementary and secondary education through a national system of state-funded schools.

For the first time, a distinction was made between the 'good' special schools run by the state, e.g. Kendriya and Navodaya Vidyalayas, model schools, Sainik schools, etc., and the rest of the government schools, ensuring that the latter now became dysfunctional schools for the poor and disadvantaged. The former were excluded from the purview of the act and, like unaided private schools, were covered only by the condition that they provide 25% admission for students from the EWS. After completion of the March 2013 deadline for meeting the infrastructural requirements stipulated by the act, less than 10% schools were found to be RTE-compliant, but the aspiration for 'private' schooling had been fuelled by the 25% quota which created an 'elite' within the ranks of the EWS.

Using government data, the NGO Pratham, in its Annual Status of Education Report (ASER, 2012), found that whereas 29.8% of lower primary students attended private schools in 2010–11, after the implementation of the RTE Act in 2010, there was a 5.8% point increase in private school enrolment. A consistent shift from government schools towards low-quality budget schools by children from the EWS resulted in private schools accounting for 23.1% of all elementary schools in 2015, up from 19.4% in

192   Madhu Prasad

2010. By 2020, ASER 2012 estimates, over 50% students will be paying for primary education.

In fact, the RTE 2009 signalled that the very idea of a national system of state-funded education for which the central and state governments would be held responsible and accountable had been abandoned.

Non-formal education and alternative 'equivalents' to schooling

The marginalisation of the majority of India's children of elementary school age (i.e. up to fourteen years) had already been signalled in 1977–78, when the centrally sponsored non-formal education (NFE) scheme was introduced on a pilot basis to support the formal system in providing education for all.[9] In 1986, the National Policy on Education (NPE 1986–92) stated that the formal education system would not be able to reach out to children up to fourteen years of age from 'diverse' socio-economic backgrounds and introduced NFE as a low-cost alternative to be treated as 'equivalent to schooling' for the working poor and children in 'difficult circumstances'. The exclusion from the formal system of education of children living in habitations with no educational facilities; working children with household responsibilities; children of migrant labour families; tribal children; and those from the 'lowered' castes, minorities and gender and disability groups within these sections, who even now constitute well over 80% of children in the relevant age group, was thus initiated.

By 1999–2000, more than 303,800 NFE centres were being run by twenty-five states/union territories and 826 voluntary agencies/non-governmental organisations (NGOs). Upper-primary-level NFE centres were being run by the state governments and NGOs, and primary-level NFE centres were being run by NGOs alone. Total enrolment in these centres was 7.4 million. These programmes were run by state governments with the involvement of voluntary groups and NGOs, which the World Bank (WB) promoted as the preferred 'delivery vehicles' for the informal schemes that governments across the under-developed countries were encouraged to substitute for formal institutional structures. Forty-one experimental and innovative projects were also being implemented by these agencies in 1999–2000. In the Ninth Five-Year Plan period (i.e. 1997–98 to 2001–2002), budget allocation for the NFE scheme amounted to 11.4% of the total budget allocation for centrally sponsored schemes in the elementary education sector. The scheme was implemented with a funding pattern of 60:40 (i.e. 60% funding support from the central government and 40% funding support from state governments) for co-education centres and 90:10 for centres for girls. In the case of NGOs, 100% of funding assistance was directly provided by the central government for opening NFE centres. This strategy, and the NGO 'lobby' that it empowered, became one of the most powerful obstacles to realising the constitutional directive of education for all. The scheme covered less than 10% of the estimated 56 million out-of-school children in the age group six to fourteen in 2000, and the transition rate from NFE centres to formal schools was very low. However, it was revised in the year 2000 and ironically renamed as the Education Guarantee Scheme (EGS) and Alternative and Innovative Education (AIE). It became part of the Sarva Shiksha Abhiyaan (SSA – Education for All Mission), from the beginning of the Tenth Five-Year Plan, i.e. 2002–03.

With the WB-initiated District Primary Education Programme (DPEP) that was initiated in 1994 (GoI, 1995), 'low-cost' practices like multi-grade teaching and reduced infrastructure steadily infiltrated the government school system as well and served to justify the denial of quality education to the vast majority of India's children. To cut costs, para-teachers, Shiksha Mitras and Acharyas in EGCs were employed on contract, with no regard to qualifications or teacher training. In most states, recruitment of full-time, trained teachers was badly affected, if not halted altogether. However, existing cadres of trained permanent teachers were required to engage in preparing and serving mid-day meals in the schools and undertaking a range of other 'official' duties in their villages, districts and states, including conducting human and animal censuses and elections from the panchayat level upwards to state assemblies and the Parliament, manning official 'missions' like polio eradication, etc., and under RTE (2009) even undertaking 'disaster management' responsibilities and procedures.

The 'missing' National Policy on Education 2016/18

The present regime's proposed National Policy on Education 2016/18 (NEP 2016/18), tantalisingly glimpsed and then speedily withdrew, in the shape of the Subramanium Committee Report and an MHRD document, *Some Inputs for Draft NEP*, promises to accelerate this process. Amendments proposed to the already flawed RTE 2009 are revealing. Two prominent and beneficial features are being dropped (GoI, 2016). First, 'alternative' schools, which need not meet the basic infrastructural and pedagogical norms laid down in the RTE 2009, are to be encouraged, and a whole body of literature has already emerged advocating the prioritisation of 'outcome-based' educational strategies instead of 'input-based' ones.[10] Second, the no-detention policy introduced by RTE 2009, which ensured that children up to fourteen years of age/Class VIII at least remained in schools, has been changed and detention re-imposed for Class V and Class VII, thereby pushing even ten-year-olds out of school. A co-related initiative aims at *selectively* making the elementary curriculum vocational for targeted backward and tribal areas. Dovetailed into the prime minister's much-publicised but miserably low-performing skill development programme with an employment rate of 0.05% for skilled trainees, and the amendments to the Child

Labour (Prohibition and Regulation) Act 1986, permitting children under fourteen years old to work in 'family enterprises' and reducing the number of banned occupations for adolescents, this education policy will reinforce caste-based occupations and ensure that the majority of India's children from the oppressed and marginalised sections are condemned to a childhood of labour and a 'future' as low-paid daily wage workers.[11]

Keeping children out of school or 'pushing' them out of the formal system of education is not a function of people's poverty or state 'shortage of funds'.[12] As the earlier account shows, it is the product of a range of socially negative attitudes and priorities that have come to dominate education policy. To segregate the poor and the disadvantaged in institutions catering only to them is a form of exclusion that reproduces entrenched social inequalities prevalent in society and results in a situation where the vast majority of children are denied their fundamental right to education, while 'privilege' uncritically masquerades as 'merit'.

Marketing a commodity called knowledge

This outcome has gained credibility because of the depiction of learning as a 'private good', of knowledge as a 'commodity' and of education as a marketable 'service'. Neoliberalism's sole organising principle and standard of value in all areas of social life commoditizes not only labour, goods and services but also culture, relationships and social institutions.

The state of globalised capitalism and consequences resulting from the imposition of neoliberal reforms across the world have had devastating effects on the economic conditions in which the vast majority of people find themselves. The world is rapidly becoming polarised into

> central and peripheral economies, with the gap between rich and poor, between the powerful and the powerless growing so large that. . . . At the start of the twenty-first century, the combined assets of the 225 richest people was roughly equal to the annual incomes of the poorest 47 per cent of the world's population (Heintz and Folbre, 2000, cited in McLaren and Farahmandpur, 2001: 345) and eight companies earned more than half the world's population (World Development Movement, 2001).
>
> (Cole, 2018: 58)

The impact on the provision of social services like education, health, public utilities, job and food security has been equally destructive. These sectors have been opened to profiteering by private capital with the application of the 'user-pays' principle, on the one hand, and by initiating public–private partnership (PPP) schemes, on the other. Public funds are transferred to private corporations, while citizens, reduced to 'consumer/clients', become mere conduits, allowing governments to smooth the process of the transfer.

According to educational statistics for the year 2016 released on 28 February 2018, by the UNESCO Institute for Statistics (UIS), the official data source for Sustainable Development Goals 4 (SDG 4) to be realised by 2030,

- The number of out-of-school children, adolescents and youth, at 263 million worldwide, i.e. one out of every five, has barely changed over five years from 2011 to 2016.
- In the primary school age group of six to eleven years, 63 million, i.e. 9%, are not in school. In 2013, the last year for which data were provided, India accounted for 2,897,747 out-of-school children at this level even three years after the RTE Act was implemented.
- Sixty-one million adolescents worldwide are out of school in the twelve to fourteen age group.
- One hundred and thirty-nine million, i.e. one out of every three, are out of school at the upper secondary stage covering fifteen- to seventeen-year-olds. The world's lowest-income countries have a 59% out-of-school rate at this level, compared to only 6% across high-income countries.

However, the effects have been felt even in advanced countries. A recent United States court judge in Michigan decided that *students at poorly performing schools did not have a constitutional right to a better education.* He dismissed a class-action lawsuit filed in September 2016 at troubled, underperforming schools in Detroit which served mostly racial minorities and which 'described schools that were overcrowded with students but lacking in teachers; courses without basic resources like books and pencils; and classrooms that were bitingly cold in the winter, stiflingly hot in the summer and infested with rats and insects'.[13]

In India the commercialisation and marketisation of education has put education outside the grasp of the vast majority of India's population.[14] The National Sample Survey Organisation's (NSSO) most recent survey on education (71st round), conducted during January to July 2014, reveals a pattern in the exclusion that is being effected.

As per the net attendance ratio (NAR), 89% of children of primary school going age of the richest fifth of the population attend school both in the rural and urban areas. The proportion drops by 10 percentage points to 79% for children in the poorest fifth of the population in rural areas and 78% in urban areas. But when it comes to secondary school, there is a sharp drop, which becomes even worse at the higher secondary level. The poorest fifth of the population have NAR of 18% (rural) and 23% (urban); the richest fifth have NAR of 53% and 66%. Also, the difference between the richest fifth and the poorest fifth in enrolment widens sharply at the higher secondary and higher educational levels. Only 6% of young people from the bottom fifth of the population attend educational levels above higher secondary in urban India, but that proportion is five times higher, at 31%, for young people from the richest fifth of the population. NAR even for urban children studying above the higher secondary levels for the middle fifth of the population is 15%, i.e. half that of the top fifth. So, compared to the top 10% of the population, even the middle class is substantially disadvantaged when it comes to higher education.

The situation is worse in rural India and continues to decline as the negative factors pile up. Data from the 2016 Central Board of Secondary Education (CBSE) Class XII exams showed that only 1,827 girls from the scheduled tribes appeared for the exam.

In lieu of a conclusion

A vibrant national system of education has to be transformational and emancipatory; it cannot reproduce and strengthen existing hierarchies and disparities. The real challenge for the education system lies in transforming a heterogeneous and diverse population into a rich learning source for the development of sensibilities that are not marked by conformism and prejudice, but rather are open to critical self-questioning. This cannot be left to the vagaries of the market where profit rules and private players respond accordingly.

On campuses across the country, the rising tide of protests against privatisation, against curbing democratic rights of students and faculty and in support of social justice have been called 'anti-national' by the present regime. We are dealing here with two opposing concepts of nation and nationhood. The first, generated through collective struggle, found expression in the civil liberties and equal rights given in the constitution. These liberties and rights are *enabling conditions* for an on-going politics of a *democratically negotiated nationalism* in which education, and particularly higher education, has a significant role to play.

The opposing Hindutva concept, espoused by the current regimes at the centre and in several states, is a communal-patriarchal construct, an ideological imposition that seeks to discipline the 'other' by communalisation, marginalisation and dispossession. Within this Hindu majoritarian concept of the nation, 'others' are second-class citizens limited by the will of a self-appointed governing class. But in a vicious circularity, 'Hindus' themselves are now defined as those who exemplify the ideology of the RSS and the Sangh Parivar! This is fundamentally anti-democratic and anti-constitutional, for it replaces the rights of citizens with the supremacist hold of a privileged group.

On 27 July 2016, HRD Minister Shri Prakash Javedkar held a closed-door, six-hour-long meeting with the RSS and its affiliates, including its student wing, the Akhil Bhartiya Vidyarthi Parishad (ABVP), to discuss the NEP 2016/18 and how to 'instill nationalism, pride and ancient Indian values in modern education'. As if this were not sufficient, military training for a ten-lakh 'youth force', which will now be raised annually to instil 'discipline' and 'nationalism' in youth from Class X onwards, is to be made compulsory for those joining the defence, para-military and police forces.[15] Conformism and a slavish mentality bred by indoctrination in a particular ideology is thereby sought to be cultivated throughout the curriculum, with no space for critical reasoning or alternative avenues of knowledge.

This is precisely the concept of knowledge promoted by votaries of an instrumentalist view of commercialised education. The commodification of knowledge requires that it be degraded to the 'acquisition of skills' required for services that are available in the market. The entire terminology of the NEP 2016/18 is devised within the framework of skill acquisition. 'Competencies' and 'outcomes' are units to be monitored, measured, graded and readied for the market. The purpose of education is the grooming of a 'human resource' to create a workforce that will enter the marketplace where only that training is 'valued', which makes the worker fulfil the expectation of being fiercely competitive in relation to fellow workers, but docile in dealings with superiors and masters.

The communalisation of education, like the commercialisation and commoditisation of education, creates and secures the anti-democratic and potentially fascist socio-political environment in which neoliberalism can flourish. Today, authoritarian governments are typically proponents of neoliberal economic thinking, espousing policies that cannot create jobs and a healthy work environment for citizens. The purpose is to concentrate financial power in fewer and fewer hands and severely restrict social spending and welfare policies which benefit the masses. To secure this path of 'development', it is necessary to destroy democratic institutions and practices, to prevent united struggles of the working people and to create an environment of fear and insecurity in which dissent is not allowed and people are trained to conform to the dominant state ideology.

Notes

1 Altaf Hussain Hali (1837–1914). Hali wrote one of the earliest works of literary criticism in Urdu, *Muqaddamah-i Shay'r-o-Sha'iri*. Its critical preface, 'the Muqaddima-i-Sher-o-Shairi', led the way to literary criticism in Urdu literature.
2 A uniform definition of literacy for British India was adopted beginning with the 1911 census – an individual was recorded as literate if he or she could read and write a short letter to a friend. Although officials point to certain problems with the post-1911 enumeration, such as enumerators on occasion adopting school standards, they do indicate that 'the simple criterion laid down was easily understood and sensibly interpreted' (Census of India 1921, Volume I – Report, Chapter VIII).

3 Notes on Indian Affairs: (1837: Vol. 2. No. XXXVII: 28).
4 Greatly influenced by social reformer Jyotiba Phule, Shahuji Maharaj was associated with many progressive and path-breaking activities during his rule (1894–1922). Primary education to all, regardless of caste and creed, was one of his most significant priorities.
5 Gokhale pointed out while introducing a bill on compulsory primary education on March 16, 1911, which was defeated in the Imperial Legislative Council, that 'His Highness began his first experiment in the matter of introducing compulsory and free education into his State eighteen years ago in ten villages at the Amreli Taluka. After watching the experiment for eight years, it was extended to the whole taluka in 1901, and finally, in 1906, primary education was made compulsory and free throughout the State for boys between the ages of 6 and 12, and for girls between the ages of 6 and 10' Natesan, G. A. (1916). Speeches of Gopal Krishna Gokhale (2nd ed.). Madras, India: (p. 725–26).
6 A great reformer in the tradition of her mother and grandmother, Sultan Jahan founded several important educational institutions in Bhopal, establishing free and compulsory primary education in 1918. During her reign, she had a particular focus on public instruction, especially female education. She built many technical institutes and schools and increased the number of qualified teachers.
7 In contrast, the School Choice National Conference (SCNC), hosted annually in New Delhi since 2009 by the Centre for Civil Society (CCS), wants government to fund 'children' not 'schools' through Direct Benefit Transfers (DBT), including voucher schemes, and transfer state funds to aided and unaided private elite and low-budget school managements alike to 'develop an education market where students can avail education of their choice'. CCS's latest initiative, National Independent Schools Alliance (NISA), advocates expansion of parental school choice and systematic competition between private and government schools, at state expense, to improve quality and outcomes for all schools. The NISA support base comprises largely budget-based private schools that face closure for failing to meet RTE (2009) input norms for recognition.
8 Whereas the 1993 judgment directed that the entire Article 45 of the Directive Principles be converted into 'an enforceable right' applicable to all children 'up to 14 years of age', the 86th Amendment introduced Article 21A in the Fundamental Rights section, providing for compulsory and free education for all children, except for those attending private unaided or minority schools, from age six to fourteen years only. The original Article 45 was retained as a directive principle but was amended with the state promising 'to endeavor to provide early childhood care and education for all children until they reach the age of 6 years'.
9 The influence of international agencies like the International Monetary Fund (IMF) was felt as the GOI negotiated the largest-ever IMF loan given to a developing country in 1980–81. Although the GOI withdrew from the loan and from implementing the IMF reform programme in 1984, the reforms process had in fact begun.
10 Outcome-based education (OBE) is an educational theory that bases each part of an educational system around specified outcomes and pedagogical methods and tools focusing on what knowledge and skills are required to reach the outcome. Planners of the course work backwards from the outcome. Students understand what is expected of them, and the faculty functions as an instructor, trainer, facilitator, and/or mentor. Potential employers can look at records of potential employees to determine if the outcomes they have achieved are necessary for the job. A holistic approach to learning is lost. Learning can find itself reduced to

something that is specific, measurable and observable. As a result, OBE is not widely recognized as a valid way of conceptualizing what learning is about.

11 A 2015 report of the International Labour Organization (ILO) puts the number of child workers in India aged between five and seventeen at 5.7 million, out of 168 million globally. More than half of India's child workers labour in agriculture and over a quarter in manufacturing – embroidering clothes, weaving carpets or making matchsticks. Children also work in restaurants and hotels and as domestic workers. With child labour rates highest among tribal and lower-caste communities, at almost 7% and 4%, respectively, the amendments to the 1986 law will disadvantage and have an adverse impact on these especially marginalised and impoverished communities.

12 Government expenditure on education as a percentage of GDP was 3.8% for India in 2012. The figure is 6.3% for Vietnam, 4.3% for Mali, 4.7% for Nepal and 5% for Rwanda, all of them poor countries. Direct tax concessions to rich individuals and companies was pegged at Rs. 128,639 crore in 2015–16. Yet school education got only Rs. 42,187 crore.

13 Top of the World: USA. Access to literacy not a constitutional right in America. *The Indian Express*. July 7, 2018.

14 An overwhelming 78%, i.e. 836 million people in India, were found to be living on a per capita consumption of less than Rs 20 a day, according to the Arjun Sengupta report on the Conditions of Work and Promotion of Livelihood in the Unorganised Sector, based on government data for the period between 1993–94 and 2004–05. The per capita consumption of the extreme poor was at Rs 12 per day. The justification for economic reforms was supposed to be the trickle-down effect but ten years of economic reforms seems to have made little difference.

15 Government discusses military training plan for disciplined 10 lakh 'force of youth'. *The Indian Express*. July 17, 2018.

References

Acharya, P. (1997). Educational ideals of Tagore and Gandhi: A comparative study. *Economic and Political Weekly*, 32(12).

Allahabad High Court. (2015). *Judgment pronounced on 18/08/2015 on a bunch of petitions, first amongst them being the WRIT No. 57476 of 2013*. Shiv Kumar Pathak and 11 Others Versus State of UP And Three Others.

Annual Status of Education Report (ASER). (2012). Annual Status of Education Report. New Delhi, India: ASER Centre/ Pratham.

Arnold, W. D. (1922). First Report. 1857. In: J. A. Richey, ed., *Selections from educational records*, Part II. Calcutta: Superintendent of Government Printing.

Biswas, A. and Aggarwal, S. P. (1994). *Development of education in India: A historical survey of educational documents before and after independence*. Delhi: Concept Publishing.

Chaudhary, S. I. (2002). *1882 Middle class and the social revolution in Bengal: An incomplete agenda*. Dhaka: The University Press Limited.

Cole, M. (2018). *Marxism and educational theory: Origins and issues*. New York: Routledge.

Davis, L. E. and Huttenback, R. A. (1986). *Mammon and the pursuit of empire: The political economy of British imperialism, 1860–1912*. New York: Cambridge University Press.

Engels, F. (1845/1975). *Speeches in Elberfeld. 8 February 1845*. Marx – Engels Collected Works, Vol. 4. Moscow: Progress Publishers, pp. 1844–1845.

Government of India. (1966). *Education and national development: Report of the education commission*. New Delhi: Ministry of Education.

———. (1967). *The Report of the Committee of Members of Parliament on Education*, New Delhi: Ministry of Education.

———. (1944). *Post-War Plan of Educational Development in India*. Central Advisory Board Of Education (CABE). New Delhi: Manager of Publications.

———. (1995) *DPEP Guidelines*. New Delhi: MHRD.

———. (2016). *National policy on education (NPE) 2016: Report of the committee for evolution of the new education policy*. New Delhi: Ministry of Human Resource Development, Government of India.

Gupta, N. (1981). *Delhi between two empires (1803–1931): Society, government, & urban growth*. Oxford: Oxford University Press.

Heintz, J. and Folbre, N. (2000). *The ultimate field guide to the U.S. economy: A compact and irreverent guide to economic life in America*. New York: New Press.

Howell, A. (1872). *Education in British India: Prior to 1854 and in 1870–71*. Calcutta: Superintendent of Government Printing, pp. 20–21.

Lee, J. W. and Lee, H. (2016). Human capital in the long run. *Journal of Development Economics*, 122, pp. 147–169.

Marriot, S. (November 1846). *Commissioner of Revenue in the Deccan, and later Member of Council, Government of Bombay, in a letter to Sir R. Grant*. India: The Duty and Interest of England to inquire into its State (Accessed on 16 January 1836).

Martin, M. (1834). *The history of British colonies*, Vol. 1: *Possessions in Asia*. London: James Cochrane and Co.

McLaren, P. and Farahmandpur, R. (2001). Educational policy and the socialist imagination: Revolutionary citizenship as a pedagogy of resistance. *Educational Policy*, 15(3), pp. 343–378.

Naik, J. P. (1975). *Equality, quality and quantity: The elusive triangle in Indian education*. Bombay: Allied Publishers.

Report of Indian Education Commission. (1882). *Calcutta: Manager of publications*. Available at: https://archive.org/details/ReportOfTheIndianEducationCommission/page/n325 (Accessed on 12 January 2018).

———. (1884). *Bombay*, Vol II. Calcutta. (1884: 140).

Weiner, M. (1991). *The child and the state in India: Child labor and education policy in comparative perspective*, 4th ed. Princeton, NJ: Princeton University Press.

———. (1994). India's case against compulsory education. *Seminar*, 413, January, pp. 83–86.

World Development Movement. (2001). *The tricks of the trade: How trade rules are loaded against the poor*. London: WDM.

Part IV

Transnational perspective on neoliberalism and education

Chapter 11

The reactionary right and its carnival of reaction

Global neoliberalism, reactionary neoconservatism: Marxist critique, education analysis and policy

Dave Hill

The first part of this chapter critically examines neoliberal and neoconservative policy globally. This differs in various national contexts, but its aims at maximising private capitalist profit do not vary. These aims are fundamental to capitalism. This maximisation of profit is at the expense of both the social wage (welfare benefits/public services) and the individual wage and working conditions and rights of workers, such as education workers. In the second section of this chapter I locate these developments more theoretically within Marxist educational analysis, referring to Western Marxist reproduction and Marxist resistance theorists such as Althusser, Gramsci, Anyon, Bowles and Gintis, Bourdieu, Apple, Willis, Giroux, McLaren, Rikowski and my own work. I conclude by briefly suggesting a socialist policy for education.

Capitalism and class war from above

Neoliberal and neoconservative policy differs in different national and historical contexts. But aim towards maximisation of profit at the expense of both the social wage (welfare benefits/public services) and the individual wage and working conditions and rights of workers, such as education workers. This intensification of the extraction of surplus value from the labour power of workers, including education workers, can be termed 'Kleptocratic Capitalism', 'Turbo-Capitalism' and 'Class War from Above' or 'Immiseration Capitalism' (Hill, 2012a, 2013, 2017a).

Commentators from across the political spectrum are in general agreement that in a vigorous 'class war from above' (Harvey, 2005; Hill, 2012b, 2013; Malott et al., 2013) since the economic crisis of the mid-1970s, ('the oil crisis'), the capitalist class has been remarkably successful in wresting back from the working class a greater and greater share of public wealth, of the share of national income and wealth, across much of the capitalist world (Picketty, 2014), with Oxfam reporting on the inequality gap widening as 42 people hold the same amount of wealth as 3.7 billion poorest, with the world's richest 1% getting 82% of the wealth generated globally in 2017 (Oxfam, 2018).

As part of the international and national divisions of labour, capitalist profitability reigns supreme, whether neoliberal-neoconservative capitalism in the Anglo-Saxon world, or in post-Soviet capitalism or in Modi's neoliberal-neoconservative India, an example of post-colonial capitalism. All are oligarchic, plutocratic and kleptocratic. The victims are the environment, workers and their rights and conditions and social rights – and regions – and their populations, which are deemed unprofitable for profit. So, in the interests of capital accumulation, of the maximisation of private oligarchic profit, whole regions are devastated, impoverished and written off. This is as true of Detroit or the South Wales valleys, of impoverished regions in Russia, Bihar and Uttar Pradesh in India, and of whole countries such as Bulgaria in the post-Soviet capitalist economies. We are witnessing the global, internal and external migrations from poverty and the crippling of the social state, along with the impoverishment, pauperisation and absolute immiseration of internal and external migrant labour – people – who live, love and labour, their sinews aching with the intensification of the extraction of surplus value from their labour power. The rich grow fatter and richer and ever more gluttonous. The poor, the migrants, the working classes die early and sick.

Some conservatives argue that inequality is not only 'natural' but that it is also 'desirable', because it fuels envy, aspiration, competition and hard work. Such arguments are global, made, for example, by the Conservatives and Liberal Democrats in the UK, the Adaletve Kalkinma Partisi (AKP) in Turkey, the Bhartiya Janata Party (BJP) in India and right-wing and centre-right governments everywhere.

And in a development that is new since the 1970s, political parties and governments that were traditionally 'labour' or 'social democratic' or left-of-centre governments – governments that in the 1940s, 1950s and 1960s had seen it as their duty to redistribute some wealth and power from the top to the bottom of society – have *also* subscribed to the neoliberal restructuring of economies.

Avowedly socialist governments, such as those of Cuba, Bolivia and Venezuela, which have by and large (though not totally) refused to travel the neoliberal road, have *not* seen these increasing inequalities. In contrast to neoliberal governments, they see their role as to make societies more equal, with both having established free health care and free education as public rights rather than as commodities to be bought and sold.

In contrast to neoliberal and neoconservative ideology (described later), the liberal democratic and social democratic analysis is that capitalism works fine, or can work fine; it just needs some reforms, some improvements. Social democratic parties, whether in their social democratic or their neoliberal incarnations, such as the Labour Party in Britain and Australia, and social democratic parties in Scandinavia and Germany, and 'socialist' parties in France, Spain and Portugal, do not want to replace capitalism – they just want to manage it better.

They cite the much more equal economies and societies of northwest Europe, such as Sweden and Finland (and, between 1945 and the mid-1970s, of Western Europe in general), and argue that societies become more equal, and happy, with regulation capitalism, with more regulation over health and medicine standards, food standards, health and safety standards and environmental and ecological protection, for example. The book *The Spirit Level*, by Wilkinson and Pickett, 2009, offers powerful evidence to support this, with the most equal societies such as the Scandinavian countries and Taiwan and Japan, with their concern for communities rather than focusing spectacularly on individuals and individualism, have far less homicide, rape, psychosis, violence and social ills than the most unequal large, rich societies such as the United States and the UK.

Where Marxists disagree with other critics of these widened social and economic inequalities is in their belief that capitalism has periodic crises, of over-accumulation, for example; of profitability for capital; of a declining rate of profit, and that in times of crisis (such as the recession/slump of the 1930s, the 'oil crisis' of the 1970s and the 'bankers' crisis' since 2008) the capitalist class will always try to tear back from the hands of the workers the benefits and living standards they and their class organisations (such as trade unions and political parties) had won in more profitable times.

That is to say that in times of economic crisis and of recession, even 'labour' and social democratic governments 'dance to the tune' of national and transnational capitalists and start cutting the real value of wages/salaries and social benefits. That it is 'the poor who pay for the crisis'.

For Marxists, capitalism is not just immoral and a case of 'oppression'. It is that capitalism is based on economic exploitation. However, most Marxists and socialists (the terms are slightly different and used differently based on historical and geographical situations) point to the need for 'agency' for action, for the need for Marxist militants and activists to work to develop class consciousness. Marx and Engels (1848) spoke the development of the working class as a (conscious) 'class for itself', instead of a 'class in itself' with economically similar positions in relationship to the ownership of the means of production and similar social relations of production, but with no sense of class unity or class struggle (Marx, 1847). Freire used the term 'conscientization' (Freire, 1993). Marxists believe in 'agentist' activism, in the need to develop strong political organisations to fight for major revolutionary social and economic change. For Marxists today, socialism and Marxism are not 'inevitable'; they have to be fought for. Marxists believe that the point is not simply to describe the world, but to change it. In Marx's words, 'The philosophers have only interpreted the world, in various ways; the point is to change it' [1845].

206 Dave Hill

Capitalism is undoubtedly for Marxists immoral. Workers die far earlier than bankers and CEOs and 'royal' families, especially the unskilled and semi-skilled manual strata of the working class, who have unhealthier lives and have inferior education and health and retirement services than the rich. And within the working class, professional and managerial strata lead longer and healthier lives in general than the poorer and the manual strata. Furthermore, capitalism deliberately encourages division within the working class (with capitalist and politicians, as well as the media, whipping up hatred and division between black and white, men and women, LGBT and straight, immigrant and non-immigrant, public-sector employees and private-sector employees). Indeed, Marxists see Fascism and Nazism in 1920s, 1930s and 1940s Europe and some examples of contemporary extreme nationalism and xenophobia since then (as with the Nazi 'Golden Dawn' party being elected to the Greek parliament in 2012 and to the European Parliament in 2014) as a throw of the dice by capitalists desperate to 'stop the red menace', to stop communism. Elsewhere, capitalist classes and the media give substantial support to nationalist, anti-immigration, right-wing parties such as the United Kingdom Independence Party (UKIP), which topped the poll in the UK the 2014 European Parliament elections.

But, to repeat, where Marxist analysis of economic, social, human rights policy and education policy differs from other critique – even of vibrant radical left democrats like Henry Giroux – is that Marxists first prioritise class analysis; second, they go beyond critique, beyond deconstruction, into reconstruction – into proposals for a fundamental change in society and economy, a socialist economy; and, third, Marxists go beyond proposal/programme into activism.

So, what are neoliberalism and neoconservatism?

Neoliberalism and (neo)-conservatism

Neoliberalism

Neoliberalism is marked, *inter alia*, by the marketisation, commodification, degradation, managerialisation and privatisation or pre-privatisation of public services (Giroux, 2004; Harvey, 2005; Hill, 2013; Hill and Kumar, 2009; Hill and Rosskam, 2009).

Elsewhere (Hill, 2003, 2006a for example) I have detailed the major characteristics of neoliberalism as follows to education:

1 Privatisation/pre-privatisation of public services such as schooling and universities.
2 Cuts in public spending, salaries, pensions and benefits.
3 Marketisation, competition between schools and between universities.

The reactionary right 207

4 Vocational education for human capital (except for the ruling class, who, in their elite private schools, are encouraged into a wider and less 'basics' driven education).
5 Management of the workforce: 'new public managerialism' in schools and colleges, with hugely increasing differentials in pay and power between managers and workforce.
6 Encouragement of competition between workers through performance-related pay and the 'busting' of national pay scales agreed to by trade unions.
7 Casualisation/'precariatisation' of public- and private-sector workers, with a decline in tenured and in full-time 'secure' jobs for teachers and university faculty.
8 Attacks on trade unions, on workers' rights and on centralised pay bargaining.
9 'Management speak', e.g. students as 'customers', 'delivering' the curriculum and the discourse of the market replacing that of social responsibility.
10 Denigration/ideological attacks on the public-sector workforce.

Neoconservatism

Neoliberalism is enforced by authoritarian neo-conservatism. Gamble (1988) talked of this in *The Free Society and the Strong State*. Neoconservatism here refers first to 'hierarchy, order and control' and second to 'traditional morality'.

First, there is the use by governments of the repressive state apparatuses (RPA) such as law, the police, the judiciary, the security services, the armed forces and the surveillance forms of management control within institutions and places of work, which are intimidating in nature. In addition to their overtly intimidatory, law enforcement, repressive function, the RPA have ideological functions and impacts (Althusser, 1971). These repressive state apparatuses currently reinforce the individualistic, competitive, 'common-sense' pro-capitalist hegemonic ideology (Gramsci, 1971) and serve to 'naturalise' capital, rendering capitalist economic relations and capitalist social relations – what Marxists term 'the capital-labour relation' – seem 'only natural'. They punish deep dissent and 'deep critique'.

Second, concerning the 'traditional morality' aspect of neoconservatism, this varies in space and time, from country to country and at different periods. It generally, but not always, includes a veneration of the family and heterosexual and married relationships. Conservative politicians and theorists vary over such matters as 'conservative social morality'. Thus, for example, some conservatives are socially liberal but not socially conservative. This is in contrast to the 'Victorian morality' of, for example, Margaret Thatcher in the UK and of Reycep Erdogan, the conservatising prime minister of Turkey,

208 Dave Hill

with his 'soft-Islamicisation' of Turkey by banning kissing on the metro, limiting birth control and availability of alcohol and bringing back and encouraging more conservative forms of dress for women, in particular, the *hijab* (veil that covers the hair). As with Thatcher in the 1980s, Erdogan is marrying this policy with intense neoliberalism, through schools and universities and in the wider society and economy (Inal and Akkamayak, 2012).

This second aspect of conservatism and neo-conservatism is that, universally, it involves and seeks to enforce an acceptance of elitism and hierarchy – and of accepting one's place in that hierarchy. That hierarchy is a racial, gender and social class hierarchy. It is, as with the evangelical Christian Trump supporters and social conservatives in the United States, as with Erdogan's governments in Turkey and as with Modi's appeals to Hindu chauvinism in India and Netanyahu's Zionism in Israel, also based on appeals to religion. In the mix, in different countries/times are ultra-patriotism, ultra-nationalism, vilification of minorities and super-exploitation of 'othered' internal and external migrants and proclaimed adherence to strict forms of personal and religious morality.

The main aspects of neoconservatism as they relate to education can be seen as:

1 Control of curricula of schools, teacher education, universities and the removal of 'dangerous' content.
2 Control of pedagogy teaching methods and pedagogic relations between teachers and students.
3 Control of students through debt and through actual or fear of unemployment.
4 Control of teachers and professors through surveillance, a culture of having to meet targets, punishment of dissidents and union activists, dismissals and closures of schools and closures of university departments.
5 Brute force and 'the security state' within schools – the use of tear gas, sound grenades, stun grenades, beatings, prosecutions, draconian sentencing and, in some countries, imprisonment and killings (e.g. murders of trade union activists in Colombia).

The relationship between neoliberalism and neoconservatism

The strength of the neoliberal alliance with (neo)-conservatism and with conservative forces is particularly strong in the United States and in Turkey. In the United States, the nexus, the alliance, between social conservatives and economic conservatives is pronounced and has been intensively analysed by writers such as Michael W. Apple (e.g. 2006), where he charts and analyses 'the conservative restoration'. This 'conservative restoration', is characterised by millions of United States citizens actually voting against their own objective economic self-interest, such as support for Obamacare, for more protection of benefits and economic rights than offered by Trump and the Republicans.

In Turkey, the Erdogan government is very nakedly pushing forward with the Islamicisation of society and the education system and with the brute-force use of the repressive apparatuses of the state, as seen in the summer of 2013 national police brutality against the Gezi Park resistance movement, resulting in eight deaths at the hands of the police. Thus, in Turkey, neoliberalism is accompanied by traditionalist, Islamic conservatism in and through the ideological state apparatuses of the media, the mosque and the education system, accompanied by the naked use of the repressive state apparatuses, such as the bullets, tear gas and chemically treated water cannons used across Turkey during the summer of 2013 (Gezgin et al., 2014).

There are also isolated states resisting neoliberalism, such as the governments and states of Cuba, Bolivia and Venezuela, and, within the Anglo-Saxon neoliberal capitalist countries, and pro-capitalist countries in general, millions of liberal-left, socialist and Marxist educators and (often the same people) anti-racist and anti-sexist activists, LGBT activists and pro-indigenous and eco-activists resisting both neoconservatism and neoliberalism.

Neoconservatism is sometimes in tension with neoliberalism. For example, with respect to schools, neoconservatives want government control of the schools' curriculum (to shut out contrarian liberal and socialist and anarchist versions of history, civics and literature, for example). Neoliberals, in contrast, want there to be a complete competitive market in schools, with each school having and developing its own 'brand' of curriculum.

Another area of disagreement between neoconservatism and neoliberalism is that, for neoliberals, profit is the overriding goal. UK Prime Minister Margaret Thatcher (1979–91) broke or substantially reduced the power not only of trade unions but also of traditional elites controlling access to the higher professions.

It is important to make clear that neoliberalism is simply the latest stage of capitalism. It is current capitalism. This critique is, *in essence*, a critique of capitalism itself, of capitalist economic relations, of capitalist social relations, of the capital–labour relation. Removing neoliberalism and (neo)-conservatism, for example, through social democratic reforms may lead to a more compassionate society with some (immensely) valuable welfare, workers' rights reforms and even a slight equalisation of income and wealth and power in society. But such reforms, although, to repeat, hugely valuable, will not remove class exploitation by the capitalist class of the labour power of the working class.

For capitalism, education is a market from which profits can be made. For the transnational and national capitalist class and their corporations and governments, nothing must get in the way of the reproduction of capitalist social relationships and capitalist economic relationships. And that

210   Dave Hill

includes resistant and alternative models and practices in public education. Hence, not only is education being marketised, privatised and softened up for privatisation and commodified, but the very curriculum and pedagogy themselves within schools and universities are being controlled, constrained and sanitised (Rikowski, 2008) to make a world safe for capitalism.

Marxist analyses of education

In the second section of this chapter I locate developments in education within Marxist educational analysis, referring to Western Marxist reproduction and Marxist resistance theorists such as Althusser, Gramsci, Anyon, Bowles and Gintis, Bourdieu, Apple, Willis, Giroux, McLaren, Rikowski and to my own work. In addition, Marx and Marxism have influenced a broad range of critical scholars, including Bourdieu and Bernstein. Such thinkers offer ideas, concepts and arguments which *complement* Marxism rather being Marxist *per se*.

Bukharin and Preobrazhensky

Marxist analysis of the role education performs in a capitalist society was set out by Bukharin and Preobrazhensky in 1920 (1920/1969):

> In bourgeois society the school has three principal tasks to fulfil. First, it inspires the coming generation of workers with devotion and respect for the capitalist régime. Secondly, it creates from the young of the ruling classes 'cultured' controllers of the working population. Thirdly, it assists capitalist production in the application of sciences to technique, thus increasing capitalist profits.

Bukharin and Preobrazhensky (1920/1969) describe each of these tasks:

> Just as in the bourgeois army the 'right spirit' is inculcated by the officers, so in the schools under the capitalist régime the necessary influence is mainly exercised by the caste of 'officers of popular enlightenment'. The teachers in the public elementary schools receive a special course of training by which they are prepared for their role of beast tamers. . . . The ministries of education in the capitalist régime are ever on the watch, and they ruthlessly purge the teaching profession of all dangerous (by which they mean socialist) elements.

In Western capitalist economies, we can say that the aim is to withhold 'critical' secondary and higher education from working-class youth. Despite the best efforts, and indeed love, of many teachers, education is perceived for working-class youth as 'skills training', devoid of 'deep critique'. There is the suppression of critical space in education, the strict control of teacher education, of the curriculum, of educational research (Hill, 2006b). Of course, many teachers resist.

Gramsci: hegemony, intellectuals and contestation

Gramsci's (1971) key concepts are the (capitalist) hegemony of ideas, the social role of teachers as intellectuals, an insistence on developing counter-hegemonic 'good sense' (as opposed to hegemonic capitalist 'common sense') in settings outside the school as well as within, the call for 'resistance' and, often forgotten, the role of the organised Marxist (in his words, communist) party.

For Gramsci, the state and state institutions such as schools, rather than being the servant of the interests of capitalism and the ruling class, were an arena of class conflict and a site where hegemony has to be continually striven for. Thus, schools and other education institutions are seen as relatively autonomous apparatuses, providing space for oppositional behaviour. For Gramsci, as for Marxists in general, education is a class struggle. Banfield (2016) notes, '[I]t is part of what Gramsci has aptly called the "war of position" (Gramsci, 1971) where the trenches of civil society are won in classrooms, workplaces, pubs and on street corners such that socialism becomes the "enlightened common sense of our age" '. For Gramsci, teachers and educators have a very special role: 'All men (*sic*) are intellectuals but not all men have in society the function of intellectuals'.

Common sense and (class conscious) good sense

For Gramsci, and indeed for millions of communist, Marxist, critical and Freirean teachers and educators (and cultural workers), historically and today, this means challenging, critically interrogating and deconstructing accepted wisdoms, curricula, pedagogies and working – as part of the working class (as 'organic intellectuals') – developing our own worldview, our own 'good sense', our own analysis, vision and programme. Gramsci's influence on the critical pedagogy movement globally (and of revolutionary critical pedagogy) has been immense (coupled with the work of Freire and of the Frankfurt School).

Other than Gramsci, the theorists referred to in this chapter are Marxist reproduction theorists. Giroux (1983) expertly summarises the differences between Marxist reproduction theorists and Marxist resistance theorists. This latter group has been very much influenced by Gramsci.

Bourdieu: schooling as cultural reproduction

Bourdieu's (1990, 1997; Bourdieu and Passeron, 1977) most useful concepts for Marxists are his theory of schooling as cultural reproduction and his concepts of habitus, cultural capital and symbolic violence, whereby schools recognise and reward middle-class/upper-class knowledge, language and body language and diminish and demean working-class and (some) minority-ethnic cultures.

For Bourdieu, the major function of the education system is to maintain and legitimise a class-divided society. In his analysis, schools are middle-class institutions run by and for the middle class. Cultural reproduction, for Bourdieu, works in three ways.

Cultural capital: knowing that

The curriculum and examinations privilege and validate particular types of 'cultural capital', the type of elite knowledge that comes naturally to middle-class and, in particular, upper-class children, but which is not 'natural' or familiar to non-elite children and school students. At the same time, and as a consequence, it disconfirms, rejects and invalidates the cultures of other groups, both social class groups and ethnic minority and immigrant groups.

Cultural capital: knowing how

There is also a hidden curriculum. This type of cultural capital is 'knowing how', how to speak to teachers, not only knowing about books but also knowing how to talk about them. It is knowing how to talk with the teacher, with what body language, accent, colloquialisms, register of voice and grammatical exactitude in terms of the 'elaborated code' of language and its associated habitus, body posture or way of behaving.

> In a number of social universes, one of the privileges of the dominant, who move in their world as a fish in water, resides in the fact that they need not engage in rational computation in order to reach the goals that best suit their interests. All they have to do is follow their dispositions which, being adjusted to their positions, 'naturally' generate practices adjusted to the situation.
>
> (Bourdieu, 1990: 108–109)

For Bourdieu, and for sociologists in general, children and teenagers bring their social-class backgrounds into school with them. This echoes Bernstein (1977) and his theory of class-specific language codes, whereby schools privilege and reward middle-class, so-called 'elaborated language' and devalue and demean working-class, so-called 'restricted language.'

Cultural reproduction through separate schooling

Third, cultural reproduction works in Britain through the separate system of schooling for the upper and upper-middle classes, nearly all of whom send their children to private (independent) schools. The system of secondary education exemplifies and reproduces class differentiation, which is rigidly separated into a flourishing, lavishly funded private sector, as compared to the demoralised, underfinanced public sector, itself divided into schools in wealthy areas and those in inner-urban/inner-city areas.

Class-based pedagogies in the classroom: Jean Anyon and Jill Duffield and her colleagues: Jean Anyon and class-based pedagogy

Anyon (2011), Bernstein, (1977) and Duffield (1998) addressed the significant social class differences in pedagogy and the hidden curriculum – the pattern of expectations and acceptable/desired norms of behaviour for children/students from different social classes.

Jean Anyon's studies of the early 1980s (summarised in Anyon, 2011) were in five schools of four different social class types (two of the schools were 'working class', one was 'middle class', one 'affluent professional' and one 'executive elite' (capitalist) class. She showed distinct differences in pedagogy and expectations of teachers of children/students from different social classes.

The working-class school

In the two working-class schools, work follows the steps of a procedure, usually mechanical, involving rote behaviour and very little decision making or choice. Steps are told to the children by the teachers and are often written on the board. The children are usually told to copy the steps as notes.

Rote behaviour was often called for in classroom work. The teachers continually gave the children orders. Only three times did the investigator hear a teacher in either working-class school preface a directive with a polite 'please' or 'let's' or 'would you'. Instead, the teachers said, 'Shut up,' 'Shut your mouth,' 'Open your books'.

The middle-class school

In the middle-class school, work is getting the right answer. If one accumulates enough right answers, one gets a good grade.

The affluent-professional school

Work is creative activity carried out independently. . . . Work involves individual thought and expressiveness, expansion and illustration of ideas. . . . The products of work in this class are often written stories, editorials and essays, or representations of ideas in mural, graph, or craft form. The products of work . . . should show individuality.

The executive-elite school

In the executive elite school, work is developing one's analytical intellectual powers. Children are continually asked to reason through a problem, to produce intellectual products that are both logically sound and of top academic quality. . . . The teachers were very polite to the children, and the investigator heard no sarcasm, no nasty remarks and few direct orders. The teachers never called the children 'honey' or 'dear' but always called them by name.

Jill Duffield and associates

Pedagogies – the teaching and learning methods used by teachers and pupils – vary according to the pupils' social class. Duffield (1998), influenced by Bourdieu, followed two classes in each of four Scottish schools through their first two years of secondary education, observing 204 lessons. They found that children in the two working-class schools spent between 3% and 6% of their time in English class discussion compared with 17% to 25% in the middle-class schools. Pupils in predominantly working-class secondary schools were given more time-consuming reading and writing tasks than children in middle-class schools and had less opportunity for classroom discussions. 'Teachers of English in the two middle-class schools were more likely to give a reading or writing assignment as homework leaving time in class for feedback and redrafting written work'.

This seems in many ways to replicate the findings of Anyon and of Bowles and Gintis' (1976) *Schooling in Capitalist America* referred to next, concerning the class-based reproductive nature of the curriculum of schools, and Bernstein's (1977) work on pedagogies in the classroom.

Bowles and Gintis: schooling as economic reproduction

Bowles and Gintis' (1976) theorised schooling as economic reproduction, whereby 'the correspondence principle' explains the way in which the hidden curriculum of schools reproduces the social (and economic) class structure of society within the school, training school students for different economic and social futures on the basis of their social and economic pasts – their parental background.

Thus, it is the 'hidden curriculum', rather than the actual 'formal' or subject curriculum, which is crucial in providing capitalism with a workforce that has the personality, attitudes and values which are most useful. The structure of social relations in education develops the types of personal demeanour, modes of self-presentation, self-image and social-class identifications which are the crucial ingredients of job adequacy. Specifically, the social relationships of education – the relationships between administrators and teachers, teachers and students, students and students and students and

The reactionary right   215

their work – replicate the hierarchical division of labour. Thus, there is a structural correspondence between the social relations of the education system and those of production.

Bowles and Gintis suggest that school values correspond to the exploitative logic of the workplace, whereby pupils learn those values necessary for them to toe the line, to fit uncomplicatedly into menial manual jobs. For such children/students, the passive subservience (of working-class pupils to teachers) corresponds to the passive subservience of workers to managers, the acceptance of hierarchy (teacher authority) corresponds to the authority of managers and the system of motivation by external rewards (that is, grades rather than the intrinsic reward of learning and discovering) corresponds to being motivated by wages rather than job satisfaction.

Althusser: schooling as ideological reproduction

Althusser's (1971) conceptualised schooling as ideological reproduction, whereby schooling as an ideological state apparatus (ISA) works to persuade children that the status quo is fair and legitimate. If that doesn't work, then schools (and other state apparatuses) also function as a repressive state apparatus (RSA), disciplining and punishing what they regard as unacceptable 'deviance' or non-conformity/rebellion. Althusser was concerned with a specific aspect of cultural reproduction, namely, ideological reproduction, with the recycling of what is regarded as 'common sense' – in particular, with an acceptance of the current capitalist, individualistic, inegalitarian, consumerist society and economy.

How does the school function as an ISA? Althusser suggests that what children learn at school is 'know-how':

> Besides these techniques and knowledges, and in learning them, children at school also learn the 'rules' of good behaviour, rules of respect for the socio – technical division of labour and ultimately the rules of the order established by class domination. The school takes children from every class at infant-school age, and then for years in which the child is most 'vulnerable', squeezed between the family state apparatus and the educational state apparatus, it drums into them, whether it uses new or old methods, a certain amount of 'know-how' wrapped in the ruling ideology in its pure state.
>
> (Althusser, 1971)

Rikowski: schooling as the development of labour power and the crucial role of teachers

Rikowski (2001, 2002) theorised the crucial role of schooling (at all levels) of developing labour power: first, skills, and second, attitudes, personality characteristics and potential suitable for capitalism. For Rikowski (2001)

216 Dave Hill

'teachers and trainers are implicated in socially producing the single commodity – labour-power – on which the whole capitalist system rests. This gives them a special sort of social power' which includes 'the power to subvert, to teach against capital'.

For Rikowski (2001, 2002) schools do not just play a major role in reproducing educational, social, cultural and economic inequality; schools, colleges and universities – education – 'is a key process in the generation of the capital relation; this is the skeleton in capitalist education's dank basement' (2001):

> The substance of capital's social universe is value. Or, more specifically, capital's existence rests on surplus value -Labour-power, the capacity to labour (or labour capacity) is the primordial form of social energy within capital's social universe.
>
> (Rikowski, 2001)

Rikowski highlights two aspects to the social production of labour power: skills and willingness to use those skills (attitude). First, for Rikowski (2001) there is 'the development of labour power *potential*, the capacity to labour effectively within the labour process'. Second, 'the development of the willingness of workers to utilise their labouring power, to expend themselves within the labour process as value-creating force'. He points to the focus on 'attitudes' in recruitment studies and 'the exhortations of employers that schools must produce 'well motivated' young people, with sound attitudes to work, recruits who are 'work-ready' and embody 'employability'.

Rikowski ascribes a special place for teachers, trainers and educators, because they are crucial to 'producing the single commodity – labour-power – on which the capitalist system rests. This gives them a special sort of *social power*. They work at the chalkface of capital's weakest link, labour-power'. Hence, 'teachers are in a special position regarding their capacity to disrupt and to call into question the capitalist class relation'. They can subvert and colonise hegemonic curricula and pedagogies and 'insert principles of social justice into their pedagogy' (2001).

Socialist education

I conclude by (very briefly) suggesting a socialist policy of principles for education.

In brief, these are:

1 A democratically controlled public education service (i.e. with no private schools or universities)
2 'Comprehensive' in nature (what in India is called 'the common school', i.e. with no selective schools)

The reactionary right   217

3   With no charges to students (i.e. free education)
4   Fully and adequately funded by the state (local and/or national)
5   With free, nutritious, balanced school meals for every child to combat hunger, poor diets and obesity
6   With well-trained/educated and well-paid teachers and a teacher education system focusing not only on pedagogy/effective learning but also on critical thinking, teaching 'how to think' not 'what to think', and social and economic and environmental justice
7   That prioritises in the school both the hidden curriculum and formal curriculum, as well as social and economic justice, ecological and environmental justice and literacy, with critical interrogation using Marxist analysis
8   That includes creative studies/subjects for all in addition to 'basic' subjects
9   That is secular education, not religious
10 That has aims beyond the important aim of vocational education, into broader cultural, social and community education and into the development of an economically productive, critical and egalitarian citizenry (Hill, 2010)

In doing so, I recognise both the power of resistance but also its limitations, as well as the need for more comprehensive economic, political and social change – the change from capitalism to socialism.

The anti-hegemonic, socialist, Marxist struggle must take place in arenas outside the classroom, school and education apparatus and needs, as I and others argue (e.g. in Hill, 2012b, 2017b), a (Marxist) analysis, activism, organisation, party (socialist Marxist) programme. And that analysis must be a Marxist class analysis. This is a revolutionary Marxist programme to replace, overcome, overthrow and go beyond capitalism, to abolish the labour–capital relation and to progress into a democratic socialist society. In this, in the future, youth and education and cultural workers have, together with political parties, trade unions and social movements, a major role to play.

References

Anyon, J. (2011). *Marx and education*. London: Routledge.
Apple, M. (2006). *Educating the right way: Markets, standards, god, and inequality*. London: Routledge.
Althusser, L. (1971). Ideology and State apparatus. In: L. Althusser, ed., *Lenin and philosophy and other essays*. London: New Left Books.
Banfield, G. (2016). *Critical realism for Marxist sociology of education*. London: Routledge.
Bernstein, B. (1977). Class and pedagogies: Visible and invisible. In: B. Bernstein, eds., *Class, codes and control*, Vol. 3. London: Routledge and Kegan Paul.

218 Dave Hill

Bourdieu, P. (1990). *In other words: Towards a reflexive sociology.* Stanford, CA: Stanford University Press.

Bourdieu, R. (1997). The forms of capital. In: A. Halsey and H. Lauder, et al. eds., *Education: Culture, economy, society.* Oxford: Oxford University Press.

Bourdieu, R. and Passeron, J. (1977). *Reproduction in education, society and culture.* London: Sage Publications.

Bowles, S. and Gintis, H. (1976). *Schooling in capitalist America.* London: Routledge and Kegan Paul.

Bukharin, N. and Preobrazhensky, Y. (1920/1969). *The ABC of communism.* London: Penguin Books. Available at: www.marxists.org/archive/bukharin/works/1920/abc (Accessed on 19 December 2017).

Duffield, J. (1998). Learning experiences, effective schools and social context. *Support for Learning,* 13(1), pp. 3–8.

Freire, P. (1993). *Pedagogy of the oppressed.* New York: Continuum.

Gamble, A. (1988). *The free society and the strong state.* Basingstoke: Palgrave MacMillan.

Gezgin, U. B., İnal, K. and Hill, D. eds. (2014). *The Gezi revolt: People's revolutionary resistance against neoliberal capitalism in Turkey.* Brighton: Institute for Education Policy Studies.

Giroux, H. (1983). Theories of reproduction and resistance in the new sociology of education: A critical analysis. *Harvard Education Review,* 53(3), pp. 257–293.

———. (2004). *The terror of neoliberalism: Authoritarianism and the eclipse of democracy.* Boulder, CO: Paradigm Publishers.

Gramsci, Antonio. (1971). *Selections from the Prison notebooks.* New York: International Publishers Co.

Harvey, D. (2005). *A brief history of Neoliberalism.* Oxford: Oxford University Press.

Hill, D. (2003). Global neoliberalism, the deformation of education and resistance. *Journal for Critical Education Policy Studies,* 1(1). Available at: www.jceps.com/index.php?pageID=article&articleID=7 (Accessed on 12 April 2018).

———. (2006a). Education services liberalization. In: E. Rosskam, ed., *Winners or losers? Liberalizing public services.* Geneva: ILO, pp. 3–54. Available at: www.ieps.org.uk/PDFs/DaveHill-2006-EUCATIONSERVICESLIBERALIZATION.pdf (Accessed on 23 December 2017).

———. (2006b). Class, the crisis of neoliberal global capital, and the role of education and knowledge workers. *Firgoa Universidade Publica.* Available at: http://firgoa.usc.es/drupal/node/47262 (Accessed on 20 November 2017).

———. (2010). *A socialist manifesto for education.* Available at: www.ieps.org.uk/PDFs/socialistmanifestofored.pdf (Accessed on 23 December 2017).

———. (2012a). Immiseration capitalism, activism and education: Resistance, revolt and revenge. *Journal for Critical Education Policy Studies,* 10(2). Available at: www.jceps.com/index.php?pageID=article&articleID=259 (Accessed on 23 December 2017).

———. (2012b). Fighting Neoliberalism with education and activism. *Philosophers for Change.*1 March. Available at: https://philosophersforchange.org/2012/02/29/fighting-neoliberalism-with-education-and-activism/ (Accessed on 19 December 2017).

———. ed. (2013). *Immiseration capitalism and education: Austerity, resistance and revolt.* Brighton: Institute for Education Policy Studies.

———. ed. (2017a). *Class, race and education under Neoliberal capitalism*. New Delhi: Aakar Books.

———. (2017b). The Role of Marxist Educators Against and Within Neoliberal Capitalism. *Insurgent Scripts*, January. New Delhi: Insurgent Scripts. Available at: http://insurgentscripts.org/the-role-of-marxist-educators-against-and-within-neoli beral-capitalism/ (Accessed on 26 January 2018).

Hill, D. and Kumar, R. eds. (2009). *Global neoliberalism and education and its consequences*. New York: Routledge.

Hill, D. and Rosskam, E. eds. (2009). *The developing world and state education: Neoliberal depredation and egalitarian alternatives*. New York: Routledge.

Inal, K. and Akkaymak, G. eds. (2012). *Neoliberal Te of the AKP. Transformation of education in turkey: Political and ideological analysis of educational reforms in the ag*. New York: Palgrave Macmillan.

Malott, C., Hill, D. and Banfield, G. (2013). Neoliberalism, immiseration capitalism and the historical urgency of a socialist education. *Journal for Critical Education Policy Studies*, 11(4). Available at: www.jceps.com/index.php?pageID=article& articleID =311 (Accessed on 3 November 2017).

Marx, K. (1845). *Theses on Feuerbach*. Available at: www.marxists.org/archive/ marx/works/1845/theses/ (Accessed on 19 December 2017).

———. (1847). *The poverty of philosophy*. Available at: www.marxists.org/archive/ marx/works/1847/poverty-philosophy/ (Accessed on 10 January 2017).

Marx, K. and Engels, K. (1848). *The communist manifesto*. Available at: www. marxists.org/archive/marx/works/download/pdf/Manifesto.pdf (Accessed on 28 December 2017).

Oxfam (2018). *Press release: Even it up*. Available at: www.oxfam.org/en/pressroom/ pressreleases/2018–01–22/richest-1-percent-bagged-82-percent-wealth-created-last-year (Accessed on 19 December 2017).

Picketty, T. (2014). *Capital in the twenty-first century*. Cambridge, MA: Harvard University Press.

Rikowski, G. (2001). *After the manuscript broke off: Thoughts on Marx, social class and education*. A paper prepared for the British Sociological Association Education Study Group Meeting, King's College London, June 23. Available at: www. leeds.ac.uk/educol/documents/00001931.htm (Accessed on 19 January 2017).

———. (2002). Fuel for the living fire: Labour-power! In: A. Dinerstein and M. Neary eds., *The labour debate: An investigation into the theory and reality of capitalist work*. Aldershot: Ashgate.

———. (2008). The compression of critical space in education today. *The flow of ideas*. Available at: www.flowideas.co.uk/?page=articles&sub=Critical%20Space% 20in%20Education (Accessed on 20 February 2018).

Wilkinson, R. and Pickett, K. (2009). *The spirit level: Why more equal societies almost always do better*. London: Allen Lane.

Chapter 12

The agonies of neoliberal education

What hope progress?

Tom G. Griffiths

The title of this chapter borrows directly from a paper by Immanuel Wallerstein (1994) titled, *The Agonies of Liberalism: What Hope Progress?* I do that to highlight the insight and inspiration that Wallerstein's world-systems analysis continues to offer to our understanding of neoliberal capitalism that we are collectively experiencing, and in turn to our individual and collective efforts to imagine and advance alternatives. Counter-intuitively, that work identified the collapse of historical socialism not as the triumph of capitalism, but as a maker in the decline of the cultural framework of liberalism that was shared across capitalist and socialist states within the framework of a single, capitalist world-economy. The shared framework referred to was one that focused on the delivery of linear, and seemingly endless, national economic growth and 'development', overseen by rational policymakers in political power, harnessing scientific and technological revolution, and leading to the utopian goal of material abundance for all at some point over the horizon. The failure of 'liberalism' as defined to deliver on these promises, across political contexts, forms part of the wider structural crisis of the capitalist world-system that Wallerstein and others present as reaching absolute limits, whose resolution can only be via the transition towards an alternative, but uncertain, world-system.

In this chapter I will draw on world-systems analysis as way of understanding some key features of systems of mass schooling, including as one of many theoretical arguments for a critical education/critical pedagogy that might help prepare citizens with the critical knowledge, skills and dispositions needed to contribute to a non-capitalist transition. Most importantly, the chapter will draw on this perspective to critique the ongoing strength or prevalence of human capital theory in educational policy, reducing the primary purpose of mass schooling to the preparation of skilled, productive, disciplined labour. Further, the chapter explains how, within the dominant neoliberal framework, this official primary purpose of mass schooling emphasises individual economic benefits from schooling over broader, collective, social and cultural benefits, which helps to advance the neoliberal

The agonies of neoliberal education   221

core policy of reducing the public provision of education and constructing this, and other areas of social policy, as private and individual responsibilities, things to be purchased by individuals. I conclude with some reflections on the ways educators and activists use human capital logic to argue for expanded public provisions of and investments in education and the associated tensions involved. Acknowledging the realities of public policy debates with governments committed to neoliberal policy prescriptions, I advocate alternative approaches for educators and activists that emphasise alternative primary purposes of mass education, with the potential to contribute to wider anti-systemic movements.

World-systems analysis and mass schooling

In the mid-1990s I began a doctoral research project of secondary schooling in Cuba, inspired by foundational work focused on the ways in which schools operate, through their institutional, curricular and pedagogical practices, to sort people into differential social and economic trajectories and social class positions through the differential distribution of various educational credentials. This has been identified as critical education/critical pedagogy and the new sociology of education (e.g. Apple, 1979; Bowles and Gintes, 1976; Young, 1971). Grounded in these large areas of scholarship, that research was driven by an expectation that under Cuban socialism, schooling would be directed towards alternative social functions and the reproduction of a more equal and more just socialist society.

In the subsequent research, what I encountered was high schools that looked like a sort of global Western/industrialised/'norm' of the modern high school, with classrooms with desks and chairs, a chalkboard and teacher desk at the front, and with teachers 'instructing' students in these classes in traditional school subjects, with a common transmission-of-knowledge approach to pedagogy. The pedagogical patterns were familiar, involving teachers at the front of the class imparting information for students to copy from the board and memorise for later reproduction. There was a systemic emphasis on standardised testing to assess students' acquisition of knowledge, teachers' transmission of knowledge, and conventional compartmentalising of knowledge across subject disciplines. Schools were differentiated across sub-systems, some with highly competitive entry as pre-university institutes, others preparing students for vocational trajectories.[1]

I raise the Cuban case not to deal with it in a thorough way (see for example Griffiths, 2005, 2009), but to note how that work, and the broader case of education under historical socialism, can be understood in part through world-systems analysis. This approach responds to other work within the field of comparative and international education that has explained policy convergence in terms of an emerging world culture, arguing that the operation of a capitalist world-economy must be a part of any causal explanation (Griffiths and Arnove, 2015). The focus on this perspective is to locate nation-states and their national development projects within their participation in the capitalist world-economy.

From a world-systems analysis perspective, we see the consolidation of human capital theory as a driving force for the expansion of mass education across political systems tied to projects for national economic development within the capitalist world-economy. World-systems analysis built on dependency theory, and a larger argument about the emergence and subsequent trajectory of a single capitalist world-economy. Capitalism is understood as beginning with the crisis of feudalism in the 14th century, and a 'conjuncture of secular trends, an immediate cyclical crisis, and climatological decline' (Wallerstein, 1974: 37). These conditions led initially to a European world-economy, based on a capitalist mode of production, in the 'long 16th century', spanning 1450–1640. The development of a single capitalist world-economy was based in the accompanying geographical expansion of agricultural production, driven both by the nobility seeking to restore income levels and by increased activity of merchants trading in staple goods (Wallerstein, 1974).

The argument here is that a single capitalist world-economy developed over time, incorporating geographical areas through trade in necessities or staples and rise of the local bourgeoisie to manage the inter-dependent trade between areas, which in turn contributed to the strengthening of state machineries to oversee this. The capitalist world-economy involved a single division of labour and incorporated multiple political systems across ostensibly sovereign nation-states, particularly in the post-colonial period, operating in a formal interstate system and associated international institutions. This involved economic decisions within incorporated areas being oriented towards participation within the world economy, while political decisions of areas and units within the world economy were also oriented towards smaller structures and units of legal control, whether states, city-states, or empires (Wallerstein, 1974: 67).

Building on dependency theory, world-systems analysis locates and explains differential levels of 'development' in terms of countries'/nation-states' location within the capitalist world economy such that the development of some countries rests, in part, on the under-development of others, as articulated in Andre Gunder-Frank's (1966) famous essay. Wallerstein elaborates this in terms of core, semi-peripheral, and peripheral zones or areas of the world-economy, with particular types of economic activity associated with these areas, facilitating the flow of surplus from peripheral to core areas. According to this argument, the gradual expansion and incorporation of further geographical areas of the world was driven by this distribution of surplus and accumulation of capital by incorporating more of the available labour into production chains (Wallerstein, 1989).

The agonies of neoliberal education   223

This hierarchical structure of core, semi-peripheral, and peripheral zones is, for Wallerstein, a further defining feature of the capitalist world economy, whereby

> the economic factors operate within an arena larger than that which any political entity can totally control. This gives capitalists a freedom of maneuver that is structurally based. It has made possible the constant economic expansion of the world-system, albeit a very skewed distribution of its rewards.
>
> (Wallerstein, 1974: 348)

Part of the enduring strength of the capitalist world-system lies in the associated incorporation of multiple cultures and political systems with multiple forms of labour control, operating and seeking to maximise national outcomes within the world economy. In this account the modern nation-state seeks to create state structures and machinery 'sufficiently strong to defend the interests of one set of owner-producers in the world-economy against other sets of owner-producers as well as, of course, against workers' (Wallerstein, 1980: 114).

Clearly, the state is constructed to service the interests of the capitalist class, building structures and mechanisms intended to provide some sectors of capital with a comparative market advantage and, with it, increased profits/capital accumulation. The strength of the state thus becomes a critical element in determining the structural location of a nation-state within the hierarchical world economy. This framework both acknowledges the intent, and imperative, of states across the system to achieve and maintain measures of national economic development and the reality of the capitalist world-economy that requires some areas or states to remain in a state of relative 'underdevelopment' as a structural part of its normal operation.

With respect to the nature and spread of systems of mass education, one of the critical elements of this perspective is the associated creation of what Wallerstein calls a shared cultural framework of centrist liberalism, described as 'a set of ideas, values, and norms that were widely accepted throughout the system and that constrained social action thereafter' (Wallerstein, 2011: xvi). Some of the core features of this cultural framework, shared across political systems and nation-states, included:

> A belief in sovereign, independent nation-states operating through an inter-state system; a belief in linear, and endless, national economic growth and development as a possibility (if not inevitability); a belief in the universal nature and power of scientific and technological knowledge and advances; a belief in the capacity of sovereign nation-states, via rational policymakers in positions of power, to apply this knowledge to their administration of development projects; a belief in the need for a

224 Tom G. Griffiths

strong state machinery, and associated infrastructure, to undertake this work; and a promise of endless growth, progress and development, with the utopia of material abundance for all at some point over the horizon. As eloquently expressed by Wallerstein (1995: 103):

The possibility of the (economic) development of all countries came to be a universal faith, shared alike by conservatives, liberals, and Marxists. The formulas each put forward to achieve such development were fiercely debated, but the possibility itself was not. In this sense, the concept of development became a basic element of the geocultural underpinning of the world-system. . . .

Both conservatives and socialists accepted the world-scale liberal agenda of self-determination (also called national liberation) and economic development (sometimes called the construction of socialism).

The point here is not to deny so-called 'underdeveloped' states like Cuba the right to 'development', nor the aspiration and policy intent to achieve 'catch-up' development to approximate something like the levels of material wealth and well-being found in the core, so-called 'industrialised' or 'developed' countries of the world economy. Indeed, exercising this universal right is arguably a part of what drove the Soviet Union's massive programme of university educational aid for students from 'underdeveloped' and newly independent states (see Griffiths and Charon Cardona, 2015). That programme was explicitly about providing the absent 'conscience money of the West' (Bach, 2003: 6) that had directly, largely through colonial rule, consciously contributed to states' underdevelopment while extracting wealth and surplus value generated in the peripheral, colonial countries. The Soviet Union stepped in, with accompanying geopolitical considerations, seeking to advance the cause of socialism and win over graduates, and through them their home countries, to the socialist bloc. But a major part of the programme's logic was based in human capital theory, providing the formal education of professionals with the necessary knowledge and skills to oversee and deliver the development projects of former colonies.

Wallerstein's (1995) essay, and his and others' extensive scholarship under the banner of world-systems analysis offered, provides a way of understanding and explaining points of apparent policy convergence between nation-states' systems of mass schooling, including across historical socialist and capitalist contexts, and across the full range of diverse political systems more broadly. Identifying this convergence in terms of the normal operation of the capitalist world-economy remains something I am developing in my own work (e.g. Griffiths, 2009, 2013, 2015). Within the capitalist world-economy, nations' systems of mass schooling are seen as a part of wider projects of national economic development, which in turn are shaped by nation-states' efforts to achieve the 'centrist liberalism' promises of national

The agonies of neoliberal education 225

development within the hierarchical and inherently unequal capitalist world-economy.

Human capital theory and neoliberalism

The outline of world-systems analysis and its potential contribution to an understanding of the nature and spread of systems of mass education, set out earlier, clearly indicates the economic imperative on nation-states operating with the world economy. The post-war rise of human capital theory in the 1950s and 1960s aligned closely with the structural economic development imperative, fuelled further by post-war reconstruction and by the colonial legacy of underdevelopment that newly independent states confronted. Theodore Schultz's (1961) paper, *Investment in Human Capital*, elaborated the human capital case for investments in education, observing that '[i]t simply is not possible to have the fruits of a modern agriculture and the abundance of modern industry without making large investments in human beings' (16). Schultz (1961) was almost apologetic in this paper about the potentially dehumanising or alienating effects of 'looking upon human beings as capital goods' (2), but concluded that capitalism and the development of capitalists depended upon the acquisition of knowledge and skills that investments in education provided.

The basic logic of human capital theory is that a measurable rate of return on investments made in education can be calculated. This return on investments is two-fold: 1) an individual return (via the subsequent exchange of the educational credential attained for higher socio-economic status) and 2) a return to the nation via the more highly skilled, qualified, more productive labour force, improving the nation's competitiveness within the world economy and generating higher levels of national economic growth. Schultz's work raised dilemmas for capitalist countries in the Cold War context, in which the socialist bloc was prioritising publicly funded education for all, and had led the way in what others would subsequently term lifelong education (Steiner-Khamsi, 2006). Part of the dilemma, as discussed by Fleming (2017), was how to deal with the question of this form of capital being embodied in individuals and the acknowledgement of a return to individuals and how this should be understood and handled in policy. Fleming (2017) cites disagreements between Schultz and the anti-communist free-market ideologue Milton Friedman, the latter opposing ideas of such investments being treated as public goods, with returns being retained in the public sphere through taxation, for example, and instead arguing that individual recipients of this return 'should bear some or all of the investment costs'.

The clear alignment between human capital theory and Rostow's (1959) universal stages of economic growth, as set out in his 'non-communist manifesto', are readily apparent. Rostow stressed that the universal model of growth was not inevitable, but dependent on the correct 'patterns of choice'

(15) made by policymakers. His work extended to a justification/apology for colonial intervention and rule, arguing that:

> Without the affront to human and national dignity caused by the intrusion of more advanced powers, the rate of modernization of traditional societies over the past century-and-a-half would have been much slower than, in fact, it has been.
>
> (Rostow, 1959: 6)

Preparing human capital with the required knowledge, skills, dispositions, and discipline for the envisaged economic 'take-off', 'drive to maturity', and 'high-mass consumption' arguably entrenched this way of viewing and conceptualising the primary purposes of mass education.

Vally and Spreen (2012) noted the rise of human capital theory in the 1960s and its subsequent waning as part of the Marxist and dependency theory critiques of modernisation theory in the 1970s and 1980s. This major critique continued in world-systems analysis as reviewed earlier, and is supported by a growing scholarship pointing to the central contradictions of capitalism (e.g. Harvey, 2014), its subsequent transition towards something else (e.g. Mason, 2015; Wallerstein et al., 2013), and the associated incapacity of education to deliver employment, let alone meaningful and rewarding employment (Blacker, 2013; Collins, 2013). Despite these developments, human capital theory continued, and continues to be, the dominant official policy basis for education, whether for maintenance or expansion of mass schooling, or for post-school specialised and higher education. Under neoliberal policy frameworks, the development myths of modernisation theory and Rostow's work continue to be perpetuated and renewed, as though the decades of demonstrable failure of capitalism to deliver the material benefits of development to the majority had not occurred.

The logic that prevails, I argue, falsely promises upward social mobility for all individuals, and for all nations, through the returns on educational investments and the preparation of more qualified, more productive workers. Quite apart from debates about the source of educational investments and the distribution of returns on these investments, this sort of policy perpetuates the underlying problem, as identified by Vally and Spreen (2012: 179), whereby 'education is perceived as a panacea for problems that have their root causes elsewhere in the wider economy and society'. It deflects attention away from the root causes of social and economic inequalities within and between nations that characterise capitalism and seeks to perpetuate the liberal myth of linear progress and development for all states, if they would only apply the right policies and adopt the right sort of governance, as packaged and advocated by international agencies promoting neoliberal prescriptions.

Long-standing critical education work continues to provide the grounding for how this sort of dominant human capital logic, under neoliberal capitalism, works to legitimise inequalities and locate blame for poverty, for under- and unemployment, for a nation's 'underdevelopment', within individual students and parents; within schools and teachers; and within national policymakers/governments. If education is the panacea, as the World Bank, the United Nations, the IMF, and other international institutions continue to claim, then inadequate investment in education, or failure within its systems, is the problem.

This dominant narrative intersects with and reinforces the associated myth of meritocracy, entrenching blame for failure, for disadvantage, for under-performance, at the individual and whole country level (Bloodworth, 2016). In a recent discussion piece, Ye Liu (2016) describes a 'meritocratic dystopia' in which Michael Young's egalitarian commitments to 'greater equality in opportunities' as the necessary basis for the distribution of rewards based on merit were lost and meritocracy came to be associated with high-stakes standardised testing. She concludes that one logical outcome of a 'mature meritocracy' would see social status and well-being determined by a narrow measure of merit, with extreme social inequality a 'necessary by-product' for those left behind, allowing 'no alibis for failure'. We are arguably already living in some form of this sort of 'meritocratic dystopia'. Warmington (2015: 274) adds:

> Those who have benefited from the education system and now find themselves in good fortune tend to believe that 'what worked for them (a college education) must work for others, including and perhaps especially the poor' (*CD*, 166). The fact is, however, that not everyone can learn their way out of poverty because, as Marsh's figures show, late capitalism still operates a very large low-wage economy. The economic system that makes some affluent is the same system that locks others into poor work.

The political bind of human capital logic

The meritocratic and neoliberal myths of something approaching universal, upward social mobility, dependent in large part on individual ability and effort, permeate through public policy across the world, from early child-care through to university education. For example, in the case of Australia, the Council of Australian Governments (2009) generated an overarching framework for the provision of early childhood education across the country, entitled *Investing in the Early Years – A National Early Childhood Development Strategy*. Its stated vision, set out in the first paragraph of the policy framework, is 'to ensure that by 2020 all children have the best start in life to create a better future for themselves and for the nation' (4). Smith et al. (2016) cite this and similar approaches to the governing of early childhood education in New Zealand and the United States, noting how

> the creeping edu-capitalism shifts early years education and care further from a socialist endeavour and collectivism to individualistic capitalism under corporate business models, for profit, and to seeing childhood and education as a new, profitable investment.
>
> (126)

Even before children commence school, then, the primary purpose of childcare and child development in childcare is to prepare children for schooling and to begin their preparation for work and labour, as well as the narrowed definition of their lives and sense of being as units of human capital for the economy.

The United Nations Sustainable Development Goals, which replaced the partially achieved Millennium Development Goals, set out what is in many ways a laudable agenda to further extend the basics of what we might understand as markers of 'development' – ending poverty and hunger; providing decent housing with adequate and clean water, sanitation, and ecologically sustainable electricity supplies; reduced inequalities; and peace with justice – and gives attention to the intersection of the 17 identified goals (United Nations, 2017). Importantly, current UN Secretary General António Guterres refers in the forward to the 2017 report to the aspiration to 'free humanity from poverty, secure a healthy planet for future generations, and build peaceful, inclusive societies as a foundation for ensuring lives of dignity for all' (United Nations, 2017: 2). With respect to the push to universalise quality education, he adds that 'if all children in low-income countries completed upper secondary school by 2030, per capita income would increase by 75 per cent by 2050 and we could advance the fight to eliminate poverty by a full decade' (2). When it comes to the goal of reducing inequality within and between countries, the SDG report cites efforts to reduce the cost of remittances, to further increase the voting shares of developing countries in the IMF, and to further reduce tariffs on exports from low developed countries (LDCs).

One of the binds that educators and activists confront in our efforts to work for change from within these systems is a tendency to rely on human capital arguments in our efforts to appeal to policymakers and to public opinion shaped by a lifetime of this sort of policy thinking, to defend and expand the provision of public funding for education. This extends to all levels of education and is a well-established feature of school and university reforms. In response to policies like the Council of Australian Governments (2009) framework, we increasingly see advocates for early childcare education and its expansion citing and relying on claimed future economic benefits of this early preparation for schooling, whether in terms of the formation of future productive workers or the future reduction in social welfare costs that this early educational intervention is said to provide. For example, the Australian website from the Early Learning: Everyone Benefits group, www. everyonebenefits.org.au, notes that:

> All children benefit from early learning but particularly vulnerable children, who experience multiple adversities of poverty, neglect, domestic violence or live with parents with mental illness or drug and alcohol addictions. These are the children who benefit the most from the stability of a safe early learning environment, who are able to get the support they need to understand and manage their emotions and learn good social skills.

This group also highlights James Heckman's work, from a two-page 'fact sheet' titled: *Invest in Early Childhood Education & Development: Reduce Deficits and Strengthen the Economy*, citing economic returns on investments in early childcare education (Heckman, 2018).

As with the development of human capital theory in the 1960s, this sort of advocacy for educational spending as an investment that will reap future economic returns suggests governments should make these investments. Activists defending public education rely on this. But as we know, the neoliberal policy framework also works directly against the public provision of services in general, including educational services, in favour of the individual purchase of such services from private providers. Neoliberalism as a policy framework privileges market principles and competition in all spheres of social life, including education, in its advocacy for an ever-reducing role for government and the provision of public services by government. Calls to reduce taxation (particularly on the wealthiest sectors of society) and correspondingly reduce public expenditure on services follow, whereby individuals (under the neoliberal myth of maximal individual choice) select and purchase formerly public services from private providers, adding to the profits of companies providing these services. This foundational premise of neoliberal education policy rests on neoliberal economics more broadly which seeks to reduce taxes, and with them, state expenditure on all public services, in favour of increasingly privatised provision of such services to be purchased by individuals, which in turn generates profits for private companies providing formerly public services (Hill, 2005, 2013). Down's (2006) synthesises this logic and succinctly captures the idea here as being

> wedded to the idea that the market should be the organising principle for all political, social and economic decisions. This involves trade and financial liberalisation, deregulations, the selling off of state

corporations, competition, heavy tax cuts, and a shifting of the tax burden from the top to the bottom.

(96)

Wallerstein (2003) described this sort of neoliberal utopia that policymakers continue to put forward as a 'mad fantasy' that sets out to redefine

the good society as the one characterized by the predominance of an unfettered free flow of the factors of production, all in non-governmental hands, and most especially the free flow of capital.

(221–22)

Revolutionary reforms

Human capital logic is used to support the neoliberal dystopian fantasy. It cites individual social and economic benefits that will accrue to individuals from their participation in formal education and attainment of educational credentials, leading arguably to increasingly strident claims that to provide this material advantage with public funds is unfair/unjust when the benefits go to the individual. In this context of the ongoing neoliberal assault/counter-offensive, appeals to human capital return-on-investment arguments for public educational provisions, expansion, and improvement risk exacerbating public reductions in educational provision, spending, and 'investments' by inadvertently reinforcing claims of individual benefit, and hence the need for individual investments. More fundamentally, our reliance on these arguments endorses the myth that upward social mobility and development is possible for all within the existing international system and world economy.

As with any collective political action within the current neoliberal phase of the capitalist world-system, however, we struggle with the associated tensions, risks, and contradictions at every turn. The UN and its SDG agenda does not call for the transformation and replacement of the capitalist world-system with an alternative that can better achieve its goals; nor is it likely to in the foreseeable future. But even within these frameworks that are creations of, and dedicated to the preservation of, the capitalist world-system, we can find opportunities to advocate alternative agendas. At one level, many of us might publicly support and actively work to help achieve the goals of universal quality education, based on some common ground with UN Secretary General Guterres, for example. Moreover, even within the narrowed, human capital argument for EFA, it is possible to find some statements of alternative visions which, for example, hint at a rights-based approach to universal quality education, as articulated by Katarina Tomasevski (2003), and, of course, which rest upon Article 26 of the Universal Declaration of Human Rights (United Nations, 1948). For example, former

The agonies of neoliberal education   231

UK Prime Minister and now UN Special Envoy for Global Education Gordan Brown recently noted that

> Delivering an education to all – and not just some children – is the civil rights struggle of our time. . . . Confronted by the largest refugee crisis since the close of the Second World War, and with education receiving less than 2 per cent of humanitarian aid, it is vital we marshal the funds to provide an education for all children – especially those left out and left behind: refugee children.
>
> (cited in UN News Centre, 2017)

Former Prime Minister of New Zealand and now UNDP Administrator Helen Clarke is similarly is quoted as saying:

> In our world, knowledge is power, and education empowers. It is an indispensable part of the development equation. It has intrinsic value – extending far beyond the economic – to empower people to determine their own destiny. That is why the opportunity to be educated is central to advancing human development.
>
> (cited in UNESCO, 2016: 13)

My argument here is that we can and should be critical of the limited and flawed human capital logic underpinning SDGs and similar international organisations' policies for expanded mass education, but this does not mean we should completely disregard them and their potential to assist the cause of achieving universal education that raises critical consciousness in ways that support the transformation of capitalism. Under neoliberal conditions, we are condemned to act in response to the associated attacks on public education, and so engage in political struggles to defend, maintain, and even improve public provisions of education.

But the human capital logic that underpins mainstream policy is fundamentally and irretrievably flawed under existing political and economic structures. Worse still, appeals to it risk further promoting and legitimising public policy that seeks to shift the cost of such services from the state to individuals, citing individual benefits, as noted earlier. If we are to advance anything like the 'revolutionary reforms' that de Sousa Santos (2008) identified and advocates with respect to education, then we need to base our arguments in an alternative logic. Within the ongoing neoliberal counter-offensive, this alternative might simply be a radical re-statement of quality education as a human right, along the lines of that advanced by countries like Venezuela as part of its anti-neoliberal politics of 21st-century socialism (Griffiths, 2010a, 2010b). Social democratic initiatives like those advanced in that case become revolutionary, but achievable, short-run reforms in the larger struggle for liberatory education and social transformation. Similarly,

232 Tom G. Griffiths

we might advocate for the benefits of a universal, quality, liberal arts education like that developed by Martha Nussbaum (2012) and her 'human development paradigm'.

Arguing for expanded public education as a human right and as a public good may, where necessary, linking such arguments with mainstream figures and institutions as suggested earlier. This activity can help build a larger movement that acknowledges the failure of universalised human capital arguments, and so is open to the need for and task of constructing alternative systems. These are alternatives in which all can make meaningful contributions and in which all actively work to raise students' critical understanding of these realities. On this grounding we can develop students' knowledge, skills, and dispositions needed to both imagine more equal, just, democratic, and peaceful alternatives and to take action to contribute to their realisation. The contemporary crises that confront capitalism are expanding the potential support for such alternatives, in the same way that neoliberal austerity is making the idea of socialism in developed capitalist states like the UK, and even the United States, almost mainstream. From the bleakness of neoliberal capitalism and pending ecological catastrophe, there is a realistic hope for system changing progress.

Note

1 Care is needed to acknowledge significant points of difference, such as the systemic application of the 'work-study' principle, illustrated most emphatically in the *Escuelasen el campo* (Schools in the Countryside), which were full boarding schools for students located in areas of agricultural production and with part of the school day dedicated to students' productive work, which in turn was envisaged to help finance the expansion of these secondary schools across the country. This phenomenon has also received quite a bit of attention from academic researchers, including work tracking and comparing its application in countries like Tanzania and Zimbabwe.

References

Apple, M. (1979). *Ideology and curriculum*. London: Routledge & Kegan Paul.

Bach, Q. V. S. (2003). *Soviet aid to the third world: The facts & figures*. East Sussex: The Book Guild.

Blacker, D. J. (2013). *The falling rate of learning and the Neoliberal Endgame*. Winchester: Zero Books.

Bloodworth, J. (2016). *The myth of meritocracy: Why working-class kids get working-class jobs*. London: Biteback Publishing.

Bowles, S. and Gintes, H. (1976). *Schooling in capitalist America: Educational reform and the contradictions of economic life*. New York: Basic Books.

Collins, R. (2013). The end of middle-class work: No more escapes. In: I. Wallerstein, R. Collins, M. Mann, G. Derlugian, and C. Calhoun eds., *Does capitalism have a future?* Oxford and New York: Oxford University Press, pp. 37–69.

Council of Australian Governments. (2009). *Investing in the Early Years – A National Early Childhood Development Strategy* Available at: www.startingblocks.gov.au/media/1104/national_ecd_strategy.pdf (Accessed on 26 September 2017).

de Sousa Santos, B. (2008). Depolarised pluralities. A left with a future. In: P. Barrett, D. Chavez, and C. Rodríguez-Garavito eds., *The new Latin American left: Utopia Reborn*. Amsterdam: Pluto Press, pp. 255–272.

Down, B. (2006). A critical pedagogy of vocational education and training in schools and communities struggling with shifts in the global economy. *Learning Communities: International Journal of Learning in Social Contexts*, 3(1), pp. 94–120.

Fleming, P. (2017). *What is human capital?* Available at: https://aeon.co/essays/how-the-cold-war-led-the-cia-to-promote-human-capital-theory (Accessed on 28 December 2017).

Frank, A. G. (1966). The development of underdevelopment. *Monthly Review*, 18(7), pp. 17–31.

Griffiths, T. G. (2005). Learning 'to be somebody'. Cuban youth in the special period. *International Journal of Learning*, 11, pp. 1267–1274.

———. (2009). 50 Years of socialist education in revolutionary Cuba: A world-systems perspective. *Journal of Iberian and Latin American Research*, 15(2), 45–64.

———. (2010a). Las reformas curriculares y la educación Bolivariana: Una perspectiva del análisis sistema-mundo [Curricular reform and Venezuela's Bolivarian education: A world-systems perspective]. *Ensayo y Error*, XIX(38), pp. 117–139.

———. (2010b). Schooling for twenty-first-century socialism: Venezuela's Bolivarian project. *Compare*, 40(5), pp. 607–622. doi:10.1080/03057920903434897

———. (2013). Wallerstein's world-systems analysis. In: T. G. Griffiths and R. Imre eds., *Mass education, global capital, and the world: The Theoretical lenses of István Mészáros and Immanuel Wallerstein*. New York: Palgrave Macmillan, pp. 67–98.

———. (2015). Critical education for systemic change: A world-systems analysis perspective. *Journal for Critical Education Policy Studies*, 13(3), pp. 163–177.

Griffiths, T. G., and Arnove, R. F. (2015). World culture in the capitalist world-system in transition. *Globalisation, Societies and Education*, 13(1), pp. 88–108. doi:10.1080/14767724.2014.967488.

Griffiths, T. G. and Charon Cardona, E. T. (2015). Education for social transformation: Soviet university education aid in the cold war capitalist world-system. *European Education*, 47(3), pp. 226–241. doi:10.1080/10564934.2015.1065390

Harvey, D. (2014). *Seventeen contradictions and the end of capitalism*. London: Profile Books.

Heckman, J. (2018). Invest in early childhood development: Reduce deficits, strengthen the economy. *Heckman: The economics of human potential*. Available at: https://heckmanequation.org/resource/invest-in-early-childhood-development-reduce-deficits-strengthen-the-economy/ (Accessed on 15 June 2018).

Hill, D. (2005). Globalisation and its Educational discontents: Neoliberalisation and its impacts on education workers' rights, pay and conditions. *International Studies in Sociology of Education*, 15(3), pp. 257–288.

———. ed. (2013). *Immiseration capitalism and education: Austerity, resistance and revolt*. Brighton: Institute for Education and Policy Studies.

Liu, Y. (2016). The truth about meritocracy: It doesn't make society fairer. *The Conversation*. Available at: https://theconversation.com/the-truth-about-meritocracy-it-doesnt-make-society-fairer-65260 (Accessed on 22 December 2017).

Mason, P. (2015). *Postcapitalism: A guide to our future*. London: Allen Lane.

Nussbaum, M. C. (2012). Education for profit, education for democracy. In M. C. Nussbaum, ed., *Not for profit: Why democracy needs the humanities*. Princeton and Oxford: Princeton University Press, pp. 13–26.

Rostow, W. W. (1959). The stages of economic growth. *The Economic History Review*, 12(1), pp. 1–16.

Schultz, T. W. (1961). Investment in human capital. *The American Economic Review*, 51(1), pp. 1–17.

Smith, K., Tesar, M. and Myers, C. Y. (2016). Edu-capitalism and the governing of early childhood education and care in Australia, New Zealand and the United States. *Global Studies of Childhood*, 16(1), pp. 123–135.

Steiner-Khamsi, G. (2006). The development turn in comparative education. *European Education*, 38(3), pp. 19–47.

Tomasevski, K. (2003). The promise of the 1948 universal declaration of human rights. In: K. Tomasevski ed., *Education denied: Costs and remedies*. London and New York: Zed Books, pp. 36–50.

UN News Centre. (2017). *World leaders gathered at UN commit to boosting investment in education*. Available at: www.un.org/sustainabledevelopment/blog/2017/09/world-leaders-gathered-at-un-commit-to-boosting-investment-in-education/ (Accessed on 2 March 2018).

UNESCO. (2016). *Education 2030 incheon declaration: Towards inclusive and equitable quality education and lifelong learning for all*. Available at: http://unesdoc.unesco.org/images/0024/002456/245656E.pdf (Accessed on 20 December 2017).

United Nations. (1948). *The universal declaration of human rights*. Available at: www.un.org/en/documents/udhr/index.shtml (Accessed on 22 October 2017).

———. (2017). *The sustainable development goals report 2017*. New York: United Nations.

Vally, S. and Spreen, C. A. (2012). Human Rights in World Bank Education Strategy. In: S. J. Klees, J. Samoff, and N. P. Stromquist eds., *The world bank and education: Critiques and alternatives*. Rotterdam: Sense Publishers, pp. 173–187.

Wallerstein, I. (1974). *The modern world-system I: Capitalist agriculture and the origins of the European world-economy in the sixteenth century*. New York: Academic Press.

———. (1980). *The modern world-system II: Mercantilism and the consolidation of the European world-economy, 1600–1750*. New York: Academic Press.

———. (1989). *The modern world-system III: The second era of great expansion of the capitalist world-economy, 1730–1840s*. San Diego, CA: Academic Press, Inc.

———. (1994). The agonies of liberalism: What hope progress? *New Left Review*, (204), pp. 3–17.

———. (1995). *After liberalism*. New York: The New Press.

———. (2003). *The decline of American power*. New York: The New Press.

———. (2011). *The modern world-system IV: Centrist liberalism triumphant, 1789–1914*. Berkeley: University of California Press.

Wallerstein, I., Collins, R., Mann, M., Derlugian, G. and Calhoun, C. (2013). *Does capitalism have a future?* Oxford and New York: Oxford University Press.

Warmington, P. (2015). Dystopian social theory and education. *Educational Theory*, 65(3), pp. 265–281.

Young, M. F. D. ed. (1971). *Knowledge and control: New directions for the sociology of education*. London: Collier-Macmillan.

Chapter 13

Analysing educational change

Towards an understanding of patterns of historical and cultural refraction

Ivor Goodson

This chapter reports some of the findings from four-year studies of educational reforms in seven European countries undertaken for the European Commission. The countries covered are England and Wales, Ireland, Portugal, Spain, Finland, Sweden and Greece, and the research was conducted and reported from 2004 to 2014.

The aim of the Professional Knowledge project was to understand how plans for educational reform and restructuring impinged on patterns of professional knowledge with particular regard to teaching and health professionals (nurses and doctors).

In this chapter I concentrate primarily on the education sector. The methodological basis of the research is fairly complex, as would be expected in a multi-disciplinary, multi-national study, but the full methodological armoury can be reviewed at the Profknow (2002–2008) website (www.prof know.net) (Goodson and Lindblad, 2011).

Broadly, the research study employed a narrative approach to studying two kinds of narratives. First, what were called 'systemic narratives'; these comprised the main documentary sources of the restructuring and reform initiatives in each national and regional area. To bring this closer to the educational settings, however, these 'systemic narratives' were juxtaposed against what were called 'work life narratives'. 'Work life narratives' focused on life history interviews with a range of teachers employed in schools, primarily secondary schools, in the national settings. Where possible, the life history interviews covered a cohort plan so that the different generations of teachers were given a chance to develop their narratives according to the historical period in which they had worked. Cohorts therefore covered three broad time spans: teachers who had begun work in the 1960s and 1970s, those who had begun work in the 1980s and 1990s and those who had recently begun work.

The two sections that follow review 'systemic narratives' in relationship to particular historical periods, and the final section looks at teachers' work–life narratives in relationship to these systemic reforms.

Historical periods and systemic narratives

Our work on studying generations, as originally planned, led us to conceptualise historical periods of restructuring. The work uses the French historical methodology developed by the *Annaliste* school of historians. They focus on particular conjunctures where broad-based restructuring is promoted. It is possible to identify particular historical periods where maximal 'windows of opportunity' for broad-based restructuring exist (for an extended commentary on historical periodisation and education see Goodson, 2005).

For this reason, it is crucial, when dealing with educational transitions and reform initiatives, to identify and understand historical periodisation and its conceptual and methodological limitations. The definition of periods allows us to define the possibility for professional action and professional narratives at particular points in historical time. We have found in the Profknow project that the capacities for action and narrative construction differ greatly according to the historical periods studied. Moreover, we can begin to see how each country, and in some cases regions, has different systemic trajectories. These historical trajectories mean restructuring approaches each state or region from a different angle, so to speak. Both historical periods and systemic trajectories can be seen as refracting centralised restructuring initiatives. Studying translation and diffusion gives us access to the processes of refraction.

Because of the complexity of historical periodisation, we asked each national team to prepare their own historical analysis. This periodisation tells us important facts about changes in education and health care in their respective national contexts. But they also tell us about the manner in which different national teams organise their ways of dealing with these state institutions. Their perceptions of welfare state developments are themselves therefore periodised.

We enclose a summary chart of these perceptions. Although we have employed the term 'dictatorship' in the Southern European cases, our national team referred instead to internal 'transitions' within those periods and to growing patterns of modernisation.

Nonetheless, the late evolution of welfare states in the south stands in sharp juxtaposition to the post-war social democracies in the north. Sweden, Finland and England saw fast expansion after 1945. But England and Ireland moved rapidly into reform mode through the 1980s. This neoliberal style of restructuring then becomes a broad-based movement across all seven countries in the 1990s, but building on sharply different trajectory foundations (Table 13.1).

These rather basic definitions of periodisation nonetheless serve some general purposes. They show the clear distinction between the Southern European states and the Northern European states with regard to their historical trajectories. In the southern nation-states dictatorship came to an

Analysing educational change 237

Table 13.1 Periodisation in national contexts

National case	Periods
England	1945–1979: Progressive narrative on welfare state expansion. 1979–1997: Marketisation narrative. 1997–2007: Narrative of the middle way: targets, tests and tables.
Finland	1945–1969: Preparatory phase building the welfare state. 1970–1989: The golden age. 1990–2007: Restructuring.
Greece	1945–1967: Post-war period. 1967–1974: Dictatorship. 1975–1989: Welfare state building. 1991–2007: Restructuring.
Ireland	1970–1986: The demise of the apprenticeship and increasing secularisation. 1987–1997: Envisioning the future partnership as a new approach. 1997–2007: Opening the floodgates of reform.
Portugal	1945–1974: Dictatorship. 1974–1976: Revolutionary period. 1977–1985: Normalisation. 1985–2007: Restructuring.
Spain	1939–1976: Dictatorship. 1977–1990: Normalising. 1990–2000: Welfare state building. 2000–2007: Restructuring.
Sweden	1945–1975: Welfare state expansion – services for all. 1975–1992: Decentralisation and deregulation. 1992–2000: Marketisation. 2000–2007: Quality agenda.

end in the mid-1970s and 'welfare state' patterns slowly began to emerge. At more or less the same time the north established welfare states that were coming under pressure to marketise and reform. England and Ireland led this neoliberal agenda pattern of restructuring in the 1980s; other countries began the same agenda in the 1990s.

Hence, when that which Meyer calls the 'world movement' of neoliberal educational reforms started in all countries in the 1990s, they began on very different historical foundations. The historical trajectories of each nation-state effectively reformulated and refracted this neoliberal reform agenda in starkly different ways. This is reflected in the juxtaposition of these systemic narratives to teachers' work–life narratives in each country.

Before we review the work–life narratives, it may be worth providing the Profknow summary of neoliberal reform initiatives. The following summary is drawn from Beach's work on the Profknow project and accords with

238 Ivor Goodson

much of the research work characterising this period of restructuring (e.g. Ball, 2007) (Table 13.2).

Of course, restructuring of systems is not achieved by the enunciation of policy discourse; restructuring works only in association with teachers' work–life narratives and practices.

We have seen that neoliberal reforms constitute a world movement and delineated some of the key characteristics of the world movement in the current conjuncture. This conjuncture was discerned in the first section, when we looked at historical periodisation. This became a generalised movement in the mid-1990s as it continued to increase in terms of force.

Table 13.2 Main features of public service restructuring in the case studies

- Decentralisation.
- Development of an emphatic discourse of privatisation and marketisation (habituation).
- Standardisation of instruction and assessment.
- Sacrifice of the critical mission of professional education/training to practical and technical training in economic interests.
- Conversion of public services to private.
- Business takeover of education and care supply and teacher and nursing supply.
- The creation of quasi-markets for consolidating the processes of privatisation.
- Authorities forming agencies for contracting out services to private suppliers.
- Costs of administration shifted from costs of public ownership and control to costs of managing and monitoring outsourced delivery.
- Increased costs from franchise effects (un-/under-employment) on public employees.
- The increased objectification of labour and increases in the value form of labour.
- A dissemination of a view of learners and care recipients as economically rational, self-interested individuals and the reconstruction of supply in line with this vision.
- A redefinition of democracy in terms of consumer choice.
- An increased objectification of teachers and nurses, learners and patients, care and curricula and (increasingly) professional education and educators as factors of production.
- The creation of a labour buffer (surplus army of labour) in the education and care sectors at the same time as (at least in some education sectors) posts are increasingly difficult to fill and notoriously difficult to maintain continuity in.
- Increased class differences in terms of education and care supply and consumption: i.e. in terms of who provides care and to/for whom.
- Increased inequalities in service work conditions.
- Increases in quick training programmes to maximise economic gains.
- Increases in judgment of performances according to consumer values.

Crucially, however, we saw how the restructuring of educational systems in European nation-states builds on different trajectorial foundations and historical periodisation. There turn out to be critical zones of refraction in understanding how restructuring initiatives are translated and diffused in a specific milieu.

Work–life narratives

We discerned a range of responses when juxtaposing systemic narratives and work–life narratives. In the next section, we provide examples from most of our case study countries. But this should not be taken to mean countries react monolithically to restructuring initiatives. There are a variety of *points of refraction*, or milieu membranes, through which restructuring policies must pass – national systems, regional systems, school board systems – right through to individual schools and individual classrooms and teachers. This means that a wide range of responses are possible, even if certain national characteristics of responses can be evidenced.

Figure 13.1 provides a framework for analysing the various main configurations found when juxtaposing system narratives and teachers' and nurses' work–life narratives.

A number of national case studies highlight the different juxtapositions, but, as noted, this is not to argue that national responses are monolithic. The English case study, for instance, finds compelling evidence of integration and of restructuring affecting professional change towards what we call 're-framed' professionals.

The report notes:

> Teachers and nurses are trapped in the gap between government rhetoric and political narratives about choices and entitlements and the reality of the classroom or the hospital situation.
>
> The interviews highlight the unease of professionals with overriding national policies. Using choice and competition as methods of raising standards in public services is seen as intrinsically contradictory and causing greater inequalities in society and taking professionals away from the aims of putting clients first. However, the lack of a national underlying oppositional ideology (with socialism having been dropped by the Labour Party) leads to inward motivation and increased professional localism.

England poses an interesting case, given the historical periods and trajectories we have evidenced earlier. One of the countries to build up a strong welfare state after 1945, England became a leader in neoliberal restructuring initiatives aimed at transforming, if not dismantling, this welfare system.

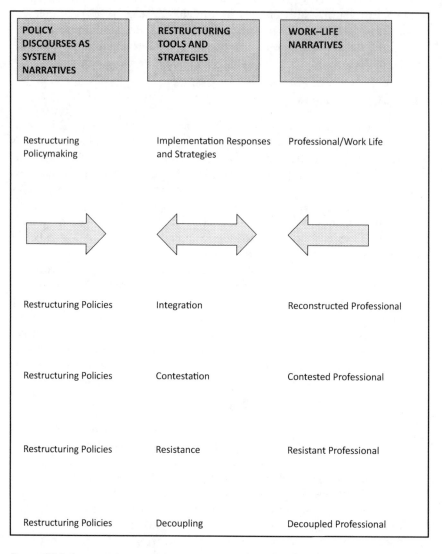

Figure 13.1 Juxtaposing system narratives and work–life narratives

In Sweden and Finland, the welfare system has proved more durable and politically sustainable. Hence, both the Swedish and Finnish studies show how restructuring has been contested and often, if attempted, sidestepped by professionalism.

The slogan *personality is the most important instrument of work* is predominant among Finnish teachers, indeed the practicing teachers emphasise that the long science-based teacher education, except practical training periods, provides only a theoretical foundation for professional work. For them the most important source of knowledge is the practical activities, common sense, everyday experiences and learning by doing. In addition, personal hobbies and activities outside the school are valued as well. Indeed according to some recent studies, the opportunities to draw on personal interests and to exercise independent judgement are among the most important motivations for being a teacher.

This example is common in the established welfare societies of Sweden and Finland as they once were in England. The belief in professional autonomy being motivating and creative leads to loosely coupled or decoupled restructuring strategies. Significantly Finland, where professional autonomy is deeply entrenched and restructuring policies are least intensive, produces highly successful educational indicators. This appears to be an efficient and motivated professional system which builds on a belief in professional expertise, judgment and commitment. Without these elements, it is difficult to see restructuring working smoothly, however intensive and politically promoted it might be.

Certainly, restructuring has the features of a world movement that political elites are promoting, but we can see how the different historical periodisations and trajectory crucially refract this process. In Sweden and Finland, deeply entrenched systems of social democracy and professional expertise appear to have more enduring leverage than in England and Ireland.

Now let us turn to the very different historical periodisations and trajectories in Southern Europe. As we noted, these countries – Portugal, Spain and Greece – came late to welfare systems and social democracy. Hence, the restructuring world movement enters these societies at a different stage and at a different angle. The result of this trajectory of engagement is clear in the way that restructuring initiatives are refracted.

In Portugal, contestation and resistance seem endemic. The report is eloquent and very clear on this point:

> The strategies developed by the teaching profession have been mainly reactive: they express mostly a systematic rejection of the initiatives proposed by the central administrator than a proactive and anticipatory presentation of new forms of structuring and promoting the professional group. . . . Only recently (since the end of the 1980s) have the unions discussed a structure for the teaching career, but even then, they have done so . . . in a primarily reactive manner, trying to keep things the way they were and resisting any attempts of change, rather than proposing structural changes that might improve the quality of professional practice and its outcomes.

This Portuguese response shows how the role of periods and trajectories is a vital conceptual tool in understanding how restructuring initiatives are received by professional groups, received and then refracted. The periodisation and trajectories in Greece have considerable similarities and, for the older generation who knew the revolutionary period, can be clearly evidenced. Here, though, generational restrictions can more clearly be drawn than was the case in Portugal, where generational conformity seems more substantial.

> Generational differences in the professional strategies towards restructuring are expressed as differentiated attitudes towards intensification of working conditions.
>
> Senior teachers and nurses tend to ignore the pressures and they use experience and collegial learning as the main way to cope with new demands at work and compensation for the lack of up-to-date knowledge. Working conditions are experienced as more intense and pressurising on the part of the middle aged teachers. Hierarchies among this age group are more peculiar since their formal qualifications vary substantially (some of them having two years initial education, some others four years plus additional university 'equation' training). Younger teachers and nurses tend to come from a richer socioeconomic background and they all have university qualifications. They experience restructuring not as part of historical consciousness regarding the transitions the profession is undergoing but as a frustrating client-oriented working environment. Personnel shortages add to this feeling.
>
> Substantial generational differences refer to the confidence in syndicalism as an effective professional strategy. In both the teaching and the nursing professions, the older generation is aware of the contribution of collective action in proposing and defending professional strategies. However, the younger generation of nurses and teachers are not interested in syndicalism and do not become active members partly because the image of syndicalism has faded as part of the more general mistrust in politics.

The Spanish case study is a beautifully constructed analysis of some of the complexities and refractions of restructuring when viewed from the local level. Their analysis confirms the essential point about periodisation and trajectories and generations.

> Talking about restructuring both in education and in health requires us to talk briefly about structuring. As we have already said, the very late development of Welfare State in Spain has to be acknowledged when dealing with restructuring. Only doing this one can understand the specificity of the Spanish case, which is something like a compressed and anomalous history of the Welfare State in Europe. Public health

and education institutions were firstly developed in democracy in the 1990s. Before that, as we know, there were timid build-ups by Franco's regime. Up until 1967 in health and 1970 in education there was not a comprehensive system for providing basic services to most citizens. So basically what we see during the 1990s is the building of the kind of welfare institutions that most European countries developed after the Second World War. A decade later, the first clear symptoms of their dismantling were manifest.

The report shows responses that are quite like aspects of the Portuguese and Greek (certainly the older generation) work–life narratives.

The recent history of the Spanish educational system just mentioned provided a concrete picture of restructuring from a system narrative. However, it failed to be identified as a meaningful player for the teachers themselves. A high degree of scepticism and cynicism was observed regarding the impact of policies in everyday practices. First, our evidence shows that the Spanish teachers we studied perceived their profession and their work on a daily, personal basis rather than embedded in large socio-political contexts. Therefore, restructuring was not thought of as a kind of local expression of global dynamics, so a very interesting gap remains between their conception of the system and the theoretical causes and explanations some theorists of the field may put forward. Even when explicitly drawing attention to changes in the legislation from our side, this was not perceived as influencing day-to-day business, either because changes are too cosmetic or lack the necessary time to become applied practice. The educational projects associated with the different political parties were met with a dismissive shrug, unable to affect their working conditions for the better. What happens on the level of politics is perceived as having little or nothing to do with the real necessities in the school.

Sophia:

> I don't care about a lot of political things, but in your daily life. . . . That's also why I believe a little less each day in political things. I mean, the little I know, they disappoint me so much that beyond my daily life, why should I care about politics.

Rosa's view is similar:

> In her eyes it is not that the actual laws don't function but rather that they are missing the necessary resources to be actually implemented.

The Spanish case points to the conceptual complexity of professional responses and highlights the differences between the teachers and nurses noted earlier and between diverse local settings. Their warning against conceptual over-generalisation is important.

By comparing our cases, it becomes apparent how varied and often contradictory the processes of 'restructuring' are. They comprise many facets, temporalities and scales.

Thus, it is clear how historical periods and trajectories operate in identifiable ways to refract restructuring initiatives. We have clear evidence that the main responses delineated in the earlier chart of restructuration, contestation, resistance and decoupling can be found in our case studies. Moreover, our work on generational periodisation and trajectories is of some utility in understanding the pattern of responses.

Theory is always of specific rather than general use. We, too, need to be parsimonious with our general ambitions. But if there is a message to those in governing agencies who sponsor restructuring initiatives, it would be to advise a similar caution in promoting over-centralised, over-generalised expectations and edicts. We have seen how a world movement like restructuring has been widely promoted in Europe. We have also seen how the response has varied immensely and how sensitivity to generations, periodisation and national trajectories helps explain the process of refraction.

At the end point of the multi-layered refraction process sits the individual or professional. Still, we should remember a key player, probably the key player, in the process. Alienate your professional groups, and your restructuring rhetoric will remain just that – political rhetoric. Let us end then with a recognition of the central and inestimable value of the professional contribution of teachers and nurses in the actual delivery of that about which the rest of us pronounce. The professional teacher was described in this way by an experienced Finnish teacher educator who remembers Finland's exemplary performance in education:

> Good teacher hood is a personal quality, not a skill learnable by heart. Already at the classroom door one could see if the teacher trainee had enough charisma, enthusiasm, aura and know-how. That was completed by an easy and respectful attitude towards the pupils. Theory could not help if the sentiment was wrong.

Indeed, theory could not help if the sentiment was wrong – neither one is tempted to add restructuring if the antecedent trajectory or professional sentiment is wrong.

The question of personal refraction is of increasing importance as institutional sites become saturated by monetised and commodified transactions. New domains have to be sought out and activated. One clear area is the domain of what we might think of as 'the meaning of life'. The purchase of a third superyacht would not replace issues of moral purpose and basic humanity for most people when considering the meaning of our short lives. Only the most brazenly greedy and unreflective would embrace that as constituting a meaningful life. So, the question of 'the meaning of life' continues

Analysing educational change 245

to elude the neoliberal market society. It is the question that will not go away, and, despite its pervasive take-over of our institutions, the market society has often failed to win 'hearts and minds'.

So, our 'life politics' – the way we pursue our life, our moral judgments, our human interactions, our ongoing social projects and our purposes – remain a precious, indeed, sacred, site for re-interpretation. I found in one of my journals this unattributed quote from Paul Goodman:

> Suppose you had the revolution you are talking and dreaming about. Suppose your side had won and you had the kind of society you wanted. How would you live, you personally in that society? Start living that way now!

Of course, in a market society such personal utopias may prove contested and precarious, but the effort to live in a way that is respectful of our better instincts for humanity is itself a pre-figurative statement. To live in a way that is consistent with our beliefs and ideals is itself a victory and one that provides models and modalities for other personal projects and collective actions.

Modelling can be a huge influence, as the example of Muhammed Ali shows. Remember his often-quoted statement, a statement right against the grain of the existing structure of American society:

> I am America. I am the part you won't recognise. But get used to me – black, confident, cocky; my name, not yours, my religion not yours; my goals, my own. Get used to me.

This was Ali's life politicism, intensely contested and precarious. But look at his influence and read it in the recent obituaries, the sheer scale of influence of his personal life politics.

The African American playwright August Wilson (1990) has talked about these kinds of 'life politics' and especially the process of 'coming to know' they facilitate:

> We found ourselves in a world that did not recognise our language or our customs, did not recognise our gods, and ultimately did not recognise our humanity. Once you understand that you have an intrinsic sense of self-worth from the way your idea of pleasure and pain all those things go into your mythology, your history. All of these things go into the makeup of a culture and I think that it is crucial that we as Black Americans keep this alive. Now what the society has told us that if you are willing to deny that, if you are willing to deny the fact that you're Africa, if you are willing to give up your culture and adopt the cultural values of the dominant society, which is European. Then you

can participate better in American society, go to school and have decent jobs and have decent housing etc. That's at a tremendous cost, that's at the loss of self. I think that the vast majority of the 35 million Americans have rejected that social contact. They want their social contract that will allow them to participate in society as African people with their culture intact.

There is, of course, a tension at the heart of the argument for 'life politics' as a site of refraction. But we know our institutions are being saturated by market mantras and mentalities. It is hard to find our moral bearings within them – for finding a way through an institution where the management strata are being created and consolidated to facilitate neoliberal dogma is difficult. It presents us with what we have called 'a crisis of positionality' (Goodson, 2014).

This is why in spite of the dangers of individualism, the site of personal life politics is so important. When our institutions are market-saturated, we have to begin elsewhere. Paul Mason (2016: 36) has written cogently about the tension at the heart of life politics. He says:

> It accepts, in a way our grandfathers would have found hypocritical and intolerable, the self as the centre of the world: it understands work on the self as a contribution to collectivity.

This new collectivity links with our notion of working horizontally, not vertically. If the managerial elites are in place to instantiate market mentalities, vertical hierarchical action is essentially redundant. Mason says:

> If we all have better, less angry, more educated selves, the society we build will cohere without any need for rigid hierarchies. And its concept of human liberation is based more on freedom that on economic well-being.
>
> (Ibid)

Horizontal refraction and personal refraction then provide the seed beds for new virtues and visitors. They are our 'resources of hope' in resisting the current march towards what Marquant calls 'a kind of seedy barbarism' (Marquand, 2015).

We need to begin a 'long march' in the opposite direction, and strategies for refraction, reinterpretation and re-imagination are our starting point.

Conclusion

Alongside this report of empirical findings, I have provided some speculative comments on patterns of historical refraction. In these instances, refraction refers to the capacity for global patterns to be re-directed and re-ordered by their setting in historical periods and cultural contexts. Hence, global initiatives which follow similar intentions and directions can end up moving in unintended directions and sequences. Although in some ways refraction is similar to the concept of re-contextualisation, the work focuses not only on the external changes in local and professional cultures and in personal contexts but also on internal changes in perceptions and narratives. In addition, as the 'external relations' of change, we try to elicit evidence on the 'internal affairs' of change.

In terms of a focus on new capitalism, it is perhaps instructive to reflect that the economic profession itself is highly subject to refraction. Fourcade's (2009) recent study, *Economists and Societies*, develops a historical and sociological study of the developments of the economist professional discourse in three countries.

Basically, she argues that within each nation, a distinctive professional culture has developed. In the United States, this is characterised by a unique federal structure in which relationships with the state are held at bay by the traditions of autonomy in universities and economic departments. This makes for a profoundly different pattern to that found in France and the UK. In France, the economists are more immersed in the culture of the state and are characterised as public administrators trained and educated in the 'grand corps d'état'. In Britain, the elitist pattern of economist training comes from an amalgam of Oxbridge training and the institutional infrastructure of the government, the civil service and the major London banks.

Thus, although in some ways the new capitalism poses similar questions for economists studying the new world order, each nation's economists pursue this from a different historical and political trajectory. Hence, 'despite all the talk about globalisation, each country wants to find economic solutions that suit its historical paths and conditions' (Hess, 2009: 54).

This pursuit of national solutions can be seen in the Profknow report. Broadly, the English and Irish have pursued the neoliberal agenda in the fastest and deepest manner. More recently, in the Southern European countries, with their less well-established social democratic structures, we see 'the market' driving towards an abandonment of these visions, though the result on the front line of education is less coherent or conclusive. In the most historically grounded social democratic systems of Sweden and Finland, the response has been more in line with a vision of trusting professionals, and most clearly in the Finnish case underpinning 'good teacherhood' and professional judgment.

Because neoliberalism has pushed more for transparency over accountability and educational results, it seems strange that they have not drawn any lessons from the PISA study of educational standards. These show with deafening clarity that those that have pursued neoliberal reforms in the fastest and deepest manner, such as England, perform very poorly in terms of

248 Ivor Goodson

educational standards. Meanwhile, those that have defended a social democratic vision and explicitly valued professional autonomy, such as Finland, have produced top-rate educational standards, and it would seem time to seriously scrutinise the neoliberal orthodoxy in the field of education.

References

Ball, S. J. (2007). *Education plc: Private sector participation in public sector education.* London: Routledge.

Fourcade, M. (2009). *Economists and societies: Discipline and profession in the United States, Britain, and France, 1980s to 1990s.* Princeton: Princeton University Press.

Goodson, I. F. (2005). The long waves of reform. In *Learning, curriculum and life politics.* London and New York: Routledge, pp. 105–129.

Goodson, I. F. (2014). *Curriculum, personal narrative and the social future.* London and New York: Routledge.

Goodson, I. F. and Lindblad, S. eds. (2011). *Professional knowledge and educational restructuring in Europe.* Rotterdam: Sense Publishers.

Hess, A. (2009). The backstory of the credit crunch. *Times Higher Education,* December 17/24.

Mason, P. (2016). Paul Mason on why the left must be ready to cause a commotion. *The New Statesman.* 23–29 September.

Marquand, D. (2015). *Mammon's kingdom: An essay on Britain, now.* London and New York: Penguin.

Profknow (Professional Knowledge in Education and Health). 2002–2008. *Restructuring work and life between state and citizens in Europe* (funded by the EU. University of Brighton – UK, University of Gothenburg – Sweden, National and Kopodistorian University of Athens – Greece, University of Joensuu – Finland, University of Barcelona – Spain, University of the Azores – Portugal, St. Patrick's College, Dublin City University – Ireland, University of Stockholm – Sweden). www.profknow.net (Accessed on 3 January 2018).

Wilson, A. (1990). *Interview with Melvyn Bragg on the South Bank Show* (Series 2: Episode 25). Available on Sky: http://go.sky.com/vod/content/SKYENTERTAIN MENT/content/videoId/fdea6ff4605a0510VgnVC M1000000b43150a (Accessed on 10 January 2017).

Chapter 14

Combating educational inequality[1]
Competing frameworks

Vikas Gupta

Different national variants of the modernist discourse and practice on education – for instance, Germany, France, and the USA in the nineteenth century and the USSR and China in the twentieth century – historically demonstrated that establishment of a common structural apparatus or system of education is a necessary (if not sufficient) prerequisite for the integration of diverse pedagogic, epistemological, and linguistic activities and for preparing cohesive national societies transcending the intercommunity and class divides and the rift between the state and the community. This modernist paradigm also sought to homogenise and 'officialise' curricular knowledge. Of course, such a thrust for a common structural apparatus and homogenisation of curricular knowledge did not alleviate existing inequalities, stratifications, and segregations completely anywhere. Instead, due to this integrationist and homogenising tendency inbuilt into the modernist projects of nation building and the force of prevalent societal asymmetries, a range of structural, social, epistemological, and linguistic inequalities continued to characterise the educational sphere, such as the coercive streaming of students for specific kinds of curriculums, preservation of special arrangements of education in the name of exceptions, and an orientation of education that helped in the reproduction of traditional hierarchies through the dissemination of particular cultural capital. Even there differences existed between the ideal objectives and grassroots reality and between metropolitan cities and rural areas. The religious question was also settled differently in these countries whilst evolving secular systems of education (Soysal and Strang, 1989). The modernist paradigm has been found to contain a strong tendency for reproduction due to the selective nature of its epistemological and linguistic dimensions (Bourdieu, 1973; Bowles and Gintis, 1947; Willis, 1981). Research even exposed the manner in which the bureaucratic structures of formal education in industrial societies have been essentially hostile to the genuine human sensibilities (Illich, 1971).

Nonetheless, within this modernist paradigm focusing on state-led integration of educational order, public provisioning of education was generally regarded as more capable of achieving desired objectives than leaving

250 Vikas Gupta

this task in the hands of any other agency. Recognising this advancement becomes a crucial research agenda at a juncture when the state is trying to withdraw from such a responsibility, as elaborated in this chapter. Moreover, a comparison with the nineteenth-century British or Indian situation would reveal that the countries which followed this modernist paradigm of state-centric common schooling still achieved greater success in building a more equitable system of education for the pupils of different classes and communities under the state's auspices.

Now a different model, based upon the neoliberal policy framework, has been acquiring poignant salience in recent decades which focuses on redressing specific or disaggregated forms of educational inequalities in the form of the inclusion of some hitherto excluded people within different levels of a systemic structure, whilst it seeks to make the system all the more stratified by avoiding any meaningful discussion on the structural question altogether. Thus, it neither seeks to establish structural equality by over-throwing hierarchical stratification which reproduces existing order, nor does it recognise the need to adopt the analytical lens of a broader and aggregate spectrum of inequality experienced simultaneously by differently excluded groups forming the overwhelming majority within a given social system. Instead, without taking these equalising structural measures, it intends to further augment the epistemological and linguistic homogeneity. Of course, the trend of epistemological homogenisation had begun under the modernist paradigm. Therefore, as a reaction, in the second half of the previous century, various scholarly as well as ground-level official and non-official efforts began to deal with the rampant suppression of diversity by the modernist paradigm in the form of securing some space for the cultures, knowledges, and languages of variously marginalised people, or the plural ethos of a child's milieu. The neoliberal paradigm–engendered homogeneity is not only thwarting those efforts; it is much more damaging than the one unleashed by its modernist counterpart. In other words, neoliberalism poses a more serious threat not only to the diversity of knowledges and languages but to the entire society by augmenting existing inequalities due to certain contradictions lying at its heart.

Focusing on the question of inequalities in school education, this chapter shows how the neoliberal framework seeks to significantly alter those academic preferences which so far enjoyed some kind of consensus amongst progressive intellectuals. It shows how the area where greater uniformity was to this point considered desirable within a certain progressive discourse, now the stratification is being augmented by ignoring the structural questions altogether; and where until, quite recently, heterogeneity was conceived as worthy of appreciation and engagement (the domain of languages and knowledges), homogeneity is once again dominant. The chapter also shows that the doctrine of individual (or consumer) choice is being propagated against the compulsion-based state interventions in education in a period when the state is becoming more repressive of freedom in all other aspects of human life.

In a federal polity like India, some contrary examples might at times be visible here and there. However, the earlier mentioned contradictions of the neoliberal paradigm appear to be the unmistakable leading direction of contemporary Indian education policy and practice.

Still, the dominant pattern was not uncontested in the past; nor are the opposition and counter-voices absent today. The Scandinavian countries are still trying to carve a different path despite the neoliberal challenge. Socialist countries like China, despite many changes in recent years, are still maintaining common schooling. Even in India, Bhutan is investing in an equitable system of education, and that, too, under a dynastic rule. The protests are quite frequent in the United States as well as in the UK against the neoliberal restructuring of education. In fact, the objective conditions of the contestation of educational inequality (due to its immensely heightened levels) have matured perhaps so much today that the long-cherished idea of 'common schooling' was recently articulated in a *suo motu* manner within a quite radical judgment of the Allahabad High Court (AHC) on primary education (AHC, 2015) in India as well. Therefore, this chapter takes up the characteristic features of this radical judgment on primary education (AHC, 2015) and the challenges before its implementation as a thematic plot in which it tries to expose some of these contradictions of contemporary Indian education. However, the AHC judgment is to be seen only as an example of a particular kind of vision; otherwise, the idea of equitable quality compulsory education is much older and comprehensive. Similarly, the challenges in the path of the implementation of this AHC verdict, as analysed in this chapter, are not difficulties exclusive to this judgment; these represent obstacles in the path of building a public-funded equitable education system in the entire country today.

Piercing structural inequality and the key features of AHC judgment

Like in other parts of the world, in India, the direct role of the state in the sphere of education historically emerged only during modern period. Different models of educational arrangements were historically known to England and India. Out of these diverse models, a particular one was chosen for India by the colonial state in collaboration with the traditional elites allied with the Raj. Through the Educational Despatch of 1854, it was assured that the state does not desire to see a scenario where all institutions are established and run by it alone. On the contrary, the state adopted only a transient role. Hence, there emerged a relatively unified apparatus of education composed of institutions established by religious foundations, social reformers, nationalists, and the colonial state. Reading the report of the Indian Education

Commission chaired by W. W. Hunter, or other annual reports of the provincial governments, or the five-yearly reports of the central government would reveal that schools could be classified as state-founded and -maintained institutions (a relatively smaller category if the second and third categories are merged), aided institutions, unaided institutions recognised by the state, and unaided and unrecognised institutions. There were even different schools for different categories of students, such as schools for the sons of landlords, native princes, factory or railway workers, girls, handicapped, tribals, oppressed castes, Europeans and Eurasians, 'criminals' or 'potential criminals', etc. There were divisions along the lines of language, such as schools that imparted education in English and schools that used different vernaculars or classical languages for educating children. There were also differences amongst 'district schools' and 'village schools' in terms of their purposes, class clientele, medium of education, and textbooks. These institutions were differently endowed, catered to specific sections, and at times had a different orientation and differentiation at the level of the curriculum (Gupta, 2015). There is also evidence to suggest that very often, even within a single school, different sitting arrangements were made for the students of different caste backgrounds (Constable, 2000).

The state continued to possess a 'minimalist' role in the sphere of education in post-independence India too. It created a vast network of various kinds of educational institutions, but the share of directly state-established and -managed institutions remained limited, and government at best played the role of a regulator granting recognition and some financial assistance. Even though the state could not bring about a fundamental transformation in the nature of education, it could keep the costs within the reach of middle classes. Hence, the benefits too remained restricted mostly in the hands of upper and middle classes and dominant groups. Despite the expansion of the education system over last 200 years, this has remained the dominant trend (Gupta, 2014).

However, with the view to mark a change at the level of the system of education from its colonial legacy, the Kothari Commission recommended the establishment of a 'common school system based on the concept of neighborhood schools' (CSSNS) and allocation of 6% of GDP for education (Ministry of Education, 1966). In the NPE 1968, the GoI accepted the recommendation for CSSNS without actually institutionalising it or raising the expenditure to the recommended level (GoI, 1968).

In the subsequent period, we find that rather than establishing CSSNS, the government has been augmenting structural inequality even within the public system of education. For instance, the NPE 1986, although it did not explicitly reject the recommendation for CSSNS, it did provide new layers in the system in the form of Navodaya and Central schools for a special category of students, on one hand, and non-formal education for the huge category of 'deprived children', on the other (GoI, 1986). Besides this, under various flagship programmes, such as DPEP and SSA, and various euphemisms, such as venture schools, Education Guarantee Scheme (EGS), alternative education, and equal schools (single-teacher schools), central and state governments, in collusion with international agencies of global capital and religious organisations, have further augmented the layers of substandard schools for the education of the masses of this country. This inequality and disparity have been legitimised under the pretext of community-based arrangements of education and withdrawal of the state through school mergers, closures, and PPP. On the other hand, for the better-off sections of the population, in the name of merit, newer layers are being created, such as Pratibha Vikas Vidyalaya and model schools.

Of course, some enabling laws were passed during the third and fourth decades of the twentieth century for compulsory primary education, but not much could be achieved due to the reluctance of the colonial state, opposition by the dominant social interests, and the differing priorities of the nationalist leaders who occupied provincial governments. Thereafter, elementary education was also conceived as a fundamental right initially by the constituent assembly, but finally was shifted by them to 'directive principles of state policy' under Article 45 of the Indian constitution. Of course, it was non-justiciable for individuals. However, the provision was not that weak either, as it was a directive for state policy inserted in the Indian constitution at the culmination of the nationalist fervour of anti-colonial resistance, perhaps with the hope that the post-independence Indian nation-state would take up the task of providing education quite seriously in the manner some Western nations took it at the eve of their modern development, such as post-revolutionary France; certain states like Prussia, which later became part of Germany; and different states in the United States during the late eighteenth and nineteenth centuries. All these Western nations had evolved, although with slightly varying frameworks of compulsory common education as an essential instrument of nation building, Christian or secular instruction, the civic ideology of revolution, or the cultural codes of capitalism.

Although the idea of compulsory education did not acquire this kind of centrality in the policy framework of the post-independence Indian nation-state, nonetheless, it secured much faster expansion than what India witnessed under a colonial regime. Moreover, education was recognised as a fundamental right by the Supreme Court of India in 1993 in the famous Unni Krishnan judgment (Supreme Court, 1993), which subsequently led to the 86th Amendment act in the constitution of India in 2001 and the legislation of the RTE Act in 2009 by the Indian Parliament (GoI, 2009). The Unni Krishnan judgment undoubtedly played an important role in this transition. However, thereafter, the legislative fruition of the need to recognize elementary education as a fundamental right took more than fifteen years. Over this preparatory period, purging of the more radical aspects of an hitherto undefined concept called the fundamental right to education also took place, with the view to adapt it to the already existing system, in particular by neutralising the tension it could have posed if it was combined with another fundamental right, namely the equality before the law. For instance, the RTE Act 2009 provided legal sanction to a multi-layered system through its recognition of different existing categories of schools, wherein masses and classes were subjected to differential arrangements.

It is therefore not a surprise if within a period of just five years, on 18 August 2015, Justice Sudhir Agarwal of AHC felt that necessary arrangements for the exercise of the right to education were not provided by the class of decision makers to the schools of the masses because of this multi-layered system of education. In his view, the pathetic situation existed because the interests of decision makers were not tied to the schools of 'common men'. Therefore, Justice Agarwal directed the Uttar Pradesh (UP) government to ensure that the government servants, semi-government servants, local bodies, representatives of the people, the judiciary, and all such persons who receive any perk, benefit, salary, etc., from the state exchequer or public fund send their children to primary schools run by the UP Board of Basic Education alone (AHC, 2015: Section 90). Contrary to the generally prevalent assimilationist tendency of gradualism, even for such a mammoth change, the AHC judgment directed the UP government to submit a compliance report within a period of six months, so that the new arrangements could be enforced from the following academic session beginning in April 2016 onwards (AHC, 2015: Section 94). The judgment went to the extent of directing the government to make penalty provisions for those who would violate this directive of a 'common-men's school'. For example, the judgment directed that if a child is sent to a primary school not maintained by the board, the amount of fee, etc., paid to such a privately managed primary school shall be deposited in the government funds every month, so long as education in other kinds of primary school is continued. As if this penalty was not enough, the AHC instructed that such a person, if in service, should also be made to forego other benefits like increment and promotional avenues for certain period, as the case may be. And it said that this is only illustrative (AHC, 2015: Section 90).

The court's rationale behind such an unusually strong directive was that after more than sixty-five years of independence, these 'common men's schools' (which, according to said judgment, 90% of children in the relevant age group attend) are still struggling to have basic amenities, because government servants send their kids to primary schools with a better infrastructure and other facilities which belong to elite and semi-elite private schools. It alleged that the public administration therefore has no actual desire to see these schools function (AHC, 2015: Section 84). Not only the rationale but also the strong tenor of the judgment is evident in the assertion that

> After more than 65 years of independence, these Schools are still struggling to have basic amenities for children.
>
> (AHC, 2015: Section 84)

The judgment builds the rationale through four argumentative instruments, which, by implication, also expose the illegality and unconstitutionality of the existing differential arrangements of education through the manner in which these negatively affect the implementation and exercise of constitutional provisions and fundamental rights:

> First, provisioning of 'common-men's schools' by the government is in a shabby condition owing to the absence of 'real administrative involvement', because the decision makers do not have any direct stake in these institutions as they send their children in the schools of 'elite' and 'semi-elite' categories.
>
> (AHC, 2015: Section 84)

> Second, the situation will improve if those who are duty-bound to administer these institutions are compelled to send their children to these 'common-men's schools'.
>
> (AHC 2015: Section 86)

> Third, it will also boost social equation.
>
> (AHC 2015: Section 87)

Fourth, the judgment aptly remarks that the state and central government both are harping every time and very frequently on the need for an improved primary school, but their intention has not resulted in execution and reality at the grassroots level (AHC, 2015: Section 85). Different schemes of education have been launched by the government, but the situation continues to be worrying. Hence, the court is compelled to provide the directive of the 'common-men's school'.

Although due to space constraints, I am not reproducing here the data pertaining to educational participation and withdrawal, the position of the AHC can be easily corroborated with the alarming picture evident in the pathetic infrastructural indicators, extreme dropout rates, absenteeism, and other critical symptoms still prevalent in the state, as regularly documented in the State Report Cards prepared under DISE by NUEPA. What can we then expect from the AHC judgment? Why is such a stern judgment not implemented long after the elapse of the six-month deadline? Is it merely because the bureaucracy and public representatives do not want their kids to mingle with their counterparts from the lower orders of society? Does it only cover the bureaucracy and public representatives? Are there other powerful stumbling blocks as well? Is the anticipated compulsion unprecedented and unwarranted suspending the 'right to choose'? If so, it is also equally interesting to examine why the judgment is not challenged at any higher level of the judiciary – in the double bench of the same High Court or in the Supreme Court of the nation.

Of course, the judgment initially triggered so much optimism that one activist knocked on the door of Supreme Court to get it endorsed for the entire nation (Sharma, 2015). However, I have not been able to find any update on this appeal. In fact, a lot of confusion exists even amongst the staunch activist supporters of this judgment with regard to the state government's subsequent legal measures to get it repealed. Thus, even the general ignorance that exists with regard to subsequent legal proceedings on this issue (if any) further testifies to the quandary elaborated next.

Tea-table conversations, Internet discussions, and newspapers were flooded with diverse and often polarised opinions, euphoria, and alarm on this verdict of the AHC when it was pronounced. For instance, in the national dailies in English, two representative critics of the said judgment were (Kapur, 2015) and (Sabharwal, 2015) and two illustrative favourable opinions were (Gupta and Giri, 2015) and (Kumar, 2015). Besides this, one of the Hindi dailies (Hastakshep, 2015) contained a compilation of somewhat varying but mostly favourable articles on this judgment, such as those by Anil Sadgopal, Ashok Aggrawal, and the present author. However, subsequently, silence has prevailed within academia on the failure of the UP government to implement this judgment. Why is it so? Of course, this is a mystery to be researched elsewhere. Nonetheless, one possible hint could be provided here with the view to arrive at some tentative answer that could be further explored elsewhere. Perhaps this silence is caused by the impact of the neoliberal ideology, which is trying to destroy faith in the ability of the public system of education (and state systems for other amenities) to deliver. Academia (and perhaps the judiciary as well) is also part of this victimisation of perspective engendering despair amongst them. Neoliberalism has made them also an unwitting accomplice.

Whatever it is, and rather than engaging with specific expositions of individual scholars mentioned earlier, as undertaking such an exercise would be difficult in a single chapter, this chapter takes up for discussion only the broad trends of this discourse within a particular argumentative framework. Let us first try to understand some salient features of the AHC judgment. Thereafter, I will expand further the discussion on its significance, as well as the challenges in its implementation.

First, even though the judgment used the term 'primary education', it implied 'elementary education' (from Class I to VIII instead of Class I to V).

Combating educational inequality   257

It is called in UP lower primary and upper primary, and together covers a minimum of eight years instead of five.

Second, the category of parents covered under the AHC judgment included a vast majority of society, not merely *babus* (clerks), civil servants, and politicians. It used terms like semi-government employees and those who receive any 'perk or 'benefit'. Thus, it covered all those who took on any kind of contract work from the government or received any form of advantage from the state – a much larger and almost omnipresent and infinite category then the simple expression 'government employees'. It thus cuts across various socio-economic, cultural, linguistic, and religious boundaries.

Third, the AHC judgment harps upon the radical doctrine of equality in an era where a tapered practice of inclusion has become the buzzword in policy framework and governance practices. The contemporary framework of inclusion seeks to accommodate certain people at different levels of a multi-layered system of differently endowed institutions, ranging from government schools for elite categories to ordinary village schools maintained by gram panchayats; from high-fee-charging private schools to low-budget schools run and managed by religious trusts, corporate houses, and other non-governmental organisations (NGOs); exclusive institutions established in the name of 'special schools' for Dalits, tribals, and the disabled; home-based education for the 'severely disabled' and some other categories of students; and non-formal or alternative education schemes for those still left out of this iniquitous ladder. Within such an inclusion framework, the prospects of a child's participation at any particular step of this hierarchical order of schooling depend upon a variety of factors, such as:

- Parents' social status and paying capacity;
- State's reliance on reimbursement schemes, siphoning public funds to private schools;
- The paradox of first assigning huge tax exemptions to corporate houses and then seeking their legitimacy through tokenistic 'corporate social responsibility' (CSR) formulas; and
- The dominant notions of a child's physical/mental capacities, merit, talent, or ability, which are reinforced through scholarships and charities and controlled via different educational expenditures (Gupta, 2014).

Of course, it would be an interesting question to explore elsewhere whether this segregation is possible due to the tapered practice or due to the inherent weakness of the doctrine of inclusion, or as a result of the shift away from equality principle. However, it can be underlined here that contrary to the contemporary trend of hierarchical inclusion, this judgment tries to achieve 'social equation' (AHC, 2015: Section 87) within the framework provided by the doctrine of equality as it seeks to place a vast majority within an equitable educational order through the instrument of 'common men's schools'.

Fourth, the AHC judgment appears to be sterner than even the RTE Act of the GoI (2009) in terms of its intention to seek time-bound implementation. For instance, the RTE Act could be implemented by respective states of the Indian union only when they framed and notified relevant rules applicable within their area of jurisdiction after 1 April 2010. There was no deadline given for the same. Therefore, for many years, many states did not try to implement the RTE Act. However, as stated earlier, because it was such a mammoth change, the AHC judgment directed the UP government to submit a compliance report within six months and make penalty provisions for those who violated the directive of the 'common men's school' (AHC, 2015: Section 94).

Further, the AHC judgment unequivocally invoked the framework of compulsion on part of the state, whilst on the other hand, within the RTE framework, it is not clear to date whose primary responsibility it is – the principal/teacher, parents, or a particular officer – to ensure that the children in the relevant age group are sent to school regularly. Moreover, in the RTE Act (GoI, 2009), it is not made clear unequivocally who will be penalised, by whom, when, and how much for the failure of a government or local body maintaining a school to adhere to the standards and norms prescribed in the schedule. Instead, these are explicitly excluded in Section 18 (1). Sections 18 and 19 are exclusively concerned with the recognition procedure to be followed for private and aided schools. Sections 8 (G) and 9 (H) of the RTE Act (2009) also do not make any such provision for government schools. The RTE Act demands time-bound compliance of the norms and standards specified in the schedule as a mandatory condition only as part of the procedure and rules for recognition of private and aided schools, which thereby does not apply to the institutions fully under the control of the government or local bodies. Hence, notwithstanding Ashok Agarwal's positive response to such a query in an interview (Rajalakshmi, 2011: 16–17), the question itself was indicative of the doubt that prevails on this issue.

Perhaps this cliché is the source of prevalent dormancy on the part of the concerned departments of the government to undertake a structural transformation of their own schools with urgency and dispatch: steps which should have been otherwise considered essential for a fundamental right to be realised. Similarly, the critics of RTE Act who favour the model of 'budget primary schools' (BPS) also allege that it does not compel the government to adhere to the norms and standards as prescribed therein with regard to its own schools (Thakore, 2018). The three-year education agenda of NITI Aayog (NITI Aayog, 2017: 135–143) favouring an outcome measurement–based approach instead of making any commitment for better financial and human resources as inputs for improvement is yet another attempt to abdicate the state's responsibility to provide an educational infrastructure. If the infrastructural requirements were perceived as mandatory for government schools, perhaps the NITI Aayog would have found it difficult to adopt such an approach against inputs and the norms and standards.

Of course, we can make an alternative and liberal interpretation of the RTE Act (GoI, 2009) by reading the silence to mean that the norms and standards prescribed in the schedule are binding for every school, because as distinct from Section 18 of the act, the schedule does not make any exceptions. Even the fact that the schedule is annexed with the RTE Act implies – if seen in the context of the spirit of a fundamental right to education – that it is binding on every school. It can also be argued that for equitable quality education, compliance with the norms and standards as enshrined in the schedule is essential for every school and that there should be parity amongst government, aided, and unaided private schools; otherwise, it would amount to a violation of the fundamental right to equality as enshrined in Article 14 of the Indian constitution.

Yet, the point underscored so far is that such a line of reasoning would be an exceptionally liberal interpretation of the RTE Act (GoI, 2009); otherwise, a close reading of the sections cited allows constructing a somewhat different case, which means that the present judgment (AHC, 2015) is sterner than the RTE Act. It is perhaps obvious for a judgment trying to ensure implementation of a fundamental right as a condition of its extreme and massive violation by the custodian agency itself.

Anil Sadgopal, through many arguments, has pointed out the deleterious impact of the RTE Act (Sadgopal, 2009, 2010, and 2013). Though these have been vindicated by recent events, the supporters of this act might still rightly argue that this legislation has made it possible for the judiciary to make radical interpretations as and when it intends to do so. There have been a few examples of more progressive readings of the act than what has been demonstrated by its outright opponents. The AHC judgment could be one case in point. Nonetheless, it might be apt to ask whether the judgment draws strength from the general recognition of education as a fundamental right, rather than from the specific provisions of the RTE Act (2009) as such.

Fifth, one common view is that the AHC provided such a strong direction for a 'common-men's school' only as a 'suo motu judicial cognizance' by inserting a 'parting note' in the judgment. It is true that none of the petitions for which the said verdict was issued by the AHC had demanded to send everyone to a 'common-men's school'. The petitioners were only concerned about different issues related to the appointment of teachers to posts. Nonetheless, it can be argued that the core issue of these petitions, the appointment of teachers, is an integral part of the fundamental right to education. Hence, implicitly the judgment relied on the constitutional framework where education has now acquired the status of a fundamental right (AHC, 2015: Section 84), in so far as it finds the cause of a faulty procedure of the appointment of teachers and their compromised quality within the careless attitude of the state officials, as they did not have a direct stake in these schools (AHC, 2015: Section 86).

In those other parts of the verdict dealing with the legal issues in the appointment of teachers, the AHC bench astutely carried out the juridical interpretations of the issues involved. However, the paragraphs which provide the directive for a 'common-men's school' did not invoke legal evidence in the form of fundamental rights and directive principles of state policy as enshrined in the Indian constitution. It did not refer to any national education policy either – so much so that it did not invoke the reports of the Kothari Commission (GoI, 1966) and Common School System Commission (Government of Bihar, 2007). Both of these could have been very helpful to ensure greater legitimacy of the verdict for a 'common-men's school'.

Similarly, the AHC judgment did not cite any international experiences or practices to justify its directive. For instance, it does not explicitly interrogate the constitutionality and legality of differential arrangements for education in the manner as in the historical case of *Brown v. the Board of Education* in the United States in 1954, which is considered a catalyst for alleviating educational segregation there (Brown vs Board of Education, 1954).

However, the absence of explicit invocation of an existing legal framework should not necessarily entail its inapplicability if the judgment is challenged in the higher court of law, provided it is based on a rational interpretation of solid available evidence. It should be possible to utilize the examples of the legal framework referred to earlier if the verdict is challenged on those grounds in a court of law, provided the appellate court grants permission to bring these aspects up for discussion. Moreover, it should be considered a valid and constitutional prerogative of the court to take 'judicial cognizance' of the malady and ensure that the fundamental rights are exercised by citizens without any hindrance. It is all the more warranted because whilst other fundamental rights are preventive, the right to education is affirmative, necessitating a priori arrangements.

There are some other concerns which would require attention if an equitable system of schooling is to be built as mandated by the AHC judgment. For instance, schools have not been made accessible for physically, mentally, or visually disabled children even though they constitute a significant proportion of our population, ranging from the national census enumerations of little less than 3% (Registrar General and Census Commissioner of India, 2011) to international estimations of more than 10% (WHO, 2011). As per the NSSO surveys, many of them, particularly in the urban areas, attend special schools. They attend mainstream schools in the rural areas, as special schools are almost non-existent there. The key indicators in the DISE data reveal every year that the drop-out rate is highest amongst children with disabilities in comparison to any other social category: sixty-six out of one hundred leave school after Class V. Hence, the state would be required to adopt a time-bound roadmap to make all of its schools fully accessible for the inclusive education of these disabled children within 'common-men's schools' conceived by the AHC; otherwise, the compulsion might push more disabled children out. Of course, one option for the state is to grant relaxations to all such groups on the grounds of unfeasibility. However, it would imply continuation of differential arrangements in perpetuity in violation of not only the fundamental right to equality as enshrined in the Indian constitution but also the rights as upheld in various national and international legislations for persons with disabilities (GoI, 1995, 2007, 2016; UNO, 2007). The other possibility is to promote 'home-based education'. However, it would be exclusionary and discriminatory and in violation of the spirit of the genuine right to education, even though the RTE Amendment Act 2010 has sanctioned it (Gupta, 2013).

Similarly, there are innumerable treatises exposing the masculine, casteist, communal, classist, urban, and inhumane orientation of the existing education system. Therefore, even if all children are sent to the same school, it might not create 'social equation' if the nature of education continues to remain prejudicial and discriminatory. Further, the children with better childhood care and access to preschool might still continue to enjoy an edge in these schools over their underprivileged peers, as the judgment is silent on preschool education. Therefore, without changing the nature of education, and without addressing the early childhood care–related issues effectively, real transformation cannot be achieved. Of course, if the AHC verdict is implemented, it will release the potential of facilitating the interaction of different classes, groups, communities, and sexes within the same spatial enclosure of the school. However, this should be regarded as the first step in the direction of democratising the orientation of education. The next step also will have to be taken immediately. For instance, when the government of Soviet Russia decided to introduce equal education for all immediately after the 1917 revolution, structural changes were carried out alongside pedagogical, epistemological, and linguistic transformations, and for these, the government recognised full autonomy of the communes and their schools to make innovations in accordance with the new principles yet making them locally relevant (Fitzpatrick, 1970).

Even though different classes, groups, communities, and sexes are sent to receive education within the same spatial enclosure of 'common-men's schools', the objective of complete social mingling might be attained in a limited manner, because the nature of localities in India (or in UP) is not necessarily so heterogeneous everywhere. There are areas of heavy concentration of particular communities. Localities are also often subdivided in terms of the class status of its inhabitants. The service elite does not live everywhere. Moreover, because most of the officials (of higher grades) send their children live in cities, the degree of its impact in rural areas is likely to remain limited. Therefore, fixing a particular radius as the intake area may reproduce in many cases the same social composition in school too.

Nonetheless, different kinds of government servants and public representatives are present or appointed in the rural areas: security guards and police, health workers, Anganwadi workers, village panchayat representatives, block development officers (BDOs), rural bank employees, etc. Many of them presently send their kids to a private school either in the village or in the nearby town. Many of them decide to live in the town even though they are posted in the village, primarily to ensure the education of their children in a better private school there. This scenario might change if it becomes mandatory for them to send their kids to a government school as directed by the AHC. Moreover, these contingent issues can be addressed by defining the catchment area with appropriate sensitivity and through the maintenance of an index of socio-cultural diversity, as recommended by the Justice Sachchar Committee (GoI, 2006). Such an attempt would create a much better scenario than what exists today.

It might be argued that the AHC verdict not only curtails the choice of parents (who happen to be government servants, public representatives, or the beneficiary of perquisites from the state) to admit their kids in the school of their preference but also the right of their children to study in their preferred school, even though the latter is not bound by any service conditions. However, a counter-argument could run like this: until children have acquired the age of eighteen years, parents are their custodians and are legally entitled to take decisions on their behalf. Moreover, parents serving the government also claim reimbursement of their children's tuition fee, medical expenses, Leave Travel Concession (LTC), Home Town Leave Travel Concession, House Rent Allowance, etc. from the state exchequer. These parents do not mind traveling with their children in Air India for LTC, as travel by private airlines is prohibited. When public servants and public representatives can take so many benefits from the government for their children, and when they can respect the limitation on their choice if it grants them some privileges, the state can also impose reasonable restrictions on the freedom of these parents to select schools for their kids. Moreover, apart from these government servants, public representatives, and others who profit from the state exchequer, the history of compulsory education and the growth of common schooling in the West – broadly in the same period when the doctrines of freedom and equality were developed within the modern political discourse – provide many precedents for compulsions imposed on the entire population. Still, if the curtailment of choice is problematic because of the currently prevalent poor condition of ordinary government schools, then the AHC judgment sees the solution in the improvement of these schools by linking the interests of decision makers with the interests of the rest of the stakeholders. Hence, if these schools would improve, the objection would automatically die out. After all, most of the parents are happy to get their children admitted in KVS (central schools) run by the government, because they are better maintained. Moreover, notwithstanding flagrant violations of the provision, the freedom to select a school is restricted: every state government and local body have fixed catchment areas of schools and have introduced point systems. There are already many significant restrictions on the right to freedom of public servants and representatives governed by the code of conduct, such as their right to expression; to political participation, out-station, or overseas journey; and to practice a parallel profession, albeit outside their duty hours. There is no hue and cry on these limitations. Above all, seeing through the logic of democracy founded on the principle of equality, it appears ironic that compelling children of public servants and representatives to attend state institutions appears to be unreasonable when a great majority of the poor population is practically compelled to do so anyhow.

Moreover, even the six freedoms listed in Article 19 (1) of the Indian constitution do not include the freedom to choose a school. The term 'choice' is a recent arrival in educational discourse. We do not know of the precedents of such an established principle prior to the contemporary neoliberal discourse on education. In any case, the value of the fundamental rights of citizens should be placed higher than the notion of individual choice. If democracy stands for the 'greatest good for the greatest number', then we cannot favour the right to freedom of a select few, mostly from well-to-do families, over the right to equality of the remaining majority, mostly composed of a deprived and poorer population. If there is a clash between the right to freedom of a few and the right to equality of many, it becomes more important in a democratic nation to ensure the latter. However, it seems that the actual conflict is not between principles of freedom and its anti-thesis, the compulsion. The real factors protecting the inertia are embedded in the sociology of power: the tension between the privileges of the 'haves' consisting of upper caste, middle and upper class, non-tribal, majority community and the non-privileges of the 'have-nots' comprising poorer classes, religious minorities, Dalits, tribals, and the disabled.

Some of the leading national newspapers (*The Times of India*, 2015; *The Indian Express*, 2015) reported the welcoming attitude of the basic education minister of the government of UP then formed by the Samajwadi Party. This makes it all the more surprising that the AHC judgment was not implemented. One of these reports also stated that the minister, whilst supporting the verdict, attacked BJP (Bharatiya Janata Party), the main opposition party in the state at the time of the AHC verdict and ruling at the centre, because they opposed the 'Equal Education Bill' in 1977, as they wanted to ensure space for RSS-run schools. Education being a concurrent subject and BJP forming both the union and the state government now, the agenda to create greater scope for RSS-run schools has acquired a greater poignancy. This is patently clear in the efforts of the present union government to adopt a new education policy for the nation (Gupta, 2016). The BJP-led NITI Aayog's three-year action agenda of education, as discussed earlier, seeks to expand the market of education in the hands of non-state players. Therefore, the BJP-led government has pushed the AHC judgment under

264 Vikas Gupta

the carpet. It is true that this judgment was pronounced six months after the release of the themes and questions for the new NEP. However, the core issue of the judgment, common public provisioning of education, has been there since the report of the Kothari Commission (GoI, 1966) and the NPE 1968 (GoI, 1968). The NPE 1986 (GoI, 1986) also did not discard the idea, though it diluted it by instituting newer layers within the system of education. The government of Bihar also constituted a Common School Commission (Government of Bihar, 2007). Still, we did not find any echo of this issue in the consultations for the new NEP, or in the Draft NEP Inputs 2016 (barring some reference to it in the Report of the Subramaniam Committee), or in the document of NITI Aayog, because these have altogether avoided questions pertaining to structural inequality reproducing social inequity. It is otherwise politically desirable that the policymakers explore implications and possibilities created by the judiciary, an organ of the state, and an important pillar of democracy, particularly when they are drafting legislation on a social issue of universal relevance, such as education. Moreover, education is a subject of concurrent list, where states and the centre both are entitled to legislate. Therefore, the centre must be aware of the developments taking place in the states.

Structural asymmetries, social inequalities and the privatisation of education

Even though the AHC judgment is not a radical step like the nationalisation of private schools, it nonetheless strikes an atypical note in today's context of privatisation, as it is close to reflecting the millenarian expectation once expressed by the Kothari Commission about the gradual withering of private schools if the quality of government schools could be maintained at a satisfactory level (Ministry of Education, 1966). Of course, there was a time when, notwithstanding all systemic problems with state-run institutions, the exclusion of marginalised students, and the resultant monopoly of the better of sections, governmental institutions were generally considered the benchmark in terms of quality and trust juxtaposed with private institutions with uncertain credentials. If a government institution existed within a locality, permission was not given for opening another recognised private educational institution there. Only when a student was expelled from a government institution or did not get admission would he seek refuge in a private one. The AHC also observed that

> The recruitment of thousands of posts at a time used to commence but got trapped in huge litigation due to unmindful, irregular and casual approach of the official(s) responsible for managing such recruitment, lack of accountability and credibility as well as sincerity.
>
> (AHC, 2015: Section 79)

This is the transition from the state-centric 'welfare model' to the 'neoliberal model' of privatisation.

A range of scholars, such as Adam Smith, the godfather of mercantilism, (Smith, 1976: 709–710) to Nobel laureate Amartya Sen and his co-author Jean Dreze (Dreze and Sen, 2002), have cautioned us to keep education outside the market logic. However, neoliberalism has brought a swift change to our common sense, breeding a generalised and overdrawn contempt for the public and praise for the private for its managerial efficiency. Now the managerial capacity and the quality of educational services provided by the government are weighed negatively by NGOs, other publicists of privatisation, the ordinary recipients of public services, and even by the state itself. For instance, the Annual Status of Education Reports (ASER) of Pratham underline the dismal standards of learning and pathetic infrastructure prevalent in government schools. However, Pratham exhibits no interest in decoding the fundamental structural reasons for this purported difference between governmental and private institutions. It does not deconstruct both categories – government and private – to reveal the internal heterogeneity of standards. Scholars have also underlined various methodological problems in the findings and arguments of the supporters of private education (Bhatty, 2015; Vellanki, 2015).

Similarly, interventions (Tooley et al., 2007, Jain and Dholakia, 2009, 2010) have advocated the need to rely on a private initiative in education. Their arguments were also countered by various scholars (Sarangapani, 2009; Ramachandran, 2009; Jain and Saxena, 2010; and Kumar, 2010).

Still, quite opposite from the compulsion-based framework of the AHC verdict, the Centre for Civil Society (CCS) has been very powerfully running the 'school choice' campaign by organising high-profile annual conferences. This campaign demands the following: 'fund students, not schools'; 'develop an education market where all avail quality education of their choice'; 'right to education of choice'; 'vouchers'; 'learning outcomes'; and 'autonomy and accountability'. However, their argument of 'choice' is not about the individuals who are placed on an equal level to select one amongst many similar options of equitable quality education available to them. Within their framework, the state will, at best, make some economically underprivileged children capable of making some payment to private schools through vouchers, but the hierarchy of the private school system will remain intact and the state system of education will be gradually abandoned. Hence, their voucher-supported paying capacity will enable them to mostly access the BPS and will take away their state-maintained schools. The private BPS (with a poor infrastructure and low-paid contractual teachers) would be available to the bulk masses of this nation through a voucher-based state reimbursement system. On the other hand, for the better-off section, the bigger corporate houses, such as the Goenkas, the Ambanis, and others, are opening their exuberantly charged schools with magnificent buildings. The CCS does not even consider the possibility that some 'disadvantaged' children might be incorporated in these schools under the 25% quota provided within the RTE Act, because, as elaborated next, they are in opposition to such regulation of private schools by the state. In fact, their demand for autonomy is actually a camouflage for deregulation. Within this framework, the state-owned and -run schools will be converted into private schools under the scheme of 'public–private partnership', and thus the government schools would be an ever-diminishing category. Similar or inclusive within the BPS category are the schools opened by religious organisations of the right wing, such as the ekal vidyalayas of the RSS, which will benefit from the withdrawal of the state from its direct role under the 'school choice model'.

The activists are also critiquing this model. For instance, the All-India Forum for Right to Education (AIFRTE), which is a platform of more than seventy-five organisations and individuals, staged an opposition outside the venue of the fourth school choice campaign on 4 December 2018. In its handbill prepared for this purpose, it argued that the 'school choice' model intends to reproduce, aggravate, and legitimize inequalities, because in the context of different and unregulated fee structures of various schools, rich and poor students would ultimately go to separate schools, despite being provided with school vouchers by the state. The AIFRTE demanded a 'Directly (and Fully) State-Funded Common School System Based on Neighborhood School Guaranteeing Equitable quality Education to All' (AIFRTE, 2012).

Thus, the growth of the private sector in education has its supporters as well as detractors. Whereas the supporters ground their arguments in comparative studies of students' learning gains in the non-state and state-run schools, its detractors ground their arguments in the social justice discourses and the essential role of the state to ensure equitable distribution of quality education to all children. The supporters of privatisation view education as predominantly a private good, and the detractors as a public good (Muzaffar and Sharma, 2011: 4).

Hence, the debate is in no way settled in favour of a neoliberal political economy of privatisation of school education. It shows that even the term 'quality' needs to be defined carefully in order to engage systematically with the supposition that the education provided by the private schools is really better. In fact, the same ASER surveys highlighting the quality deficit of government schools also contain the data which reveal (though not emphasised by Pratham) that even the private schools are not doing much better in this regard. Moreover, this debate clarifies that both the private and the public sector are not internally homogenous: they are marked by stark stratifications of every kind. The supporters of privatisation of school education also need to refine their methodology for analysing the cost aspect of government schooling, as the expenditure from the state exchequer feeds into private schools as well.

Still, the arguments of the proponents of privatisation – even though effectively contested – have started receiving a lot of importance in the corridors of power. For instance, the Union Ministry of Human Resource Development (MHRD), which is responsible for education in the entire nation, began to valorise the private sector for its natural and essential managerial efficiency, implying the inevitable deficiency of the government sector (MHRD, 2007). The MHRD propagated such an understanding, side-lining all successful benchmark institutions of its own – IIM (Indian Institute of Management), IIT (Indian Institute of Technology), IIIT (Indian Institute of Information and Technology), AIIMS (All-India Institute of Medical Science), central schools (KVS), Navodaya Vidyalayas, etc.

Moving further, the mid-term appraisal of the previous Five-Year Plan (Planning Commission, 2010: Chapter 6) and the XII Five-Year Plan (Planning Commission, 2013: Vol 3, Ch 21) underlined the need to promote non-governmental profit-making organisations in the sphere of education. The three-year action agenda of NITI Aayog for 2017–20 (NITI Aayog, 2017: 135–143) in fact shows no interest in making any commitment for greater allocation for the government school education sector to improve its infrastructural aspects. Instead, it advocates a significant shift from an 'input-based approach' to an 'outcome measurement–based approach'. It seeks to provide the government as well as the private sector a level playing field in school education without undertaking to nourish the former to make it genuinely competitive (Ibid, 135–143). On the contrary, in such a scenario, the 'outcome-based approach', which is generally based on the mechanical testing of learning levels by outside agencies, is likely to shift the attention away from infrastructural improvement and expedite the process of closing, merging, or transferring government schools into the PPP mode. We do not have a nationwide objective assessment of infrastructural indicators of private schools. Nonetheless, it is clear that the private school sector, a very heterogeneous field, includes a major chunk of the BPS, whose capacity to maintain reasonably good infrastructure is likely to be constrained by financial reasons. For instance, NISA has been claiming that due to the imposition of the 'norms and standards' under the RTE Act, many BPS have been closed down (Thakore, 2018): of course, there has been no effort to establish veracity of the figures cited by them.

There are striking similarities in the framework adopted by NITI Aayog and the one propagated by the lobby for privatisation of education. This includes the advocacy of PPP, a voucher system and other modes of reimbursement to private schools by the state, the unregulated freedom of BPSs and the schools opened by the bigger corporate houses, and the preference for the output measurement approach over input-based assessment. For instance, like the NITI Aayog, the National Independent School Alliance (NISA) and its parent organisation, the CCS, favour BPS; condemn the RTE Act for its norms and standards and other methods of regulating private schools; and favour and outcome-based approach. Even though the quality of education cannot be reduced to mere provision of a better infrastructure, we cannot say that it is unnecessary altogether. Still, they don't want the infrastructural norms and standards to be a parameter to judge the quality of an educational institution. They both discuss the need to establish an independent agency for testing the outcomes. Whilst the NITI Aayog covertly upholds the profit-making objective in school education, the NISA-CCS also combined the bigger corporate investors in education to uphold it in unmistakable and overt terms.

Despite the verdict of the Supreme Court upholding the constitutional validity of the provision for a 25% percent quota for disadvantaged children under the RTE Act 2009, the discourse around it, as well as plethora of subsequent petitions seeking its implementation, have ultimately promoted the idea of the superiority of private schools as an oxymoron. This has provided a further push to the race of admitting children in these private schools not only under the 25% quota reserved for economically weaker sections under the RTE Act 2009 but also in general. Even though the Supreme Court might have conceived the disputed question of the 25% quota as a measure designed for social justice and endorsed it, by doing so, it practically shifted the attention of a large number of well-intentioned education workers, activists, and lawyers away from the real necessity of strengthening the public system of education to the task of ensuring the share of the disadvantaged in private schools. It has thus strengthened the generalised public perception regarding the better-quality education in private schools (Supreme Court, 2010; Patnaik, 2012–13; Teltumbde, 2012).

Earlier, the Supreme Court had worked out a harmonious interface between education and the right to live with dignity in the famous Unnikrishnan judgment (SC, 1993), which bolstered the claim of individual citizens to name education as a fundamental right from the state. However, the TMA Pai judgment (Supreme Court, 2002) protected the rights of the managers of educational institutions. Still, if properly seen, this judgment cannot counteract the constitutional safeguard provided in the form of a provision that the state can restrict exercise of this right 'in the interest of public order'. Yet this judgment is being deployed by the NISA-CCS lobby in support of the interests of school managers against state regulation. The NISA-CCS lobby also believes that the minority judgment was right and not the majority judgment of the Supreme Court which upheld the 25% quota in private schools under the RTE Act in 2010. They also treat the 25% quota in private schools as the state abdicating its responsibility, and therefore they demand scrapping the RTE Act (Thakore, 2018). However, they don't demand an alternative arrangement of a fully and directly state-funded common education system. Instead, they want the freedom of their schools from state regulation, not only to spread education in the manner they wish but also to earn a profit.

Homogeneity of language and knowledge

Another very important factor determining the choice of private schools is parents' desire to obtain English-medium education for their kids. English-medium education is perceived to be crucial for upward mobility up the social and professional ladders. However, besides the fact that such a view perhaps represents a narrow view of upward mobility, learning a particular language, such as English, is one thing and utilising the mother tongue located in the multi-lingual context of the child's milieu as the medium of education is another. They are not exclusive. Proficiency in any language of the world, such as Hindi, Sanskrit, Urdu, or even English, could be obtained without necessarily adopting it as the medium of education. Even though this path might require additional effort at some level of an individual's life to acquire advanced-level acquaintance with any particular discourse in a given language, still, it would be a more democratic approach to protect different languages and the treasures of knowledge contained therein. After all, the attainment of proficiency in a particular language mainly requires appropriate arrangements for its teaching and learning as one of the subjects of the school curriculum, giving the child access to additional literature, and exposure to actual communication in it.

Since the colonial period, there has existed in India a socially segregated, stratified, and hierarchical structure of education along the lines of language, such as institutions that imparted education in English, local vernaculars, or classical languages (Chavan, 2013). Still, during the colonial period (and also during a greater part of the post-independence phase), most of the students were educated in the regional languages at the school level. English was denied to most of them (Naregal, 2001). However, English continued to enjoy a hegemonic place as the medium of higher education for all and the medium of school education for the elites, despite all evidence presented by various vernacular educators to prove that non-English languages can be used for all purposes. As a result, in due course, English also started eroding the option of the vernacular medium at the school level (Chavan, 2013; Chaudhary, 2013; Naregal, 2001).

An analysis of the constitutional assembly debates has demonstrated how the multilingual and multicultural ethos that is constitutive of Indian society was largely ignored, and because the focus was so much on containing the existing political safeguards available to the religious and backward minorities, how the rights of linguistic minorities were largely compromised (Agnihotri, 2015). He points out that when members raised issues about the medium of instruction in education in the case of minorities, migrants, or metropolitan cities such as Delhi, their voices did not receive the attention they deserved. The pleas to include languages such as Mundari, Gondi, and Oraon in the schedule of languages were not entertained (Agnihotri, 2015: 48). Even in the directive principles of state policy, there are no specific directions concerning minority languages. Only in Article 46 is it proposed that the 'State shall promote with special care the educational and economic interests of the weaker sections of the people, in particular, of the Scheduled Castes and the Scheduled Tribes'. The issue of language in the case of persons with disability was not even addressed (Agnihotri, 2015: 55).

Still, until quite recently, the ordinary government schools in the state of UP, as well as in most other parts of the country, followed their respective regional languages (if not necessarily the mother tongues and the multilinguality of the child's milieu) as the medium of education. They also arranged for learning one or two additional languages as per the 'three language formula'. Even though the regional languages could not replace English in higher education, they surely emerged during the second half of the nineteenth century as an optional medium of education. 'Over a period of time, the 8th schedule languages have acquired a special status in the Indian polity in terms administration, education, films and literary awards' (Agnihotri, 2015: 55).

Of course, one of the many difficulties faced in language arrangements for education has been the divide between the fluid colloquial languages of the child's milieu, on one hand, and the officialised, standardised, and therefore often heavily Sanskritised language used in the school, on the other. The status and the nature of Hindi/Hindustani-Urdu has been another contentious issue showing mainly how the modernist paradigm of homogenisation and standardisation of languages and the politics on this question have sharpened language identities and segregated them from each other. Moreover, the officially adopted regional languages in any state are not always the mother tongues of students. Further, the gap between the language of the school and that of the child's milieu is likely to be higher in the case of socially marginalised, ethnically excluded, and religious/linguistic minority groups. The question of linguistic plurality is also essentially linked with the pedagogic aspects of the learner's construction of knowledge from his or her own milieu. Moreover, language speakers are essentially multi-lingual, and languages are much more fluid than frozen.

It is in this context that the NCERT noted in a position paper little more than a decade ago:

> (I)n a country like India, most children arrive in schools with multilingual competence and begin to drop out of the school system because, in addition to several other reasons, the language of the school fails to relate to the languages of their homes and neighborhoods. It is imperative that we make provisions for education in the mother tongue(s) of the children and train teachers to maximize the utilization of the multilingual situation often obtaining in the classroom as a resource.
>
> (NCERT, 2006)

However, the RTE Act (GoI, 2009) adopted a somewhat ambiguous position on the medium of education, which could be utilised in any direction: mother tongues as medium of education, or regional languages, or English. It provides that the 'child's mother tongue, as far as practicable' (GoI, 2009: section 29, para 2, clause F) should be adopted as the medium of education. Of course, a progressive reading of the act would be favourable to mother tongues. However, its provision is not sturdy enough to undo the language hierarchy inherited from the history of the colonial as well as early post-independence phase of the constitutional assembly and is too weak to stop the neoliberal drive to massively introduce English as the medium of education at all levels, from elementary to higher education.

This linguistic hierarchy combined with class and caste/ethnic stratification is being contemporarily exacerbated by the neoliberal market in many ways. At the level of the individual, whosoever can afford it intends to send his or her children to English-medium schools. Budget private schools (allegedly as substitutes to dysfunctional state-run schools) offering the English medium of education (of course, in differing success) have rapidly emerged in every corner of the country in recent years. Some children learn in English-medium schools and others develop a sense of deprivation, denial, or discrimination. Therefore, there has also emerged a group of intellectuals championing the cause of Dalit Bahujans and is demanding the governments provide English-medium education, as it believes that the same is necessary to fight Brahminical oppression and domination under the 'chaturvarna system of languages'. Even a temple of an English goddess has been erected in the state of UP (Babu, 2017).

In order to satisfy this neoliberalism-augmented desire of at least some sections of the masses, the central government, many state governments, and the municipal corporations are trying to introduce English as the medium of education in the entire school or in certain sections of each class. For instance, the central government, in partnership with state governments, has been following a scheme of establishing 6,000 English-medium model schools in the entire country. Similarly, the Delhi Directorate of Education and the Municipal Corporations have been converting section (A) of different classes into the English medium. (It may be also interesting to underline here that it is the same government of Delhi under the Aam Aadmi Party [AAP] that has divided students into different sections of classes as per their supposed mental capabilities and have prescribed for the supposedly weaker students a different course of studies and examination.)

The veteran Socialist Party leader and former chief minister of UP, Mulayam Singh Yadav, often reportedly spoke against expensive English-medium schools and opposed English as a foreign language of privilege (I. Jain, 2017a). However, on the contrary, his son, Akhilesh Yadav, who subsequently became the chief minister of the same province, decided in

272 Vikas Gupta

2014 to convert one government primary school in each district into an English-medium institution as a pilot project. According to a media report, he was concerned over the growing tendency among parents not to send their children to government schools where the medium of education is Hindi. He believed that only those parents who cannot afford education in English-medium schools send their children to government schools. He was worried that even though every year, children from state-run schools excel not only in academics but also in other spheres of education, still, there is a declining trend in the enrolment of students in government schools (Joshi, 2014).

At present, the BJP is the ruling party in the state of UP. The positive response to the initiative of the former Samajwadi Party government to set up government primary English-medium schools in every district of the state and the increased attendance prompted the current BJP government to plan many more schools in the state (Mullick, 2018). Accordingly, the Department of Basic Education in UP issued a circular on 5 January 2018 directing its education bureaucracy to identify five schools in each block (total number of blocks being over 820 in the entire province) to be converted into English-medium education schools. Unlike the case of the implementation of the AHC judgment, where the government did not initiate even any explorations, in this case, it is so desperate that within less than twenty days, on 24 January 2018, it issued a follow-up circular asking the education bureaucracy to submit the list of identified schools within a week's time. The entire exercise of identifying about 5,000 schools, selecting 25,000 teachers and principals (from the available pool), their training, and appointment were to be completed by 18 March 2018 so that these schools might be ready on the first day of the next academic session in April 2018.

However, the survey of the language problem hints at the possibility that the introduction of English as the medium of education in schools catering to a diversified student population might push the subaltern students out. Second, such a decision introduces another layer within an already stratified system of schooling. The infrastructurally better schools are being identified for this purpose, and the rest will be condemned for poor outcomes in comparison with these institutions. Moreover, this way of negotiating class/caste/language inequality is merely illusory, because it leaves most of the poor children to study with their poor peers, whilst richer children learn with their affluent friends. Both rich and poor get half an experience and half the learning devoid of a fuller exposure to reality and, therefore, it is harmful for both of them. It also needs to be recognised that no developed countries in the world (other than those which remained under the yoke of British imperialism) have ever shown such a mania of English with the view to access modern universal knowledge.

It is therefore a significant challenge for the state to resolve this social tension and conflict in terms of the language question by adopting an equitable policy of the mother tongue medium of education grounded in the multi-linguality of a child's milieu. At the same time, there is a need to take a broader view of language plurality, what Alok Rai demonstrated as Hindi within quotation marks and Hindi without quotation marks (Rai, 2001), instead of reducing it to a question of Hindi versus English or Hindi versus Urdu. Otherwise, the parents from linguistic or religious minority communities or those inhabitants of UP who do not identify Hindi as their mother tongue might justifiably argue that the implementation of the AHC judgment would compromise their fundamental right to protect and promote their language and culture if the state does not persuasively commit to ensure through a proper roadmap that its 'common-men's schools' will take care of this responsibility of optimising diversity and minimising disparity of all kinds, including that of language. Even though the AHC verdict is silent on the language question, the judicial developments on this issue in the state of Karnataka are quite instructive of such a difficulty to be faced by other states, including UP.

The government of the state of Karnataka started to introduce the Kannada language as the medium of education uniformly in all schools within the province in 1982. Until early 1990s, the measures of the state government with regard to the Kannada medium of education at the primary level were by and large upheld by the judiciary (the High Court of the state as well as the Supreme Court of India), except that the High Court disallowed in 1984 the mandatory introduction of Kannada medium at secondary level of school education. A double bench of Supreme Court upheld the government decision to introduce Kannada as the medium of primary education compulsorily in all schools on the grounds that the state is the best judge as far as language policy is concerned and that the court shall not interfere with it. Accordingly, in 1994, the government of Karnataka issued a language policy providing for the mother tongue or Kannada to be the medium of instruction in primary schools (Bangalore Mirror, 2014; Pai, 2018).

However, in subsequent decades, we have witnessed some kind of reversal in the position of the judiciary with regard to the role of the state on the language question, now favouring the choice of the individual. When the language policy of the Karnataka government was opposed by the group of private schools, a full bench of the High Court said in 2008 that the state can only regulate and not restrict the right of the students and their parents to choose the medium of instruction, and accordingly it struck down a particular clause of the order issued within the framework of the language policy of 1994 which made it applicable to non-governmental schools (Bangalore Mirror, 2014; Pai, 2018; Chitra, 2008). Thereafter, the state government filed an appeal in the Supreme Court of India. A division bench of the Supreme Court referred the matter in 2013 to a larger constitutional bench, as in 1993, another division bench had ruled in favour of the government's position on the compulsory introduction of the mother tongue as medium of primary education in all schools (Bangalore Mirror, 2014; Pai, 2018).

The five-judge bench of the Supreme Court partly reversed the earlier orders in 2014 and judgments. According to their interpretation, Article 19(1)(a) of the constitution of India covered the fundamental right of parents to choose the medium of instruction in which their children study in schools and that the state cannot impose any language, including the mother tongue of the students, as the medium of instruction in private and unaided schools. According to this judgment, the state has no power under Article 350A of the constitution to compel the linguistic minorities to choose their mother tongue only as a medium of instruction in primary schools (Bangalore Mirror, 2014; Pai, 2018).

However, in this judgment of 2014, the Supreme Court granted that the government-run schools can have any language as the medium of education. Therefore, if state governments decide to, they can continue providing education in mother tongues, at least at the elementary level, as an interim measure, expecting its extension into higher levels in due course. However, within each state, there is another variety of government schools, which are established by the central government (the central schools, Navodaya Vidyalayas, and model schools) and which follow CBSE (Central Board of Secondary Education) or ICSE (Indian Certificate of Secondary Education) boards. Compulsory introduction of the mother tongue medium of education is presented as particularly problematic in regard to this category of government schools (Aravind, 2018; Prajwal, 2017; Sumaya, 2018).

The syllabus of these schools linked with all-India boards generally attract students aspiring to join those lucrative degree courses for which centralised tests have been instituted, such as medicine and engineering. Centralised tests have the inbuilt tendency to favour homogenised knowledge and language. The stakeholders of these schools which are affiliated with central boards also prefer English as the medium of education. Hence, apart from English-medium private schools, even the stratification present within the government school system in any state constitutes a barrier in the introduction of the mother tongue medium of education. Moreover, the children of migrant populations, particularly those whose parents come to a specific state as part of the short-term transfer policy of their public or private employers, are generally presented as yet another group which will be hit hard by the imposition of a law which makes learning in the mother tongue compulsory for all children (*The Times of India*, 2018a; Aravind, 2018; Prajwal, 2017; Sumaya, 2018).

At the same time, it also needs to be recognised that if the government follows the policy of mother tongues as the medium of education in its own schools and private schools and schools affiliated with centralised boards are allowed to introduce English-medium instruction, it creates a particular kind of social divide. Those who can afford to pay the fees to secure an English-medium education in private schools in order to join a tiny service sector create a negative outlook on the mother tongue within the rest of the society. They, too, begin to aspire for English-medium education. Unfortunately, now the governments as well as the judiciary are interpreting this socio-structural phenomenon as a matter of an individual's choice.

After losing the battle in the Supreme Court on the mandatory introduction of the Kannada medium of primary education in all schools, the government of Karnataka opted for a new but significantly compromised path. It passed the Kannada Language Learning Act in 2014, which came into force on 29 April 2015 (Karnataka Government (2015). Under this legislation, Kannada is required to be mandatorily taught as the first or second language out of three languages from Class I to Class X in all schools. It covers all schools, whether established and run by the state government or private investors. Kannada is to be taught whether the school follows the state board's curriculum and examination, or the all-India boards, or even the international curriculum. Starting with Class I in 2017–18, Kannada is to be introduced in these schools gradually in different phases, up to Class X by 2027.

As per the media reports, the private schools and schools affiliated with the central government might challenge in the judiciary the language policy adopted by the government of Karnataka in 2015 (Tanu, 2017; *The Times of India*, 2018a). Their problems are by and large the same that I have summarised earlier in the context of the introduction of a mother tongue medium of education at the primary stage. On the other hand, realising these legal and structural barriers, former Karnataka chief minister Siddharmaiah wanted to mobilize other state governments to pressurize the central government for a constitutional amendment facilitating mother tongues as the medium of education (Bahadur, 2016). Nana Patil even presented a bill in Lok Sabha in 2016 unsuccessfully trying to make an amendment in the constitution of India to mandatorily impose mother tongues as the medium of education (Patil, 2016). However, such champions of mother tongues often lack an equally vocal stand on the question of promoting structural equality through the establishment of a common school system and the locally relevant curricular knowledge contesting the epistemological-linguistic hegemony being perpetuated through its homogenisation and centralisation.

Another related instrument for promoting homogeneity in education is the institutionalisation of a singular textbook for the entire country. The textbook regime commenced under the colonial period, when the provincial textbook committees were convened to prepare lists of books in each subjects to be studied by students to pass examinations. The setting up of the provincial textbook committees was part of the project of the 'officialisation of knowledge'.[2] Even though multiple textbooks were approved for each subject in every province, this process unleashed a drive for the homogenisation, standardisation, and officialisation of curricular knowledge. Thus began a flattening process overriding epistemological heterogeneity and linguistic diversity. The common driving force for this could be seen in a certain kind of Eurocentric paradigm of modernity and officialisation of educational knowledge. Because the capacity to acquire this flattened knowledge was considered merit, the supportive measures, such as scholarships, fee concessions or waivers, hostels, and similar other educational facilities, as well as students' progression to the next stage in the ladder of classes, were tied to it.

However, it should be noted that although the process commenced under colonialism in the mid-nineteenth century, it was completed only in the second half of the twentieth century, with the 'nationalisation of textbooks'. The nineteenth century undoubtedly marked a watershed in the 'officialisation' of curricular knowledge. Still, reports of provincial as well as central textbook committees in the nineteenth century reveal that the state control on textbooks had not acquired finality in this period. A lot of unapproved textbooks remained in circulation, and a large number of institutions were kept out of any mandatory requirement to use only the approved textbooks. Even the government schools were provided a list of approved textbooks for each subject to choose from, rather than introducing only one textbook. Sometimes the state-commissioned authors wrote textbooks, but mostly writers privately wrote textbooks and applied for approval from the provincial textbook committees, with the view to ensure larger readership, fame and financial gain.

This process of the 'officialisation of knowledge' achieved the next major breakthrough in the second half of the twentieth century, when respective states of the Indian union began to establish their monopoly through a single prescribed textbook for each subject and that, too, only written by commissioned authors under their auspices (Goyal and Sharma, 1987). During the early 1960s, people complained that provincial textbooks often contained retrogressive, orthodox, and communal tenets. In order to combat this problem, the central government decided to prepare model textbooks. For this purpose, it established the NCERT. Of course, its purpose was not to replace provincial textbooks, but to provide a model to be emulated as a guideline. However, many states began adopting the NCERT textbooks directly.

Still, as of now, there are two kinds of textbooks, those which are prepared by provincial-level bodies and those which are prepared at the national level. Besides this, there are private schools, which often use different textbooks in certain classes. Therefore, the next major step, currently under the consideration of the government of India, is the complete centralisation of curricular knowledge through the introduction of only one national textbook for each subject to be studied in all schools (Gupta, 2016). One recorded proposal in the minutes of a meeting held on 21 March 2015 chaired by the union minister for HRD was that books of NCERT with a uniform syllabus could be made applicable to all schools in the states. The draft of the NEP released for public input in 2016 recommended in clause (3) of section 4.5 that

> For science, mathematics and English subjects, a common national curriculum (meaning textbook here) will be designed. For other subjects, such as social sciences, a part of the curricula will be common across the country and the rest will be at the discretion of the states.

Hence, the Draft NEP 2016 intended to take away the right of the states to have fully their own curriculum for social sciences and other disciplines. Within this framework, states would be left to only insert some parts within the overall framework determined by the central government. On the other hand, this control of the central government would be absolute in natural sciences, mathematics, and English. Thus, it also wrongly implies that in natural sciences and mathematics, the local context does not matter at all. It needs to be recognised that this process of 'officialisation' implies complete central control over the notion of 'worthy knowledge' and that it does not go well with the idea of epistemological autonomy of learners, educators, and writers; it is antithetical to the diversity of Indian society.

Still, the government of Uttarakhand has recently decided to replace state-level textbooks with the NCERT textbooks, including the textbooks on the environment. The government of Gujarat has also announced a phase-wise programme of the replacement of state-level textbooks with those of the NCERT (Sharma, 2017; *India Today*, 2017). The UP government has replaced the state-level textbooks, as well as some others being used in madarsas, with those written by the NCERT in the name of modernisation (Agrwal, 2018; *Financial Express*, 2018; *The Times of India*, 2017). Rajasthan also announced the replacement of state-level textbooks with the NCERT textbooks about a decade ago. However, later on, although it retained the state-level textbooks, it has been introducing many controversial changes in them, in accordance with the ideology of RSS, which has the support of the current central government led by the BJP (*The Hindu*, 2010; Jain, 2017b; and *The Times of India*, 2018b).

The introduction of common all-India tests for various admissions after the senior secondary examination, such as engineering, medicine, management, etc., has emerged as a new factor hastening this process of homogeneity of curricular knowledge and language. Neoliberalism has the tendency to centralize all educational knowledge and assessment through common tests. It is becoming a global phenomenon. However, it is contrary to any notion of rational engagement with knowledge and assessment of merit. It is helping in the preservation of the interests of the dominant classes through the increased proliferation of the coaching business. This is being legitimised in the name of the tokenistic inclusion of some students from the marginalised section whilst actually excluding the bulk of them.

278 Vikas Gupta

Even with all its disparities, admission to MBBS seats in state government counselling in Tamil Nadu was accessible to many downtrodden sections, as it was based on the state board marks. Only the rich elites who can spend lakhs of rupees at coaching centres can now have access to a medical education. Anitha was a seventeen-year-old student who killed herself at her home on 1 September 2017, after losing her medical seat due to the NEET exam. She was denied a seat in medicine even though she got very good marks in her state board exams (1176 out of 1200). In Anitha's own words, 'When nobody gets equal opportunities, who are they deceiving by saying single exam for all?' According to an undated write-up of the Ambedkar-Periyar Study Circle (an independent student body recognised by IIT, Madras), it was NEET that pushed Anitha to suicide.

Notes

1 I thankfully acknowledge generous grants received for the research utilized in this paper from Indian Council of Historical Research, TRG on Education and Poverty in India (Max Weber Foundation, Germany), University of Delhi and Charles Wallace Trust for India.
2 The term 'officialization of knowledge' has been derived from Michael W. Apple (2000).

References

Agnihotri, R. K. (2015). Constituent assembly debates on language. *Economic and Political Weekly*, L(8), February 21, pp. 47–56.

Agrwal, P. (2018). NCERT textbooks to be 'optional' for UP Madrassa students; Books to be available in Urdu. *The Times of India*, January 5. https://timesofindia. indiatimes.com/city/lucknow/uttar-pradesh-madrassas-to-have-ncert-books-yogi-govt/articleshow/61342533.cms (Accessed on 4 July 2018).

AIFRTE. (2012). *No to Anti-Constitutional 'School Choice' Model of PPP, Voucher Scheme, Commercialization, and Profiteering in Education!*, handbill issued on 03/12/2012.

Allahabad High Court. (2015). *Judgment pronounced on 18/08/2015 on a bunch of petitions, first amongst them being the WRIT No. 57476 of 2013*. Shiv Kumar Pathak and 11 Others Versus State of UP And Three Others.

Apple, M. W. (2000). *Official knowledge: Democratic education in a conservative age*, 2nd ed. New York: Routledge, First Published 1993.

Bangalore Mirror. (2014). State cannot make Kannada mandatory language in private, unaided schools. *Bangalore Mirror Bureau*, May 6, 2014. https://bangaloremirror. indiatimes.com/bangalore/others/kannada-language-primary-education-banga lore-karnataka-constitution-kannada-primary-education-constitution-of-india-fundamental-rights-language-of-parents-choice-ruling-victory-english-medium-schools/articleshow/34741617.cms (Accessed on 22 June 2018).

Bhat, P. (2017). Kannada made 1st or 2nd language in all Karnataka schools: Parents and student question move. *The News Minute*. 17 October. www.thenewsminute.

com/article/kannada-made-1st-or-2nd-language-all-karnataka-schools-parents-and-teachers-question-move (Accessed on 16 July 2018).

Bhatty, K., Anuradha, D. and Rathin, R. (2015). The public education system and what the costs imply. *Economic and Political Weekly*, 50(31), 1 August.

Bourdieu, P. (1973). Cultural reproduction and social reproduction. In: Richard Brown, ed., *Knowledge, education and cultural change*. London: Tavistock.

Bowles, S. and Gintis, H. (1947). *Schooling in capitalist America: Educational reform and the contradictions of economic life*. London, Henley: Routledge & Kegan Paul.

Brown vs Board of Education. (1954). Brown vs Board of Education of Topeka. *United States Report*, 347, 483.

Chatterjee, S. (2018). Mandatory Kannada rule. *The News Minute*, January 31. www.thenewsminute.com/article/mandatory-kannada-rule-cbse-schools-approach-karnataka-hc-solution-75664 (Accessed on 22 June 2018).

Chavan, D. (2013). *Language politics under colonialism: Caste, class and language pedagogy in Western India*. Newcastle upon Tyne: Cambridge Scholars Publishing.

Chaudhary, I. K. (2013). Sanskrit learning in colonial Mithila: Continuity and change. In: Deepak Kumar, Joseph Bara, Nandita Khadria, and CH. Radha Gayathri, eds., *Education in Colonial India: Historical Insights*. New Delhi: Manohar, pp. 125–144.

Constable, P. (2000). Sitting on the school verandah: The ideology and practice of 'untouchable' educational protest in the late nineteenth-century Western India. *Indian Economic and Social History Review*, 37(4), pp. 383–422.

Desai, R. B. (2016). Karnataka wants Constitutional amendment to make mother tongue compulsory in schools. *The Hindu, Raichur*, December 02, www.thehindu.com/news/national/karnataka/Karnataka-wants-Constitutional-amendment-to-make-mother-tongue-compulsory-in-schools/article16742504.ece (Accessed on 22 June 2018).

Dreze, J. and Sen, A. (2002). *India: Development and participation*. New Delhi: Oxford University Press.

Financial Express. (2018). *UP: Adityanath government approves introduction of NCERT books in madrasas*. New Delhi, May 23. www.financialexpress.com/india-news/up-adityanath-government-approves-introduction-of-ncert-books-in-madrasas/1177680/ (Accessed on 4 July 2018).

Fitzpatrick, S. (1970). *The commissariat of enlightenment: Soviet organization of education and the arts under lunacharsky October 1917–1921*. Cambridge: Cambridge University Press.

GoI. (1968). *National policy on education*. New Delhi: Government of India.

———. (1986). *National policy of education 1986*. New Delhi: Ministry of Human Resource Development, Government of India.

———. (1995). *The persons with disabilities* (Equal Opportunities, Protection of Rights and Full Participation) Act, Government of India.

———. (2006). *Social, economic and educational status of the Muslim Community of India: A report of Prime Minister's high level committee under cabinet secretariat*. Chairperson: Justice Rajindar Sachar.

———. (2009). *The Right of Children to Free and Compulsory Education Act*.

———. (2016). *The Rights of Persons with Disabilities Act*.

Government of Bihar. (2007). *Report of common school system commission*, June 8. http://teacher-ed.hbcse.tifr.res.in/documents/common-school-commission-bihar-report (Accessed on 20 September 2015).

Goyal, B. S. and Sharma, J. D. (1987). *A study of the evolution of the textbook*. New Delhi: NCERT.

Gupta, A. and Giri, A. (2015). Will Sending Kids of Govt. Servants to State-Run Schools Stop The Rot. *The Pioneer*, 29 August. www.dailypioneer.com/columnists/oped/will-sending-kids-of-govt-servants-to-state-run-schools-stop-the-rot.html (Accessed on 20 September 2015).

Gupta, V. (2013). Discourse and politics of home-based education. *Reconstructing Education*, (Joint Issue), 1(4), Sept-Dec, 2012 & 2(1), January-March, pp. 11–16.

———. (2014). Changing discourses on inequality and disparity: From welfare state to neoliberal capitalism. In: R. Kumar, ed., *Education, state and market: Anatomy of neoliberal impact*. New Delhi: Aakar, pp. 19–57.

———. (2015). *Aspects of structure of education and curricular knowledge in colonial India*, Paper Presented in the XXXVIII Indian Social Science Congress at Visakhapatnam (29 March–2 April 2015) on the theme of 'Knowledge Systems, Scientific Temper and the Indian Peoples'.

———. (2016). Politics of the guarded agenda of new education policy. *Economic and Political Weekly*, L1(42), October 15, pp. 59–69.

Hany Babu, M. T. (2017). Breaking the chaturvarna system of languages: The need to overhaul the language policy. *Economic and Political Weekly*, 52(23), June 10, pp. 112–119.

Hastkshep. (2015). Weekly Supplement of Hindi newspaper Rashtriya Sahara, Saturday, 29 August.

Illich, I. (1971). *Deschooling society*. New York: Harper and Row.

India Today. (2017). Schools in Gujarat replicate NCERT textbooks. *New Delhi*, February 8. www.indiatoday.in/education-today/news/story/gujarat-replicate-ncert-textbooks-959610-2017-02-08 (Accessed on 5 July 2018).

Jain, I. (2017a). UP to have 5,000 English-medium 'sarkari' schools'. *Times of India*, 7 October 2017. https://timesofindia.indiatimes.com/city/lucknow/up-to-have-5000-english-medium-sarkari-schools/articleshow/60985800.cms (Accessed on 22 June 2018).

Jain, S. (2017b). Rajasthan Textbooks Revised to Glorify Modi Government. *The Wire*, June 16. https://thewire.in/education/rajasthan-textbooks-revised-glorify-modi-government (Accessed on 16 July 2018).

Jain, M. and Sadhana, S. (2010). Politics of low cost schooling and low teacher salary. *Economic and Political Weekly*, 45(18), pp. 79–80.

Jain, P. S. and Ravindra, H. D. (2009). Feasibility of implementation of right to education act. *Economic and Political Weekly*, XLIV(25), pp. 38–43.

———. (2010). Right to education act and public-private partnership. *Economic and Political Weekly*, XLV(8), pp. 78–80.

Joshi, S. (2014). U.P. govt. to open English-medium schools. *The Hindu*, Lucknow, 29 November 2014. www.thehindu.com/news/national/other-states/up-govt-to-open-englishmedium-schools/article6646342.ece (Accessed on 22 June 2018).

Kamal, A. S. (2018). Karnataka govt. makes Kannada medium compulsory: Here's why it is a terrible idea. *Firstpost*. 1 April www.firstpost.com/india/kannada-in-primary-schools-how-karnataka-got-its-mother-tongue-theory-wrong-2182269.html (Accessed on 23 June 2018).

Kapur, A. (2015). The Wrong Way to Fix Government Schools, *Business Standard*, September 3, www.business-standard.com/article/punditry/the-wrong-way-to-fix-government-schools-115090201545_1.html (Accessed on 20 September 2015).

Karnataka Government. (2015). The Kannada Language Learning Act, 2015, Karnataka' Act No. 22 off 2015, *First Published in the Karnataka Gazette Extraordinary on the Second day of May, 2015* (Received the assent of the Governor on the Twenty Ninth day of April, 2015).

Kulkarni, T. (2017). Many CBSE Schools Add Another Subject to Accommodate Kannada. *The Hindu*, Bengaluru, 20 November. www.thehindu.com/news/national/karnataka/many-cbse-schools-add-another-subject-to-accommodate-kannada/article20557202.ece (Accessed on 16 July 2018).

Kumar, K. (2015). A Common Schooling System Would Bring Us Together as a Society, *Hindustan Times*, Sep 02, 2015 www.hindustantimes.com/analysis/a-common-schooling-system-would-bring-us-together-as-a-society/article1-1386498.aspx (Accessed on 20 September 2015).

Kumar, S. M. (2010). Is there a case for school vouchers? *Economic and Political Weekly*, XLV(7), pp. 41–46.

MHRD, and GOI. (2007). *Public Private Partnership (PPP) in education: A concept note*.

Ministry of Education, GoI. (1966). *Education and national development*. New Delhi: Ministry of Education, GoI.

Mullick, R. (2018). UP government set to run 5k English medium primary schools, *Hindustan Times*. Lucknow, 2 April 2018. www.hindustantimes.com/lucknow/up-government-set-to-run-5k-english-medium-primary-schools/story-KzuEVGl S9Y3UlJ7e3eEPjP.html (Accessed on 22 July 2018).

Muzaffar, I. and Ajay, S. (2011). Public-private debates in education: Whither private without a public? *Journal of Social and Policy Science*, 1(2), June 2011, pp. 1–25.

Nana, P. and Shri, A. T. (M.P.). (2016). *The Basic and Primary Education* (Compulsory Teaching In Mother Tongue), Bill No. 98 of 2016, New Delhi, 3 March 2016.

Naregal, V. (2001). *Language politics, elites, and the public sphere*. New Delhi: Permanent Black.

NCERT. (2006). *Position paper, national focus group on teaching of Indian languages*. New Delhi: NCERT.

NITI Aayog. (2017). *India: Three year action agenda 2017–18 to 2019–20*. New Delhi: Government of India.

Pai, T. V. M. (2018). *This language policy, good or bad, Deccan Chronicle*, Jun 15. www.deccanchronicle.com/nation/current-affairs/150617/this-language-policy-good-or-bad.html (Accessed on 25 June 2018).

Patnaik, R. (2012–2013). The supreme court verdict in favor of 25% reservation in private unaided schools. *Reconstructing Education*, 1(4), 2(1), pp. 5–11.

Planning Commission. (2010). *Mid-Term Appraisal of Eleventh Five Year Plan 2007–12*. http://planningcommission.nic.in/plans/mta/11th_mta/chapterwise/chap6_edu.pdf (Accessed on 20 September 2015).

———. (2013). *Twelfth Five-Year Plan (2012–2017). GOI. First published, Sage Publications India*. http://planningcommission.gov.in/plans/planrel/12thplan/pdf/12fyp_vol3.pdf (Accessed on 20 September 2015).

Rai, A. (2001). *Hindi nationalism*. Delhi: Orient Longman.

Rajalakshmi, T. K. (2011). The Interview with Senior Advocate Ashok Agarwal. *Frontline*, July 15, pp. 16–17.

282 Vikas Gupta

Ramachandran, V. (2009). Right to education act: A comment. *Economic and Political Weekly*, Xliv(28), pp. 155–157.

Ramani, C. V. (2008). Mother Tongue as the Medium of Instruction. *The Hindu*. Karnataka, February 20. www.thehindu.com/todays-paper/tp-national/tp-karna taka/Mother-tongue-as-the-medium-of-instruction/article15170042.ece (Accessed on 23 June 2018).

Registrar General and Census Commissioner India. (2011). *Census of India, Ministry of Home Affairs*, Government of India.

Sabharwal, M. (2015). Because elites opt out. Is forcing government servants to send their kids to government schools absurdity or common sense? *The Indian Express*, 28 August 2015 http://indianexpress.com/article/opinion/columns/because-elites-opt-out/ (Accessed on 20 September 2015).

Sadgopal, A. (2009). *Sansad Mein Shiksha Ka Adhikaar Chhenanewala Bill*. Bhopal: Kishore Bharati.

———. (2010). Right to education act Vs right to education. *Social Scientist*, 38(9–12), pp. 17–50.

———. (2013). *Shiksha men PPP: Sarvajanik Niji bhagedariya Nav Udarwadi Loot*. Bhopal: Kishore Bharati.

Sarangapani, P. M. (2009). Quality, feasibility and desirability of low cost private schooling. *Economic and Political Weekly*, XLIV(43), pp. 67–69.

Sharma, R. (2017). *NCERT textbooks to replace GCERT in classes III, V and VII*. *The Indian Express*. Ahmedabad, 28 June. https://indianexpress.com/article/cities/ahmedabad/ncert-textbooks-to-replace-gcert-in-classes-iii-v-and-vii-4725 405/ (Accessed on 5 July 2018).

Sharma, S. (2015). Implement Allahabad HC order across country, RTI activist to SC. *Tribune News Service*. 26 August 2015. www.tribuneindia.com/news/haryana/courts/implement-allahabad-hc-order-across-country-rti-activist-to-sc/124372.html (Accessed on 20 September 2015).

Smith, A. (1976). *The wealth of nations*. Oxford: Clarendon Press.

Soysal, Y. and Strang, D. (1989). Construction of the first mass education systems in nineteenth-century Europe. *Sociology of Education*, 62(4), pp. 277–288.

Supreme Court of India. (1993). Judgment pronounced on 14/05/1993 in the matter of Unnikrishnan P. J. And Others versus State of A. P. And Others. Review Petition Nos. 483 of 1993 in Writ Petition No. 678 of 1993. Etc.

———. (2002). Judgment pronounced on 31/10/2002 in the matter of T.M.A.Pai Foundation & Ors Versus State Of Karnataka &Ors in Writ Petition (civil) 317 of 1993.

———. (2010). Judgment pronounced on Writ Petition (C) No. 95 Of 2010, Society For Un-Aided Private Schools Of Rajasthan Vs U.O.I. & Anr.

Teltumbde, A. (2012). RTE: A symbolic gesture. *Economic and Political Weekly*, XLVII(19), pp. 10–11.

Thakore, D. (2018). Why the RTE Act Should Be Scrapped. *Educationworld*. (April). www.educationworld.in/Magazine/EWIssueSection.aspx?Issue=EducationWorld_April_2018&Section=Cover_Story Browsed on (Accessed on 6 June 2018).

The Hindu. (2010). *Rajasthan to go for NCERT Syllabus*, 7 April. www.thehindu.com/todays-paper/tp-national/tp-otherstates/Rajasthan-to-go-for-NCERT-sylla bus/article16016500.ece (Accessed on 5 July 2018).

The Indian Express. (2015). *Minister to write to officials: Admit your kids in govt schools.* 27 August. http://indianexpress.com/article/cities/lucknow/minister-to-write-to-officials-admit-your-kids-in-govt-schools/ (Accessed on 20 September 2015).

The Times of India. (2015). Allahabad HC order an opportunity to improve standard of education, The Times of India. 26 August 2015, http://timesofindia.indiatimes.com/home/education/news/Allahabad-HC-order-an-opportunity-to-improve-standard-of-education/articleshow/48686084.cms (Accessed on 20 September 2015).

———. (2017). Uttar Pradesh Madrassas to have NCERT books: Yogi govt. *The Times of India*, Lucknow 30 October.

———. (2018a). Devnani's 'revisionist' ideas, NDA schemes guide NCERT books. The Times of India, Jaipur, 3 June. http://timesofindia.indiatimes.com/articleshow/64434992.cms?utm_source=contentofinterest&utm_medium=text&utm_campaign=cppst (Accessed on 16 July 2018).

———. (2018b). *Rule to make Kannada mandatory in schools still in limbo*, April 17. https://timesofindia.indiatimes.com/city/bengaluru/rule-to-make-kannada-mandatory-in-schools-still-in-limbo/articleshow/63790595.cms (Accessed on 16 July 2018).

Tooley, J., Dixon, P. and Gomathi, S. V. (2007). Private schools and the millennium development goal of universal primary education: A census and comparative survey in Hyderabad, India. *Oxford Review of Education*, 33(5), pp. 539–560.

UNO (United Nations Organization). (2007). United Nations Convention on the Rights of Persons with Disabilities (UNCRPD).

Vellanki, V. (2015). Government vs private schools in ASER 2014: Need to avoid binaries. *Economic and Political Weekly*, 50(7), February 14.

WHO. (2011). *World disability report.* World Health Organization (Who).

Willis, P. (1981). *Learning to labor: How working class kids get working class jobs.* New York: Columbia University Press.

Index

Note: Page numbers in **bold** indicate a table on the corresponding page, and page numbers in *italics* indicate a figure on the corresponding page.

Aam Aadmi Party (AAP) 10, 57, 271
accountability 9, 26–27, 31–37, 39–40, 61, 81, 91, 119, 247, 264–265
action research 13, 138–141, *141*, 149–151
aim(s): of education 6, 7, 8, 11, 14, 27, 29, 40, 83, 91–100, 103–105; social 6, 40
Allahabad High Court (AHC) 18, 187, 251; AHC judgment 18, 251, 254–264, 272, 273
All India Forum for Right to Education (AIFRTE) 266
Althusser, L. 165–166, 203, 207, 210, 215
Annual Status of Education Report (ASER) 45, 117–118, 191, 265
assessment 3, 8, 11–12, 31, 32, 39, 55, 57, 63–64, 103, 108–109, 114, 116–120, 267, 277; *see also* learning outcome(s) (LOs)

Bombay Plan 9
budget private schools/budget primary schools (BPS) 57, 258, 265–267, 271; *see also* low-fee private schooling (LFPS)

capitalism: alternatives to 172; capitalist class 163, 172, 188–189, 203, 205–206, 209, 213, 216, 223; capital-labour relations 169, 207, 209; global/globalised capitalism 14, 194, 253; immiseration 203
Central Advisory Board of Education (CABE) 117, 185

Central Board of Secondary Education (CBSE) 196, 274
classroom practice(s) 13, 59, 131, 132
cluster resource centre (CRC) 35, 139–141, 149, 151
common school system 2, 4, 6, 18, 29, 33, 52, 56, 73, 77, 252, 260, 266, 275; common men's school 188, 254, 255, 257–261, 273
consensualisation 14–15, 154, 156, 165–167; consensualised reproduction 154–173
constitution: constitutional assembly 269, 271; constitutional provision(s) 66, 255; of India/Indian 1, 66, 124, 253, 259, 260, 261, 263, 274, 275
contestation 40, 211, 241, 244; of educational inequality 251
critical educators/critical education 7, 8, 15, 17, 27, 82, 166, 173, 220, 221, 227
critical pedagogy 8, 13, 14, 141, 151, 167, 169–171, 173, 211, 220, 221
curriculum: hidden 16, 212–214, 217; National Curriculum Framework (NCF) 8, 116; officialisation of curricular knowledge 275–276

directive principles of state policy 46, 53n4, 67, 253, 260, 269
discipline 16, 39, 59, 102, 124, 126, 129, 131–132, 196–197, 220, 221, 226, 277
District Information System for Education (DISE) 67, 78, 255, 260

286 Index

District Primary Education Programme (DPEP) 2, 28, 193
Draft NEP 2016 80, 91–107, 264, 277

economically weaker section (EWS) 4, 28, 47, 191, 268
educability, notion of 137, 140–142, 147, 149, 150
education *see* elementary education
educational crisis 5, 18
education policy: educational reforms 3, 13, 17, 28, 35, 92, 235, 237; elementary education policy 5, 6, 18–19, 27, 30, 56, 59, 72, 83; school education policy 57
education workers 17–19, 85, 203, 268
elementary education: equitable 3, 4, 15, 19, 66–85; as a fundamental right 45, 46, 50, 253–254, 259, 268; primary education 30, 57, 75, 185, 188, 192, 193, 198nn4–6, 251, 253, 256, 273, 275; public education 2–5, 10, 18, 28, 29, 46, 55–64, 68, 73, 77, 81, 82, 84, 104, 123, 210, 216, 229–232; as a public good 1, 11, 66–85; school education 2–12, 14, 26, 28, 38–39, 45, 47, 49–52, 56, 57, 67, 68, 71, 74, 78, 80, 82, 83, 85, 100, 108, 112, 116, 155, 177, 189, 199n12, 250, 261, 266, 267, 269, 273; universalisation of 35, 66, 177, 179
employable skills 97, 99–100, 103, 105, 106
examination: system 8, 12, 108, 109–111, 113–117, 120n1; utility of 111; *see also* public examination
exclusion 8, 13, 15, 16, 67, 68, 71, 83–85, 138, *139*, 177–197

fascisation 14, 159, 164, 173n1; fascised rule of capital 154–173
freedom 1, 3, 15, 25, 26, 34, 93, 101, 102, 106, 113, 126, 127, 132, 167, 169, 178, 185, 186, 188–190, 223, 246, 251, 262–263, 267, 268
Freire, P. 205, 211

Giroux, H. 16, 169, 171, 203, 206, 210, 211
global neoliberalism *see* neoliberalism

government schools *see* school(s)
Gramsci, A. 16, 163, 172, 203, 207, 210, 211

Hill, D. 9, 14, 16, 17, 27, 159, 160, 172, 173n1, 203, 206, 217, 229
human capital theory 9, 17, 220, 222, 224–226, 229; human capital logic 221, 227, 230, 321

inclusion 1, 4, 28, 47, 53n4, 67, 81, 84, 250, 257, 277; inclusive teaching and learning methodology 13
inequality: social 57, 71, 227; structural 6, 39, 84, 150, 251, 252, 264
in-service training 151; *see also* teacher training/teacher education

knowledge-based economy and society (KBES) 11, 83, 96, 105
knowledge, curricular 249, 275–277; commodification of 6, 26, 124, 155, 197, 206; homogenisation of 249; officialisation of 275–276
Kumar, R. 3, 8, 13, 14, 25–26, 67, 72, 83

learning outcome(s) (LOs) 3, 6–7, 31, 47, 57, 60, 63–64, 80, 81, 98, 119, 265; student learning 6, 80
low-fee private schooling (LFPS) 3, 29

market 1, 4–9, 11, 25–27, 29–32, 33, 34, 38, 39, 40, 43, 50, 51, 77, 80, 82–84, 100, 103, 116, 124, 126, 129, 130–131, 155–157, 172, 177–178, 180, 194–197, 198n7, 207, 209–210, 223, 225, 229, 245–247, 263, 265, 271
Marxist education: Marxist critique 203; Marxist educational analysis 9, 14, 16, 203, 210; Marxist educators 16, 209
mass schooling 220, 221, 224, 226
mentor teacher programme 59; mentor teacher 59–60
Ministry of Human Resource Development (MHRD) 48, 267
model schools *see* school(s)
modernity 12, 124–133, 181, 276; modernist paradigm 249, 250, 270
mother tongue, as medium of education 185, 269–275

National Policy on Education
(NPE): 1986 2, 30, 83, 192;
2016 91, 193
neoconservatism 206–209
neoliberal educators 26, 50, 51, 79
neoliberalism: global 7, 17, 203;
neoliberal policy shifts 25, 39, 40,
85; neoliberal reforms 190, 194,
238, 247; neoliberal restructuring
7, 9, 15, 17, 204, 239, 251; *see
also* capitalism, global/globalised
capitalism
new public management (NPM) 26
NITI Aayog 6, 37, 82–84, 258,
263–264, 267–268
no-detention policy (NDP) 91, 118
non-formal education (NFE) 3, 74,
192, 252
non-state stakeholding 78; non-state
actors 10, 46–51, 73

para-teachers 2, 190, 193
periodisation 236–239, **237**,
241–242, 244
policy: analysis 7, 11, 15, 17; changes
3, 5, 7, 9, 27, 29, 30; context 6, 7, 9,
18, 27, 37–40, 78, 82, 83; discourses
240; making 6, 9, 15, 38, 58, 75;
neoliberal policy framework 7, 226,
229, 250; reform 9, 37, 39; shifts 3,
5, 7, 11, 18, 27, 29, 30, 34, 39, 40,
72, 73, 79, 83, 85; text(s) 6, 8, 11,
38, 39, 72, 74; trends 14, 16, 72;
wisdom 2, 37, 40, 74, 78
primary education *see* elementary
education
private schools *see* school(s)
privatisation 1–6, 11, 12, 16, 17, 25,
26, 37, 39, 43, 44, 72, 74, 78, 83,
85, 123, 155, 158, 179, 196, 206,
210, **238**, 264–267; *see also*
school(s)
Programme of Action (POA) 31
public education *see* elementary
education
public examination 108–109, 113–114,
119, 120, 120n1
public-private partnership 4, 9, 43, 44,
53, 194, 266
public services 9, 25, 26, 203, 206, 229,
239, 265

quality: concept of 26, 30–33, 266; of
education 2, 3, 26, 28, 31–33, 39,
45, 47, 48, 50–52, 55–57, 62, 64,
74, 76, 77, 82, 84, 96, 97, 127, 268,
190, 191, 193, 228, 230, 231, 259,
261, 265, 266, 268

refraction 17, 236, 239, 244, 246–247
resistance 9, 16, 51, 100, 108, 114,
117, 119, 120n1, 154–156, 180,
203, 209–211, 217, 241, 244, 253
restructuring policies 239, *240*, 241;
structural adjustment programme
(SAP) 2, 28
right to education 46, 53n3, 75–78,
127, 179, 188, 191, 194, 254,
259, 260, 261, 265, 266; Right of
Children to Free and Compulsory
Education Act (RTE Act) 2009 4,
28, 29, 46, 47, 51, 53n5, 61, 68, 76,
108, 119, 177, 191, 195, 253, 254,
258–259, 266–271
Rikowski, G. 203, 210, 215–216

Sadgopal, A. 1, 4, 28, 29, 51–52, 66,
68, 76–77, 81, 256, 259
sanskara 13, 138, 151n1
Sarva Shiksha Abhiyan (SSA) 3, 28, 59
school(s): equitable system of schooling
4, 82, 260; government 4, 57, 58, 64,
67, 68, 77, 82, 117, 122, 126, 193,
262, 267, 274; model 48; private 3, 10,
47, 56, 77, 122, 126, 129, 155, 191,
262, 265, 267; public 46, 51, 112,
130; state 78; types of 8, 45, 68, 74
school education *see* elementary
education
school management committee(s)
(SMCs) 61
socialism: socialist education 216;
socialist policy for education
16, 203
social justice 1, 5, 8, 11, 13–15, 39, 66,
71, 77, 80, 84, 95, 102, 105, 116, 151,
170, 172, 189, 196, 216, 266, 268
state: colonial 29, 109, 114, 132, 251,
253; modern 178–179; neoliberal 5,
38, 83; policy 15, 28, 46, 53n4, 66,
67, 253, 260, 269
structural adjustment programme *see*
restructuring policies

Sustainable Development Goals (SDGs) 228
systemic narratives 235–237, 239

teacher training/teacher education 35, 59, 142, 149, 150, 193

universalisation of school education (UEE) 177

Washington Consensus 1, 4, 8
welfare: of citizens 44; policies 5, 84, 197; regimes 14; sectors 2; societies 241; state 25, 236–237, 237, 239, 242; systems 241; welfarism 5
Winch, C. 26, 33, 51, 92, 93, 104
work–life narratives 235, 237, 238, 239–246, *240*
world-systems analysis 9, 220–222, 224–226

Printed in the United States
By Bookmasters